AROUND UNTER DEN LINDEN
See pp54–69

NORTH OF THE CENTRE
See pp98–111

EAST OF THE CENTRE
See pp86–97

North of the Centre

East of the Centre

Around Unter den Linden

Museum Island

Tiergarten

Kreuzberg

0 metres 1000

0 yards 1000

KREUZBERG
See pp136–145

MUSEUM ISLAND
See pp70–85

W9-BCN-870

EYEWITNESS TRAVEL GUIDES

BERLIN

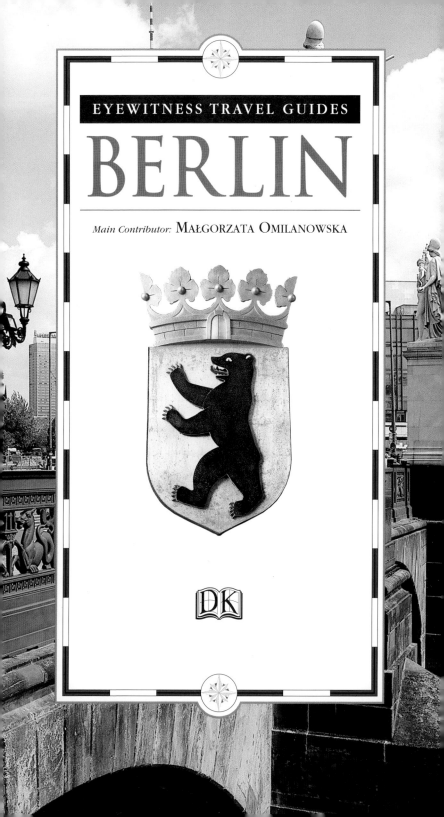

EYEWITNESS TRAVEL GUIDES

BERLIN

Main Contributor: Małgorzata Omilanowska

DK

LONDON, NEW YORK,
MELBOURNE, MUNICH AND DELHI
www.dk.com

Produced by Wydawnictwo Wiedza i Życie, Warsaw
MANAGING EDITOR Ewa Szwagrzyk
SERIES EDITOR Joanna Egert
DTP DESIGNER Pawel Pasternak
CONSULTANT Nils Meyer
ILLUSTRATIONS Andrzej Wielgosz,
Lena Maminajszwili, Dorota Jarymowicz
PHOTOGRAPHY Dorota and Mariusz Jarymowicz
CORRECTION Bożena Leszkowicz
PRODUCTION Anna Kożurno-Królikowska, Ewa Roguska
CONTRIBUTORS Małgorzata Omilanowska, Christian Tempel
MAPS Maria Wojciechowska, Dariusz Osuch (D. Osuch i spółka)

Dorling Kindersley Limited
EDITORS Nancy Jones, Esther Labi, Hugh Thompson
SENIOR EDITOR Helen Townsend

Reproduced by Colourscan, Singapore
Printed and bound by South China Co. Ltd., China

First American Edition, 2000
04 05 10 9 8 7 6 5 4
Published in the United States by DK Publishing, Inc.
375 Hudson Street, New York, New York, 10014
Reprinted with revisions 2002, 2003, 2004

Copyright © 2000, 2003 Dorling Kindersley Limited, London

ALL RIGHTS RESERVED. NO PART OF THIS PUBLICATION MAY BE REPRODUCED,
STORED IN A RETRIEVAL SYSTEM, OR TRANSMITTED IN ANY FORM OR BY ANY
MEANS, ELECTRONIC, MECHANICAL, PHOTOCOPYING, RECORDING OR OTHERWISE,
WITHOUT THE PRIOR WRITTEN PERMISSION OF THE COPYRIGHT OWNER.

Library of Congress Cataloging-in-Publication Data

ISSN 1542-1554
ISBN 0-7894-9430-2
FLOORS ARE REFERRED TO THROUGHOUT IN ACCORDANCE WITH EUROPEAN USAGE;
IE THE "FIRST FLOOR" IS THE FLOOR ABOVE GROUND LEVEL.

**The information in this
Dorling Kindersley Travel Guide is checked annually.**
Every effort has been made to ensure that this book is as up-to-date
as possible at the time of going to press. Some details however, such
as telephone numbers, opening hours, prices, gallery hanging
arrangements and travel information are liable to change. As a result
of the return of the German government to Berlin, and the large
amount of construction work under way, whole areas of the city are
in a constant state of change. The publishers cannot accept
responsibility for any consequences arising from the use of this book,
nor for any material on third party websites, and cannot guarantee
that any website address in this book will be a suitable source of
travel information. We value the views and suggestions of our readers
very highly. Please write to: Publisher, DK Eyewitness Travel Guides,
Dorling Kindersley, 80 Strand, London WC2R 0RL, Great Britain.

CONTENTS

HOW TO USE
THIS GUIDE 6

A child's drawing of Berlin's Fernsehturm (Television Tower), Siegessäule and Funkturm (Radio Tower)

INTRODUCING
BERLIN

PUTTING BERLIN ON
THE MAP 10

THE HISTORY OF
BERLIN 16

BERLIN AT A GLANCE 28

BERLIN THROUGH
THE YEAR 48

Bomb-damaged Kaiser-Wilhelm-
Gedächtnis-Kirche (see pp152–3)

The Spree river passing by the Nikolaiviertel *(see pp88–9)*

Chicken fricassée with crayfish *(see p231)*

Modern architecture by the former Checkpoint Charlie *(see p141)*

Berliner Dom *(see pp76–7)*

HOW TO USE THIS GUIDE

THIS DORLING KINDERSLEY travel guide helps you to get the most from your visit to Berlin. It provides detailed practical information and expert recommendations. *Introducing Berlin* maps the city and the region, and sets it in its historical and cultural context, and describes events through the entire year. *Berlin at a Glance* is an overview of the city's main attractions. *Berlin Area by Area* starts on page 52. This is the main sightseeing section, which covers all of the important sights, with photographs, maps and illustrations. *Greater Berlin* covers the nearby historic city of Potsdam, as well as three walking tours. Information about hotels, restaurants, shops and markets, entertainment and sports is found in *Travellers' Needs*. The *Survival Guide* has advice on everything from using Berlin's medical services, telephones and post offices to the public transport system.

FINDING YOUR WAY AROUND THE SIGHTSEEING SECTION

Each of eight sightseeing areas in Berlin is colour-coded for easy reference. Every chapter opens with an introduction to the area of the city it covers, describing its history and character, and has a *Street-by-Street* map illustrating typical parts of that area. Finding your way around the chapter is made simple by the numbering system used throughout. The most important sights are covered in detail in two or more full pages.

Each area has colour-coded thumb tabs.

1 Introduction to the area
For easy reference, the sights in each area are numbered and plotted on an area map. To help the visitor, this map also shows U- and S-Bahn stations, main bus and tram stops and parking areas. The area's key sights are listed by category, such as Museums.

Locator map

A locator map shows where you are in relation to other areas in the city centre.

A suggested route takes in some of the most interesting and attractive streets in the area.

2 Street-by-Street map
This gives a bird's-eye view of interesting and important parts of each sightseeing area. The numbering of the sights ties up with the area map and the fuller description of the entries on the pages that follow.

Stars indicate the features that no visitor should miss.

BERLIN AREA MAP

The coloured areas shown on this map *(see inside front cover)* are the eight main sightseeing areas used in this guide. Each is covered in a full chapter in *Berlin Area by Area (see pp52–205)*. They are highlighted on other maps throughout the book. In *Berlin at a Glance*, for example, they help you locate the top sights. They are also used to help you find the position of three walks *(see pp198–205)*.

Numbers refer to each sight's position on the area map and its place in the chapter.

Practical information provides everything you need to know to visit each sight. Map references pinpoint the sight's location on the *Street Finder* map *(see pp300–323)*.

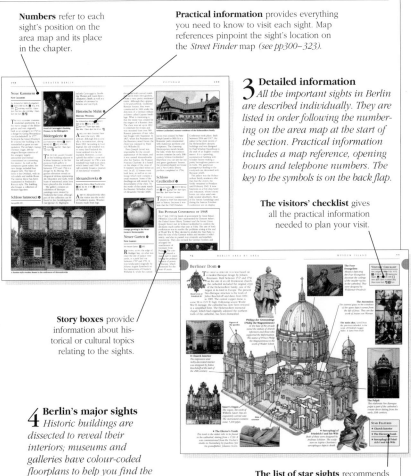

3 Detailed information
All the important sights in Berlin are described individually. They are listed in order following the numbering on the area map at the start of the section. Practical information includes a map reference, opening hours and telephone numbers. The key to the symbols is on the back flap.

The visitors' checklist gives all the practical information needed to plan your visit.

Story boxes provide information about historical or cultural topics relating to the sights.

4 Berlin's major sights
Historic buildings are dissected to reveal their interiors; museums and galleries have colour-coded floorplans to help you find the most important exhibits.

The list of star sights recommends the places that no visitor should miss.

INTRODUCING
BERLIN

Putting Berlin on the Map

Berlin, the capital of the Federal Republic of Germany, has a population of approximately 3.5 million and covers 889 sq km (343 sq miles). Situated in the eastern part of the country, in the middle of the Brandenburg region, Berlin occupies the flatlands on the banks of the Havel and Spree rivers, which merge in the Spandau district. The whole city is criss-crossed with numerous canals.

KEY

☐	Berlin and Environs
----	Ferry route
••••	National border
✈	Airport
═	Autobahn (motorway)
▬	Major road
—	Railway
⚓	Ferry terminal

An aerial view of the centre of Berlin, showing the Tiergarten and Unter den Linden *(see p12)*

Berlin and Environs

Tourist attractions in central Berlin are described on pages 54–165, and there is also a Streetfinder on pages 300–323 to help you find the sights. Places of interest in the outer districts of Berlin and in Potsdam are described on pages 166–205.

Greater Berlin

BERLIN IN ITS PRESENT FORM was created in 1920, through an amalgamation of several towns and villages surrounding the historic centre. It now consists of 12 administrative districts, some of which were formerly separate municipalities, such as Spandau. The city is surrounded by recreational areas, including lakes and woodlands. To the southwest lies the city of Potsdam with its splendid palaces, which can be reached easily by public transport.

Niederschönhausen

PANKOW

Schönholz

96

Prenzlau

Eberswalde

Malchow

Wartenberg

Heinersdorf

96a

109

WEISSENSEE

VEDDING

Gesundbrunnen

PRENZLAUER BERG

Prenzlauerberg

HOHEN-
SCHÖNHAUSEN

Lehrter Stadtbf.

MITTE

Friedrichstr.
2/5

Alexanderpl.

96a

LICHTENBERG

Potsdamerpl.

1

FRIEDRICHSHAIN

1/5

Ostbahnhof

Lichtenberg

Frankfurt/Oder

KREUZBERG

179

Ostkreuz

Friedrichsfelde

Rummels-
burger
See

Karlshorst

Flughafen
Tempelhof

See next page

TREPTOW

NEUKÖLLN

Spree

96a

TEMPELHOF

100

Baumschulenweg

Schöneweide

Britz

KEY

Central Berlin

Built-up area

Outer suburbs

Airport

Railway station

Autobahn (motorway)

Major road

Minor road

Railway line

Motorway under construction

Mariendorf

96

Buckow

0 kilometres   2

0 miles   1

101

Jüterbog

Zossen

Schönefeld

Central Berlin

CENTRAL BERLIN is divided into eight colour-coded sightseeing areas. The historic core is located along the eastern and northern banks of the Spree river, around the grand boulevard Unter den Linden and on Museum Island. West of the centre is the sprawling green Tiergarten. To the south is Kreuzberg, an area renowned for its alternative lifestyle. Further west is Kurfürstendamm, the centre of former West Berlin. Finally, at the edge of the city centre is the summer residence of the Prussian kings, the Schloss Charlottenburg.

Around Schloss Charlottenburg
The Baroque Charlottenburg Palace, named after Sophie Charlotte (wife of Friedrich III), is one of Berlin's greatest tourist attractions. Its magnificent rooms contain many beautiful objects (see pp156–65).

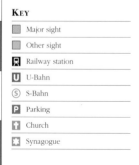

Kulturforum, Tiergarten
The Kulturforum is a cluster of interesting museums and libraries. It is also the home of the Berlin Philharmonic (see pp112–35).

Around Kurfürstendamm
The Kurfürstendamm, or Ku'damm as it is often called, is the main thoroughfare of western Berlin. This area contains numerous shops, restaurants, bars and cinemas (see pp146–55).

KEY

▆	Major sight
▆	Other sight
🚇	Railway station
Ⓤ	U-Bahn
Ⓢ	S-Bahn
🅿	Parking
✝	Church
✡	Synagogue

Berliner Dom, Museum Island
*On this island are Berlin's Protestant
cathedral, with its Neo-Baroque interior
and massive dome, and
a museum complex
(see pp70–85).*

**Rotes Rathaus,
East of the Centre**
*This monumental
town hall, which
replaces the former
medieval Rathaus,
dates from the 1860s.
It is decorated with
terracotta bas-reliefs,
(see pp86–97).*

CHAUSSEESTR.

Hamburger
Bahnhof

INVALIDENSTR.

HANNOVERSCHESTR.

TORSTR.

RSTR.

REINHOLDTALER STR.

TORSTR.

WEINMEISTERSTR.

FRIEDRICHSTR.

ORANIENBURGER STR.

ALTE SCHÖNHAUSER STR.

MÖLLSTR.

M I T T E

Alter Jüdischer
Friedhof

KARL-LIEBKNECHT-STR.

OTTO-BRAUN-STR.

FRIEDRICH-LIST-UFER

ROSTR.

LUISENSTR.

Spree

Pergamon-
museum

**Bahnhof
Alexanderplatz**

KARL-MARX-ALLEE

J.-F.-DULLES-ALLEE

SCHEIDEMANNSTR.

ENTLASTUNGSSTR.

DOROTHEENSTR.

Zeughaus

Fernsehturm

SCHILLINGSTR.

UNTER DEN LINDEN

*Altes
Museum*

**Berliner
Dom**

Marienkirche

BURGSTR.

GRUNERSTR.

STRASSE DES 17. JUNI

Tiergarten

G A R T E N

BEHRENSTR.

BEBEL-
PLATZ

FRANZÖSISCHE STR.

MARKGRAFENSTR.

WERDER

RATHAUSSTR.

BREITE STR.

STRALAUER STR.

MÜHLENDAMM

NEUE ROSSSTR.

INSELSTR.

TIERGARTENSTR.

**Kunstgewerbe-
museum**

*Gemälde-
galerie*

SIGISMUNDSTR.

LENNÉSTR.

WILHELMSTR.

LEIPZIGER STR.

WALLSTR.

GERTRAUDENSTR.

NEUE JAKOBSTR.

BRÜCKENSTR.

HEYDT STR.

STAUFFENBERGSTR.

STRESEMANNSTR.

KOCHSTR.

ORANIENSTR.

GENTHINER

LÜTZOWSTR.

POTSDAMER STR.

KURFÜRSTENSTR.

DERNEWITZSTR.

FLOTTWELLSTR.

ANHALTER STR.

SCHÖNEBERGER STR.

STRESEMANNSTR.

FRIEDRICHSTR.

LINDENSTR.

GITSCHINER STR.

K R E U Z B E R G

BLÜCHERSTR.

PRINZENSTR.

HORNSTR.

GROSSBEERENSTR.

ZOSSENER STR.

URBANSTR.

BAERWALDSTR.

YORCKSTR.

YORCKSTR.

GNEISENAUSTR.

KREUZBERGSTR.

Viktoriapark

KATZBACHSTR.

MEHRINGDAMM

DUDENSTR.

**Galeries Lafayette,
Friedrichstrasse**
*This department store
combines history
with ultra-modern
architecture (see
pp54–69).*

Viktoriapark, Kreuzberg
*This park is situated on a hill in the
Kreuzberg district, whose inhabitants include many Turks and
eccentric artists (see pp136–45).*

0 metres		500
0 yards		500

THE HISTORY OF BERLIN

BERLIN IS ONE OF THE YOUNGER *European capitals. The first written reference to the small fishing settlement of Cölln appeared in the year 1237. Together with the equally insignificant settlement of Berlin on the opposite bank of the Spree river, it was to become first a successful trading city under the control of the Margraves of Brandenburg, then capital of Prussia, and finally, the capital of Germany. Following World War II and the 1949 armistice, Berlin became a central arena for the Cold War. In 1991, after the fall of the Berlin Wall, the city became the capital of the newly-united Federal Republic of Germany.*

EARLY SETTLEMENTS

During the first centuries AD the banks of the Spree and Havel rivers were inhabited by various tribes, most notably the Germanic Semnones. By the end of the 6th century the Semnones were competing for land with Slavic tribes, who built forts at what are now the Berlin suburbs of Köpenick *(see p175)* and Spandau *(see p185)*. Five hundred years later the Slavic tribes were finally defeated following the arrival of the warlike Saxon, Albrecht the Bear of the House of the Ascanians, who became the first *Markgraf* (Margrave, or Count) of Brandenburg. The banks of the Spree river were now resettled with immigrants from areas to the west including the Harz mountains, the Rhine valley and Franconia.

Statue of Albrecht the Bear

BEGINNINGS OF THE MODERN CITY

Berlin's written history began in the early 13th century, when the twin settlements of Berlin and Cölln grew up on opposite banks of the Spree river, around what is now the Nikolaiviertel *(see p90)*. Trading in fish, rye and timber, the towns formed an alliance in 1307, becoming Berlin-Cölln, a deal celebrated by the construction of a joint town hall.

Following the death of the last Ascanian ruler in 1319, Brandenburg became the object of a long and bloody feud between the houses of Luxemburg and Wittelsbach, with devastating effects for the area's inhabitants. In 1411 the desperate townspeople appealed to the Holy Roman Emperor for help, receiving in response Friedrich von Hohenzollern as the town's special protector. Then in 1415 Rome duly rewarded Friedrich by naming him Elector of Brandenburg, a fateful appointment that marked the beginning of the 500-year rule of the House of Hohenzollern.

TIMELINE

1134 Investiture of Albrecht the Bear	
1197 First mention of Spandau	
1237 First written reference to Cölln	
1307 Signing of the treaty between Cölln and Berlin	
1359 Berlin and Cölln join Hanseatic League	
1415 Friedrich von Hohenzollern appointed Elector of Brandenburg	

1150   1200   1250   1300   1350   1400

1157 Albrecht the Bear defeats Slavic tribes and is crowned Margrave of Brandenburg

1209 First documented mention of Köpenick

c.1260 Berlin is enlarged

1244 First written reference to the settlement of Berlin

Silver denarius of 1369

◁ **Adolf von Menzel's symbolic painting *Borussia*, or *Prussia* (1868), at the Ephraim-Palais**

Deposition from the Cross (c.1520), a pane of a Gothic polyptych from the time of the Reformation

THE EARLY HOHENZOLLERNS

In 1432 Berlin and Cölln were formally unified. By 1443 Elector Friedrich II, son of Friedrich I, had begun construction of the town's first castle, the future Stadtschloss *(see p 71)*. This was part of his plan to make Berlin-Cölln the capital of Brandenburg and to reduce the powers and privileges of its citizens. Despite fierce opposition from the local population, the castle was built. By 1448 all opposition had been violently crushed, and in 1451 the castle became the Elector's official residence. To symbolize the consolidation of Hohenzollern power, he added an iron chain and padlock around the neck of the city's heraldic bear.

By the time Friedrich's nephew Johann Cicero became

Elector in 1486, Berlin-Cölln was formally established as the capital of the March of Brandenburg.

REFORMATION AND THE THIRTY YEARS' WAR

During the first half of the 16th century, the radical religious ideas of Martin Luther (1483–1546) spread quickly throughout the whole of Brandenburg. In 1539 the new Protestantism was adopted by the Elector, Joachim II Hector, and most of the town's aldermen.

For a time the city grew fast, boosted by the arrival of religious refugees from the Netherlands, as well as Italian artists invited by the subsequent elector, Joachim Georg. However, successive epidemics of the bubonic plague occurred in 1576, 1598 and 1600, checking the town's growth. The effect was compounded by the advent of the Thirty Years' War which raged from 1618 to 1648, turning the whole of the Holy Roman Empire into a bloody battlefield. In 1627 the Elector of Brandenburg had fled, relocating his court to the less exposed town of Königsberg. By 1648 the population of Berlin-Cölln had fallen to just 6,000, its population being decimated by famine and disease.

BERLIN UNDER THE GREAT ELECTOR

The fortunes of Berlin were turned by the arrival of Friedrich Wilhelm von Hohenzollern, who ascended the Brandenburg throne in 1640. Under the rule of this man, later known as the Great Elector, Berlin experienced a period of an unprecedented growth. The city's population

A falconer on a 16th-century tile

TIMELINE

1432 Unification of Cölln and Berlin

1486 Elector Johann Cicero makes Berlin his permanent residence

1539 Elector Joachim II converts to the Protestant faith

| 1415 | 1465 | 1515 | 1565 |

1447–8 Berlin rebellion against the Elector

1442 Construction begins on the royal castle in Cölln

1594 Building of the Spandau citadel completed

Tankard in the shape of Berlin's heraldic bear (1562)

The former Stadtschloss (Berlin Castle), with Lange Brücke in the foreground, c.1685

rose to 20,000 by 1688 at the end of Friedrich Wilhelm's long reign.

In 1648 work started on the modern fortification of the city. The Lustgarten *(see p74)* was established opposite the Stadtschloss and the road later to become known as Unter den Linden *(see p60)* was planted with lime trees. The city's economic power increased following the building of the canal linking the Spree and Oder rivers, which turned Berlin into the hub of all Brandenburg trade.

Berlin began to expand in all directions with the creation of new satellite towns – first Friedrichs-werder, then Dorotheen-stadt and Friedrichstadt, all between 1650 and 1690. They would all be absorbed into a unified city of Berlin in 1709.

In 1671 several wealthy Jewish families expelled from Vienna settled in Berlin, while following the 1685 Edict of Potsdam, large numbers of French Huguenots flocked to Brandenburg, forced out of their homeland after Louis XIV repealed the Edict of Nantes. Both these events came to play a major role in the future development of the city.

**Friedrich II
(1740–86)**

THE CAPITAL OF PRUSSIA

The successor to the Great Elector, Friedrich III inherited the title in 1688. Thirteen years later he raised Branden-burg's status to that of a kingdom, and was crowned King Friedrich I of Prussia. Ambitious and with a taste for luxury, Friedrich became a powerful patron of the arts. Under his rule Berlin acquired its Academies of Fine Arts and Science. Artists transformed the castle into a Baroque palace. The Zeughaus *(see pp58–9)* and the sum-mer palace or Schloss in Lietzenburg, later renamed Charlottenburg *(see pp160–61)*, were built at this time.

The next ruler of Prussia, Friedrich Wilhelm I (1713–40), was unlike his father and soon became known as the "Soldier-King". His initiatives were practical: Berlin was further expanded and encircled with a new wall, not for defence but as a measure against the desertion of conscripted citizens. Pariser Platz *(see p67)*, Leipziger Platz *(see p126)* and Mehring-platz *(see p144)* were all built at that time, and the popu-lation reached 90,000.

The next king was Friedrich II (1740–1786), otherwise known as Frederick the Great or "Alter Fritz" (Old Fritz). An educated man who appreciated art, he oversaw the city's transforma-tion into a sophisticated cultural centre. He was also an aggres-sive empire builder, sparking the Seven Years' War of 1756–63 with his invasion of Silesia, during which Berlin was briefly occupied by Austrian and Russian troops. The city's devel-opment continued, however, and at the time of Friedrich II's death in 1786, its population numbered 150,000.

The Baroque Period

BERLIN'S BAROQUE PERIOD lasted from the second half of the 17th century to the end of the 18th, and saw the expansion of Berlin-Cölln from a small town, devastated by successive epidemics of bubonic plague and the ravages of the Thirty Years' War, into a rich and cosmopolitan metropolis. Population growth was rapid, aided by the official amalgamation of Berlin-Cölln with the previously independent communities of Dorotheenstadt, Friedrichstadt and Friedrichs-werder. New city walls were built, as were many substantial buildings, including the Akademie der Künste, the Charité and Schloss Charlottenburg.

EXTENT OF THE CITY

▨ *1734*   ☐ *Today*

Flute Concert
This painting by Adolf von Menzel shows the arts-loving King Friedrich II (1740–86) giving a flute recital for his guests in the music room of the Schloss Sanssouci.

Nikolaikirche

Frederick the Great
The famous French-born portrait painter, Antoine Pesne, created this portrait of Friedrich II of Prussia, heir to the Prussian throne, in 1739.

Rococo Tureen
This elaborate silver tureen, decorated with a gilded lemon, was made in the Berlin workshop of Georg Wilhelm Marggraf und Müller in 1765.

Stadtschloss
(Royal Palace)

Love in the Italian Theatre (1714)
French painter Jean-Antoine Watteau (1684–1721) was a favourite with King Friedrich II, and as a result many of his works can still be seen in Berlin.

Rondell (now Mehringplatz)

Oktogon (now Leipziger Platz)

Zeughaus (Former Arsenal)
The splendid Baroque Zeughaus was completed in 1730. Used to store weapons until 1875, it will house the Deutsches Historisches Museum. This view of it was painted in 1786 by Carl Traugott Fechhelm.

King Friedrich I
This medallion bears the likeness of the first King of Prussia (1688–1713). The work of sculptor and architect Andreas Schlüter (1660–1714), it adorns the king's tomb.

Quarré (now Pariser Platz)

BERLIN IN 1740
This map shows the layout of the city's 18th-century fortifications, with various landmark buildings. Contrary to today's convention, this map was drawn with the north pointing down, rather than up.

Unter den Linden

BAROQUE ARCHITECTURE IN BERLIN

Many of Berlin's Baroque buildings have been destroyed, but in the city centre some fine examples still exist. Don't miss the Zeughaus *(see pp58–9)*, two fine churches in Gendarmenmarkt – the Deutscher Dom and the Französischer Dom *(see pp64–5)* – the Parochialkirche *(see p97)* and Sophienkirche *(see p104)*. Another Baroque highlight, even though it is largely a reconstruction, is Schloss Charlottenburg *(see pp158–9)* with its delightful park.

Schloss Charlottenburg

Antique scroll depicting the grand boulevard of Unter den Linden, 1821

BEGINNINGS OF THE MODERN ERA

By the time Friedrich Wilhelm II (1786–97) ascended the throne of Prussia, the country's era of absolute rulers was nearing an end. New trends associated with Romanticism were gaining popularity, and there was an explosion of ideas from outstanding personalities such as writers Gotthold Ephraim Lessing (1729–81) and Friedrich and August-Wilhelm von Schlegel.

Throughout Europe, French Emperor Napoleon Bonaparte (1769–1821) was waging war, defeating the Prussians in 1806 at the battles of Jena and Austerlitz. As French troops moved in to occupy Berlin, Friedrich Wilhelm took his court to Königsberg, while Berlin's pride, the horse-drawn chariot *(Quadriga)* crowning the Brandenburg Gate, was dismantled and taken to Paris.

By the end of 1809 the royal court had returned to Berlin, and, having received huge reparations, Napoleon and his troops finally left the city. In 1814 the *Quadriga* was returned to Berlin, and a year later Napoleon was defeated at Waterloo. Granted the mineral-rich lands of the Rhineland and Westphalia at the subsequent Congress of Vienna, Prussia enjoyed rapid industrialization during the next 30 years, particularly in Berlin. By 1837 August

Portrait of Friedrich Wilhelm IV

Borsig had opened his locomotive factory in the city, and in 1838 the first train ran on the Berlin–Potsdam railway.

Many outstanding buildings were designed at this time by Karl Friedrich Schinkel *(see p187)*, including the Neue Wache *(see p60)* and the Schauspielhaus, renamed the Konzerthaus *(see p64)*. Berlin University (now Humboldt Universität) was established in 1810 and became a major seat of learning, attracting famous lecturers such as philosophers Georg Hegel (1770–1831) and Arthur Schopenhauer (1788–1860).

In 1844, however, recession hit Europe, leaving a quarter of all Prussians in poverty. Hunger riots rocked the city in April 1847 and by 1848 Berlin saw a people's uprising in which over 250 demonstrators were shot dead by the Prussian army.

BUILDING AN EMPIRE

In 1861 Friedrich Wilhelm IV (1840–1861) was forced by madness to cede the throne to his brother, Wilhelm (1861–1888). Otto von Bismarck was soon appointed Chancellor, with a foreign policy to install Prussia in Austria's place at the head of all German-speaking states. In 1864 Prussia declared war on Denmark, and successfully acquired Schleswig-Holstein.

TIMELINE

1791 Building of the Brandenburg Gate completed

1799 Foundation of the Bauakademie

1810 Berlin University established

1831 Cholera epidemic breaks out

1844 Opening of the Berlin zoo (Zoologischer Garten)

1785   1800   1815   1830   1845

Enamelled box, mid-18th century

1806 Beginning of the 2-year French occupation of Berlin

1830 Opening of the Altes Museum

1838 Opening of the Berlin–Potsdam railway line

In 1866, following war with Austria, Prussia established dominance over the North German Confederation, an association of 22 states and free towns. In 1870 Prussia went to war with France, annexing the provinces of Alsace and Lorraine. Bismarck's next move was the proclamation of a German Empire on 18 January 1871, with Berlin as its capital and King Wilhelm I as Kaiser (Emperor). Thanks to the colossal reparations paid by France, and the abolition of trade barriers, Berlin now entered another period of rapid industrial growth, accompanied by a population explosion. By 1877 Berlin's population had grown to one million; by 1905 it was two million.

Poster advertising the Berlin Secession Exhibition of 1900, by Wilhelm Schulz

TRIUMPH AND DISASTER

The late 19th century saw an explosion of scientific and cultural achievement in the city, including the completion of a new sewage system in 1876, dramatically improving public health. By 1879 electric lamps lit the streets

Berlin's original Reichstag (parliament) building, constructed in 1894

and in 1881 the first telephones were installed. A year later the first urban train line, the S-Bahn, was opened. Berlin's cultural and scientific life flourished, headed by such outstanding personalities as writer Theodor Fontane, painter Adolf von Menzel and bacteriologist Robert Koch. In 1898 Max Liebermann *(see p67)* founded the hugely influential Berlin Secessionist movement, with members including Käthe Kollwitz and Max Slevogt.

As the city prospered, political developments in Germany and throughout Europe were moving towards the stalemate of 1914. Initially, the outbreak of World War I had little effect on the life of Berlin, but the subsequent famine, strikes and total German defeat led to the November Revolution in 1918, and the abdication of Kaiser Wilhelm II.

The Berlin Congress of 1878 by Anton von Werner

Mosaic by Martin-Gropius-Bau

Capital of the German Empire

O N 18 JANUARY 1871, Berlin became the capital of the newly-established German Empire, fulfilling the expansionist ambitions of the Prussian Chancellor Otto von Bismarck. Bringing together many previously independent German-speaking regions, the new Empire stretched beyond the borders of present-day Germany, into what are now France, Poland, Russia and Denmark. Massive reparations paid by France after her defeat in the Franco-German war of 1870 stimulated the rapid growth of a fast-industrializing Berlin, accompanied by an explosion of scientific and artistic invention. Standing at just 300,000 in 1850, by 1900 the city's population had reached 1.9 million.

EXTENT OF THE CITY

■ 1800	☐ Today

House of Hohenzollern
Mosaics depicting the Hohenzollern rulers decorate the bombed remains of the Kaiser-Wilhelm-Gedächtnis-kirche (see pp152–3), completed in 1895.

The Stadtschloss
The Stadtschloss was the royal residence at the declaration of the Prussian Empire in 1871. Decorating the Rathausbrücke, in the foreground, was the magnificent statue of the Great Elector, now in the courtyard of Schloss Charlottenburg (see pp160–61).

Prussian nobles

Members of Parliament

Riehmers Hofgarten
In the late 19th century a huge number of buildings were erected, from tenement blocks to grand buildings like this one.

Neptunbrunnen
This exuberant fountain (see p92) created by sculptor Reinhold Begas in 1891 was a present to Wilhelm II from the Berlin town council.

Hackescher Markt Station
Formerly called Bahnhof Börse, this is one of Berlin's first S-Bahn stations, built to a design by Johannes Vollmer and opened in 1902.

Vase with Portrait of Wilhelm II
Designed by Alexander Kips and bearing a portrait of Kaiser Wilhelm II, this vase was mass-produced at the Berlin Königliche-Porzellan-Manufaktur. Pieces were often presented to visiting heads of state.

Empress Augusta Victoria

Heir to the throne, Wilhelm

Black mourning clothes for women and black armbands for men were obligatory after the deaths of the two Kaisers, Wilhelm I and Friedrich III, in 1888.

Diplomatic corps

Prussian Chancellor Otto von Bismarck

Kaiser Wilhelm II

OPENING OF THE REICHSTAG
This enormous canvas, painted by Anton von Werner in 1893, portrays Kaiser Wilhelm II giving a speech to the Members of Parliament, nobles and other dignitaries at the official opening of the Reichstag. This important event took place only 11 days after the coronation of the new Kaiser.

Charlotte Berend
The arts flourished in the years before World War I. This 1902 portrait of an actress is by Berlin artist Lovis Corinth.

The burning of one of the thousands of buildings belonging to Jews on *Kristallnacht*, November 1938

THE WEIMAR REPUBLIC

On 9 November 1918 two politicians simultaneously proclaimed the birth of two German Republics. Social democrat Philipp Scheidemann announced the founding of a Democratic Republic, while hours later Karl Liebknecht, founder of the German communist movement, declared the Free Socialist Republic of Germany. Rivalries between the two groups erupted in January 1919 in a week of rioting, crushed by the Freikorps army who also brutally murdered communist leaders Karl Liebknecht and Rosa Luxemburg.

In February 1919 the National Assembly elected Social Democrat Friedrich Ebert President of the German Republic. In 1920 urban reform dramatically increased the size of Berlin, causing the population to swell to 3.8 million. Berlin, like the rest of the country, fell on hard times, with rising unemployment and rampant hyper-inflation.

At the same time, the city became the centre of a lively cultural life. Leading figures in theatre included Max Reinhardt and Bertolt

Ein Volk, ein Reich, ein Führer!

Nazi propoganda poster of Hitler, printed in 1938

Brecht, while from the UFA film studio came such classics as *The Cabinet of Dr Cagliari* and *Metropolis*. Jazz was popular, and the Berlin Philharmonic gained worldwide fame. Architecture flourished with Walter Gropius and Bruno Taut, while Berlin scientists Albert Einstein, Carl Bosch and Werner Heisenberg were all awarded the Nobel Prize.

THE THIRD REICH

The world stock-market crash of October 1929 and the ensuing Depression put the fragile German democracy under great pressure, paving the way for extremist politicians. On 30 January 1933 Adolf Hitler was appointed Chancellor. The Reichstag fire in February was used as a pretext to arrest communist and liberal opponents, and by March 1933 Hitler's Nazi (National Socialist German Workers) Party was in control of the Reichstag. Books by "un-German" authors were burned in front of the Alte Bibliothek, and works of art deemed to be "degenerate" were removed from museums.

Inferno (1946), Fritz Koelle

The 1936 Olympic Games in Berlin were meant as a showcase for Aryan supremacy. Although Germany won 33 gold medals, the real hero was the black US athlete Jesse Owens, with four gold medals.

The effects of the Nazi regime were felt particularly by Jews and intellectuals, many of whom were

TIMELINE

	1926 The Funkturm (radio tower) is opened			
1919 Proclamation of the Weimar Republic			**1938** Kristallnacht on the night of 9–10 November	**1945** Germany surrenders on 8 May
		1930 Opening of the Pergamonmuseum		**24 June 1948–12 May 1949** Soviet blockade of Berlin

| **1920** | | **1930** | | **1940** | | **1950** | | **19** |

| | **1928** Premiere of *The Threepenny Opera* by Bertolt Brecht | | **1933** Hitler accedes to power | | **1942** Wannsee Conference | |
| | **1920** Urban reform creates Greater Berlin | | **1939** Outbreak of World War II on 1 September | | *Poster depicting the German race* | |

Bilder deutscher Rassen 1

Nordische Rasse

forced to emigrate. On the night of 9–10 November 1938, known as *Kristall-nacht* (Night of the Broken Glass), thousands of synagogues, cemeteries, Jewish homes and shops throughout Germany were looted and burned.

WORLD WAR II

Hitler's invasion of Poland on 1 September 1939 signalled the start of World War II. For the citizens of Berlin, food shortages were followed in August 1940 by British air raids. By 1941 the goverment policy of the mass deportation of Jews to concentration camps had begun. Other groups targeted included homosexuals, priests and Romany gypsies. In January 1942, at a conference held in a villa in Wannsee *(see p181)* it was decided to embark on a systematic extermination of all European Jews. The unsuccessful attempt to assassinate Hitler in 1944 ended up with Nazis murdering many members of the German resistance.

After nearly four years of bitter warfare, the tide began to turn against the Germans. In April 1945 more than 1.5 million Soviet soldiers invaded Berlin. On 30 April Hitler committed suicide, and Germany conceded defeat.

BERLIN DIVIDED

The Potsdam Conference of 1945 *(see p199)* divided Berlin into four sectors, occupied respectively by Soviet, US, British and French troops. This put the devastated city at the centre of the Communist-Capitalist Cold War. On 24 June 1948 the Soviet authorities, in their attempt to annex the whole city, introduced a blockade of its Western sectors. The Allies responded with the Berlin Airlift, which thwarted the Soviet plans. On 12 May 1949 the blockade was lifted.

Historic buildings at the Gendarmenmarkt destroyed by British and American bombs, 1945–6

The same year saw the birth of the Federal Republic of Germany, with its capital in Bonn, and the German Democratic Republic (GDR), with the capital in East Berlin. West Berlin remained as a separate enclave. On 17 June 1953 workers' strikes in the GDR and East Berlin turned into an uprising which was bloodily crushed by the authorities. In their attempt to staunch the ever-rising flood of refugees, the GDR authorities decided in 1961 to surround West Berlin with a wall, and shoot at anyone attempting to cross it.

The political changes which occurred all over Eastern Europe in 1989 led to the fall of the Berlin Wall and the opening of the frontiers between the two republics. On 3 October 1990, Germany was officially reunified and Berlin once again became the capital. The government moved here in 1991.

Celebrations as the Berlin Wall falls, 9 November 1989

1961 Construction of the Berlin Wall on 13 August

1971 "Basic Treaty" allows travel from West to East Berlin

1987 Celebration of Berlin's 750th anniversary

1990 Official reunification of Germany, 3 October

1994 Allies leave Berlin

1970	1980	1990	2000

Trabant – the most popular car in the GDR

1991 Berlin becomes the German captial, 20 June

1989 Fall of the Berlin Wall, 9 November

1999 The Federal German Parliament assembles at the rebuilt Reichstag in April

BERLIN AT A GLANCE

MORE THAN 150 PLACES of interest are described in the *Area by Area* section of this book. These include a range of sights from historic monuments, such as the Nikolaikirche *(see p90)*, to modern landmarks like the ambitious showcase architecture of the new Potsdamer Platz district *(see p126);* from the peace of the Botanical Garden *(see p177)* to the noisier charms of Berlin's long-established zoo *(see p150)*. To help you make the most of your stay, the following 16 pages provide a time-saving guide to the very best that Berlin has to offer. Museums and galleries, historic buildings, parks and gardens, modern architecture, the legacy of the divided city and famous Berliners all feature in this section. Below is a top ten selection of attractions that no visitor should miss.

BERLIN'S TOP TEN ATTRACTIONS

Pergamonmuseum
See pp80–83.

Schloss Charlottenburg
See pp160–61.

Kungstgewerbe-museum
See pp118–21.

Gemäldegalerie
See pp122–5.

Nikolaiviertel
See pp88–9.

Zoologischer Garten
See p150.

Brandenburger Tor
See p67.

Fernsehturm
See p93.

Reichstag
See p134.

Kaiser-Wilhelm-Gedächt-nis-Kirche See pp152–3.

◁ Interior of the Reichstag *(see p134)*, with its new dome designed by Sir Norman Foster

Berlin's Best: Museums and Galleries

BERLIN BOASTS SOME of the finest museum collections in the world. Since 1990 many of the collections previously split between East and West Berlin have been brought together in new venues. One example is the Gemäldegalerie collection, a

Ancient Greek vase magnificent collection of Old Master paintings. Berlin's major museum complexes are located on Museum Island, around Schloss Charlottenburg, at the Kulturforum and at Dahlem.

Kunstgewerbemuseum
The arts and crafts collection at the Kunstgewerbemuseum (see pp118–21) is among the most interesting in Europe. One of its many treasures is this 17th-century gold elephant-shaped vessel.

Around Schloss Charlottenburg

Tiergarten

Around Kurfürstendamm

Gemäldegalerie
This world-famous collection illustrates the history of European painting from the 13th to the 18th centuries. Originally part of a triptych, The Adoration of the Magi (1470) was painted by Hugo van der Goes (see pp122–5).

Museumszentrum Dahlem
This huge complex houses several museums devoted to ethnography and non-European art (see p178).

0 metres	750
0 yards	750

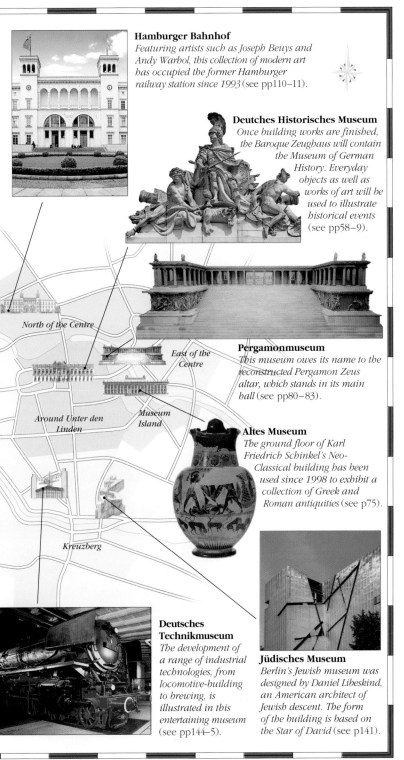

Hamburger Bahnhof
*Featuring artists such as Joseph Beuys and
Andy Warhol, this collection of modern art
has occupied the former Hamburger
railway station since 1993 (see pp110–11).*

Deutches Historisches Museum
*Once building works are finished,
the Baroque Zeughaus will contain
the Museum of German
History. Everyday
objects as well as
works of art will be
used to illustrate
historical events
(see pp58–9).*

North of the Centre

East of the
Centre

Pergamonmuseum
*This museum owes its name to the
reconstructed Pergamon Zeus
altar, which stands in its main
hall (see pp80–83).*

Around Unter den
Linden

Museum
Island

Altes Museum
*The ground floor of Karl
Friedrich Schinkel's Neo-
Classical building has been
used since 1998 to exhibit a
collection of Greek and
Roman antiquities (see p75).*

Kreuzberg

**Deutsches
Technikmuseum**
*The development of
a range of industrial
technologies, from
locomotive-building
to brewing, is
illustrated in this
entertaining museum
(see pp144–5).*

Jüdisches Museum
*Berlin's Jewish museum was
designed by Daniel Libeskind,
an American architect of
Jewish descent. The form
of the building is based on
the Star of David (see p141).*

Exploring Berlin's Museums

Majolica plate,
Kunstgewerbe-
museum

DESPITE BEING DAMAGED during World War II, Berlin's numerous museums are still among the finest, and the most heavily subsidized, in the world. Many collections were split up when the city was partitioned in 1946, and although the process of bringing them together again is under way, some collections are still scattered around different sites, and many of the older museums are undergoing refurbishment.

Picasso's *Head of the Faun* (1937)
in the Sammlung Berggruen

ANCIENT ART

THE ART OF ANCIENT Egypt is shown at the **Ägyptisches Museum** (Egyptian Museum). The jewel of this museum is the bust of Queen Nefertiti. Works of art from Ancient Greece and Rome are kept in the 19th-century **Altes Museum** (Old Museum). Another large collection of antiquities can be found in the **Pergamonmuseum**, where visitors can see several reconstructed architectural wonders, including the Pergamon Zeus altar and the Market Gate from Miletus. The museum also holds an impressive collection of Middle Eastern art, including a reconstruction of the Babylonian Ishtar Gate.

Bust of Nefertiti,
Ägyptisches
Museum

German and Italian sculpture will be housed in the **Bode-museum**, due to open in 2004 following refurbishment. The **Alte Nationalgalerie** (Old National Gallery), which has been undergoing refurbishment, displays 18th- and 19th-century art, including paintings by the German Romantics, amongst which are famous landscapes by Caspar David Friedrich. Other highlights can be seen at the nearby Altes Museum building.

A collection of sculpture from the late-16th to the mid-19th centuries can be seen in the **Schinkel-Museum**. The **Neue Nationalgalerie** (New National Gallery) is filled with late 19th- and early 20th-century paintings and sculpture. Art Nouveau and Art Deco works are featured at the **Bröhan-Museum**, while works by modern greats, such as Pablo Picasso, Paul Klee and Georges Braque, are on show at the **Sammlung Berggruen** (Berggruen Collection).

The **Brücke-Museum** displays the works of German Expressionists, and contemporary art is exhibited in the **Hamburger Bahnhof**.

Arts and crafts, from the Middle Ages to the present, are displayed at the **Kunstgewerbemuseum** (Museum of Applied Arts). The **Bauhaus-Archiv** displays applied arts by members of the influential inter-war Bauhaus movement.

FINE ART AND DESIGN

BERLIN'S LARGEST collection of 13th- to 18th-century European painting is displayed in the **Gemäldegalerie** (Picture Gallery). Here are works by old masters including Dürer, Rembrandt, Titian, Botticelli and Caravaggio. In the same museum complex is the **Kupferstichkabinett**, with drawings and prints from the Middle Ages to the present.

Old masters can also be seen in the **Jagdschloss Grune-wald**, a Renaissance palace home to German and Dutch paintings from the 14th to 19th centuries. A large collection of predominantly 17th-century paintings is housed in the **Bildergalerie** (Gallery of Paintings) in Potsdam.

Étienne Chevalier with St Stephen by Jean Fouquet, Gemäldegalerie

NON-EUROPEAN ART

THOSE INTERESTED in Asian art should visit the **Museums-zentrum Dahlem**. This complex houses three large collections: the Museum für Ostasiatische Kunst (Museum of East Asian Art), the Museum für Indische Kunst (Museum of Indian Art) and the Ethnologisches Museum (Museum of Ethnography), which explores the heritage of non-European nations.

The **Museum für Islamische Kunst** (Museum of Islamic Art) is located in the same building as the Pergamonmuseum.

Totem pole, Ethnologisches Museum

HISTORY

THE COLLECTION of the **Deutsches Historisches Museum** (Museum of German History) traces German history from the Middle Ages to the present. The **Hugenotten-museum** (Huguenot Museum), located in the tower of the Französischer Dom, charts the history of the city's Huguenots.

The **Centrum Judaicum** (Jewish Centre) in the Neue Synagoge (New Synagogue), and the **Jüdisches Museum** (Jewish Museum), in a new building by Daniel Libeskind, are devoted to Jewish history and cultural heritage.

Berlin has several museums associated with World War II. The **Topographie des Terrors** (Topography of Terror) exhibition is displayed at the site of the former Gestapo and SS headquarters. A deeply shocking collection of documents concerning the Holocaust is kept at the **Haus der Wannsee-Konferenz**. The tools of terror used on the citizens of the German Democratic Republic can be seen at the **Stasi-Museum**, while the **Haus am Check-point Charlie** (House at Checkpoint Charlie) museum tells the stories of those who crossed the Berlin Wall. The **Alliierten Museum** focuses on life during the Cold War.

TECHNOLOGY AND NATURAL HISTORY

THE **Museum für Natur-kunde** (Museum of Natural History) contains the world's biggest dinosaur skeleton. Also popular with visitors is the **Deutsches Technik-museum** (German Technology Museum), in a large site around a former railway station. German movie history (including original costumes worn by divas such as Marlene Dietrich) is presented at the **Filmmuseum Berlin**. Those interested in technology should also visit the **Museum für Post und Kommunikation** (Museum of Post and Communications).

SPECIALIST SUBJECTS

BERLIN IS not short of specialist museums. There are museums devoted to laundry, sugar and even hemp. Lovers of theatre and literature can visit the one-time home of Bertolt Brecht (1898–1956), now the **Brecht-Weigel Gedenkstätte** (Brecht-Weigel Memorial). Worth a visit to see the magnificent Wurlitzer organ alone is the **Musikinstrumenten-Museum** (Musical Instruments Museum). The outdoor **Domäne Dahlem** (Dahlem Farm Museum) shows 300 years of local farm life and exhibits old-fashioned tools.

A wide array of exhibits in the Musikinstrumenten-Museum

Berlin's Best: Historic Architecture

BERLIN IS A RELATIVELY new city. It expanded slowly until the first half of the 19th century, and then grew with increasing rapidity from around 1850 onwards. Although many of the city's finest architectural treasures were destroyed by World War II bombing, it is still possible to discover many interesting historic buildings (for more information, *see pp36–7*). In nearby Potsdam *(see pp190–205)* you can visit the splendid Schloss Sanssouci. Set in magnificent parkland, the palace was built for Friedrich II (1740–1786) and extended by subsequent rulers.

Schloss Charlottenburg
The construction of this Baroque royal palace at Charlottenburg was begun in 1695. Subsequent extension works took place throughout the 18th century (see pp160–61).

Around Schloss Charlottenburg

Tiergarten

Around Kurfürstendamm

Schloss Bellevue
This Rococo palace by Philipp Daniel Boumann is now the official residence of the President of the Federal Republic of Germany.

The Reichstag
This massive Neo-Renaissance building was designed in 1884 by Paul Wallot. Its elegant new dome is the work of British architect Norman Foster (see p134).

Schloss Sanssouci
This small palace was the favourite residence of Friedrich II.

Neues Palais
The Neues Palais combines elements of Baroque and Neo-Classical style.

POTSDAM PALACES

The summer palace of Schloss Sanssouci gives its name to Potsdam's Park Sanssouci, a royal complex with highlights including the grand 18th-century Neues Palais and the small but charming Schloss Charlottenhof.

0 metres	750
0 yards	750

Brandenburger Tor
*This Neo-Classical gate stands at
the end of Unter den Linden.
Crowned by a Quadriga (chariot)
driven by the Goddess of Victory, it
is the symbol of Berlin (see p67).*

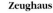

Zeughaus
*Upon completion of re-
building, this Baroque
arsenal will house the
Deutsches Historisches
Museum (see pp58–9).
Its courtyard will contain
masks of dying warriors
by sculptor Andreas
Schlüter (1660–1714).*

Marienkirche
*This Gothic church,
founded in the 13th
century, contains a
striking 15th-century
mural. It is one of the
city's oldest buildings
(see pp94–5).*

North of the Centre

East of the
Centre

Around Unter
den Linden

Museum
Island

Kreuzberg

Rotes Rathaus
*Berlin's main Town Hall is named
"red" after the colour of its brick
exterior, not the political
persuasion of the Mayor (see p90).*

Berliner Dom
*This enormous cathedral, built
between 1894 and 1905, is an
example of the Neo-Renaissance
style in Berlin (see pp76–7).*

Konzerthaus
*Built in 1820 to replace a theatre
destroyed by fire, this beautiful building
on the Gendarmenmarkt was designed by
Karl Friedrich Schinkel (see pp64–5).*

Exploring Berlin's Historic Architecture

U NTIL THE INDUSTRIAL REVOLUTION of the late 19th century, Berlin was little more than a small town surrounded by villages. As a result, the city's oldest buildings are concentrated in the central core around Unter den Linden and along the Spree river, an area which suffered heavy damage during World War II. Older country residences, however, as well as some important newer buildings, can be seen in former villages such as Wedding and Charlottenburg, which now form part of Greater Berlin.

14th-century Gothic doorway of the Nikolaikirche in the Nikolaiviertel

MIDDLE AGES AND RENAISSANCE

T HE **Nikolaikirche** is the oldest building in central Berlin. The base of its massive front tower is Romanesque and dates back to about 1230, although the church itself is Gothic and was built between 1380 and 1450. The second Gothic church in the city centre is the **Marienkirche**. Nearby are the ruins of a **Franciscan friary**, and the **Heiliggeistkapelle**. Many medieval churches outside the city centre have survived the war. Among the most beautiful is the late-Gothic **Nikolaikirche** in Spandau, dating

from the early 15th century. A further ten village churches, most dating from the 13th century, can be found hidden among high-rise apartment buildings. **St Annen-Kirche** in Dahlem, however, still enjoys an almost rural setting.

The few surviving secular structures include fragments of the **city walls** in the city centre, and the **Julius-turm** in Spandau, a huge, early 13th-century tower which stands in the grounds of the Spandau Citadel. Berlin's only surviving Renaissance buildings are the **Ribbeckhaus** with its four picturesque gables, the **Jagdschloss-Grunewald**, a modest hunting lodge designed by Casper Theyss in 1542, and the **Spandau Citadel** (or fortress), a well-preserved example of Italian-style military defence architecture. Finished in 1592, the construction of the Citadel was begun in 1560 by Christoph Römer using plans by Italian architect Francesco Chiaramella da Gandino. It was brought to completion by Rochus Guerrini Graf zu Lynar (the Count of Lynar).

BAROQUE EXPANSION

T HE THIRTY YEARS' WAR (1618–48) put a temporary stop to the town's development, and it was not until the Peace of 1648 that new building work in the Baroque style began. One of the first of the city's Baroque buildings is the late 17th-century **Schloss Köpenick**. More buildings followed, many of which survive today. They include the **Parochialkirche**, the **Deutscher Dom** and the **Französischer Dom**, as well as the magnificent **Zeughaus**, or arsenal, built between 1695 and 1730. During this period Andreas Schlüter (1664–1714) designed the now-demolished Stadtschloss (Royal Palace), while Johann Arnold Nering (1659–95) designed **Schloss Charlottenburg**. Other surviving Baroque palaces include **Palais Podewils**, **Schloss Friedrichsfelde** and **Schloss Niederschönhausen**. One of the few buildings dating from the reign of Friedrich Wilhelm I (1713–40) is the **Kollegienhaus** at Lindenstrasse No. 14 , designed by Philipp Gerlach and built in 1733. During the reign of Friedrich II (1740–86), many buildings were erected in the late Baroque and Rococo styles. These include **Schloss Sanssouci** in Potsdam and the **Alte Bibliothek** building on Unter den Linden, which completed the Forum Fridericianum project, now better known as Bebelplatz *(see pp56–7).*

Detail of the Zeughaus

NEO-CLASSICISM AND ROMANTICISM

T HE NEO-CLASSICAL architecture of the late-18th and early-19th centuries has given Berlin much of its basic form. One dominant figure of this period was Carl Gotthard Langhans (1732–1808), creator of the **Brandenburg Gate** and of **Schloss Bellevue**. Even more influential, however, was Karl

Renaissance-style defence, the Citadel building at Spandau

Friedrich Schinkel *(see p187)*. His work includes some of Berlin's most important public buildings, including the **Neue Wache**, the **Altes Museum** and the **Konzerthaus**. Many of Schinkel's residential commissions are also still standing, with some such as **Schloss Klein Glienicke** and **Schloss Tegel** open to the public. Schinkel's Neo-Gothic work includes **Schloss Babelsberg** and the **Friedrichswerdersche Kirche**.

Elegant Neo-Classicism at Karl Friedrich Schinkel's Schloss Klein Glienicke

INDUSTRIALIZATION AND THE MODERN AGE

THE SECOND HALF of the 19th century was a time of rapid development for Berlin. After Schinkel's death, his work was continued by his students, Ludwig Persius (1803–45) and Friedrich August Stüler (1800–65). Stüler designed the Neo-Classical **Alte Nationalgalerie** between 1866 and 1876. Some splendid Neo-Romanesque and Neo-Gothic churches and several notable public buildings in various styles were also produced at this time. The spirit of the Italian Neo-Renaissance is seen in the **Rotes Rathaus** designed by Hermann Friedrich Waesemann, and in the **Martin-Gropius-Bau**, by Martin Gropius in 1877. Late Neo-Renaissance features are used in Paul Wallot's **Reichstag** building and in Ernst von

Decorative frieze on the Martin-Gropius-Bau

Ihne's **Statsbibliothek** building. Julius Raschdorff's **Berliner Dom** shows Neo-Baroque influences. Much of the religious architecture of the period continued in the Neo-Gothic style, while Franz Schwechten designed the **Kaiser-Wilhelm-Gedächtnis-Kirche** in the Neo-Romanesque style. Many structures of this period are built in the modernist style inspired by the industrial revolution, the textbook example being the huge power station, **AEG-Turbinenhalle**, designed by Peter Behrens in the 1890s.

BETWEEN THE TWO WORLD WARS

THE GREATEST architectural achievements of this period include a number of splendid housing estates, such as the **Hufeisensiedlung** designed by Bruno Taut and Martin Wagner in 1924, and **Onkel-Toms-Hütte** in Zehlendorf. An interesting example of the Expressionist style is Erich Mendelsohn's **Einsteinturm** in Potsdam. Art Deco is represented by Hans Poelzig's **Haus des Rundfunks**, the country's first Broadcasting House. Hitler's rise to power in the 1930s marked a return to the classical forms which dominated German architecture of the Fascist period. Representatives of this period include the **Tempelhof Airport** Terminal building and the **Olympia-Stadion**, built for the 1936 Olympic Games.

20th-century Neo-Renaissance detail of the massive Berliner Dom

Reminders of the Divided City

I
N 1945, AS PART OF THE post-war peace, Berlin was divided into four zones of occupation: Soviet, American, British and French. Hostilities erupted in June 1948, when the Soviets block-aded West Berlin in an attempt to bring the area under their control. The ensuing year-long standoff marked the start of the Cold War. By the 1950s, economic problems in the East had led to bloodily-suppressed riots and a mass exodus to the West. In 1961 the East German government constructed the infamous Berlin Wall *(die Mauer)* to contain its citizens. Between this time and reunification at the end of 1989, more than 180 people were shot trying to cross the Wall.

Berlin Wall
Protected to the east by land mines, the Wall, known by the East German authorities as the "Anti-Fascist Protection Wall", surrounded West Berlin and was 155 km (95 miles) long (see p168).

Memorial to Soviet Soldiers
Part of West Berlin, the area around this monument to Red Army troops killed in the 1945 Battle of Berlin was closed for many years due to attacks on its Soviet guards (see p135).

Around
Schloss Charlottenburg

Tiergarten

Around
Kurfürstendamm

0 km   1
0 miles   0.5

KEY

━━━ Berlin Wall

BERLIN BEFORE REUNIFICATION

The Wall cut the city in half, severing its main transport arteries, the S-Bahn and U-Bahn lines. West Berliners were excluded from the centre of the city. Running along the Wall was a no-man's-land, now Berlin's biggest building site.

KEY

━━━ Berlin Wall

━━━ Sector boundaries

✈ Airport

French Sector

Soviet Sector

British Sector

American Sector

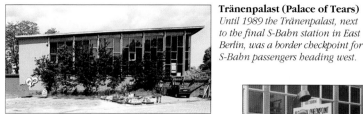

Tränenpalast (Palace of Tears)
Until 1989 the Tränenpalast, next to the final S-Bahn station in East Berlin, was a border checkpoint for S-Bahn passengers heading west.

Checkpoint Charlie
This border crossing between the American and Soviet sectors was used by foreign citizens and diplomats. It was the location of many dramatic events during the years of the Cold War.

North of the Centre

East of the Centre

Around Unter den Linden   Museum Island

Kreuzberg

East Side Gallery
The longest remaining section of the Berlin Wall became an open-air gallery in 1990, covered with an eclectic mixture of paintings by 118 artists (see p173).

Luftbrücke
This striking memorial commemorates those who died during the Berlin Airlift of 1948–9. Allied planes delivered 2.3 million tons of supplies to West Berlin in the face of the year-long Soviet blockade (see p145).

Haus am Checkpoint Charlie
This museum holds photos and other Wall memorabilia, including a selection of escape vehicles (see p140).

Berlin's Best: Modern Architecture

FOLLOWING BERLIN'S DEVASTATION in World War II, intense post-war reconstruction turned the city into a giant building site. With the help of architects from several countries the city acquired many modern structures and estates, ranked among the best in the world. The city's reunification in 1990 and the reinstatement of Berlin as the main seat of government gave rise to a second wave of building activity, carried out on a scale unprecedented in Europe. The architectural elite are participating in the design of the new Berlin, and the sites in the city centre that stood empty until 1990 are being filled with new buildings at an incredible rate.

Bauhaus-Archiv
This cubist structure was completed in 1978 to house the Bauhaus museum. It was designed much earlier by Walter Gropius (1883–1969), director of the Bauhaus art school from 1919 to 1928.

Around Schloss Charlottenburg

Tiergarten

Around Kurfürstendamm

Kant-Dreieck
This building, with its pure forms and the eccentric sail-like structure mounted on the roof, is the work of Josef Paul Kleihues.

Nordische Botschaften
Built between 1997 and 1999, the five interconnected embassies of the Scandinavian countries are an example of daring architectural design. The building's green shutters adjust to the intensity and direction of available sunlight.

Kammermusiksaal

Both the Berliner Philharmonie building (1961) and the adjacent Kammermusik-saal, or chamber music hall (1987), were designed by Hans Scharoun. The latter was built posthumously by Edgar Wisniewski, Scharoun's pupil.

Galeries Lafayette

This elegant department store in Friedrichstrasse, designed by Jean Nouvel, brings Parisian chic to the heart of Berlin.

North of the Centre

East of the Centre

Around Unter den Linden

Museum Island

Kreuzberg

Quartier Schützenstrasse

This part of the city features the work of Italian architect Aldo Rossi. With high-rise blocks and bold colour schemes, the area shows modernity and classical forms standing side by side.

| 0 metres | 750 |
| 0 yards | 750 |

Gemäldegalerie

The new Gemäldegalerie, designed by the Hilmer and Sattler Partnership, was opened in June 1998. The main hall is particularly elegant.

Sony Center

This ultra-modern steel-and-glass building was designed by German-American architect Helmut Jahn. It houses offices, entertainment venues, the Kaisersaal and Sony's European headquarters.

Exploring Berlin's Modern Architecture

A ROUND THE WORLD architects are forever designing buildings with innovative and interesting structures, but in Berlin this creative process is happening on an unprecedented scale. The city is a vast melting pot of trends and styles, where the world's greatest architects scramble for new commissions and where the buildings compete with each other in the originality of their form and in their use of the latest technology.

Haus der Kulturen der Welt in the Tiergarten

FROM 1945 TO 1970

W ORLD WAR II exacted a heavy price from Berlin. The centre was reduced to rubble and the partitioning of the city made it impossible to carry out any co-ordinated reconstruction. In 1952, East Berlin decided to develop **Karl-Marx-Allee** in the Socialist-Realist style. In reply, West Berlin employed the world's greatest architects to create the **Hansaviertel** estate. Le Corbusier built one of his *unités d'habitation*, while the American architect, Hugh A Stubbins, built the Kongresshalle (now the **Haus der Kulturen der Welt**). The West's response to the cultural venues inherited by the East Berliners, including the opera, the library and the museums, was the **Kulturforum** complex. The complex included such magnificent buildings as the **Philharmonie**, designed by Hans Scharoun, and the **Neue Nationalgalerie**, designed by Mies van der Rohe. While West Berlin acquired its huge "trade

temple"– the **Europa-Center**, constructed in 1965, East Berlin boasted its **Fernsehturm** (television tower), built in 1969.

FROM 1970 TO 1990

T HE CONTINUING rivalry, as each part of the city tried to outdo the other, resulted in the construction of East Berlin's **Palast der Republik** in 1976. The West replied with the ultramodern **Internationales Congress Centrum** in 1979. The Kulturforum complex was further extended with designs by Scharoun, including the **Kammermusiksaal** and the **Staatsbibliothek** (library). The impressive **Bauhaus-Archiv** was developed from a design by Walter Gropius. In 1987 Berlin celebrated its 750th anniversary, which in the East saw the completion of the huge **Nikolaiviertel** development, with its pre-war allusions. In the West, the IBA's 1987 scheme gave the town its enormous new post–modernist housing estates in Kreuzberg and also in the **Tegel** area.

Neue Nationalgalerie at Kulturforum designed by Mies van der Rohe

Potsdamer Platz

I N THE SHORT space of a few years a new financial and business district has sprung up on the vast empty wasteland surrounding the Potsdamer Platz. It boasts splendid constructions designed by Renzo Piano, Arata Isozaki and Helmut Jahn. As well as office blocks, the area has many public buildings, including cinemas and a theatre, as well as a huge shopping centre – the Arkaden, plus a luxury hotel, restaurants and several bars.

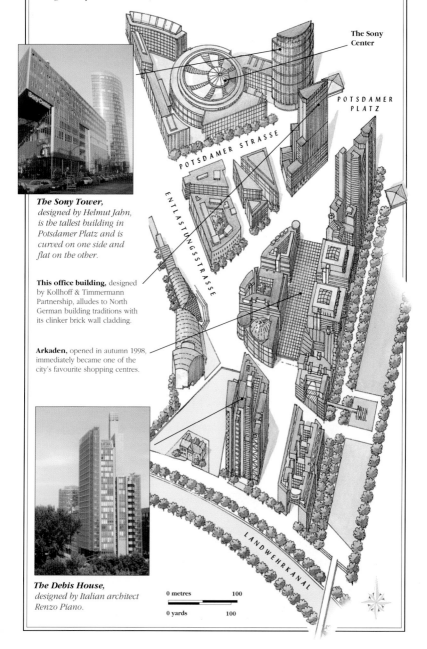

The Sony Center

POTSDAMER PLATZ

POTSDAMER STRASSE

ENTLASTUNGSSTRASSE

LANDWEHRKANAL

The Sony Tower, designed by Helmut Jahn, is the tallest building in Potsdamer Platz and is curved on one side and flat on the other.

This office building, designed by Kollhoff & Timmermann Partnership, alludes to North German building traditions with its clinker brick wall cladding.

Arkaden, opened in autumn 1998, immediately became one of the city's favourite shopping centres.

The Debis House, designed by Italian architect Renzo Piano.

0 metres   100

0 yards   100

Berlin's Best: Parks and Gardens

B ERLIN IS UNDOUBTEDLY one of Europe's greenest capital cities, with the sprawling Tiergarten at its centre. However, most of Berlin's districts have their own smaller parks and gardens, too, some of them with children's play areas and nature trails. To the west of the city is the vast Grunewald, a beautiful area of forest which contains mountain bike trails and scenic paths for walkers and cyclists. In summer, numerous lakes, rivers and canals provide excellent facilities for water sports.

Zoologischer Garten
Popular with children, Berlin's zoo has some 14,000 animals, representing 1,400 different species. It is the oldest zoo in Germany (see p150).

Schloss Charlottenburg
The well-maintained grounds of this royal palace were designed in the French Baroque style (see pp160–61).

Around Schloss Charlottenburg

Around Kurfürstendamm

Botanischer Garten
Established from 1899 to 1910 in Dahlem, this botanical garden is one of the biggest in the world (see p177).

Park Babelsberg
This vast landscaped park was designed by Peter Joseph Lenné, and now lies within the Potsdam city limits. It surrounds the picturesque Schloss Babelsberg (see pp210–11).

Tiergarten
Once a hunting reserve, this was converted into a park after 1818 by landscape designer Peter Joseph Lenné (see p132).

Monbijoupark
The park once surrounded Monbijou Palace, which was destroyed during World War II (see p103).

North of the Centre

East of the Centre

Around Unter den Linden

Museum Island

Tiergarten

Kreuzberg

Tierpark Friedrichsfelde
In 1954 the park at Schloss Friedrichsfelde was converted into the East Berlin Zoological Garden (see p174).

Britzer Garten
The landscaped park with its beautiful lime-tree avenue, surrounds the early 18th-century Schloss Britz (see p176).

Viktoriapark
This large park winds around a hill with good views of Kreuzberg. At its peak stands a memorial to the wars of liberation fought against Napoleon (see p145).

0 metres 1000
0 yards 1000

Famous Berliners

MANY OF BERLIN'S FAMOUS CITIZENS include artists and scientists who made notable contributions to the world's cultural heritage. Berlin universities were home to the most eminent German philosophers and scientists, and the thriving theatrical life of the city attracted Germany's finest writers, actors and directors. During the 1920s Berlin was also an important centre of the movie industry, attracting film stars and directors from all over Europe.

Bertolt Brecht (1898–1956)
The author of The Three-penny Opera, *Brecht founded the Berliner Ensemble in 1949 (see p108). His apartment has been turned into a museum (see p109).*

Robert Koch (1843–1910)
This noted scientist won a Nobel Prize in medicine in 1905 for his discoveries in the field of bacteriology. He became director of the Institute of Microbiology, where there is a small memorial museum.

Around Schloss Charlottenburg

Tiergarten

Around Kurfürstendamm

Herbert von Karajan (1908–89)
This famous Austrian conducted the Berlin Philharmonic from 1954 to 1989.

Marlene Dietrich (1901–92)
Hollywood's all-time great star began her career in Berlin. She is buried in the Friedenau Cemetery.

Albert Einstein (1879–1955)
Einstein was the director of the Berlin Institute of Physics from 1914 until 1933, when repressive Nazi policies forced him to leave Germany.

Jacob Grimm (1785–1863)
and Wilhelm Grimm (1786–1859)
*Best known for their children's fairy-
tales, including "Little Red Riding
Hood" and "Hänsel and Gretel", the
Brothers Grimm also began work on
the definitive German language
dictionary,* Das Deutsche Wörterbuch.

Käthe Kollwitz (1867–1945)
*Sculptor and graphic artist Käthe
Kollwitz spent much of her life in
Prenzlauer Berg. She recorded the
lives of the poor of the district, where
a monument to her now stands.*

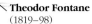

North of the
Centre

East of
the Centre

**Georg Wilhelm
Friedrich Hegel**
(1770–1831)
*Hegel was one of the
most influential phil-
osophers of the early
19th century. He taught
at Berlin University
from 1818 until his
death in 1831.*

Museum
Island

Around Unter
den Linden

Kreuzberg

Theodor Fontane
(1819–98)
*Of Huguenot ancestry,
Fontane was one of the
greatest German novelists
of the 19th century. He
also wrote theatrical
reviews for 20 years.*

**Felix Mendelssohn-
Bartholdy** (1809–47)
*Composer of the "Wedding
March" and grandson of philo-
sopher Moses Mendelssohn, Felix
Mendelssohn-Bartholdy is buried
in Kreuzberg's Friedhöfe vor
dem Halleschen Tor (see p144).*

Richard Strauss
(1864–1949)
*Now best known as a
composer, Strauss directed
the Berlin Court Opera
from 1898 to 1917.*

0 metres	750
0 yards	750

BERLIN THROUGH THE YEAR

IKE ALL MAJOR European capitals, Berlin offers a wide range of activities throughout the year. The best seasons for cultural and sporting events are spring and autumn, when the city hosts many spectacular fairs and exhibitions. During summer the city's population shrinks, as many locals head for their holiday destinations. But the weather is often pleasant, and rarely

Karneval der Kulturen

very hot, so this is a good time for serious sightseeing. In winter, although it can get quite cold, it is possible to spend time visiting museums or simply walking around the city. The streets teem with shoppers during the run up to Christmas. A more detailed programme of events can be obtained from tourist information offices *(see p278)* or on the internet at www.berlinonline.de/kultur.

The Whitsun Karneval der Kulturen in the streets of Kreuzberg

SPRING

IN SPRINGTIME, Berlin holds many interesting fairs and cultural events in its squares, parks and gardens, allowing the visitor to appreciate fully the beauty of the city as the trees and flowers burst into life. With the arrival of the warmer weather, another natural resource springs to life as cruise and rowing boats start operating on the Spree river and the city's canals.

MARCH

ITB-Internationale Tourismus-Börse *(mid Mar)*. The biggest European fair devoted to tourism where representatives from all parts of the world try to attract visitors to their countries.
Music-Biennale Berlin *(2nd week in Mar)* is a busy festival of experimental, electronic and contemporary music held on odd-number years.

Rassehunde-Zuchtschau *(weekend mid-Mar)* is a huge show for pedigree dogs and pedigree dog lovers.
Berliner Motorradtage *(end Mar)*. Motorcyclists from all over Germany converge on Berlin for this specialist event.

APRIL

Festtage *(Apr)*. A series of popular concerts and operas performed by world-class musicians in the Philharmonie and at the Staatsoper.
Easter *(exact date varies)*. Huge markets open around the Kaiser-Wilhelm-Gedächtnis-kirche, Alexanderplatz and other central locations as the city prepares for the feast.
Britzer Baumblüte *(all of Apr)* is a month-long spring festival organized in Britz, a suburb in the south of the city famous for its windmills.
Neuköllner Frühlingsfest *(all of Apr)* Hasenheide. Traditional springtime festival celebrating the new season.

MAY

German Women's Tennis Open *(early May)*. Each year this tournament attracts the world's top women players. The current strength of German tennis ensures huge crowds turn up eager to cheer on the home players.
Luft- und Raumfahrtaus-stellung Berlin-Brandenburg *(early May)*. This festival and air show of civil, military and space craft fills the skies above Schönefeld airport.
Theatertreffen Berlin *(May)*. This important Berlin theatre festival has been running since 1963, and provides a platform for theatre productions from German-speaking regions worldwide.
Karneval der Kulturen *(late May)*. For three days, the streets of Kreuzberg district are brought to life by singing and dancing in this colourful display celebrating multicultural Berlin.

Street recitation of poetry during the Theatertreffen Berlin in May

AVERAGE DAILY HOURS OF SUNSHINE

Hours
12
9
6
3
0

Jan Feb Mar Apr May Jun Jul Aug Sep Oct Nov Dec

Sunshine Chart
In Berlin, the highest number of sunny days occurs in May, but June, July and August also enjoy good weather. The cloudiest month is December, followed by January and November.

SUMMER

SUMMERTIME in Berlin is marked by many open-air events. There are concerts of classical music and opera performances, as well as open-air concerts and festivals for the young, including the famous Love Parade. It is also possible to take advantage of the good weather by taking a walk or bicycle ride in the Grunewald, or even swimming in the nearby lakes of Wannsee or Müggelsee.

An outdoor artist at work in the Potsdamer Platz

JUNE

Deutsch-Französisches Volksfest *(early Jun–mid-Jul)*. This German-French folk festival takes place near Kurt-Schumacher-Damm.
Jazz Across the Border *(throughout Jun)*. This jazz festival is organized by the Haus der Kulturen der Welt.
Konzertsommer im Englischen Garten *(mid-Jun–end Jul)* is a schedule of open-air concerts.
Christopher Street Day *(end Jun)* features a gay and lesbian parade with revellers in extravagant outfits, held around Ku'damm.

Berliner Theatermarkt an der Deutschen Oper *(end Jun)* is a programme of open days at the opera.
Open-Air-Classic *(end Jun–early Jul)*. Series of operas in Waldbühne with a gala finale in Gendarmenmarkt.

JULY

Bach Tage Berlin *(1st week in Jul)* features concerts of Johann Sebastian Bach's music, performed in concert halls throughout the city.
Love Parade *(2nd Sun in Jul)*. This huge techno-beat parade attracts youth from all over the world intent on dancing late into the night.
Heimatklänge *(mid-Jul–end Aug)*. A spectacular array of groups give open-air concerts in this world music festival; every Wednesday to Sunday.

AUGUST

Deutsch-Amerikanisches Volksfest *(30 Jul–22 Aug)*. A programme of entertainment

Berlin's world famous Love Parade techno event

with an American theme that always draws the crowds.
Berliner Gauklerfest *(late Jul–early Aug)*. Stalls on Unter den Linden selling speciality foods, while crowds are entertained by acrobats and musicians.
Kreuzberger Festliche Tage *(end Aug–early Sep)*. This is a large multi-event festival of traditional classical music held in Kreuzberg.

Prokofiev's *The Love of Three Oranges* performed in the Komische Oper

AVERAGE MONTHLY RAINFALL

Rainfall Chart
The lowest amount of rainfall occurs in February and again in April, as the temperature begins to rise. The amount of rain in September can dampen the enthusiasm of the unprepared visitor. Unexpectedly heavy cloudbursts can also occur during the summer months.

AUTUMN

AUTUMN IN Berlin is marked by major cultural events. In September the city's hotels fill with visitors arriving for the Berliner Festwochen, to hear concerts given by some of the world's top artists and to make the most of the wide range of culture on offer. Autumn is also a time for major sports events, including the Berlin Marathon, the third biggest in the world after New York and London.

SEPTEMBER

Internationales Stadionfest (ISTAF) *(first week Sep)*. International track and field event in the Olympiastadion.
Internationale Funkausstellung *(early Sep, every two years)*. High-tech media and computer fair at the Internationales Congress Centrum *(see p182)*.

Internationales Literaturfestival *(mid Sep)*. Readings, lectures and special events featuring old and new writing from around the world.
Berliner Festwochen *(throughout Sep)*. A major festival with concerts, theatre, exhibitions and meetings.
Berlin-Marathon *(3rd Sun in Sep)*. This international running event brings the city's traffic to a halt for several hours.
Art Forum in Berlin *(end Sep)*. Artists and art collectors from all over Europe gather for this five-day modern art fair.

OCTOBER

Tag der Deutschen Einheit *(3 Oct)*. Berlin celebrates the reunification of Germany

Participants in the September Berlin-Marathon

by staging an annual grand parade through the streets.
Oktoberfest *(early Oct)*. Held around Möckernstrasse, this is a slightly scaled down version of the Bavarian Festival, a celebration of beer drinking and traditional food.

NOVEMBER

Jazz Fest Berlin *(early Nov)*. Held annually since 1964, this respected jazz festival kicks off in the Haus der Kulturen der Welt *(see p134)*.
Treffen Junge Musik-Szene *(early Nov)*. Music for the younger generation.
Jüdische Kulturtage *(throughout Nov)*. A festival devoted to Jewish arts and culture with films, plays, concerts and lectures.
Internationales Reitturnier *(3rd week in Nov)*. International horse-jumping.
KinderMusik Theater Wochen *(Nov)*. This is a great feast of theatre and music for the very young, and the young at heart.

Marching through the Brandenburg Gate during Deutschland Fest

AVERAGE MONTHLY TEMPERATURE

Temperature Chart
Average maximum and minimum temperatures are shown here. The warmest months are June, July and August when the temperature exceeds 20°C. Winters are cold and temperatures can drop below –5°C in January, with the chance of heavy snow-falls or extreme frost.

WINTER

B ERLIN'S WINTERS are usually cold and the temperature can sometimes drop to below zero, with a carpet of snow lining the streets. During December, the city prepares for Christmas with many traditional markets. January brings numerous Carnival balls, while the major event in February is the great cinema gala – the Berlin Film Festival.

DECEMBER

Weihnachtsmärkte
(throughout Dec). In the month before Christmas the city is dotted with picturesque fairs and festive stalls selling Christmas gifts and regional culinary specialities.
Christmas (Weihnachten)
(25–26 Dec). As in many other European cities, Berlin's traditional celebrations include Christmas trees, present-giving, family gatherings and communal feasts.
New Year's Eve (Silvester)
(31 Dec) is celebrated in hotels, restaurants, discos, clubs and in private homes; another traditional activity is the popping of champagne corks at the Brandenburg Gate.

JANUARY

Berliner Neujahrslauf
(1 Jan). For those unaffected by the previous night's revelry, this 4-km (2.4-mile) run along the city streets starts off at the Brandenburg Gate.
Sechs-Tage-Rennen *(late Jan).* This meeting in the Velodrome features a six-day bicycle-race and other events.

Berlinale – the grand festival of world cinema

Berliner Team-Marathon
(22 Jan). Race organized by Sport Klub Charlottenburg.
Lange Nacht der Museen
(end of Jan) A series of events organized by Berlin's museums which stay open until midnight or later.
Internationale Grüne Woche
(last week of Jan). This giant fair is devoted to agriculture and food; it provides an ideal opportunity to sample delicacies from all over the world.

Christmas shopping in the KaDeWe department store

FEBRUARY

Berlinale – Internationale Filmfestspiele *(2nd and 3rd week in Feb).* This gala of cinematography attracts big movie stars and features the best films of the season. It is held in tandem with the **Internationales Forum des Jungen Films** which features low-budget movies in the Palais Podewils *(see p97)*.
Berliner Rosenmontags-konzerte is a series of classical music concerts.

PUBLIC HOLIDAYS

Neujahr New Year (1 Jan)
Karfreitag Good Friday
Ostermontag Easter Mon
Tag der Arbeit Labour
  Day (1 May)
Christi Himmelfahrt
  Ascension Day
Pfingsten Whitsun
**Tag der Deutschen
  Einheit** (3 Oct)
Weihnachten Christmas
  (25–26 Dec)

BERLIN AREA
BY AREA

AROUND UNTER DEN LINDEN

THE AREA around the grand avenue Unter den Linden is among the most attractive in Berlin. Its development started during the Baroque period with the establishment of Dorotheenstadt to the north and Friedrichstadt to the south. From the early 18th century, prestigious buildings began to appear here, and work started on the

Bas-relief from the Schadow-Haus, located on Schadowstrasse

Forum Friedericianum (later Bebelplatz). Over the following two centuries Unter den Linden became one of the city's most imposing avenues. World War II bombing took a heavy toll, but despite only partial reconstruction by the East German government, the area is still home to the highest concentration of historic buildings in Berlin.

SIGHTS AT A GLANCE

Churches
Deutscher Dom **18**
Französischer Dom **16**
Friedrichswerdersche Kirche **14**
St-Hedwigs-Kathedrale **11**

Museums and Galleries
Deutsche Guggenheim **7**
Museum für Post
    und Kommunikation **22**
Zeughaus (Deutsches Historisches Museum) (pp58–9) **1**

Streets and Squares
Bebelplatz **10**
Gendarmenmarkt **15**
Pariser Platz **24**
Unter den Linden **2**

Theatres
Admiralspalast **31**
Komische Oper **29**
Konzerthaus **17**

Maxim Gorki Theater **32**
Staatsoper Unter den Linden **12**

Historic Buildings and Sites
Alte Bibliothek **9**
Altes Palais **8**
Brandenburger Tor **25**
Holocaust Denkmal **26**
Humboldt Universität **4**
Kronprinzenpalais **13**
Mohrenkolonnaden **20**
Neue Wache **3**
Palais am Festungsgraben **33**
Reiterdenkmal Friedrichs
    des Grossen **5**
Spittelkolonnaden **21**
Staatsbibliothek **6**

Others
Ehemaliges Regierungsviertel **23**
Friedrichstadtpassagen **19**
Hotel Adlon **27**
Russische Botschaft **28**
S-Bahnhof Friedrichstrasse **30**

KEY

▢	Street-by-Street map See pp56–7
🚊	Railway station
Ⓢ	S-Bahn station
Ⓤ	U-Bahn station
Ⓟ	Parking

GETTING THERE
This area is served by S-Bahn 1, 3, 5, 7, 9 and 75; U-Bahn 6 and 9; and buses 100 and 348.

0 metres   400
0 yards   400

◁ **Sculpture of the personification of History on the plinth of Schiller's monument, Gendarmenmarkt**

Street-by-Street: Around Bebelplatz

THE SECTION OF UNTER DEN LINDEN between Schlossbrücke and Friedrichstrasse is one of the most attractive places in central Berlin. There are some magnificent Baroque and Neo-Classical buildings, many of them designed by famous architects. There are also some restored palaces that are now used as public buildings. Of particular interest is the beautiful Baroque building of the Zeughaus (the former Arsenal), which now houses the German History Museum.

Humboldt Universität
The entrance to the courtyard is framed by two guardroom pavilions and is crowned with the allegorical figures of Dawn and Dusk **4**

Staatsbibliothek
This Neo-Baroque building, designed by Ernst von Ihne, was built between 1903 and 1914. It houses a collection that dates from the 17th century **6**

Equestrian Statue of Frederick the Great
The impressive statue dates from 1851 and is the work of Christian Daniel Rauch **5**

Deutsche Guggenheim
The building, which was rebuilt after World War II, provides exhibition space for the fifth branch of the famous Guggenheim museum **7**

KEY

– – – Suggested route

Altes Palais
This Neo-Classical palace was built between 1834 and 1837 for the future Kaiser Wilhelm I. It was reconstructed after World War II **8**

Alte Bibliothek
The west side of Bebelplatz features a Baroque building with an unusual concave façade. Locals have nick-named it the "chest of drawers" **9**

★ Neue Wache
Since 1993, this monument has served as a memorial to all victims of war and dictatorship ❸

★ Zeughaus (Deutsches Historisches Museum)
A new wing designed by I M Pei has been added to this beautiful Baroque building. The Zeughaus pediment shows the Roman goddess of wisdom ❶

LOCATOR MAP
See Street Finder, maps 6, 7, 15 &16

0 metres	100
0 yards	100

Unter den Linden
This magnificent avenue was replanted with four rows of lime trees in 1946 ❷

Kronprinzenpalais
The rear elevation of the palace pavilion features a magnificent portal from the dismantled Bauakademie building ⓭

Staatsoper Unter den Linden
Unter den Linden's opera house is Germany's oldest theatre building not attached to a palace residence ⓬

★ Friedrichswerdersche Kirche
In this Neo-Gothic church, designed by Karl Friedrich Schinkel, is a museum devoted to this great architect ⓮

St-Hedwigs-Kathedrale
Bas-reliefs (1837) by Theodore Wilhelm Achtermann adorn the cathedral's supports ⓫

Bebelplatz
Designed in the 18th century as the Forum Fridericianum, this square was renamed in 1947 in honour of social activist, August Bebel. The Nazis burned books here in 1933 ❿

Zeughaus (Deutsches Historisches Museum) ❶

Warrior's mask,
courtyard arcade

T HIS FORMER ARSENAL was built in the Baroque style in 1706 under the guidance of Johann Arnold Nering, Martin Grünberg, Andreas Schlüter and Jean de Bodt. It is a magnificent structure, its wings surrounding an inner courtyard.
    Its exterior is decorated with Schlüter's sculptures, including masks of dying warriors in the courtyard. Since 1952 it has housed the German History Museum. Following a major refurbishment by the Japanese-American architect I M Pei, which includes a glass canopy for the central courtyard and a new modern wing for temporary exhibitions (that is already open), the museum will reopen in late 2004. *now open*

Europe and Asia
This group of Meissen porcelain figurines, depicting the continents, was designed by Johann Joachim Kändler.

Soldiers Plundering a House
This painting by Sebastian Vrancx dates from around 1600 and depicts a scene from the religious wars which ravaged the Netherlands during the 16th century.

GALLERY GUIDE
When the extension and refurbishment of the museum is completed, the first floor will be devoted to a new exhibition "Bilder und Zeugnisse der Deutschen Geschichte" or "Pictures and Evidence from German History" which will trace the course of German history.

Saddle
This valuable mid-15th-century saddle is decorated with graphic carved plaques made of ivory.

1st floor open?

★ Martin Luther
This portrait, painted by Lucas Cranach the Elder in 1529, will be the focal point of an exhibition devoted to the Reformation.

STAR EXHIBITS

★ Martin Luther

★ Gloria Victis

ground floor + 1st floor

Unter den Linden
Carl Traugott Fechhelm's painting shows Berlin's grandest avenue, Unter den Linden, at the end of the 18th century.

VISITORS' CHECKLIST

Unter den Linden 2. **Map** 7 A3, 16 E2. 20 30 40. & Friedrichstrasse. 100, 157, 200, 348. www.dhm.de

Steam Engine
The history of the Industrial Revolution will be illustrated with exhibits such as this 1847 steam-powered engine.

★ Gloria Victis
The death of a friend in the final days of the Franco-Prussian War (1870–71) inspired French artist Antonin Mercié to create this moving allegory.

The inner courtyard
is covered with a glass roof by I M Pei.

Prisoner's Jacket
This jacket, which once belonged to a concentration camp prisoner, will be used to illustrate the horrors of the Nazi regime.

KEY

- From the Middle Ages to the Thirty Years' War
- Baroque
- Enlightment to Unification
- Weimar Empire and Republic
- The Third Reich and World War II
- Post-1945 Era
- Non-exhibition rooms

Unter den Linden as depicted in Franz Krüger's *Opernplatz Parade* (1824–30)

Unter den Linden ❷

Map 6 E3, 6 F3, 15 A3, 16 D3.
Ⓢ *Unter den Linden.* 🚌 *100,
200, 348.*

O NE OF THE most famous
streets in Berlin, Unter
den Linden starts at Schlossplatz and runs down to Pariser
Platz and the Brandenburg
Gate. It was once the route to
the royal hunting grounds that
were later transformed into the
Tiergarten. In the 17th century
the street was planted with
lime trees, to which it owes
its name. Although removed
around 1658, they were
replanted in four rows in 1820.
  During the 18th century,
Unter den Linden became the
main street of the westward-
growing city. It was gradually
filled with prestigious buildings
that were restored after World
War II. Following the reunification of Germany, Unter den
Linden has acquired several
cafés and restaurants, as well
as many smart new shops.
This street is also the venue
for many interesting outdoor
events; it is usually crowded
with tourists and students
browsing the bookstalls around
the Humboldt Universität and
the Staatsbibliothek.

Neue Wache ❸

Unter den Linden 4. **Map** 7 A3, 16
E2. Ⓢ *Hackescher Markt.* 🚌 *100,
200, 348.* 🕐 *10am–6pm daily.*

T HIS WAR MEMORIAL, designed
by Karl Friedrich Schinkel
and built between 1816 and
1818, is considered to be one
of the finest examples of Neo-
Classical architecture in Berlin.
The front of the monument is
dominated by a huge Doric
portico with a frieze made up
of bas-reliefs depicting goddesses of victory. The triangular tympanum above the
pediment shows allegorical
representations of Battle,
Victory, Flight and Defeat.
  The building was originally
used as a royal guardhouse,
but during 1930 and 1931 it
was turned it into a monument
to the soldiers killed in World
War I. In 1960, following its
restoration, Neue Wache became the Memorial to the Victims of Fascism and Militarism.
Then, in 1993 it was rededi-
cated once again, this time to
the memory of all victims of
war and dictatorship.
  Inside the building is an
eternal flame and a granite slab
over the ashes of an unknown
soldier, a resistance fighter and
a concentration camp prisoner.
Under the circular opening in
the roof is a copy of the 20th
century sculpture *Mother with
her Dead Son*, by Berlin artist
Käthe Kollwitz, who lost her
own son in World War I.

Humboldt Universität ❹
HUMBOLDT UNIVERSITY

Unter den Linden 6. **Map** 7 A3,
16 D2. Ⓢ & Ⓤ *Friedrichstrasse.*
🚌 *100, 200, 348.*

T HE UNIVERSITY BUILDING was
constructed in 1753, for
Prince Heinrich of Prussia, the
brother of Frederick the Great.
The university was founded
in 1810 on the initiative of
Wilhelm von Humboldt. It
became the Berlin University
but was renamed in von
Humboldt's honour in 1949.
  The overall design of the
palace, with its main block
and the courtyard enclosed
within a pair of wings, has
been extended many times.
Two marble statues (1883)
by Paul Otto stand at the

WILHELM AND ALEXANDER VON HUMBOLDT

The Humboldt brothers rank among the most
distinguished Berlin citizens. Wilhelm (1767–
1835) was a lawyer and politician, occupying
various government posts. It was on his
initiative that the Berlin University (later
renamed Humboldt University) was
founded, and he conducted studies in
comparative and historical linguistics
there. Alexander (1769–1859),
a professor at the University,
researched natural science,
including meteorology, ocean-
ography and agricultural science.

Statue of Alexander von Humboldt

entrance gate and represent
Wilhelm von Humboldt (holding a book) and his brother
Alexander (sitting on a globe),
who was a famous explorer.
The entrance gate leads to the
courtyard, which was designed
by Reinhold Begas.

Many famous scholars have
worked at the University, including philosophers Fichte
and Hegel, physicians Rudolf
Virchow and Robert Koch and
physicists Max Planck and
Albert Einstein. Among its
graduates are Heinrich Heine,
Karl Marx and Friedrich Engels.

After World War II, the
University was in the Russian
sector of the divided city and
the difficulties encountered
by the students of the western
zone led to the establishment
of a new university in 1948 –
the Freie Universität *(see p179)*.

**Humboldt University courtyard
with statue of Hermann Helmholtz**

Reiterdenkmal Friedrichs des Grossen **❺**
EQUESTRIAN STATUE OF FREDERICK THE GREAT

Unter den Linden. **Map** 7 A3. Ⓢ &
Ⓤ *Friedrichstrasse.* 🚌 *100, 200, 348.*

THIS IS ONE OF the most famous monuments in Berlin,
featuring a massive bronze
statue 5.6 m (18.5 ft) in height
and standing on the centre
lane of Unter den Linden. It
was designed by Christian
Daniel Rauch and created
between 1839 and 1851. It
depicts Frederick the Great on
horseback, wearing a uniform
and a royal cloak. The base of
the high plinth is surrounded

by statues of famous military
leaders, politicians, scientists
and artists. The top tier of the
plinth is decorated with bas-
reliefs depicting scenes from
the life of Frederick the Great.
Out of line with GDR ideology,
the monument was removed
to Potsdam, where until 1980
it stood by the Hippodrome
in Park Sanssouci.

Staatsbibliothek **❻**
STATE LIBRARY

Unter den Linden 8. **Map** 7 A3, 16 D2.
🎫 *266 23 03.* Ⓢ & Ⓤ *Friedrichstrasse.* 🚌 *100, 200, 348.*
🕐 *9am–6pm Mon–Fri , 9am–1pm Sat.*

THE NUCLEUS OF the State
Library collection was the
library belonging to the Great
Elector – Friedrich Wilhelm –
founded in 1661 and situated
in the Stadtschloss. At the end
of the 18th century it was
moved to the Alte Bibliothek
building. Its current home was
designed by Ernst von Ihne
and constructed between
1903 and 1914 on the site of
the Academy of Science and
the Academy of Fine Arts.
This impressive building was

severely damaged during
World War II and underwent
extensive restoration. The
collection, numbering 3 million books and periodicals,
was scattered during the war,
including a collection of
priceless music manuscripts,
which ended up in the Jagiello-
nian Library in Cracow, Poland.

After the war only part of the
collection was returned to the
building in Unter den Linden,
and the rest was held in West
Berlin. Since reunification,
both collections are once again
under the same administration.

Deutsche Guggenheim **❼**

Unter den Linden 13–15. **Map** 7 A3,
16 D3. 🎫 *202 09 30.* 🕐 *11am–
8pm daily (to 10pm Thu).* Ⓢ & Ⓤ
Friedrichstrasse. 🚌 *100, 200, 348.* 📷

THE DEUTSCHE GUGGENHEIM
building is home to the
German branch of the New
York-based Guggenheim
Foundation. The museum does
not have its own permanent
collection, but is regularly
used to display a variety of
temporary exhibitions.

The ivy-clad Staatsbibliothek building on Unter den Linden

A window with a heraldic shield on the Altes Palais

Altes Palais ❽
THE OLD PALACE

Unter den Linden 9. **Map** 7 A3,
16 D3. Ⓢ & Ⓤ *Friedrichstrasse.*
🚌 *100, 200, 348.* ⬤ *to the public.*

THIS NEO-CLASSICAL palace,
near the former Opernplatz
(Bebelplatz), was built for the
heir to the throne – Prince
Wilhelm (later Kaiser Wilhelm
I). The Kaiser lived here all his
life. He was able to watch the
changing of the guards every
day from the ground-floor
window on the far left.

The palace, built from 1834
to 1837, was designed by Carl
Ferdinand Langhans but its
splendid furnishings were
destroyed during World War II.
The palace was subsequently
restored, and is now used by
Humboldt Universität.

Alte Bibliothek ❾
THE OLD LIBRARY

Bebelplatz. **Map** 7 A3, 16 D3. 📞 20
930. Ⓢ & Ⓤ *Friedrichstrasse.*
🚌 *100, 200, 348.*

THE OLD LIBRARY, known by
locals as the *Kommode* or
"chest of drawers" after its
curved façade, is actually one
of the city's most beautiful
Baroque buildings. It was
designed by Georg Christian
Unger and built around 1775
to house the royal library
collection. In fact, Unger based
his design on an unrealized
plan for an extension to the
Hofburg complex in Vienna,
prepared by the famous architect Josef Emanuel Fischer
von Erlach some 50 years
earlier. The concave façade of
the building is accentuated by
the insertion of three breaks,

surrounded at the top by a
row of massive Corinthian
pilasters and groupings of
heraldic shields.

Bebelplatz ❿

Map 7 A3, 16 D3. Ⓢ & Ⓤ *Friedrichstrasse.* 🚌 *100, 200, 348.*

ONCE NAMED Opernplatz
(Opera Square), Bebelplatz
was to be the focal point of
the intended Forum Frederic-
ianum, an area designed by
Georg Wenzeslaus von
Knobelsdorff to mirror the
grandeur of ancient Rome.
Although the initial plans were
only partly implemented, many
important buildings rose
around the square with the
passage of time.

On 10 May 1933 Opernplatz
was the scene of the infamous
book burning act organized by
the Nazi propaganda machine.
Some 25,000 books written by
authors considered to be
enemies of the Third Reich

were burned. These included
works by Thomas and Hein-
rich Mann, Robert Musil and
Lion Feuchtwanger.

Today, a monument at the
centre of the square, designed
by Micha Ullman in 1995,
commemorates this dramatic
event. A translucent panel
inserted into the road surface
provides a glimpse of a room
filled with empty bookshelves.
Next to it is a plaque bearing
the tragically prophetic words
of the poet Heinrich Heine,
written in 1820: "Where books
are burned, in the end people
will burn."

St-Hedwigs-
Kathedrale ⓫
ST HEDWIG'S CATHEDRAL

Bebelplatz. **Map** 7 A4, 16 D3, E3.
📞 203 48 10. Ⓢ & Ⓤ *Friedrichstr.*
🚌 *100, 200, 348.* ⬤ *10am–5pm
Mon–Sat (to 4:30pm Sat), 1–5pm Sun.*

THIS HUGE CHURCH, set back
from the road and crowned
with a dome, is the Catholic
Cathedral of the Roman Arch-
diocese of Berlin. It was built
to serve the Catholics of Silesia
(part of present-day Poland),
which became part of the
Kingdom of Prussia in 1742
following defeat in the
Silesian Wars of 1740–63.

The initial design, by Georg
Wenzeslaus von Knobelsdorff,
was similar to the Roman Pantheon. Construction began in
1747 and the cathedral was
consecrated in 1773, although

The façade of St-Hedwigs-Kathedrale featuring beautiful bas-relief sculptures work continued on and off until 1778. Its design was modified repeatedly. Later, additional work was carried out from 1886 to 1887. The cathedral was damaged during World War II, and rebuilt between 1952 and 1963.

The crypt holds the tombs of many bishops of Berlin, a 16th-century Madonna and a Pietà dating from 1420. It is also the resting place of Bernhard Lichtenberg, a priest killed in a concentration camp and beatified as a martyr by Pope John Paul II.

Bas-relief of Apollo and Mars on the façade of the Staatsoper

Staatsoper Unter den Linden ⓬

STATE OPERA HOUSE

Unter den Linden 7. **Map** 7 A3, 16 D3. 🄲 *20 35 45 55.* Ⓢ & Ⓤ *Friedrichstrasse.* 🚌 *100, 200, 348.*

THE EARLY Neo-Classical façade of the State Opera House is one of the most beautiful sights along Unter den Linden. It was built by Georg Wenzeslaus von Knobelsdorff in 1741–3 as the first building of the intended Forum Fridericianum. Following a fire, the opera house was restored from 1843 to 1844 under the direction of Carl Ferdinand Langhans, who altered only its interior.

Following wartime destruction, the opera house was rebuilt from 1952 to 1955, almost from the ground up. It has played host to famous singers, musicians and artists; one of its directors and conductors was Richard Strauss, and its stage designers included Karl Friedrich Schinkel.

The imposing façade of the Kronprinzenpalais

Kronprinzenpalais ⓭

CROWN PRINCE'S PALACE

Unter den Linden 3. **Map** 7 A3, B3, 16 E3. 🄲 *20 30 40.* Ⓢ & Ⓤ *Friedrichstrasse.* 🚌 *100, 200, 348.* 🕙 *10am–6pm Thu–Sat, Mon, Tue (to 10pm Thu).*

THIS STRIKING late-Neo-Classical palace is home to the Deutsches Historisches Museum collection while the Zeughaus (*see pp58–9*) is being restored. The palace takes its name from its original inhabitants – the heirs to the royal, and later to the imperial, throne. Its form is the outcome of numerous alterations made to what was originally a modest house dating from 1663–9. The first extensions, in the late-Baroque style, were conducted by Philipp Gerlach in 1732 and 1733. Between 1856 and 1857 Johann Heinrich Strack added the second floor. These extensions were rebuilt following World War II.

The palace served the royal family until the abolition of the monarchy. From 1919 to 1937, it was used as a branch of the Nationalgalerie. Under Communist rule it was renamed Palais Unter den Linden and became a residence for official government guests. Here, on 31 August 1990, the pact was signed paving the way for reunification.

A pavilion at the rear of the palace features the portal and terracotta slabs from the Bauakademie building, designed by Karl Friedrich Schinkel, and is currently being rebuilt as the headquarters of the German company Bertelsmann.

Joined to the main palace by an overhanging passageway is the smaller Prinzessinnenpalais (Princesses' Palace), built for the daughters of Friedrich Wilhelm III.

Friedrichswerdersche Kirche (Schinkel-Museum) ⓮

Werderstrasse. **Map** 7 B4, 16 E3. 🄲 *20 90 55 55.* Ⓢ & Ⓤ *Friedrichstrasse.* 🚌 *100, 147, 200, 348.* 🕙 *10am–6pm Tue–Sun.*

THIS PICTURESQUE church, designed by Karl Friedrich Schinkel and constructed between 1824 and 1830, was the first Neo-Gothic church to be built in Berlin. The small single-nave structure, with its twin-tower façade, resembles an English college chapel. Schinkel's original interior of the church was largely destroyed in World War II.

Following its reconstruction, the church was converted into a museum. It is currently used by the Nationalgalerie to house its permanent exhibition of sculptures from the late 16th to the mid 19th century. Highlights include a model of the famous group sculpture by Johann Gottfried Schadow, depicting the princesses Friederike and Luise (later Queen of Prussia).

Princesses Luise and Friederike in the Schinkel-Museum

Gendarmenmarkt

T HIS IS one of Berlin's most beautiful squares, created
at the end of 17th century as a market square
for the newly established Friedrichstadt. It is
named after the Regiment Gens d'Armes who
had their stables here. In 1950 it was
renamed Platz der Akademie; after
reunification the square reverted
to its original name.

Französischer Dom

JÄGERSTRASSE

GENDARMEN- MARKT

TAUBENSTRASSE

CHARLOTTENSTRASSE

Galeries Lafayette

Quartier 206

Quartier 205

0 metres   85

0 yards   85

Deutscher Dom

Schiller's Monument
*The poet's monument stands
in the centre of the square, in
front of the Konzerthaus.*

Französischer Dom ⑯

FRENCH CATHEDRAL

Gendarmenmarkt 6. **Map** 7 A4, 16
D4. ☎ 204 15 07. Ⓤ *Stadtmitte or
Französische Strasse.* **Museum** ☎ 20
64 99 22. ◯ *noon–5pm Tue–Sun.*
▨ **Viewing Platform** ☎ 20 62 872.
◯ *9am–7pm daily.* ▨ **Church**
◯ *noon–5pm Tue–Sun (from 11am
Sun).* ✝ *Sun 10am.*

A LTHOUGH THE TWO churches
on the opposite sides of
Schauspielhaus seem identical,
they differ from each other
quite considerably. Their only
common feature is the front
towers. The French cathedral
was built for the Huguenot
community, who found refuge
in protestant Berlin following
their expulsion from France
after the revocation of the
Edict of Nantes. The modest

**Side elevation of the Französischer
Dom, built for Huguenot refugees**

church, built between 1701
and 1705 by Louis Cayart and
Abraham Quesnay, was
modelled on the Huguenot
church in Charenton, France,
which was destroyed in 1688.
The main entrance, on the
west elevation (facing

Charlottenstrasse), leads to an
uncomplicated interior with a
rectangular nave and semi-
circular sections on both sides.
It features a late-Baroque
organ from 1754.
   The structure is dominated
by a massive, cylindrical
tower which is encircled by
Corinthian porticoes at its base.
The tower and porticoes were
designed by Carl von Gontard
and added around 1785, some
80 years after the church was
built. It houses the Huguenot
Museum, which details the
history of the Huguenots in
France and Brandenburg.
Well-educated and highly
skilled, they played a crucial
part in Berlin's rise as a city of
science, craft and commerce.
The French language they
brought with them survives to
this day in many words used
in the Berlin dialect.

The interior of the Konzerthaus, formerly the Schauspielhaus

Konzerthaus ⑰
CONCERT HALL

Gendarmenmarkt 2. **Map** 7 A4, 16 D4. 🛈 20 30 921 01. 🚇 Stadtmitte.

A LATE NEO-CLASSICAL jewel, this magnificent theatre building, known until recently as the Schauspielhaus, is one of the greatest achievements of Berlin's best-known architect, Karl Friedrich Schinkel. It was built between 1818 and 1821 around the ruins of Langhan's National Theatre, destroyed by fire in 1817. The portico columns were retained in the new design. Schinkel was responsible not only for the architectural structure but also for the interior design, right down to the door handles. Following bomb damage in World War II, it was reconstructed as a concert hall with a different interior layout. The exterior was restored to its former glory. The Konzerthaus is now home to the Berlin Symphony Orchestra.

The theatre façade includes a huge Ionic portico with a set of stairs that was only used by the middle classes (the upper classes entered via a separate entrance where they could leave their horse-drawn carriages). The whole building is richly decorated with sculptures alluding to drama and music. These include statues of musical geniuses mounted on lions and panthers, as well as figures representing the Muses and a Bacchanal procession. The façade is crowned with the sculpture of Apollo riding a chariot pulled by griffins.

In front of the theatre stands a shining, white marble statue of Friedrich Schiller. It was sculpted by Reinhold Begas, and erected in 1869. Removed by the Nazis during the 1930s, the monument was finally returned to its rightful place in 1988. Schiller's head was copied by the sculptor from a bust of the poet created in 1794 by Johann Heinrich Dannecker. The statue is mounted on a high pedestal surrounded by allegorical figures representing Lyric Poetry, Drama, Philosophy and History.

Deutscher Dom ⑱
GERMAN CATHEDRAL

Gendarmenmarkt 1. **Map** 7 A4, 16 D4. 🚇 Stadtmitte or Französische Strasse. 🛈 22 73 04 31. **Exhibition** ⏱ Sep–May: 10am–6pm Wed–Sun (to 10pm Tue); Jun–Aug: 10am–7pm Wed–Sun.

T HE CATHEDRAL at the southern end of the square, to the left of Konzerthaus, is an old German Protestant-Reformed church. It was designed by Martin Grünberg and built in 1708 by Giovanni Simonetti. The design was based on a five-petal shape, and in 1785 it acquired a dome-covered tower identical to that of the French cathedral.

Burned down in 1945, the church was finally rebuilt in 1993. Its exterior was painstakingly reconstructed, including its sculpted decorations. The interior is now modern and has been adapted as an exhibition space. On display is "*Wege, Irrwege, Umwege*" ("Paths, Confusions, Detours"), an exhibition about Germany's parliamentary democracy.

Sculpture from the Deutscher Dom

Friedrichstadt-passagen ⑲
FRIEDRICHSTADT PASSAGES

Friedrichstrasse Quartiere 205, 206, 207. **Map** 6 F4, 15 C4. 🚇 Französische Strasse or Stadtmitte.

T HIS GROUP of passages is part of a huge development of luxury shops, offices, restaurants and apartments built in recent years along Friedrichstrasse.

Quartier 207 is the famous Galeries Lafayette, a branch of the French department store occupying a charming building designed by Jean Nouvel and constructed almost entirely of glass. The building's axis is formed by an inner courtyard, which is defined by two glass cones with their bases facing each other. The highly reflective glass panes, together with the multicoloured stands that are clustered around the structure, make an extraordinary impression on the visitor.

The next passage, Quartier 206, has offices and smart luxury boutiques, and is the work of the American design team Pei, Cobb, Freed & Partners. The building owes its alluring, but somewhat nouveau-riche appearance to the use of forms inspired by Art Deco architecture, including sophisticated details and expensive stone cladding.

The southernmost building in the complex, and the largest passage, is Quartier 205, which is the work of Oswald Mathias Ungers.

The exterior and main entrance of Quartier 206

Mohren-kolonnaden 20

Mohrenstrasse 37b and 40/41.
Map 6 F5, 15 B5. **U** *Mohrenstrasse.*

DESIGNED BY Carl Gotthard
Langhans, these Neo-
Classical arcades resting on
twin columns were constructed
in 1787. They originally surrounded a bridge that spanned
the moat around the city of
Berlin. The bridge has since
been demolished, and the
arcades have been incorporated into buildings of a much
later architectural style located
on Mohrenstrasse.

A copy of one of the original Spittelkolonnaden in Leipziger Strasse

In 1979, a copy of one of the
colonnades was erected in
Leipziger Strasse, using
elements from the original.

One of the original arcades
known as the Mohrenkolonnaden

Spittelkolonnaden 21

Leipziger Strasse. **Map** 7 B5, 16 E5.
U *Spittelmarkt.*

IN THE VICINITY of Spittelmarkt
is a picturesque Baroque-
Neo-Classical colonnade
squeezed between several
20-storey tower blocks. These
tower blocks were erected to
obscure the view of the Axel
Springer Publishers' building,
which stood on the opposite
side of the Berlin Wall.
   A pair of such semicircular
colonnades, designed by Carl
von Gontard and built in
1776, originally surrounded
Spittelmarkt. The southern
one was demolished in 1929,
and the northern one was
destroyed during World War II.

Museum für Post und Kommunika-tion 22

**MUSEUM OF POST AND
TELECOMMUNICATIONS**

Leipziger Strasse 16. **Map** 6 F5,
15 C5. **U** *Stadtmitte* 🚌 148.
🚊 20 29 40. ⏰ *9am–5pm Tue–Fri,
11am–7pm Sat–Sun.* ● *Mon.*

THE POST OFFICE museum,
founded in 1872, is the
world's oldest establishment
of its kind. A dozen or so
years after it was founded, it
moved into the corner of the
huge building constructed for
the main post office. The office
wings, with their modest
Neo-Renaissance elevations,
contrast with the museum
premises, which has a grand
Neo-Baroque façade that is
richly decorated with sculptures. The museum's rooms
house exhibits that illustrate
the history of postal and
telecommunication services.

Ehemaliges Regierungsviertel 23

Wilhelmstrasse, Leipziger Strasse,
Voss Strasse. **Map** 6 E5. **U**
Potsdamer Platz, Mohrenstrasse.

WILHELMSTRASSE, and the area
situated to the west of it
up to Leipziger Platz, was the
former German government
district, where the main
departments had offices from
the mid-19th century until
1945. The building at Voss
Strasse No. 77 was once the
Reich's Chancellery and Otto
von Bismarck's office. From
1933, it served as the office of
Adolf Hitler, for whom the
building was specially
extended by Albert Speer.
   In the spring of 1945 the
square was the scene of fierce
fighting, and after World War
II most of the buildings had
to be demolished. Among
those that survived are the
former Prussian Landtag
offices – the huge complex
occupying the site between
Leipziger and Niederkirchner
Strasse. This building in the
Italian Renaissance-style was
designed by Friedrich Schulz,
and constructed from 1892 to
1904. It consists of two seg-
ments: the one on the side of
Leipziger Strasse (No. 3–4)
once housed the upper
chamber of the National
Assembly (the Herrenhaus)
and is now used by the
Bundesrat. The building on
the side of Niederkirchner
Strasse (No. 5) was once the
seat of the Landtag's lower
chamber, and is now the
Berliner Abgeordnetenhaus
(House of Representatives).
   The second surviving complex is the former Ministry of
Aviation (Reichsluftfahrtminis-
terium), at Leipziger Strasse
No. 5, built for Hermann
Göring in 1936 by Ernst
Sagebiel. This awesome building is typical of architecture
of the Third Reich.

Pariser Platz ㉔

Map 6 E3, 15 A3.
Ⓢ *Unter den Linden.* 🚌 *100, 200.*

THIS SQUARE, at the end of Unter den Linden, was created in 1734. Originally called Quarrée, it was renamed Pariser Platz after 1814, when the *Quadriga* sculpture from the Brandenburg Gate was returned to Berlin from Paris.

The square, enclosed on the west by the Brandenburg Gate, was densely built up until World War II. Most buildings, including the Academy of Fine Arts and the house of painter Max Liebermann, were destroyed in 1945.

Following reunification, the square was redeveloped. Twin houses designed by Josef Paul Kleihues now flank the Brandenburg Gate. On the north side of the square are the Dresdner Bank building and the French Embassy. On the south side are the US Embassy, the DG Bank head office and the Akademie der Künste (Academy of Fine Arts). The east end of the square is closed by the bulk of the Adlon Hotel.

Brandenburger Tor ㉕
BRANDENBURG GATE

Pariser Platz. **Map** 6 E3, 15 A3.
Ⓢ *Unter den Linden.* 🚌 *100, 200.*

THE BRANDENBURG GATE is the quintessential symbol of Berlin. This magnificent Neo-Classical structure was designed by Carl Gotthard Langhans and modelled on

---

MAX LIEBERMANN (1849–1935)

One of the greatest German painters, Max Liebermann was also one of the most interesting and controversial figures of Berlin's élite circles at the start of the 20th century. A sensitive observer as well as an outstanding portraitist, Liebermann was famously stubborn – he could stand up even to the Kaiser himself. From 1920 he was president of the Akademie der Künste (Academy of Fine Arts), but in view of his Jewish origin he was removed from office in 1933. He died just two years later, alone, and his wife committed suicide to escape being sent to a concentration camp.

A frieze from the Brandenburg Gate

the entrance to the Acropolis in Athens. It took from 1788 to 1795 to complete. A pair of pavilions, once used by guards and customs officers, frames its powerful Doric colonnade, crowned with an entablature. The bas-reliefs depict scenes from Greek mythology, and the whole structure is crowned by the sculpture *Quadriga*, designed by Johann Gottfried Schadow. The *Quadriga* was originally regarded as a symbol of peace. In 1806, during the French occupation, it was dismantled on Napoleon's orders and taken to Paris. On its return in 1814, it was declared a symbol of victory, and the goddess received the staff bearing the Prussian

eagle and the iron cross adorned with a laurel wreath.

The Brandenburg Gate has borne witness to many of Berlin's important events, from military parades marking the birth of the Second Reich and Hitler's ascent to power. It was here, too, that the Russian flag was raised in May 1945, and on 17 June 1953 that 25 workers demonstrating for better conditions were killed.

The gate, located in East Berlin, was restored between 1956 and 1958, when the damaged *Quadriga* was rebuilt in West Berlin. Until 1989 it stood watch over the divided city. Between 2000 and 2002 the Brandenburg Gate was meticulously restored.

Holocaust Denkmal ㉖
HOLOCAUST MEMORIAL

Ebertstrasse. **Map** 6 E3, 15 A3.
Ⓢ *Unter den Linden.* 🚌 *100, 200.*

IN 2001 THE CONSTRUCTION of a memorial for the Jews killed by the Nazis between 1933 and 1945 began. Designed by US architect Peter Eisenmann, the memorial will stand next to the Brandenburg Gate and include an underground information centre on the genocide.

Oskar Kokoschka's *Pariser Platz in Berlin* (1925–6), Nationalgalerie

The luxurious interior of the Adlon Hotel

Hotel Adlon ②

Unter den Linden 77. **Map** 6 E3,
6 E4, 15 A3, 15 B3. 🄲 *226 10.*
Ⓢ *Unter den Linden.* 🚌 *100, 200.*

CONSIDERED TO BE the most
important society venue
in Berlin, the original Hotel
Adlon opened its doors to the
public in 1907. Its luxurious
suites were once used by the
world's celebrities, including
Greta Garbo, Enrico Caruso
and Charlie Chaplin. The
hotel suffered bomb damage
in World War II, and was
demolished in 1945. A new
building bearing the same
name was opened in a blaze
of publicity on 23 August 1997.
   Today, it is once again the
best address in town. Comfort,
discretion and lavish interiors
featuring exotic timber, marble
and heavy silk, still tempt
visitors despite high prices.
Those who cannot afford to
stop for a night should at
least drop in for a cup of
coffee in the main hall. In this
hall stands the only authentic
remnant of the former Adlon
Hotel, an elegant black
marble fountain decorated
with elephants, which once
stood in the orangery.

Russische Botschaft ②

RUSSIAN EMBASSY

Unter den Linden 63/65. **Map** 6 F3, 15
B3. Ⓢ *Unter den Linden.* 🚌 *100, 200.*

THE MONUMENTAL, white
Russian Embassy building
is an example of the Stalinist
"wedding cake" style, or

Zuckerbäckerstil. Built between 1948 and 1953, it was
the first postwar building
erected on Unter den Linden.
It is built on the site of a
former palace that had
housed the Russian
(originally Tsarist)
embassy from 1837.
   The building is the
work of the Russian
architect Anatoli
Strizhevsky. This
structure, with its
strictly symmetrical
layout, resembles the
old Berlin palaces of
the Neo-Classical period.
The sculptures that
adorn it, however,
belong to an altogether
different era: the gods
of ancient Greece
and Rome have been
replaced by working-
class heroes.

**Statue of a worker
on the Russian
Embassy building**

Komische Oper ②

COMIC OPERA

Behrenstr. 55/57. **Map** 6 F4, 15 C3.
🄲 *47 99 74 00.* Ⓤ *Französische-
strasse.* Ⓢ *Unter den Linden.*
🚌 *100, 200, 348.*

LOOKING AT the modern
façade of this theatre it is
hard to believe that it hides
one of Berlin's most im-
pressive interiors. Originally
called the Theater Unter den
Linden, the theatre was built
in 1892 by the internationally
famous Viennese architectural
practice of Ferdinand Fellner
and Hermann Helmer. It has
served as a variety theatre
and as the German National
Theatre in the past, and has
only housed the Komische
Oper since World War II.
The postwar reconstruction
deprived the building of its
former façades but the
beautiful Viennese
Neo-Baroque interior
remained, full of
stuccoes and gilded
ornaments. Parti-
cularly interesting are
the expressive and
dynamically posed
statues on the pilasters
of the top balcony – the
work of Theodor Friedel.
   The Komische Oper is
one of Berlin's three
leading opera comp-
anies. Its repertoire
consists mainly of
light opera.

Crowded balconies and the plush interior of the Komische Oper

S-Bahnhof Friedrichstrasse ⬛

Map 6 F2, 6 F3 & 15 C2.

O NE OF THE CITY'S most famous urban railway stations, Bahnhof Friedrichstrasse used to be the border station between East and West Berlin. It was built in 1882 to a design by Johannes Vollmer. In 1925 a roof was added, covering the hall and the platforms.

The original labyrinth of passages, staircases and checkpoints no longer exists but it is possible to see a model of the station at the Stasi-Museum *(see p174)*. Now used as a theatre, the only remaining structure from the original station is the special pavilion once used as a waiting room by those waiting for emigration clearance. It earned the nickname Tränenpalast, the "Palace of Tears", as it is here that Berliners from different sides of the city would say goodbye to each other after a visit.

Admiralspalast ⬛

Friedrichstr. 101–102. **Map** 6 F2, 15 C1. 🇺 and 🇸 *Friedrichstrasse.*

T HE ADMIRALSPALAST was built in 1911 to house an indoor swimming pool and an ice-rink. Designed by Heinrich Schweitzer, the main façade is punctuated by Doric half-columns and inlaid with bas-relief slabs made of Istrian marble. Quite different in style, the façade on Planck-strasse is also interesting. It was designed by Ernst West-phal and includes various exotic overlapping motifs.

The area around Friedrich-strasse was once well known for its excellent theatres, and in 1922 part of the Admirals-palast was converted to house the Metropol-Theater. Through this and subsequent remodelling works the building has retained its original façade. The Metropol-Theater specialized in variety and musical productions until it was declared bankrupt in 1997.

Part of the building, which is in urgent need of refurbishment, is now used by one of

A window of the Admiralspalast decorated with marble slabs

the best political cabarets in Berlin, Die Diestel, which hails from East Berlin.

Maxim Gorki Theater ⬛

Am Festungsgraben 2. **Map** 7 A3, 16 E2. 🇨 20 22 11 29. 🇺 & 🇸 *Friedrichstrasse.* 🚌 *100, 200, 348.*

T HE MAXIM GORKI theatre was once a singing school or *Sing-Akademie.* Berlin's oldest concert hall, it was built in 1827 by Karl Theodor Ottmer, who based his design on drawings by Karl Friedrich Schinkel. This modest Neo-Classical building, with its attractive façade resembling a Greco-Roman temple, was well known for the excellent acoustic qualities of its concert hall.

Many famous composer-musicians performed at the Maxim Gorki Theater, including violinist Niccolò Paganini and pianist Franz Liszt. In 1829, Felix Mendels-sohn-Bartholdy conducted a performance of the *St Matthew*

Maxim Gorki Theater occupying the oldest concert hall in Berlin

Passion by Johann Sebastian Bach, the first since the composer's death in 1750. Following reconstruction after World War II, the building is now used as a theatre.

Palais am Festungs-graben (Museum Mitte) ⬛

FESTUNGSGRABEN PALACE (MITTE MUSEUM)

Am Festungsgraben 1. **Map** 7 A3, 16 E2. 🇨 20 84 000. 🇸 *Friedrich-strasse.* 🚌 *100, 200, 348.* 🚋 *6, 8.* 🕐 *1–5pm Mon–Fri, 1–8pm Sat, 11am–5pm Sun.*

T HE PALACE IN Festungsgraben is one of the few structures in this part of town that has maintained its original interior decor. Built as a small Baroque palace in 1753, it owes its present form to major extension work, carried out in 1864 in the style of Karl Friedrich Schinkel, by Heinrich Bürde and Hermann von der Hude.

The late Neo-Classical style of the building is reminiscent of Schinkel's later designs. The interior includes a magnificent double-height marble hall in the Neo-Renaissance style and modelled on the White Room in the former Stadtschloss *(see p71)*. In 1934 one of the ground-floor rooms was turned into a music salon, and many musical instruments were brought here from the 19th-century house (now demo-lished) of wealthy merchant and manufacturer Johann Weydinger (1773–1837).

MUSEUM ISLAND

T HE LONG ISLAND that nestles in the tributaries of the Spree river is the cradle of Berlin's history. It was here that the first settlements appeared at the beginning of the 13th century – Cölln is mentioned in documents dating back to 1237 and its twin settlement, Berlin, is mentioned a few years later (1244). Not a trace of Gothic and Renaissance Cölln is left now: the island's character was transformed by the construction of the Brandenburg

Bas-relief from the façade of the Berliner Dom

Electors' palace, which served as their residence from 1470. Over the following centuries, the palace was converted first into a royal and later into an imperial palace – the huge Stadtschloss. Although it was razed to the ground in 1950, some interesting buildings on the island's north side have survived, including the huge Berliner Dom (cathedral) and the impressive collection of museums that give the island its name – Museumsinsel.

SIGHTS AT A GLANCE

Museums and Galleries
Alte Nationalgalerie **7**
Altes Museum p75 **6**
Bodemuseum **10**
Galgenhaus **19**
Historischer Hafen Berlin **13**
Märkisches Museum **14**
Neues Museum **8**
Pergamonmuseum pp80–83 **9**

Streets, Squares and Parks
Lustgarten **5**
Märkisches Ufer **15**
Schlossplatz **1**

Historic Buildings
Berliner Dom pp76–7 **4**
Ermeler-Haus **16**
Gertraudenbrücke **17**
Marstall **11**
Nicolai-Haus **18**
Ribbeckhaus **12**
Schlossbrücke **3**

Other Buildings
Palast der Republik **2**

KEY

▨	Street-by-Street map *See pp72–3*
U	U-Bahn Station
🚌	Bus terminus
P	Parking

GETTING THERE

The easiest way to get to Museum Island and Schlossplatz is to walk from Hackescher Markt S-Bahn station, or to take a bus, either the 100, 157 or the 348. The Breite Strasse district is served by buses 147 and 257, while the south end of the island can be reached by U-Bahn line 2, going to Spittelmarkt, and by buses 142 and 147 to Märkisches Ufer.

0 metres	400
0 yards	400

◁ **The elegant Bodemuseum, with the Fernsehturm (Television Tower) in the background**

Street-by-Street: Museum Island

O N THIS ISLAND ARE the pretty Lustgarten and the Berliner Dom (Berlin Cathedral). It is also where you will find some of the most important museums in the east of the city. These include the Bodemuseum, the Altes Museum, the Alte National-galerie and the splendid Pergamonmuseum, famous for its collection of antiquities and visited by crowds of art-lovers from around the world.

Bodemuseum
The dome-covered rounded corner of the building provides a prominent landmark at the tip of the island ❿

Railway bridge, also used by the S-Bahn.

★ **Pergamonmuseum**
The museum is famous for its reconstruction of fragments of ancient towns, as well as the original friezes from the Pergamon altar ❾

AM KUPFER-GRABEN

Alte Nationalgalerie
The equestrian statue of King Friedrich Wilhelm IV in front of the building is the work of Alexander Calandrelli ❼

BODESTRASSE

Schlossbrücke
Under the GDR regime this unusual bridge was called Marx-Engels-Brücke ❸

Neues Museum
The building, which once housed a collection of Egyptian antiquities, is currently in the final stages of reconstruction ❽

0 metres   100

0 yards   100

STAR SIGHTS
★ **Pergamonmuseum**
★ **Altes Museum**
★ **Berliner Dom**

KEY

– – – Suggested route

★ **Altes Museum**
The corners of the central building feature figures of Castor and Pollux, heroes of Greek myth also known as the Dioscuri **6**

LOCATOR MAP
See Street Finder, maps 7 &16

Lustgarten
The 70-ton granite bowl was the biggest in the world when it was placed in the garden in 1828 **5**

★ **Berliner Dom**
The Neo-Baroque interior of the Berlin Cathedral features some extravagant late 19th-century furnishings **4**

Palast der Republik
Originally the home of the East German parliament, this controversial building is to be torn down **2**

BODESTRASSE

LUSTGARTEN

KARL–LIEBKNECHT STR.

OSSBRUCKE

SCHLOSSPLATZ

Schlossplatz
Excavations conducted here have unearthed the cellars of the demolished Stadtschloss **1**

Schlossplatz ❶

Map 7 B3, 16 F3. ⑤ *Hackescher Markt.* 🚌 *100, 200, 348.*

THIS SQUARE was once the site of a gigantic residential complex known as Stadtschloss (City Castle). Built in 1451, it served as the main residence of the Brandenburg Electors. It was transformed from a castle to a palace in the mid-16th century when Elector Friedrich III (later King Friedrich I) ordered its reconstruction in the Baroque style. The building works (1698–1716) were overseen initially by Andreas Schlüter and then by Johann von Göthe and Martin Heinrich Böhme.

The three-storey residence, designed around two courtyards, was the main seat of the Hohenzollern family for almost 500 years until the end of the monarchy. The palace was partly burned during World War II, but after 1945 it was provisionally restored and used as a museum. In 1950–51, despite protests, the palace was demolished and the square was renamed Marx-Engels-Platz under the GDR. Now all that remains of the palace is the triumphal-arch portal that once adorned the façade on the Lustgarten side. This is now incorporated into the wall of the government building, the Staatsratgebäude, erected in 1964 on the square's south side. The building's décor features the remaining

The surviving Stadtschloss portal fronting a government building

original sculptures, including the magnificent atlantes by the famous Dresden sculptor Balthasar Permoser. Their inclusion was not due to appreciation of their artistic merit, but rather to their propaganda value: it was from the balcony of the portal that in 1918 Karl Liebknecht proclaimed the birth of the Socialist Republic *(see p26)*.

In 1989 the square reverted to its original name. In 1993 a full-scale model of the palace was built out of cloth stretched over scaffolding. After a lengthy debate, it was decided not to rebuild the palace, instead incorporating the remaining fragments into a new museum complex.

Palast der Republik ❷
PALACE OF THE REPUBLIC

Map 7 B3, 16 F2. ⑤ *Hackescher Markt.* 🚌 *100, 200, 348.*

BUILT ON THE SITE of the Stadtschloss in 1976, the Palast der Republik was once considered one of East Berlin's most prestigious buildings. Although it housed the GDR parliament, it was also accessible to the public. It boasted restaurants, a theatre, a discotheque, sports facilities and a large hall. In 1990 the discovery that asbestos had been used in its construction led to its closure. Now cleaned, the building awaits demolition since plans to partly dismantle it and integrate key elements, such as the parliamentary chamber, into a new building on Schlossplatz have been abandoned.

Schlossbrücke ❸

Map 7 B3, 16 E2. ⑤ *Hackescher Markt.* 🚌 *100, 200, 348.*

THIS IS ONE of the town's most beautiful bridges, connecting Schlossplatz with Unter den Linden. It was built in 1824 to a design by Karl Friedrich Schinkel *(see p187).*

Sculptures on the Schlossbrücke

Statues were added to the top of the bridge's sparkling granite pillars in 1853. These figures were also created by Schinkel and made of white Carrara marble. The statues depict tableaux from Greek mythology, such as Iris, Nike and Athena training and looking after their favourite young warriors. The wrought-iron balustrade is decorated with intertwined sea creatures.

Berliner Dom ❹
BERLIN CATHEDRAL

See pp76–7.

Lustgarten ❺

Map 7 B3, 16 E2. ⑤ *Hackescher Markt.* 🚌 *100, 200, 348.*

THE ENCHANTING garden in front of the Altes Museum looks as though it has always been here, but in its present form it was established as recently as 1998 to 1999.

Used to grow vegetables and herbs for the Stadtschloss until the late-16th century, it became a real *Lustgarten* (pleasure garden) in the reign of the Great Elector (1620–88). However, its statues, grottoes, fountains and exotic vegetation were removed when Friedrich Wilhelm I (1688–1740), known for his love of military pursuits, turned the garden into an army drill ground.

Following the construction of the Altes Museum, the ground became a park, designed by Peter Joseph Lenné. In 1831 it was adorned with a monolithic granite bowl by Christian Gottlieb Cantian, to a design by Schinkel. The 70-ton bowl, measuring nearly 7 m (23 ft) in diameter, was intended for the museum rotunda, but was too heavy to carry inside.

After 1933, the Lustgarten was paved over and turned into a parade ground, remaining as such until 1989. Its current restoration is based on Lenné's designs.

Altes Museum 6

THE MUSEUM BUILDING, designed by Karl Friedrich Schinkel, is undoubtedly one of the world's most beautiful Neo-Classical structures, with an impressive 87-m (285-ft) high portico supported by 18 Ionic columns. Officially opened in 1830, this was one of the first purpose-built museums in Europe, built to house the royal collection of paintings and antiquities. Following World War II, the building was only used to display temporary exhibitions. Since 1998 the Altes Museum has housed parts of the Antikensammlung, a magnificent collection of Greek and Roman antiquities.

VISITORS' CHECKLIST

Am Lustgarten (Bodestrasse 1–3).
Map 7 B3. ⬛ 20 90 55 55.
Ⓢ Hackescher Markt. ⬛ 100, 200, 348. ⬛ 10am–6pm Tue–Sun. ⬛ ⬛ ⬛

Andochides' Amphora
The amphora is decorated with the figures of wrestlers, a common motif.

Pericles' Head
This is a Roman copy of the sculpture by Kresilas that stood at the entrance to the Acropolis in Athens.

Staircase

The monumental colonnade at the front of the building dominates the façade.

Main entrance

GALLERY GUIDE
The ground floor galleries house Greek and Roman antiquities; the first floor is used for temporary exhibitions.

Mosaic from Hadrian's Villa
(c.117–138)
This colourful mosaic depicts a battle scene between centaurs and a tiger and lion. The mosaic comes from a floor of Hadrian's Villa, near Tivoli on the outskirts of Rome.

The stately rotunda is decorated with sculptures and ringed by a colonnade. Its design is based on the ancient Pantheon.

KEY

⬜	Greek and Roman antiquities
⬜	Temporary exhibitions

Berliner Dom **❹**

Royal crest of
Friedrich III

T HE ORIGINAL BERLINER DOM was based on a modest Baroque design by Johann Boumann. Built between 1747 and 1750 on the site of an old Dominican church, the cathedral included the original crypt of the Hohenzollern family, one of the largest in its kind in Europe. The present Neo-Baroque structure is the work of Julius Raschdorff and dates from 1894 to 1905. The central copper dome is some 98 m (321 ft) high. Following severe World War II damage, the cathedral has now been restored in a simplified form. The Hohenzollern memorial chapel, which had originally adjoined the northern walls of the cathedral, has been dismantled.

Phil.d.Grossm.

Figures of
the apostles

**Philipp der Grossmütige
(Philip the Magnanimous)**
At the base of the arcade stand the statues of church reformers and those who supported the Reformation. The statue of Prince Philip the Magnanimous is the work of Walter Schott.

★ Church Interior
The impressive and richly-decorated interior was designed by Julius Raschdorff at the start of the 20th century.

Sauer's Organ
The organ, the work of Wilhelm Sauer, has an exquisitely carved case. The instrument contains some 7,200 pipes.

**Main
entrance**

★ The Elector's Tomb
This tomb is the oldest relic to be found in the cathedral, dating from c.1530. It was commissioned from the Vischer's studio in Nuremberg by Joachim I for his grandfather, Johann Cicero.

The Four Evangelists
Mosaics depicting the Four Evangelists decorate the ceilings of the smaller niches in the cathedral. They were designed by Woldemar Friedrich.

VISITORS' CHECKLIST

Am Lustgarten. **Map** 7 B3, 16 F2.
20 26 91 19. (S) *Hackescher
Markt.* 100, 200, 348.
9am–8pm (7pm in winter) daily
(from noon Sun). Sun.

The Ascension
The stained glass in the windows of the apses depict scenes from the life of Jesus. They are the work of Anton von Werner.

The main altar, saved from the previous cathedral, is the work of Friedrich August Stüler. It dates from 1820.

The Pulpit
This elaborate Neo-Baroque pulpit is part of the cathedral's ornate decor dating from the early 20th century.

★ Sarcophagi of Friedrich I and his Wife
Both of these were designed by Andreas Schlüter. The sculpture on Sophie Charlotte's sarcophagus depicts death.

STAR FEATURES

★ **Church Interior**

★ **The Elector's Tomb**

★ **Sarcophagi of Friedrich I and his Wife**

Arnold Böcklin's *The Island of the Dead*, 1883, Alte Nationalgalerie

Alte Nationalgalerie ❼

OLD NATIONAL GALLERY

Bodestrasse 1–3. **Map** 7 B2, 16 E1.
C 20 90 55 55. **Ⓢ** Hackescher Markt, Friedrichstrasse. 🚌 100, 200, 348.
🚊 1, 2, 3, 4, 5, 13, 53, 58. **◯** 10am–6pm Tue–Sun (to 10pm Thu).

THE NATIONALGALERIE building was erected between 1866 and 1876 and designed by Friedrich August Stüler, who took into account the sketches made by Friedrich Wilhelm IV. The building is situated on a high platform reached via a double staircase. On the top stands an equestrian statue of Friedrich Wilhelm IV, the work of Alexander Calandrelli in 1886. The façade of the building is preceded by a magnificent colonnade, which becomes a row of half-columns higher up. The decorations are in keeping with the purpose of the building – the tympanum features Germania as patroness of art, while the top is crowned with the personification of the arts.

The museum was originally intended to house the collection of modern art that had been on display since 1861 in the Akademie der Künste *(see p67)*. After World War II the collection was split up. Part of it was shown in West Berlin, where the Neue Nationalgalerie was erected for this purpose

(see p126). This building was then renamed Alte (meaning Old) Nationalgalerie.

Following the reunification of Germany, the modern art collections were merged again. The current collection includes works of masters such as Adolph von Menzel, Wilhelm Leibl, Max Liebermann and Arnold Böcklin. Other works include paintings by the Nazarene Brotherhood and the French Impressionists. There is also no shortage of sculptures, including works by Christian Daniel Rauch, Johann Gottfried Schadow and Reinhold Begas. Two new exhibition halls now present paintings (formerly shown at the Schloss Charlottenburg) from the German Romantic era, as well as works by Caspar David Friedrich, Karl Friedrich Schinkel and Karl Blechen.

Neues Museum ❽

NEW MUSEUM

Bodestrasse 1–3. **Map** 7 B2, 16 E2.
Ⓢ Hackescher Markt or Friedrichstrasse. 🚌 100, 200, 348. 🚊 1, 2, 3, 4, 5, 13, 53, 58. **◯** until 2005.

THE NEUES MUSEUM was built on Museum Island in order to relieve the Altes Museum, which was already very

crowded. The building was erected between 1841 and 1855 to a design by Friedrich August Stüler. Until World War II it housed a collection of antiquities, mainly ancient Egyptian art. The monumental building's beautiful rooms were decorated to complement the exhibitions they contained. Wall paintings by Wilhelm von Kaulbach depicted key events in world history.

Façade statue, Neues Museum

In 1945 the building was badly damaged and it took a long time to decide if it would be feasible to rebuild it. Reconstruction work has started, based on designs by David Chipperfield. When the reconstruction is complete it will once again house the collection of Egyptian art, although the exact interior decor will not be restored. The building will serve not only as a venue for exhibitions, but it will also contain an information centre for the whole Museum Island (Museumsinsel) complex.

Pergamonmuseum ❾

See pp80–81.

Bodemuseum ⑩

Monbijoubrücke. (Bodestrasse 1–3).
Map 7 A2, 16 D1, 16 E1. ☏ *20 90
55 55.* Ⓢ *Hackescher Markt or
Friedrichstrasse.* 🚌 *100, 200, 348.*
⬤ *until 2006.*

THE FOURTH MUSEUM building
on the island was erected
between 1897 and 1904. It was
designed by Ernst von Ihne to
fit the wedge-shaped end of
the island. The interior was
designed with the help of an
art historian, Wilhelm von
Bode, who was the director
of the Berlin state museums
at the time. The museum
displayed a rather mixed
collection that included some
Old Masters. Its original name,
Kaiser Friedrich Museum, was
changed after World War II.
Following the reassembling of
the Berlin collections, all of
the paintings were put in the
Kulturforum *(see pp122–3),*
while the Egyptian art and the
papyrus collection were
moved to the Ägyptisches
Museum (Egyptian Museum)
at Charlottenburg *(see p164).*

Following its refurbishment
the building will once again
house its collection of coins,
medals and Byzantine art. It
will also have the reassembled
collection of sculptures, which
include the works of Tilman
Riemenschneider, Donatello,
Gianlorenzo Bernini and
Antonio Canova. A copy of
the magnificent equestrian
statue of the Great Elector,
Friedrich Wilhelm, by Andreas
Schlüter will once again take
its place in the old hall.

Marstall ⑪

THE ROYAL STABLES

Schlossplatz/Breite Strasse 36–37.
Map 7 B3, C3, C4, 16 F3.
Ⓤ *Spittelmarkt.* 🚌 *143, 148.*

THIS HUGE COMPLEX, occupying the area between the
Spree and Breitestrasse, south
of Schlossplatz, is the old
Royal Stables block. The
wing on the side of Breite
Strasse is a fragment of the
old structure built in 1669. It
was designed by Michael
Matthias Smids and is the
only surviving early Baroque
building in Berlin. The wings
running along Schlossplatz
and the Spree river were built
much later, between 1898 and
1901. Although they were
designed by Ernst von Ihne,
these buildings are reminiscent
of the Berlin Baroque style –
probably because von Ihne
modelled them on designs by
Jean de Bodt from 1700.

Ribbeckhaus ⑫

RIBBECK'S HOUSE

Breite Strasse 35. **Map** 7 C4.
Ⓤ *Spittelmarkt.* 🚌 *143, 148.*

FOUR IDENTICAL, picturesque
gables crown central Berlin's
only surviving Renaissance
building. The house was built
c.1624 for Hans Georg von
Ribbeck, a court counsellor,
who sold it shortly afterwards
to Anna Sophie of Brunswick.
The architect Balthasar Benzelt
converted the house for her
in 1629. After her death in

**The Ribbeckhaus, central Berlin's
only surviving Renaissance building**

1659, the house passed to her
nephew Elector Friedrich
Wilhelm. As crown property,
the building later housed
various state administrative
offices. When another storey
was added, the row of gables
was retained by royal decree.

The house also has an
interesting late-Renaissance
portal, ornamented with the
date and coat of arms of the
first owners – von Ribbeck
and Katharina von Brösicke
his wife. This was replaced
in 1960 with a copy. Original
features of interest include the
beautiful wrought-iron grilles
on the ground-floor windows.

Historischer Hafen Berlin ⑬

HISTORIC PORT OF BERLIN

Märkisches Ufer. **Map** 8 D4.
☏ *21 47 32 57.* Ⓤ *Märkisches
Ufer.* Ⓢ *Jannowitzbrücke.* 🚌 *240,
265.* ⬤ *1 Apr–31 Oct: 2–6pm
Tue–Fri, 11am–6pm Sat & Sun.* ♿

MOORED ON THE south shore
of Museum Island, in an
area called Fischerinsel, and
opposite the Märkisches Ufer
are several examples of boats,
barges and tug-boats which
operated on the Spree river at
the end of the 19th century.
These craft constitute an open-
air museum which was once
located in the Humboldt Port.
One of the boats is now used
as a summer café, while
another, the *Renate Angelika,*
houses a small exhibition
illustrating the history of
inland waterway transport.

The Bodemuseum designed by Ernst von Ihne

Pergamonmuseum ●

THE PERGAMONMUSEUM WAS BUILT between 1912 and 1930 to a design by Alfred Messels and Ludwig Hoffmann. It houses one of the most famous collections of antiquities in Europe, and owes its name to the famous Pergamon Altar which takes pride of place in the main hall. The three independent collections – the Museum of Antiquities (Greek and Roman), the Museum of Near Eastern Antiquities and the Museum of Islamic Art – are the result of intensive archaeological excavations by German expeditions to the Near and Middle East at the end of the 19th and beginning of the 20th century.

★ **Pergamon Altar** *(170 BC)*
This scene, featuring the goddess Athena, appears on the large frieze illustrating a battle between the gods and the giants.

Roman Mosaic *(3rd or 4th century AD)*
This ancient mosaic was found at Jerash, Jordan. A second part of it is in the collection of the Stark Museum of Art, Texas.

Non-exhibition rooms

First floor

The Goddesss Athena
This enchanting Hellenistic sculpture of the goddess Athena is one of many displayed in the museum.

Ground floor

Main entrance

Assyrian Palace
Parts of this beautifully reconstructed palace interior, from the ancient kingdom of Assyria, date from the 12th century BC.

Aleppo Zimmer
(c.1603)
This magnificent panelled room comes from a merchant's house in the Syrian city of Aleppo.

VISITORS' CHECKLIST

Bodestrasse 1–3 (entrance from Am Kupfergraben). **Map** 7 A2, B2, 16 E1, E2. ☎ *20 90 55 55.*
Ⓢ *Hackescher Markt or Friedrich-strasse.* 🚌 *100, 200, 348.*
◗ *10am–6pm Tue–Wed, Fri–Sun, 10am–10pm Thu.* ● *1 Jan, Tue after Easter and Pentecost, 24–25 & 31 Dec.* 🚫 🄰 🄱 🄿 🄽
♿ 🄱 🄾 *without flash.*

GALLERY LAYOUT
The central section of the ground floor houses reconstructions of ancient monumental structures, and the left wing is devoted to the Antiquities of Greece and Rome. The right wing houses the Museum of Near Eastern Antiquities; the first floor of the right wing houses the Museum of Islamic Art.

Façade of the Mshatta Palace *(744 AD)*
This fragment is from the southern façade of the Jordanian Mshatta Palace, presented to Wilhelm II by Sultan Abdul Hamid of Ottoman in 1903.

★ **Market Gate from Miletus** *(c.120 AD)*
This gate, measuring over 16 m (52 ft) in height, opened on to the southern market of Miletus, a Roman town in Asia Minor.

★ **Ishtar Gate from Babylon**
(6th century BC)
Original glazed bricks decorate both the huge Ishtar gate and the impressive Processional Way that leads up to it.

STAR EXHIBITS

★ **Pergamon Altar**

★ **Market Gate from Miletus**

★ **Ishtar Gate from Babylon**

KEY

☐ Antiquities (Antikensammlung)

☐ Near Eastern Antiquities (Vorderasiatisches Museum)

☐ Islamic Art (Museum für Islamische Kunst)

☐ Non-exhibition rooms

Exploring the Pergamonmuseum

OPENED IN 1930, the Pergamonmuseum is the newest museum in the Museum Island complex and is one of Berlin's major attractions. The building was one of the first in Europe designed specifically to house big architectural exhibits. The richness of its collections is the result of large-scale excavations by German archaeologists at the beginning of the 20th century. Currently, the museum is at the heart of a redevelopment programme, due for completion in 2010, that will considerably increase the range of large-scale exhibits on display.

Bird from Mesopotamia

The Greek goddess Persephone, from Tarentum, 5th century BC

Restored entrance hall of the Athena temple from Pergamon, 2nd century BC

COLLECTION OF ANTIQUITIES

BERLIN'S COLLECTION OF Greek and Roman antiquities (Antikensammlung) came into existence during the 17th century. Growing steadily in size, the collection was opened for public viewing in 1830, initially in the Altes Museum (see p75), and from 1930 in the new, purpose-built Pergamonmuseum. The high-light of the collection is the huge Pergamon Altar from the acropolis of the ancient city of Pergamon in Asia Minor (now Bergama, Turkey). It formed part of a larger architectural complex, a model of which is also on display in the museum. The magnificently restored altar is thought to have been built to celebrate victory in war and to have been commissioned by King Eumenes in 170 BC. Probably dedicated to the god Zeus and the goddess Athena, this artistic masterpiece was discovered in a decrepit state by German archaeologist Carl Humann who, after long negotiations, was allowed to transport the surviving portions of the altar to Berlin. The front section of the building was restored at the museum, together with the so-called small frieze, which once adorned the inside of the building, and fragments of the large frieze, which originally encircled the base of the colonnade. The large frieze has now been reconstructed around the interior walls of the museum and its theme is the Gigantomachy (the battle of the gods against the giants). The small frieze tells the story of Telephos, supposed founder of the city and son of the hero Heracles. The frieze is an attempt to claim an illustrious ancestry for Pergamon's rulers.

The collection also contains fragments of other Pergamon structures from the same period, including part of the Athena temple. Also featured here are some excellent examples of Greek sculpture, both originals and Roman copies, as well as many statues of the Greek gods unearthed at Miletus, Samos and Nakosos, and various examples of Greek ceramic art.

Roman architecture is represented by the striking market gate from the Roman city of Miletus, on the west coast of Asia Minor. The gate dates from the 2nd century AD, and shows strong Hellenistic influences. Discovered by a German archaeological expedition, it was transported to Berlin where it was restored in 1903. Also on display are a number of magnificent Roman mosaics. A huge and impressive marble

Roman marble sarcophagus depicting the story of Medea, 2nd century AD

sarcophagus dates from the
2nd century AD and is decorated with delicate bas-relief
carvings depicting the story of
the Greek heroine Medea.

Glazed-brick wall cladding from
the palace of Darius I in Susa,
capital of the Persian Empire

MUSEUM OF NEAR EASTERN ANTIQUITIES

T HE COLLECTION NOW on
display in the Museum of
Near Eastern Antiquities
(Vorderasiatisches Museum)
was made up initially of
donations from individual
collectors. However, hugely
successful excavations, begun
during the 1880s, formed the
basis of a royal collection that
is one of the richest in the
world. It features architecture,
sculpture and jewellery from
Babylon, Iran and Assyria.

One striking exhibit is the
magnificent Ishtar Gate and
the Processional Way that
leads to it. They were built
during the reign of Nebuchad-
nezzar II (604–562 BC) in the
ancient city of Babylon. The
original avenue was about
180 m (590 ft) long. Many of
the bricks used in its reconstruction are new, but the
lions – sacred animals of the
goddess Ishtar (mistress of the
sky, goddess of love and
patron of the army) – are all
originals. Although impressive
in size, the Ishtar Gate has in
fact not been reconstructed in
full and a model of the whole
structure shows the scale of

the original complex. Only
the inner gate is on display,
framed by two towers. Dragons
and bulls decorate the gate,
emblems of the Babylonian
gods, Marduk, patron of the
city, and Adad, god of storms.

The collection also includes
pieces from the neighbouring
regions of Persia, Syria and
Palestine including a gigantic
basalt sculpture of a bird from
Tell Halaf and a glazed wall
relief of a spear bearer from
Darius I's palace in Susa.
Other Mesopotamian peoples,
including the Assyrians and
the Cassians, are represented
here too, as are the inhabitants
of Sumer in the southern part
of the Babylonian Empire
with pieces dating from the
4th century BC.

MUSEUM OF ISLAMIC ART

T HE HISTORY OF the Museum
of Islamic Art (Museum
für Islamische Kunst) begins
in 1904 when Wilhelm von
Bode launched the collection
by donating his own extensive
selection of carpets. He also
brought to Berlin a 45-m
(150-ft) long section of the
façade of a Jordanian desert
palace. The façade, covered
with exquisitely carved limestone cladding, was presented
to Kaiser Wilhelm II in 1903
by Sultan Abdul Hamid of
Ottoman. The palace was part
of a group of defence fortress-
es and residential buildings
dating from the Omayyad
period (AD661–750). These
were probably built for the
Caliph al-Walid II.

Another fascinating exhibit
is a beautiful 13th-century
mihrab, the niche in a

Brilliantly-glazed *mihrab* from a
Kashan mosque built in 1226

mosque that shows the
direction of Mecca. Made in
the Iranian town of Kashan
renowned for its ceramics, the
mihrab is covered in lustrous
metallic glazes that make it
sparkle as if studded with
sapphires and gold.

The collection's many vivid
carpets come from as far
afield as Iran, Asia Minor,
Egypt and the Caucasus. Highlights include an early 15th-
century carpet from Anatolia
decorated with an unusual
dragon and phoenix motif
and, dating from the 14th
century, one of the earliest
Turkish carpets in existence.

Other rooms hold collections
of miniature paintings and
various objects for daily use.
An interesting example of
provincial Ottoman archi-
tecture is an exquisitely-
panelled early 17th-century
reception room, known as the
Aleppo Zimmer, which was
once part of a Christian
merchant's house in the
Syrian city of Aleppo.

17th-century carpet with flower motif from western Anatolia

The exterior of the Märkisches Museum, echoing a medieval monastery

Märkisches Museum ⓮

Am Köllnischen Park 5. **Map** 8 D4.
🅲 308 660. **Ⓤ** Märkisches Museum.
Ⓢ Jannowitzbrücke. 🚌 240, 265.
⏺ 10am–6pm Tue-Sun. 🎫
Presentation of mechanical musical
instruments 3pm Sun.

T HIS ARCHITECTURAL pastiche
is a complex of red brick
buildings that most resembles
a medieval monastery. It was
built between 1901 and 1908
to house a collection relating
to the history of Berlin and
the Brandenburg region, from
the time of the earliest settlers
to the present. Inspired by the
brick-Gothic style popular in
the Brandenburg region, architect Ludwig Hoffmann included
references to Wittstock Castle
and to St Catherine's Church
in the city of Brandenburg. In
the entrance hall, a statue of
the hero Roland stands guard,
a copy of the 15th-century
monument in the city of
Brandenburg. The main hall
features the original Gothic
portal from the Berlin residence of the Margraves of
Brandenburg (see pp17–19),
demolished in 1931. Also
featured is a horse's head from
the Schadow *Quadriga*, which
once crowned the Branden-
burg Gate (see p67). A further
collection in the same building
is devoted to the Berlin theatre
during the period 1730 to 1933,
including many posters, old
programmes and stage sets.
One of the galleries houses
some charming old-time
mechanical musical instruments, which can be heard
playing during special shows.
The Märkisches Museum is
a branch of the Stadtmuseum
Berlin organization, and those
who wish to find out more

about the history of the city
can visit other affiliated
museums and monuments
such as the Nikolaikirche (see
pp90–91), the Ephraim-Palais
(see p91) and the Knoblauchhaus (see p91). Surrounding
the museum is the Köllnischer
Park, home to three brown
bears, the official city mascots,
and an unusual statue of
Berlin artist Heinrich Zille.

Märkisches Ufer ⓯

Map 8 D4. **Ⓤ** Märkisches Museum.
Ⓢ Jannowitzbrücke. 🚌 240, 265.

O NCE CALLED Neukölln am
Wasser, this street, which
runs along the Spree river, is
one of the few corners of
Berlin where it is still possible
to see the town much as it
must have looked in the 18th
and 19th centuries. Eight
picturesque houses have been
meticulously conserved here.
Two Neo-Baroque houses
at No. 16 and No. 18, known
as Otto-Nagel Haus, used to
contain a small museum
displaying paintings by Otto
Nagel, a great favourite with
the communist authorities.
The building now houses the
photographic archives for the

state museums of Berlin. A
number of picturesque garden
cafés and fashionable restaurants make this attractive area
very popular with tourists.

The Baroque interior of the
Ermeler-Haus

Ermeler-Haus ⓰
ERMELER HOUSE

Märkisches Ufer 10. **Map** 7 C4.
Ⓤ Märkisches Museum.
Ⓢ Jannowitzbrücke. 🚌 240, 265.

W ITH ITS HARMONIOUS Neo-
Classical façade, Märk-
isches Ufer No. 12 stands out
as one of the most handsome
villas in Berlin. This house
was once the town residence
of Wilhelm Ferdinand Ermeler,
a wealthy merchant and shop-
keeper, who made his money
trading in tobacco. It originally
stood on Fischerinsel on the
opposite bank of the river, at
Breite Strasse No. 11, but in
1968 the house was dismantled and reconstructed on this
new site. The house was remodelled in 1825 to Ermeler's
specifications, with a decor

Barges moored alongside Märkisches Ufer

that includes a frieze alluding to aspects of the tobacco business. Restorers have recreated much of the original façade. The Rococo furniture dates from about 1760 and the notable 18th-century staircase has also been rebuilt.

A modern hotel has been built to the rear of the house facing Wallstrasse, using Ermeler-Haus as its kitchens while the first-floor rooms are used for special events.

Gertrauden-brücke **⑰**

St Gertrude's Bridge

Map 7 B4, 16 F4.
U Spittelmarkt. 🚌 143, 147.

ONE OF Berlin's more interesting bridges, this connects Fischer Island with Spittel-markt at the point where St Gertrude's Hospital once stood. The Gertrauden-brücke was designed by Otto Stahn and built in 1894.

Standing in the middle of the bridge is a bronze statue of the hospital's patron saint, St Gertrude, by Rudolf Siemering. A 13th-century Christian mystic, St Gertrude is shown here as a Benedictine abbess. Leaning over a poor youth she hands him a lily (symbol of virginity), a distaff (care for the poor), and a vessel filled with wine (love). The pedestal is surrounded by mice, a reference to the fact that Gertrude is patron saint of farmland and graves – both popular environments for mice.

Statue of St Gertrude

Nicolai-Haus **⑱**

Brüderstr. 13. **Map** 7 B4, 16 F4. **C** 20 45 81 64. **U** Spittelmarkt. 🚌 143, 148. ◯ 10am–6pm Tue–Sun.

BUILT AROUND 1710, the Nicolai-Haus is a fine example of Baroque architecture with the original, magnificent oak staircase still in place.

The house owes its fame, however, to its time as the home and bookshop of the publisher, writer and critic Christoph Friedrich Nicolai (1733–1811). Nicolai acquired the house around 1788 when he had it rebuilt to a Neo-Classical design by Karl Friedrich Zelter to become a bookshop and major German cultural centre.

One of the outstanding personalities of the Berlin Enlightenment, Nicolai was a great supporter of such revolutionary talents as the Jewish philosopher Moses Mendelssohn *(see p102)* and the playwright Gotthold Ephraim Lessing (1729–81). Other regular literary visitors to the Nicolai-Haus at this period included Johann Gottfried Schadow, Karl Wilhelm Ramler and Daniel Chodowiecki, all of whom are commemorated with a wall plaque.

Between 1905 and 1935 the building housed a museum devoted to Gotthold Ephraim Lessing. Today the rear wing features a fine staircase from the Weydinger-Haus, demolished in 1935. Installed in the Nicolai-Haus in the late 1970s, the staircase previously stood in the nearby Ermeler Haus *(see p84)*.

East German fashion now on show in the Märkisches Museum *(see p84)*

Galgenhaus **⑲**

Gallows House

Brüderstrasse 10. **Map** 7 B4, 16 F4.
C 240 02 162. **U** Spittelmarkt.
🚌 143, 148. ◯ 10am–6pm
Tue–Sun. ⓰

LOCAL LEGEND HAS IT that an innocent girl was once hanged in front of this building, which dates from 1700. It was originally built as the presbytery of the now vanished church of St Peter. Redesigned in the Neo-Classical style around 1805, the front portal and one of the rooms on the ground floor are all that remain of the original Baroque structure.

Today the Galgenhaus houses an archive of historic photographs. These reveal the ways in which Berlin has developed over the years through changes in its buildings and monuments.

CÖLLN

An ancient settlement in the area called Fischerinsel at the southern end of Museum Island, the village of Cölln has now been razed almost to the ground. Not even a trace remains of the medieval St Peter's parish church. Until 1939, however, this working-class area with its tangle of narrow streets maintained a historic character and unique identity of its own. This vanished completely in the 1960s when most of the buildings were demolished, to be replaced with prefabricated tower blocks. A few historic houses, including Ermeler-Haus *(see p84)*, were reconstructed elsewhere, but the atmosphere of this part of town has changed forever.

An engraving of old Cölln

EAST OF THE CENTRE

THIS PART of Berlin, belonging to the Mitte district, is the historic centre. A settlement called Berlin was first established on the eastern bank of the Spree river in the 13th century. Together with its twin settlement, Cölln, it grew into a town. This district contains traces of Berlin's earliest history, including the oldest surviving church (Marienkirche). In later centuries, it became a trade and residential district, but the Old Town (the Nikolaiviertel)

The organ-grinder at Gerichtslaube

survived until World War II. The GDR regime replaced the huge apartment buildings and department stores just to the north with a square, Marx-Engels-Forum, and built the Fernsehturm (television tower). Their redevelopment of the Nikolaiviertel was controversial – buildings were faithfully rebuilt but were grouped rather than being placed in their original locations. The area still offers cosy mews and alleys, which are surrounded by postwar high-rise blocks.

SIGHTS AT A GLANCE

Churches
Franziskaner Klosterkirche ⑮
Heiliggeistkapelle ⑩
Nikolaikirche ❸
Marienkirche ⑪
Parochialkirche ⑰

Historic Buildings
Ephraim-Palais ❻
Gaststätte "Zur letzten Instanz" ⑱
Gerichtslaube ❼
Knoblauchhaus ❹
Palais Podewils ⑯
Palais Schwerin and Münze ❺
Rotes Rathaus ❶
Stadtgericht ⑭
Stadtmauer ⑲

Others
Alexanderplatz ⑬
Fernsehturm p93 ⑫

Neptunbrunnen ❾
Nikolaiviertel ❷
Marx-Engels-Forum ❽

KEY

▢ Street-by-Street map
See pp88–9

🚊 Railway station

Ⓢ S-Bahn station

Ⓤ U-Bahn station

🅿 Parking

0 metres   400

0 yards   400

GETTING THERE
This part of the city is served by S-Bahn 3, 5, 7 and 9, with stations at Hackescher Markt, Alexanderplatz and Jannowitzbrücke. Alexanderplatz is the interchange for U-Bahn routes 2, 5 and 8. Buses 100 and 157 run along Karl-Liebknecht-Strasse; buses 142 and 257 along Grunerstrasse.

◁ **Detail from the Neptunbrunnen (Neptune Fountain)**

Street-by-Street: Nikolaiviertel

ST NICHOLAS' QUARTER, or the Nikolaiviertel, owes its name to the parish church whose spires rise above the small buildings in this part of town. The Nikolaiviertel is full of narrow alleys crammed with popular restaurants, tiny souvenir shops and small museums. The district was once inhabited by artists and writers, but now it is usually filled with tourists looking for a place to rest after an exhausting day of sightseeing – particularly in the summer. Almost every other house is occupied by a restaurant, inn, pub or café, so the area is quite lively until late at night.

Bear on façade of the Rathaus

Nikolaikirche
The church is now a museum, with its original furnishings incorporated into the exhibition ❸

Gerichtslaube
The replica arcades and medieval courthouse now contain restaurants ❼

POSTSTRASSE

SPREEUFER

St George Slaying the Dragon
This statue once graced a courtyard of the Stadtschloss.

0 metres   75

0 yards   75

Knoblauchhaus
This Biedermeier-style room is on the first floor of the building, which is one of the few to survive World War II damage ❹

★ **Ephraim-Palais**
A feature of this palace is the elegant façade. Inside there is also an impressive spiral staircase and balustrade ❻

★ Rotes Rathaus
This monumental town hall, which once stood in a densely built-up area, now rises from an empty square ❶

LOCATOR MAP
See Street Finder, maps 7 & 8

NORTH OF THE CENTRE

EAST OF THE CENTRE

MUSEUM ISLAND

The Stadthaus, built in 1911 by Ludwig Hoffmann, now houses some of the departments of the Town Hall.

★ Nikolaiviertel
The narrow alleys of this district were a source of inspiration for Gotthold Ephraim Lessing, who lived here from 1752 to 1755 ❷

The Hemp Museum is a small museum specializing in all aspects of the hemp plant.

Palais Schwerin and Münze
The palace façade is decorated with a Neo-Classical frieze by Johann Gottfried Schadow, depicting the development of metal processing and coin minting ❺

STAR SIGHTS

★ Ephraim-Palais

★ Rotes Rathaus

★ Nikolaiviertel

SPANDAUER STRASSE

MÜHLENDAMM

JÜDENSTRASSE

MOLKEN MARKT

STRALAUER STRASSE

ROLANDUFER

KEY
— — — Suggested route

Canal locks on the Spree

Red-brick walls giving the Red Town Hall its name

Rotes Rathaus ❶
RED TOWN HALL

Rathausstr. 15. **Map** 7 C3. 90 26 0. Alexanderplatz. Klosterstrasse. 100, 143, 148, 200, 348. 9am–6pm Mon–Fri.

THIS IMPRESSIVE structure is Berlin's main town hall. Its predecessor was a much more modest structure and by the end of the 19th century, it was insufficient to the needs of the growing metropolis.

The present building was designed by Hermann Friedrich Waesemann, and the construction went on from 1861 until 1869. The architect took his main inspiration from Italian Renaissance municipal buildings, but the tower is reminiscent of Laon cathedral in France. The walls are made from red brick and it was this, rather than the political orientation of the mayors, that gave the town hall its name. The building has a continuous frieze known as the "stone chronicle", which was added in 1879. It features scenes and figures from the city's history and the development of its economy and science.

The Rotes Rathaus was badly damaged during World War II and, following its reconstruction (1951–58), it became the seat of the East Berlin authorities. The West Berlin magistrate was housed in the Schöneberg town hall (see p177). After the reunification of Germany, the Rotes Rathaus became the centre of authority, housing the offices of the mayor, the magistrates' offices and state rooms. The forecourt sculptures were added in 1958. These are by Fritz Kremer and depict Berliners helping to rebuild the city.

Nikolaiviertel ❷

Map 7 C3, C4. & Alexanderplatz. Klosterstrasse. 100, 143, 148, 200, 348.

THIS SMALL AREA on the bank of the Spree, known as the Nikolaiviertel (St Nicholas Quarter), is a favourite place for strolling, for both Berliners and tourists. Some of Berlin's oldest houses stood here until they were destroyed in World War II. The redevelopment of the whole area, carried out by the GDR government between 1979 and 1987, was an interesting, if somewhat controversial, attempt to recreating a medieval village. With the exception of one or two restored buildings, the Nikolaiviertel consists of newly built replicas of historic buildings.

The narrow streets of the Nikolaiviertel tempt the visitor with their small shops, as well as many cafés, bars and restaurants. One of the most popular is Zum Nussbaum, a historical inn that was once located on Fischer Island. The original building, dating from 1507, was destroyed but was subsequently reconstructed at the junction of Am Nussbaum and Propststrasse.

The interior of the Nikolaikirche, one of Berlin's oldest churches

Nikolaikirche ❸

Nikolaikirchplatz. **Map** 7 C3. 24 00 20. & Alexanderplatz. Klosterstrasse. 100, 143, 148, 200, 348. 10am–6pm Tue–Sun. (free Wed).

THE NIKOLAIKIRCHE is the oldest sacred building of historic Berlin. The original structure erected on this site was started probably around 1230, when the town was granted its municipal rights. What remains now of this stone building is the massive base of the two-tower façade of the present church, which dates from c.1300. The presbytery was completed around 1402, but the construction of the main building went on until the mid-15th century. The result was a magnificent Gothic brick hall-church, featuring a chancel with an

Riverside buildings of the Nikolaiviertel

ambulatory and a row of low chapels. In 1877 Hermann Blankenstein, who conducted the church restoration works, removed most of its Baroque modifications and reconstructed the front towers.

Destroyed by bombing in 1945, the Nikolaikirche was eventually rebuilt in 1987. Today it houses an exhibition covering the history of Berlin, featuring items that escaped the ravages of war. The west wall of the southern nave contains Andreas Schlüter's monument to the goldsmith Daniel Männlich and his wife, which features a gilded relief portrait of the couple above a mock doorway.

Knoblauchhaus **❹**

Poststr. 23. **Map** 7 C3. **(** 24 00 20. **U** & **S** *Alexanderplatz*, **U** *Kloster-strasse*. 100, 143, 148, 200, 348. 10am–6pm Tue–Sun. *(free Wed)*.

THIS SMALL TOWNHOUSE in Poststrasse is the only Baroque building in Nikolai-viertel that escaped damage during World War II. It was built in 1759 for the Knoblauch family which includes the famous architect, Eduard Knoblauch. His works include, among others, the Neue Synagoge *(see p102)*.

The current appearance of the building is the result of work carried out in 1835, when the façade was given a Neo-Classical look. The ground floor houses a popular wine bar, while the upper floors belong to a museum. On the first floor it is possible to see the interior of an early 19th-century middle-class home, including a beautiful Biedermeier-style room.

Palais Schwerin and Münze **❺**

Molkenmarkt 1–3. **Map** 7 C4. **U** & **S** *Alexanderplatz*. **U** *Kloster-strasse*. 100, 143, 148, 200, 348.

THESE TWO ADJOINING houses have quite different histories. The older one, at Molkenmarkt No. 2, is Palais Schwerin, which was built by

A fine example of German Baroque architecture, the Ephraim-Palais

Jean de Bodt in 1704 for a government minister, Otto von Schwerin. Despite subsequent remodelling, the palace kept its beautiful sculptured window cornices, the interior wooden staircase, and the magnificent cartouche featuring the von Schwerin family crest.

The adjoining house is the mint which was built in 1936. Its façade is decorated with a copy of the frieze that once adorned the previous Neo-Classical mint building in Werderscher Markt. The antique style of the frieze was designed by Friedrich Gilly and produced in the workshop of JG Schadow.

Ephraim-Palais **❻**

Poststr. 16. **Map** 7 C3. **(** 24 00 20. **U** & **S** *Alexanderplatz*. **U** *Kloster-strasse*. 100, 143, 148, 200, 348. 10am–6pm Tue–Sun. *(free Wed)*.

THE CORNER ENTRANCE of the Ephraim-Palais, standing at the junction of Poststrasse and Mühlendamm, used to be called "die schönste Ecke Berlins", meaning "Berlin's most beautiful corner". This

Baroque palace was built by Friedrich Wilhelm Diterichs in 1766 for Nathan Veitel Heinrich Ephraim, Frederick the Great's mint master and court jeweller. During the widening of the Mühlendamm bridge in 1935 the palace was demolished, which may have been due in some part to the Jewish origin of its owner. Parts of the façade, saved from demolition, were stored in a warehouse in the western part of the city. In 1983 they were sent to East Berlin and used in the reconstruction of the palace, which was erected a few metres from its original site. One of the first floor rooms features a restored Baroque ceiling, designed by Andreas Schlüter. The ceiling previously adorned Palais Wartenberg, which was dismantled in 1889.

Currently Ephraim-Palais houses a branch of the Stadtmuseum Berlin (Berlin City Museum). The ground floor features ceramics from Königliche Porzellan-Manufaktur Berlin, while the first and the second floor rooms house a collection of paintings by Berlin artists.

Frieze from the façade of the Münze (the Mint)

Gerichtslaube 🄭

Poststrasse. 28. **Map** 7 C3.
Ⓤ & Ⓢ *Alexanderplatz.* Ⓤ *Kloster-strasse.* 🚌 *100, 143, 148, 200, 348.*

THIS SMALL BUILDING, with its sharply angled arcades, has had a turbulent history. It was built around 1280 as part of Berlin's town hall in Spandauer Strasse. The original building was a single storey arcaded construction with vaults supported by a central pillar. It was open on three sides and adjoined the shorter wall of the town hall. A further storey was added in 1485 to provide a hall to which the magnificent lattice vaults were added a few decades later, in 1555.

In 1692, Johann Arnold Nering refurbished the town hall in a Baroque style, but left the arcades unaltered. Then, in 1868, the whole structure was dismantled to provide space for the new town hall, the Rotes Rathaus *(see p90).* The Baroque part was lost forever, but the Gothic arcades and the first floor hall were moved to the palace gardens in Babelsberg, where they were reassembled as a building in their own right *(see pp210–11).* When the Nikolaiviertel was undergoing restoration it was decided to restore the court of justice as well. The present building in Poststrasse is only a copy of a part of the former town hall, erected on a different site from the original one. Inside is a restaurant specializing in local cuisine.

Marx-Engels-Forum 🄯

Map 7 C3, 16 F2. Ⓢ *Hackescher Markt or Alexanderplatz.*
🚌 *100, 143, 148, 200, 348.*

THIS VAST, eerily empty square, stretching from the Fernsehturm (television tower) to the Spree river in the west, was given the inappropriate name Marx-Engels-Forum (it is not really a forum). Devoid of any surroundings, the only features in this green square are the statues of Karl Marx

Statue of Karl Marx and Friedrich Engels in Marx-Engels-Forum

and Friedrich Engels. Marx sits and Engels stands, seemingly staring at the Fernsehturm. The statues, added in 1986, are by Ludwig Engelhart. The base is decorated with bas-reliefs showing the "old order" at the rear, the "world revolution from Marx-Engels to the present day" at the front, and the "dignity and beauty of free men" on the sides.

Neptunbrunnen 🄮
NEPTUNE FOUNTAIN

Spandauer Str. (Rathausvorplatz).
Map 7 C3. Ⓢ *Hackescher Markt or Alexanderplatz.* 🚌 *100, 143, 148, 200, 348.*

THIS MAGNIFICENT fountain, sparkling with cascades of running water, provides a splendid feature on the main axis of the town hall building. It was created in 1886 by Reinhold Begas, to stand in front of the southern wall of the former Stadtschloss (Berlin Castle). It was moved to its present site in 1969.

Begas, who designed it in the Neo-Baroque style, was

Neptune surrounded by goddesses personifying Germany's rivers

undoubtedly inspired by the famous Roman fountains by Bernini and the Latony fountain in Versailles. The statue of Neptune, in a dynamic pose and in the centre of the fountain, is surrounded by four figures representing Germany's greatest rivers of the time: the Rhine, the Vistula, the Oder and the Elbe. The naturalism of the composition and the attention to detail, such as the beautiful bronze fish, crayfish, snails and fishing nets, are noteworthy.

The Gothic Chapel of the Holy Spirit, seen from Spandauer Strasse

Heiliggeistkapelle 🄰
CHAPEL OF THE HOLY SPIRIT

Spandauer Strasse 1. **Map** 7 B2, 16 F2. Ⓢ *Hackescher Markt.*
🚌 *100, 143, 148, 200, 348.*

THIS MODEST Gothic structure is the only surviving hospital chapel in Berlin. It was built as part of a hospital complex in the second half of the 13th century, but was subsequently rebuilt in the 15th century. The hospital itself was demolished in 1825, but the chapel was retained. In 1906, it was incorporated into a newly erected College of Trade, designed by Cremer and Wolffenstein.

The chapel is a fine example of Gothic brick construction. Its rather modest interior features a 15th century star-shaped vault. The supports under the vault, or consoles, are decorated with half-statues of prophets and saints.

Marienkirche 🄱

See pp94–95.

Fernsehturm ⑫

T HE TELEVISION TOWER, called by the locals *Telespargel*, or toothpick, remains to this day the city's tallest structure at 365 m (1,197 ft), and one of the tallest structures in Europe. The tower was built in 1969 to a design by a team of architects including Fritz Dieter and Günter Franke, with the help of Swedish engineering experts. However, the idea for such a colossal tower in Berlin originated much earlier from Hermann Henselmann (creator of the Karl-Marx-Allee development) in the Socialist-Realist style.

VISITORS' CHECKLIST

Panoramastrasse. **Map** 7 C2. 🅲
242 33 33. Ⓢ & 🆄 Alexanderplatz. 🚌 100, 157, 200, 348. ◯
Mar–Oct: 9am–1am daily;
Nov–Feb: 10am–midnight daily.

The television antenna is visible all over Berlin.

Viewing Platform
Situated inside a steel-clad giant sphere, the viewing platform is 203 m (666 ft) above the ground.

Television Tower
The slim silhouette of the Fernsehturm is visible from almost any point in Berlin. The ticket office and elevator entrance are located at the base of the tower.

Trans-mitter aerials

The metal sphere is covered with steel cladding.

Concrete structure rising to 250 m (820 ft)

The concrete shaft contains two elevators that carry passengers to the café and viewing platform.

The elevators are small, resulting in long queues at the base of the tower.

Tele-Café
One of the attractions of the tower is the revolving café. A full rotation takes about half an hour, so it is possible to get a bird's-eye-view of the whole city while sipping a cup of coffee.

View from the Tower
On a clear day the viewing platform offers a full view of Berlin. Visibility can reach up to 40 km (25 miles).

Marienkirche ⓫

S T MARY'S CHURCH, or the Marienkirche, was first established
as a parish church in the second half of the 13th century.
Construction started around 1280 and was completed early
in the 14th century. During reconstruction works in 1380,
following a fire, the church was altered slightly but its overall
shape changed only in the 15th century when it acquired the
front tower. In 1790, the tower was crowned with a dome
designed by Carl Gotthard Langhans. The church was once
hemmed in by buildings, but today it stands alone in
the shadow of the Fernsehturm (Television Tower).
The early-Gothic hall design and the lavish decorative touches make this church one of the most
interesting in Berlin.

The Tower
*The dome that
crowns the tower
includes both
Baroque and Neo-
Gothic elements.*

Crucifixion (1562)
*This image of
Christ, flanked by
Moses and St John
the Baptist, was
painted in the
Mannerist style by
Michael Ribestein.*

Totentanz,
meaning "dance
of death", is the
name of a 22-m
(72-ft) long
Gothic wall
fresco, dating
from 1485.

Retable
*The central part of the
Gothic altar, dating
from 1510, features
figures of three
unknown monks.*

STAR FEATURES

★ **Pulpit**

★ **Baptismal Font**

**Main
entrance**

★ Pulpit
Carved from alabaster, this masterpiece by Andreas Schlüter, completed in 1703, is placed by the fourth pillar. The pulpit is decorated with bas-reliefs of St John the Baptist and the personifications of the Virtues.

VISITORS' CHECKLIST

Karl-Liebknecht-Str. **Map** 7 C2.
242 44 67. **S** Hackescher Markt.
100, 143, 148, 200, 348.
10am–4pm Mon–Thu (from noon
Sat & Sun). 1pm Mon & Tue.

Von Röbel Family Tomb
This richly decorated Mannerist-Baroque tomb of Ehrentreich and Anna von Röbel was probably built after 1630.

Main Altar
The Baroque altar was designed by Andreas Krüger c.1762. The paintings, including Deposition *from the Cross in the centre;* Christ on the Mount of Olives *and* Doubting Thomas *on the sides, are the works of Christian Bernhard Rode.*

★ Baptismal Font
This Gothic font dating from 1437 is supported by three black dragons and decorated with the figures of Jesus Christ, Mary and the Apostles.

The magnificent interior of the Stadtgericht

Alexanderplatz ⑬

Map 8 D2. 🚇 & Ⓢ *Alexanderplatz.*
🚌 *100, 143, 148, 200, 348.*

Aᴸᴇxᴀɴᴅᴇʀᴘʟᴀᴛᴢ, or "Alex" as
it is locally called, has a
long history, although it
would be difficult now to find
any visible traces of the past.
Once called Ochsenmarkt
(oxen market), it was the site
of a cattle and wool market.
It was later renamed after
Tsar Alexander I, who visited
Berlin in 1805. At the time,
the square boasted a magnificent monumental colonnade,
which was designed by Carl
von Gontard *(see pp176)*.
   With the passage of time,
many houses and shops
sprang up around the square,
and a market hall and an
urban train line were built
nearby. "Alex" had become
one of the town's busiest
spots. Its frenzied atmosphere
was captured by Alfred
Döblin (1878-1957) in his
novel, *Berlin Alexanderplatz.*
   In 1929, attempts were made
to develop the square, though
only two office buildings were
added – the Alexanderhaus
and the Berolinahaus. These
two, both by Peter Behrens,
are still standing today.

World War II erased most of
the square's buildings. It is now
surrounded by characterless
1960s edifices, including the
Forum Hotel (formerly Hotel
Stadt Berlin) and the Fernsehturm *(see p93)*. Alexanderplatz
awaits its next transformation,
which might happen soon:
a winning design has been
chosen from a competition for
the square's redevelopment.

Stadtgericht ⑭
Cᴏᴜʀᴛs ᴏғ Jᴜsᴛɪᴄᴇ

Littenstrasse 13–17. **Map** 8 D3.
🚇 & Ⓢ *Alexanderplatz* or
🚇 *Klosterstrasse.* 🚌 *148.*

Tʜɪs ɢɪɢᴀɴᴛɪᴄ building,
situated on a long stretch
of Littenstrasse, does not seem
particularly inviting, but its
interior hides a true masterpiece of the Viennese
Secession style of architecture.
At the time of its construction,
the building was the largest in
Berlin after the Stadtschloss
(see p74). The Neo-Baroque
structure, built between 1896
and 1905, was designed by
Paul Thomer and Rudolf
Mönnich, but its final shape is
the work of Otto Schmalz.

This maze-like complex, with
its 11 inner courtyards, was
partly demolished in 1969.
What remains, however, is still
worth seeing, especially the
magnificent staircase in the
form of overlying ellipses. The
staircase is an example of
Secession architecture at its
boldest. The slim Neo-Gothic
pillars and the Neo-Baroque
balustrades further enhance the
fairytale interior.

Franziskaner Klosterkirche ⑮
Fʀᴀɴᴄɪsᴄᴀɴ Fʀɪᴀʀʏ Cʜᴜʀᴄʜ

Klosterstrasse 74. **Map** 8 D3.
🚇 *Klosterstrasse.* 🚌 *148.*

Tʜᴇsᴇ ᴘɪᴄᴛᴜʀᴇsǫᴜᴇ ruins
surrounded by greenery
are the remains of an early-
Gothic Franciscan church.
The Franciscan friars settled
in Berlin in the early 13th
century. Between 1250 and
1265 they built a church and
a friary, which survived
almost unchanged until 1945.
The church was a triple-nave
basilica with an elongated
presbytery, widening into a
heptagonal section that was
added to the structure in
c.1300. Protestants took over
the church after the Reformation and the friary became a
famous grammar school,
whose graduates included
Otto von Bismarck and Karl
Friedrich Schinkel.
   The friary was so damaged
in World War II that it was
subsequently demolished,
while the church is gradually

**Ruins of the Franziskaner Kloster-
kirche (Franciscan Friary Church)**

being reconstructed. The giant Corinthian capitals, emerging from the grass near the church ruins, are from a portal from the Stadtschloss (Berlin Castle) *(see p74)*.

Façade of the twice-restored Palais Podewils

Palais Podewils

PODEWILS PALACE

Klosterstrasse 68–70. **Map** 8 D3. Ⓤ *Klosterstrasse.* 🚌 *148.*

THIS CHARMING Baroque palace, set back from the street, was built between 1701 and 1704 for the Royal Court's counsellor, Caspar Jean de Bodt. Its owes its present name to its subsequent owner, a minister of state called von Podewils, who bought the palace in 1732.

After World War II, the palace was restored twice: in 1954 and then again in 1966 after it had been damaged by fire. The carefully reconstructed building did not lose much of its austere beauty, but the interior completely changed to suit its current needs. Today, the palace serves as a cultural centre that organizes concerts and theatre performances, including ballet.

Parochialkirche ⓱

PARISH CHURCH

Klosterstr. 67. **Map** 8 D3. 📞 247 59 50. Ⓤ *Klosterstrasse.* 🚌 *148.* 🕐 *noon–8pm daily.* ✝ *10am Sun.*

THIS BUILDING was, at one time, one of most beautiful Baroque churches in Berlin. Johann Arnold

Nering prepared the initial design, with four chapels framing a central tower. Unfortunately, Nering died as construction started in 1695. The work was continued by Martin Grünberg, but the collapse of the nearly completed vaults forced a change in the design. Instead of the intended tower over the main structure, a vestibule with a front tower was built. The church was completed in 1703, but then, in 1714, its tower was enlarged by Jean de Bodt in order to accommodate a carillon.

World War II had a devastating effect on the Parochial-kirche. The interior was completely destroyed, and the tower collapsed. Following stabilization of the main structure, the façade has been restored and the inside will be complete by 2004, with some reproduced historic elements set within a plain interior. During the summer, mass is held in the church.

Gaststätte Zur letzten Instanz ⓲

INN OF THE LAST INSTANCE

Waisenstrasse 14–16. **Map** 8 D3. Ⓤ *Klosterstrasse.* 🚌 *148.*

THE SMALL STREET at the rear of the Parochialkirche leads directly to one of the oldest inns in Berlin, Zur letzten Instanz, which translates as the Inn of the Last Instance. The inn occupies one of the four picturesque houses on Waisenstrasse – the only survivors of the whole row of houses that

once adjoined the town wall. Their history goes back to medieval times, but their present form dates from the 18th century. The houses are actually the result of an almost total reconstruction carried out after World War II. This was when one of the houses acquired its spiral Rococo staircase, which came from a dismantled house on the Fischerinsel.

The Zur letzten Instanz was first established in 1621 and initially specialized in serving alcoholic beverages. Interestingly, it was frequently patronized by lawyers. Today, however, the Zur letzten Instanz is one of Berlin's finest historic pub-restaurants frequented by all types of people, not just lawyers *(see p237)*. Its interior is full of old memorabilia.

Medallion from a headstone in the Parochialkirche

Stadtmauer ⓳

TOWN WALL

Waisenstrasse **Map** 8 D3. Ⓤ & Ⓢ *Alexanderplatz or* Ⓤ *Klosterstrasse.* 🚌 *148.*

THE TOWN WALL that once surrounded the settlements of Berlin and Cölln was erected in the second half of the 13th century. The ring of fortifications, built from field-stone and brick, was made taller in the 14th century. Having finally lost its military significance by the 17th century, the wall was almost entirely dismantled. Today, some small sections survive around Waisenstrasse, because they were incorporated into other buildings.

Remains of the Berlin's Stadtmauer (old town wall)

NORTH OF THE CENTRE

Detail from
Postfuhramt

THE AREA NORTHWEST of Alexanderplatz, bounded by Friedrichstrasse and Karl-Liebknecht-Strasse, is the former Spandauer Vorstadt, so called because one of its main streets, Oranienburger Strasse, led to Spandau. The eastern part of the area is known as Scheunenviertel (Barn Quarter). In 1672, the Great Elector moved the hay barns – a fire hazard – out of the city limits. From that time it became a refuge for Jews fleeing Russia and Eastern Europe, and by the 19th century it had become the well-established centre for Berlin's Jewish community. The area also attracted artists, writers and political activists in the 1920s. Shops, hospitals, small factories and narrow streets of houses inhabited by workers and merchants gave the district its unique, lively character. After World War II the area gradually fell into decay. However, it has recently become fashionable again. Today, its newly restored houses, grand buildings and trendy restaurants stand side by side with dilapidated tenement blocks, shabby courtyards and buildings engulfed in scaffolding. The area is popular with tourists and Berliners alike, especially in the evenings.

SIGHTS AT A GLANCE

Streets and Parks
Alte and Neue
    Schönhauser Strasse ⑩
Monbijoupark ④
Oranienburger Strasse ③
Sophienstrasse ⑨

Churches and Synagogues
Neue Synagoge ①
Sophienkirche ⑧

Theatres
Berliner Ensemble ⑬
Deutsches Theater ⑭
Friedrichstadtpalast ⑫
Volksbühne ⑪

Museums
Brecht-Weigel-Gedenkstätte ⑰
Centrum Judaicum ②

Hamburger Bahnhof
    pp110–11 ⑲
Museum für Naturkunde ⑱

Cemeteries
Alter Jüdischer Friedhof ⑦
Dorotheenstädtischer Friedhof
    pp106–7 ⑯

Others
Charité ⑮
Gedenkstätte Grosse
    Hamburger Strasse ⑥
Hackesche Höfe ⑤

GETTING THERE
S-Bahn lines 3, 5, 7 and 9 run along the south of the area, with stops at Lehrter Stadtbahnhof, Friedrichstrasse and Hackescher Markt. S-Bahn lines 1 and 2 stop at Oranienburger Strasse. U-Bahn line 6 goes to Oranienburger Tor station, line 8 to Weinmeisterstrasse and line 2 to Rosa-Luxemburg-Platz.

KEY

▨	Street-by-Street map *See pp100–1*
U	U-Bahn station
Ⓢ	S-Bahn station
P	Parking
⯊	Tram stop
▭	Bus stop

◁ **The first courtyard in Hackesche Höfe**

Street-by-Street: Scheunenviertel

Until World War II Scheunenviertel lay at the heart of Berlin's large Jewish district. During the 19th century the community flourished, its prosperity reflected in grand buildings such as the Neue Synagoge, which opened in 1866 in the presence of Chancellor Otto von Bismarck. Left to crumble for nearly 50 years after the double devastations of the Nazis and Allied bombing, the district has enjoyed a huge revival since the fall of the Wall. Recently cafés and bars have opened and visitors can expect to find some of the liveliest nightlife in East Berlin.

★ Neue Synagoge
Sparkling with gold, the recently-restored New Synagogue is now used again for services ❶

The Postfuhramt
was used originally as stables for the horses that delivered the post. Its ceramic-clad façade resembles a palace more than a post office.

Centrum Judaicum
Standing next to the Neue Synagoge, the Jewish Centre houses documents relating to the history and cultural heritage of the Berlin Jews ❷

Heckmann-Höfe
Today these lavishly restored yards, the most elegant in Berlin, attract visitors with a restaurant and fashionable clothes shops.

KEY

━ ━ ━ Suggested route

STAR SIGHTS

★ Neue Synagoge

★ Hackesche Höfe

S-Bahn line

Sophienkirche
*This small Protestant church
was founded in 1712 by
Queen Sophie Luisa* **8**

LOCATOR MAP
See Street Finder maps 1 & 6

**Gedenkstätte Grosse
Hamburger Strasse**
*This modest memorial to the
Berlin Jews stands on the site
of the city's first Jewish old
people's home* **6**

Dorotheen-
städtischerfriedhof

★ **Hackesche Höfe**
*This attractive series of
interconnected courtyards
is home to many popular
entertainment venues* **5**

| 0 metres | 50 |
| 0 yards | 50 |

Alter Jüdischer Friedhof
*Now a tree-filled park, the
city's oldest Jewish cemetery
was systematically destroyed
by the Gestapo in 1943* **7**

HACKESCHER MARKT

Fernsehturm
(television
tower)

Monbijoupark
*Once the grounds of a royal palace,
this small park contains a marble bust
of the poet Adelbert von Chamisso* **4**

Neue Synagoge ❶

NEW SYNAGOGUE

Oranienburger Strasse 30. **Map** 7 A1.
📞 28 40 13 16. Ⓢ Oranienburger
Strasse. 🚋 1, 6, 13. 🕐 10am–
6pm Sun–Thu, 10am–2pm Fri.
📷 ⬤ Jewish festivals. 🚫

THE BUILDING OF THE New
Synagogue was started in
1859 by architect Eduard
Knoblauch, and completed in
1866. The design was a highly
sophisticated response to the
asymmetrical shape of the
plot of land, with a narrow
façade flanked by a pair of
towers and crowned with a
dome containing a round
vestibule. A series of small
rooms opened off the
vestibule, including an ante-
room and two prayer rooms –
one large and one small. The
two towers opened onto a
staircase leading to the
galleries, and the main hall
had space for around 3,000
worshippers. An innovative use
of iron in the construction of
the roof and galleries put the
synagogue at the forefront of
19th-century civil engineering.

With its gilded dome, this
fascinating structure was
Berlin's largest synagogue, until
9 November 1938, when it
was partially destroyed during
the infamous "Kristallnacht"
(see pp26–7). The building
was damaged further by Allied
bombing in 1943 and was
finally demolished in 1958 by
government authorities.

Reconstruction started in
1988 and was completed with
due ceremony in 1995. The
front of the building is now
used for public exhibitions by
the Centrum Judaicum.

The Centrum Judaicum, centre for research into Jewish heritage

Centrum Judaicum ❷

JEWISH CENTRE

Oranienburger Strasse 29. **Map** 7 A1.
📞 28 40 13 16. Ⓢ Oranienburger
Strasse. 🚋 1, 6, 13. 🕐 10am–6pm
(6pm in winter) Sun–Mon, 10am–6pm
Tue–Thu, 10am–5pm (2pm in winter)
Fri. 📷 ⬤ Jewish festivals. 🚫

THE ENTRANCE TO the Jewish
Centre is easy to recognize
thanks to the policemen
permanently stationed here.
All visitors must undergo a
strict security check involving
the use of a metal detector,
which is conducted by guards
who are polite but firm. The
Centrum Judaicum occupies
the former premises of the
Jewish community council,
and contains a library and
archives and a research centre
devoted to the history and
cultural heritage of the Berlin
Jews. Next door to the
Centrum, the restored rooms
of the Neue Synagoge are
used to exhibit material
relating to the local Jewish
community, including one of

the greatest of all Jewish
thinkers and social activists,
Moses Mendelssohn. Next to
the Centrum is the well-
known Oren restaurant, which
serves Jewish and Middle
Eastern cuisine (see p238).

Oranienburger Strasse ❸

Map 6 F1, 7 A1 & 7 B2.
Ⓢ Oranienburger Strasse or
Hackescher Markt. 🚋 1, 6, 13.

ORANIENBURGER STRASSE is
home to many of Berlin's
most popular nightspots.
People of all ages flock here,
spending pleasant hours in
the area's numerous cafés,
restaurants and bars. The
district has traditionally been
a centre for alternative
culture, home to the famous
state-sponsored Tacheles
centre for the arts. The life
of the Tacheles centre may
now be coming to an end,
but many good art galleries
remain in this area. As you
stroll around the district it is
worth looking out for a

The Neue Synagoge with its
splendidly reconstructed dome

MOSES MENDELSSOHN (1729–1786)

One of the greatest German philosophers
of the 18th century, Moses Mendelssohn
arrived in Berlin in 1743 and was a
central figure in the Jewish struggle
for citizenship rights. About 50 years
later the first Jewish family was
granted full civic rights, however, it
wasn't until the Emancipation Edict of
1812 that Jewish men finally became full citizens. The
grandfather of composer Felix Mendelssohn-Bartholdy, he
is immortalized in the drama "Nathan der Weise" (Nathan
the Wise) by his friend Gotthold Ephraim Lessing.

number of interesting buildings, such as the one at Oranienburger Strasse No. 71–2, which was built by Christian Friedrich Becherer in 1789 for the Great National Masonic Lodge of Germany.

Monbijoupark ❹

MONBIJOU PARK

Oranienburger Strasse. **Map** 7 B2.
Ⓢ *Oranienburger Strasse or Hackescher Markt.* 🚊 *1, 6, 13.*

THIS SMALL PARK, situated between Oranienburger Strasse and the Spree river, was once the grounds of the Monbijou Palace. Damaged by bombing during World War II, the ruined palace was finally dismantled in 1960. A rare green space in this part of the city, the well-kept park makes a pleasant place to spend some time relaxing. It features a marble bust of the poet Adelbert von Chamisso, and there is also a swimming pool for children.

Hackesche Höfe ❺

Rosenthaler Strasse 40–41. **Map** 7 B1
7 B2. Ⓢ *Hackescher Markt.*
🚊 *1, 6, 13.*

RUNNING FROM Oranienburger Strasse and Rosenthaler up as far as Sophienstrasse, the Hackesche Höfe (*Höfe* means yards) is a huge, early 20th-century complex. It is made up of an intricate series of nine interconnecting

One of the striking inner courtyards at the Hackesche Höfe

courtyards surrounded by tall and beautifully proportioned buildings. The development dates from 1906, and was designed by Kurt Berendt and August Endell, both of whom were outstanding exponents of the German Secession style.

Damaged during World War II, Hackesche Höfe has been restored recently to its original splendour. The first courtyard is especially attractive, featuring glazed facings with geometric designs decorated in fabulous colours. A whole range of restaurants, bars, art galleries, shops and restaurants can be found here, as well as offices and apartments on the upper floors. The complex also has its own theatre, the Hackesche Hoftheater, specializing in mime. For many Berliners the Hackesche Höfe has became something of a cult spot, and for visitors it is definitely a sight not to be missed.

Gedenkstätte Grosse Hamburger Strasse ❻

GROSSE HAMBURGER STRASSE MEMORIAL

Grosse Hamburger Strasse. **Map** 7 B1.
Ⓢ *Hackescher Markt.* 🚊 *1, 6, 13.*

UNTIL THE YEARS leading up to World War II, Grosse Hamburger Strasse was one of the main streets of Berlin's Jewish quarter. It was home to several Jewish schools, an old people's home and the city's oldest Jewish cemetery, established in 1672. The home was used during World War II as a detention centre for many thousands of Berlin Jews condemned to death in the camps at Auschwitz and Theresienstadt. The building was later destroyed, and in its place now stands a small monument representing a group of Jews being led to their deaths. A modest commemorative plaque is displayed nearby.

Nearby, at Grosse Hamburger Strasse No. 27, stands a Jewish school, originally founded in 1778 by Moses Mendelssohn. Rebuilt in 1906, the building was reopened as a Jewish secondary school in 1993. The empty space once occupied by house No. 15–16, which was destroyed by World War II bombing, is now an installation, *"The Missing House"* by Christian Boltanski, with plaques recording the names and professions of the former inhabitants of the house.

The Gedenkstätte Grosse Hamburger Strasse commemorating Berlin Jews murdered in the Holocaust

Alter Jüdischer Friedhof ❼

OLD JEWISH CEMETERY

Grosse Hamburger Strasse. **Map** 7 B2.
Ⓢ *Hackescher Markt.* 🚋 *1, 6, 13.*

THE OLD JEWISH CEMETERY was established in 1672 and, until 1827 when it was finally declared full, it provided the resting place for over 12,000 Berliners. After this date Jews were buried in cemeteries in Schönhauser Allee and in Herbert-Baum-Strasse. The Alter Jüdischer Friedhof was destroyed by the Nazis in 1943, and in 1945 the site was turned into a park. Embedded in the original cemetery wall, a handful of Baroque *masebas* (or tomb-stones) continue to provide a poignant reminder of the past. A new *maseba* stands on the grave of the philosopher Moses Mendelssohn *(see p102)*, erected in 1990 by members of the Jewish community.

Tombstone of Moses Mendelssohn

Sophienkirche ❽

Grosse Hamburger Str. 29. **Map** 7 B1.
🄲 *308 79 20.* Ⓢ *Hackescher Markt.*
Ⓤ *Weinmeisterstrasse.* 🚋 *13, 53.*
🕐 *May–Oct: 3–6pm Wed, 3–5pm Sat, 11:30am–1pm Sun.* ✝ *10am Sun.*

A NARROW PASSAGEWAY and a picturesque gate take you through to this small Baroque church. Founded in 1712 by

Interior of the Sophienkirche with its original 18th-century pulpit

Eighteenth-century buildings along Sophienstrasse

Queen Sophie Luisa, this was the first parish church of the newly developed Spandauer Vorstadt area *(see p99)*. Johann Friedrich Grael designed the tower which was built between 1729 and 1735.

In 1892 the building was extended to include a new presbytery, though the church still retains its original Baroque character. A modest, rectangular structure, Sophienkirche is typical of its period, with the tower adjoining the narrower side elevation. The interior still contains a number of its original 18th-century furnishings, including the pulpit and the font.

Several gravestones, some from the 18th century, have survived in the small cemetery surrounding the church.

Sophienstrasse ❾

Map 7 B1. **Sammlung Hoffmann**
Sophienstrasse 21. 🄲 *284 99 121.*
Ⓢ *Hackescher Markt.* Ⓤ *Weinmeister-strasse.* 🚋 *13, 53.* 🕐 *11am–4pm Sat, by appointment.* 📷

THE AREA AROUND Sophien strasse and Gipsstrasse was first settled at the end of the 17th century. In fact, Sophienstrasse was once the main street of Spandauer Vorstadt. The area underwent extensive restoration during the 1980s. It was one of the

first parts of East Berlin in which renovation was chosen in favour of large-scale demolition and redevelopment. Now these modest but charming 18th-century Neo-Classical buildings are home to a number of different arts and crafts workshops, cosy bars, unusual boutiques and interesting art galleries.

One building with a particularly eventful history is Sophienstrasse No. 18. The house was erected in 1852, although its striking and picturesque, terracotta double doorway dates from the time of its extensive restoration. This was undertaken in 1904 by Joseph Franckel and Theodor Kampfmeyer on behalf of the Crafts Society. Founded in 1844, the Crafts Society moved its head-quarters to Sophienstrasse in 1905. On 14 November 1918 the very same house was used as the venue for the first meeting of the Spartacus League *(see p132)*, which was later to become the Communist Party of Germany.

The main door of the house at Sophienstrasse No. 21 leads into a long row of interior courtyards running up as far as Gipsstrasse. In one of these courtyards is a private modern art gallery, the **Sammlung Hoffmann**, which can be reached by passing through a brightly-lit tunnel.

Alte and Neue Schönhauser Strasse ⑩

Map 7 B1, 7 C1. Ⓢ *Hackescher Markt.* Ⓤ *Weinmeisterstrasse.* 🚋 *1, 7.*

Ａ LTE SCHÖNHAUSER STRASSE is one of the oldest streets in the Spandauer Vorstadt district, running from the centre of Berlin to Pankow and Schönhausen. In the 18th and 19th centuries this was a popular residential area among wealthy merchants. The proximity of the neighbouring slum area of the Scheunen-viertel *(see pp100–3)* to the west, however, lowered the tone of the neighbourhood quite considerably.

For a long time, bars, small factories, workshops and retail shops were the hallmark of the neighbourhood around Alte Schönhauser Strasse. Small private shops survived longer here than in most other parts of Berlin, and until recently the largely original houses maintained much of their pre-1939 atmosphere.

Much has changed, however, since the fall of the Berlin Wall. Some of the houses have now been restored, and many old businesses have been replaced by fashionable new shops, restaurants and bars. Throughout the district, the old and the new now stand side by side. One poignant example is at Neue

The *Schwarzen Raben* restaurant on Neue Schönhauser Strasse

Schönhauser Strasse No. 14. This interesting old house in the German Neo-Renaissance style was built in 1891 to a design by Alfred Messel. The first-floor rooms were home to the first public reading-room in Berlin, while on the ground floor was a *Volkskaffeehaus*, a soup-kitchen with separate rooms for men and women. Here the poor of the neigh-bourhood could get a free bowl of soup and a cup of ersatz (imitation) coffee.

Today, ironically, the building is home to one of Berlin's most fashionable restaurants, the Schwarzen Raben *(see p239).*

Volksbühne ⑪

PEOPLE'S THEATRE

Rosa-Luxemburg-Platz. **Map** 8 D1. Ⓒ *24 06 55.* Ⓤ *Rosa-Luxemburg-Platz.* 🚌 *340.* 🚋 *1, 7, 8.*

Ｆ OUNDED DURING the early years of the 20th century, this theatre owes its existence to the efforts of the 100,000 members of the Freie Volks-bühne (Free People's Theatre Society). The original theatre was built to a design by Oskar Kaufmann in 1913, a time when the Scheunen-viertel district was undergoing rapid redevelopment. During the 1920s the theatre became famous thanks to the director Erwin Piscator (1893–1966), who later achieved great acclaim at the Metropol-Theater on Nollendorfplatz.

Destroyed during World War II, the theatre was eventually rebuilt during the early 1950s to a new design by Hans Richter.

The eye-catching façade of the Friedrichstadtpalast theatre complex

Friedrichstadt-palast ⑫

FRIEDRICHSTADT PALACE

Friedrichstrasse 107. **Map** 6 F2. Ⓒ *23 26 23 26.* Ⓤ *Oranienburger Tor.* Ⓢ *Oranienburger Strasse or Friedrichstrasse.* 🚌 *147.* 🚋 *1, 50.*

Ｍ ULTI-COLOURED glass tiles and a pink, plume-shaped neon sign make up the gaudy but eye-catching façade of the Friedrichstadt-palast. Built in the early 1980s, this gigantic theatre complex specializes in revues and variety shows. Nearly 2,000 seats are arranged around a huge podium, used by turns as a circus arena, a swimming pool and an ice-rink. In addition, a further huge stage is equipped with every technical facility. There is also a small cabaret theatre with seats for 240 spectators.

The original and much-loved Friedrichstadtpalast suffered bomb damage during World War II, and was later condemned and replaced with the existing version. Built as a market hall, the earlier building was later used as a circus ring. In 1918 it became the Grosse Schau-spielhaus, or Grand Playhouse, opening on 28 November 1919 with a memorable production of Aeschylus' *The Oresteia* directed by the extraordinary Max Reinhardt *(see p108).*

The building itself was legendary, its central dome supported by a forest of columns and topped with an Expressionist, stalactite-like decoration. An equally fantastical interior provided seating for 5,000 spectators.

Dorotheenstädtischer Friedhof ⑯

Tнis small cemetery, established in 1763, is the final resting place of many famous Berlin citizens. It was enlarged between 1814 and 1826, but in 1899, following the extension of Hannoversche Strasse, the southern section of the cemetery was sold and its graves moved. Many of the monuments are outstanding works of art, coming from the workshops of some of the most prominent Berlin architects, including Karl Friedrich Schinkel *(see p187)* and Johann Gottfried Schadow. A tranquil, tree-filled oasis, the cemetery is reached via a narrow path, leading from the street, between the wall of the French Cemetery and the Brecht-Weigel-Gedenkstätte house *(see p109)*.

Copy of Schadow's Martin Luther

★ **Johann Gottfried Schadow** (1764–1850)
Schadow created the famous Quadriga, which adorns the Brandenburg Gate.

BIRKENALLEE

Friedrich August Stüler (1800–1865)
Damaged during World War II, the grave of this famous architect was rebuilt in a colourful, post-modernist style.

Heinrich Mann
(1871–1950)
This famous German novelist died in California but was buried in Berlin. The portrait is the work of Gustav Seitz.

BRECHTWEG

Bertolt Brecht (1898–1956)
The grave of this famous playwright is marked with a rough stone. Beside him rests his wife, the actress Helene Weigel.

Hermann Wentzel (1820–1889)
This architect designed his own tombstone; the bust was carved by Fritz Schaper.

Main entrance

Friedrich Hoffmann
(1818–1900)
The tomb of this engineer, best known as the inventor of the circular brick-firing kiln, takes the form of a colonnade faced with glazed bricks.

VISITORS' CHECKLIST

Chausseestrasse 126. **Map** 6 F1.
C 461 72 79. **F** 832 51 01.
U Zinnowitzerstrasse or Oranien-
burger Tor. 340. 6, 13,
50. May–Aug: 8am–8pm;
Sep–Apr: 8am until dusk.

★ **Karl Friedrich Schinkel**
(1781–1841)
*Schinkel was the most promi-
nent German architect of his
time, and the creator of many of
Berlin's best-loved buildings.*

**Georg Wilhelm
Friedrich Hegel**
(1770–1831)
*Probably the greatest
German philosopher of
the Enlightenment era,
Hegel worked for many
years as a professor at
Berlin University.*

BIRKENALLEE

Luther's statue
is a copy of the
monument designed
by JG Schadow.

Chapel

**Johann
Gottlieb Fichte**
(1762–1814)
*A well-known
philosopher of the
Enlightenment era, Fichte
was also the first Rector of
Berlin University.*

STAR FEATURES

★ **JG Schadow**

★ **KF Schinkel**

0 metres   20

0 yards   20

Bertolt Brecht's monument in front of the Berliner Ensemble

Berliner Ensemble ⓭

Bertolt-Brecht-Platz 1. **Map** 6 F2.
🄲 *28 40 81 55.* Ⓢ & Ⓤ
Friedrichstrasse. 🚌 *147.* 🚋 *1, 50.*

Dᴇsɪɢɴᴇᴅ ʙʏ Heinrich Seeling in the Neo-Baroque style and built from 1891 to 1892, this theatre has been witness to many changes in Berlin's cultural life. First known as the Neues Theater am Schiffbauerdamm, it soon became famous for staging important premieres. In 1895 it put on the first performance of *The Weavers*, by Gerhart Hauptmann. Later on, the theatre was acclaimed for its memorable productions by Max Reinhardt. These included Shakespeare's *A Midsummer Night's Dream* in 1905 which, for the first time, used a revolving stage and real trees as part of the set. In 1928 the theatre presented the world premiere of Bertolt

Brecht's *The Threepenny Opera*. The building was destroyed during World War II and subsequently restored with a much simpler exterior, but its Neo-Baroque interior, including Ernst Westphal's decorations, survived intact. After 1954 the theatre returned to prominence with the arrival of the Berliner Ensemble under the directorship of Bertolt Brecht and his wife, the actress Helene Weigel. The move from its former home, the Deutsches Theater, to the new venue was celebrated in November 1954, by staging the world premiere of *The Caucasian Chalk Circle*, written by Brecht in 1947. After Brecht's death his wife took over running the theatre, maintaining its innovative tradition.

Deutsches Theater ⓮

Schumannstrasse 13. **Map** 6 E2.
🄲 *28 44 12 25.* **Kammerspiele**
Ⓤ *Oranienburger Tor.* 🚌 *147.*

Tʜᴇ ʙᴜɪʟᴅɪɴɢ currently used by the theatre was designed by Eduard Titz and built between 1849 and 1850 to house the Friedrich-Wilhelm Städtisches Theater. In 1883, following substantial reconstruction, it was renamed Deutsches Theater and opened with Friedrich Schiller's *Intrigue and Love*. The theatre became famous under its next director, Otto Brahm, and it was here that Max Reinhardt began his career as an actor, before

eventually becoming director from 1905 until 1933. On Reinhardt's initiative the theatre's façade was altered and in 1906 the adjacent casino was converted into a compact theatre – the Kammerspiele. At the time, the first-floor auditorium was decorated with a frieze by Edvard Munch (now in the Neue Nationalgalerie).

Another famous figure associated with the Deutsches Theater was Bertolt Brecht who, until 1933, wrote plays for it; after World War II he became the director of the Berliner Ensemble, whose first venue was the Deutsches Theater. Brecht's debut as director was his play, *Mother Courage and Her Children.*

Elegant 19th-century façade of the Deutsches Theater

Charité ⓯

Schumannstrasse 20–21. **Map** 6 E1, E2.
🄲 *450 53 61 56.* Ⓤ *Oranienburger Tor.* 🚌 *147.* ◯ *10am–5pm Tue, Thu–Sun, 10am–7pm Wed.*

Tʜɪs ʜᴜɢᴇ ʙᴜɪʟᴅɪɴɢ complex near Luisenstrasse contains the Charité hospital. Germany's oldest teaching hospital, it was first established in 1726 and has been attached to the Humboldt University *(see p60)* since its foundation in 1810. The oldest buildings of the current complex date back to the 1830s. Over the years, Charité has been associated with many famous German doctors and scientists who worked here, including Rudolf Virchow and Robert Koch.

In 1899 Virchow founded the Museum of Pathology, which occupied purpose-built premises next to the Institute of Pathology. Its collection consisted of some 23,000 specimens, which were also available for public viewing.

MAX REINHARDT (1873–1943)

This actor and director became famous as one of the 20th century's greatest theatre reformers. He worked in Berlin, first as an actor in the Deutsches Theater, and then from 1905 as its director. As well as setting up the Kammerspiele, he produced plays for the Neues Theater am Schiffbauerdamm (renamed the Berliner Ensemble) and the Schumann Circus (later to become the Friedrichstadtpalast), which was converted specially for him by Hans Poelzig. His experimental productions of classic and modern works brought him world-wide fame. Forced to emigrate because of his Jewish origins, he left Germany in 1933 and settled in the United States, where he died in 1943.

Although many artifacts were destroyed in World War II, the museum itself has survived and was reopened in 1999.

Dorotheenstädt-ischer Friedhof ⑯

See pp106–107.

Brecht-Weigel-Gedenkstätte ⑰

BRECHT-WEIGEL MEMORIAL

Chaussestrasse 125. ☎ 283 057 044. Map 6 E1. Ⓤ Zinnowitzer Strasse or Oranienburger Tor. ➡ 340. ➡ 6, 13, 50. ◻ 10am–noon Tue–Fri, also 5–7pm Thu, 9:30am–2pm Sat, 11am–6pm Sun. ◪ compulsory. Every half hour (every hour on Sun). ◕ Mon, public hols. ◪

Brachiosaurus skeleton in the Museum für Naturkunde

BERTOLT BRECHT, one of the greatest playwrights of the 20th century, was associated with Berlin from 1920, but emigrated in 1933. After the war, his left-wing views made him an attractive potential resident of the newly created German socialist state. Lured by the promise of his own theatre he returned to Berlin in 1948, with his wife, actress Helene Weigel. Working as the director of the Berliner Ensemble until his death, he concentrated mainly on the production of his plays.

In 1953 he moved into a first-floor apartment at Chaussestrasse 125 and lived here until his death in 1956. He is buried in Dorotheen-städtischer Friedhof *(see pp106–7).* His wife lived in the second-floor apartment, and after Brecht's death moved to the ground floor. She also founded an archive of Brecht's works which is located on the second floor of the building.

Museum für Naturkunde ⑱

NATURAL HISTORY MUSEUM

Invalidenstrasse 43. Map 6 E1. ☎ 20 93 85 91. Ⓤ Zinnowitzer Strasse. ➡ 147, 245. ◻ 9:30am–5pm Tue–Fri, 10am–6pm Sat & Sun. ◪

ONE OF THE BIGGEST natural history museums in the world, the collection here contains over 60 million exhibits. Occupying a purpose-built Neo-Renaissance building, constructed between 1883 and 1889, the museum has been operating for over a century, and although it has undergone several periods of extension and renovation, it has maintained its unique old-fashioned atmosphere.

The highlight of the museum is the world's largest original dinosaur skeleton which is housed in the glass-covered courtyard. This colossal 23-m (75-ft) long and 12-m (39-ft) high brachiosaurus was discovered in Tanzania in 1909 by a German fossil-hunting expedition. Six other smaller reconstructed dinosaur skeletons and a replica of the fossilized remains of an archaeopteryx, thought to be the prehistoric link between reptiles and birds, complete this fascinating display.

The adjacent rooms feature extensive collections of colourful shells and butterflies, as well as stuffed birds and mammals. Particularly popular are the dioramas – scenes of stuffed animals set against the background of their natural habitat. A favourite with young children is Bobby the Gorilla, who was brought to Berlin Zoo in 1928 as a 2-year old and lived there until 1935. The museum also boasts an impressive collection of minerals and meteorites.

Bertolt Brecht's study in his former apartment

Hamburger Bahnhof ⑲

T HIS MUSEUM is situated in a specially adapted
Neo-Renaissance building that was formerly
the Hamburg Railway station, which dates from
1847. The building stood vacant after World
War II, but following extensive refurbishment
by Josef Paul Kleihues, it was opened to the
public in 1996. The neon installation surrounding the façade is the work of Dan Flavin. The
museum houses a magnificent collection of works
by Erich Marx, with other works of contemporary
art donated by the Neue Nationalgalerie and,
from 2004, the world-renowned Flick collection.
The result is one of the best modern art museums
in Europe, which features film, video, music
and design alongside painting and sculpture.

★ **Richtkräfte** (1974–77)
*Joseph Beuys' work – often
a record of his thoughts –
created an archive of
the artist's vision.*

Untitled (1983)
*This is a fine example of Anselm
Kiefer's work, which often
attempts to come to terms
with Germany's past.*

**First
floor**

GALLERY GUIDE

*The gallery has over 10,000 sq m
(108,000 sq ft) of exhibition space.
The west wing contains works by
Beuys and the main hall is used
for special installations.*

Ground floor

Genova (1980)
*In this painting, Sandro Chia contrasts a
finely-drawn Renaissance palace with a
colourful sky full of movement and two
mysteriously floating figures.*

**Main
entrance**

Untitled (1983)
*Keith Haring uses a simple
means of expression, one
that is reminiscent of
graffiti, comic book art
and woodblock prints.*

Untitled (1990)
This painting is a fine example of Cy Twombly's distinctive style, characterized by apparently random scrawls and scribbles, rejecting traditional composition.

VISITORS' CHECKLIST

Invalidenstrasse 50/51. **Map** 6 D1.
Ⓢ *Lehrter Stadtbahnhof.* 245, 340. ☎ 20 90 55 55. ⬚ *10am–6pm Tue–Fri, 11am–6pm Sat & Sun.* ⬚ *1 Jan, Tue following Easter and Whitsun, 24, 25 & 31 Dec.* ⓦ www.hamburgerbahnhof.de

Bourgeois Bust – Jeff and Ilona (1991)
The Rococo-style marble bust by Jeff Koons depicts himself with his wife at the time, Ilona, better known as La Cicciolina. The sculpture is deliberately pretentious and tawdry.

Second floor

Not Wanting to Say Anything About Marcel (1969)
John Cage created this work after the death of his friend, the famous artist Marcel Duchamp.

★ **Mao** (1973)
This well-known portrait by Andy Warhol initially elevated the Chinese communist leader to the rank of pop icon.

First Time Painting (1961)
This work by American artist Robert Rauschenberg was created while he worked with John Cage at Black Mountain College.

KEY

 Exhibitions

STAR EXHIBITS

★ **Mao**

★ **Richtkräfte**

TIERGARTEN

Once a royal hunting estate, the Tiergarten became a park in the 18th century. In the 19th century a series of buildings, mostly department stores and banks, was erected at Potsdamer Platz. During World War II many of these buildings were destroyed. The division of Berlin changed the character of the area. The Tiergarten area ended up on the west side of the Wall, and later regained

The Caller, on Strasse des 17 Juni

its glory with the creation of the Kulturforum and the Hansaviertel. The area around Potsdamer Platz fell in East Berlin, and became a wasteland. Since reunification, however, this area has witnessed exciting development. Together with the new government offices near the Reichstag, this ensures that the Tiergarten area is at the centre of Berlin's political and financial district.

SIGHTS AT A GLANCE

Museums and Galleries
Bauhaus-Archiv **14**
Bendlerblock (Gedenkstätte Deutscher Widerstand) **12**
Gemäldegalerie pp122–5 **8**
Kunstbibliothek **6**
Kunstgewerbemuseum pp118–21 **4**
Kupferstichkabinett **5**
Musikinstrumenten-Museum **2**
Neue Nationalgalerie **9**

Districts, Squares and Parks
Diplomatenviertel **15**
Grosser Stern **17**
Hansaviertel **19**

Potsdamer Platz pp128–31 **10**
Regierungsviertel **22**
Tiergarten **16**

Historic Buildings
Haus der Kulturen der Welt **21**

Philharmonie und Kammermusiksaal **3**
Reichstag **23**
Shell-Haus **11**
Schloss Bellevue **20**
Staatsbibliothek **1**
St-Matthäus-Kirche **7**
Villa von der Heydt **13**

Monuments
Siegessäule **18**
Sowjetisches Ehrenmal **24**

KEY

▨	Street-by-Street map *See pp114–15*
U	U-Bahn station
P	Parking
🚌	Bus stop

0 metres 600
0 yards 600

◁ **One of the many charming stretches of water in the Tiergarten**

Street-by-Street: Around the Kulturforum

Sculpture by Henry Moore

T HE IDEA OF CREATING a new cultural centre in West Berlin was first mooted in 1956. The first building to go up was the Berlin Philharmonic concert hall, built to an innovative design by Hans Scharoun in 1961. Most of the plans for the various other components of the Kulturforum were realized between 1961 and 1987, and came from such famous architects as Ludwig Mies van der Rohe. The area is now a major cultural centre which attracts millions of visitors every year.

★ Kunstgewerbe-museum
Among the collection at the Museum of Arts and Crafts you can see this intricately carved silver and ivory tankard, made in an Augsburg workshop in around 1640 ❹

Kupferstichkabinett
The large collection of prints and drawings owned by this gallery includes this portrait of Albrecht Dürer's mother ❺

★ Gemäldegalerie
Among the most important works of the Old Masters exhibited in this gallery of fine art is this Madonna in Church *by Jan van Eyck (circa 1425)* ❽

Kunstbibliothek
The Art Library boasts a rich collection of books, graphic art and drawings, many of which are displayed in its exhibition halls ❻

REICHPIETSCHUFER

LANDWEHRKANAL

Neue Nationalgalerie
Sculptures by Henry Moore and Alexander Calder stand outside this streamlined building, designed by Ludwig Mies van der Rohe ❾

STAR SIGHTS

★ Gemäldegalerie

★ Kunstgewerbe-museum

★ Philharmonie

KEY

– – – Suggested route

★ Philharmonie
Its outside covered in a layer of golden aluminium, the Berlin Philharmonic concert hall is known all over the world for its superb acoustics ❸

LOCATOR MAP
See Street Finder maps 4, 5 & 6

SCHAROUNSTRASSE

MATTHÄI-
KIRCH PLATZ

POTSDAMER STRASSE

ISMUNDSTRASSE

POTSDAMER STRASSE

Musikinstrumenten-Museum
This harpsichord is part of a collection of musical instruments dating from the 16th to 20th centuries ❷

St-Matthäus-Kirche
This picturesque 19th-century church stands out among the modern buildings of the Kultur-forum ❼

0 metres   50

0 yards   50

Staatsbibliothek
Hans Scharoun designed this public lending and research library built in 1978 ❶

The main reading room in the Staatsbibliothek

Staatsbibliothek ❶

STATE LIBRARY

Potsdamer Strasse 33. **Map** 6 D5.
📞 266 23 03. Ⓢ & Ⓤ *Potsdamer Platz.* 🚌 *129, 148, 200, 348.*
🔲 *9am–9pm Mon–Fri, 9am–7pm Sat.*

AN UNUSUAL-SHAPED building with an east facing gilded dome, the Staatsbibliothek is home to one of the largest collections of books and manuscripts in Europe and is fondly referred to by Berliners as the Stabi. After World War II, East and West Berlin each inherited part of the pre-war state library collection and the Staatsbibliothek was built to house the part belonging to West Berlin. The building itself was designed by Hans Scharoun and Edgar Wisniewski and constructed between 1967 and 1978.

It is a building where the disciplines of function and efficiency took precedence to that of form. The storerooms hold about five million volumes; the hall of the vast reading room is open plan, with an irregular arrangement of partitions and floor levels; general noise and the sound of footsteps is muffled by

fitted carpets, making the interior a very quiet and cosy place in which to work.

The library itself houses more than four million books, and an excellent collection of manuscripts. In recent years the Staatsbibliothek has been formally linked to the Staatsbibliothek on Unter den Linden *(see p61)*.

Musikinstrumen-ten-Museum ❷

MUSEUM OF MUSICAL INSTRUMENTS

Tiergartenstrasse 1. **Map** 6 D5.
📞 25 48 11 78. Ⓢ & Ⓤ *Potsdamer Platz or* Ⓤ *Mendelssohn-Bartholdy-Park.* 🚌 *129, 148, 200, 348.*
🔲 *9am–5pm Tue–Fri, 10am–5pm Sat–Sun.* **Wurlitzer Organ** demonstration *noon Sat.* 📷
♿ 👪 ⏏

HIDDEN BEHIND the Phil-harmonie, in a small building designed by Edgar Wisniewski and Hans Scharoun between 1979 and 1984, the fascinating Museum of Musical Instruments houses over 750 exhibits in a collection dating

from 1888. Intriguing displays enable you to trace each instrument's development from the 16th century to the present day. You can marvel at the harpsichord of Jean Marius, once owned by Frederick the Great, and the violins made by Amati and Stradivarius.

Most spectacular of all is the silent-film era cinema organ, a working Wurlitzer dating from 1929. With a range of sounds that extends even to loco-motive impressions, the Saturday demonstrations of its powers attract enthusiastic crowds. However, during the the week the sounds of exhib-ited instruments can be heard on tapes. The museum also has an excellent archive and library open to the public.

Philharmonie und Kammer-musiksaal ❸

PHILHARMONIC AND CHAMBER MUSIC HALL

Herbert-von-Karajan-Str. 1. **Map** 6 D5.
📞 25 48 81 32. Ⓢ & Ⓤ *Potsdamer Platz or* Ⓤ *Mendelssohn-Bartholdy-Park.* 🚌 *129, 148, 200, 348.*

HOME TO ONE of the most renowned orchestras in Europe, this unusual building is among the finest postwar architectural achievements in Europe. The Philharmonie, built between 1960 and 1963 to a design by Hans Scharoun, pioneered a new concept for concert hall interiors. The orchestra's podium occupies the central section of the pentagonal-shaped hall, around which are galleries for the public, designed to blend into the perspective of the five corners.

The tent-like gilded exterior of the Philharmonie and Kammermusiksaal

The exterior reflects the interior and is reminiscent of a circus tent. The gilded exterior was added between 1978 and 1981.

The Berlin orchestra was founded in 1882, and has been directed by such luminaries as Hans von Bülow, Wilhelm Furtwängler, the controversial Herbert von Karajan, who led the orchestra from 1954 until his death in 1989, and Claudio Abbado. The current director is Sir Simon Rattle. The orchestra attained renown not only for the quality of its concerts but also through its prolific symphony recordings.

Between the years 1984 to 1987 the Kammermusiksaal, which was designed by Edgar Wisniewski on the basis of sketches by Scharoun, was added to the Philharmonie. This building consolidates the aesthetics of the earlier structure by featuring a central multi-sided space covered by a fanciful tent-like roof.

Kunstgewerbe-museum ❹

MUSEUM OF ARTS AND CRAFTS

See pp118–121.

Kupferstich-kabinett ❺

PRINT GALLERY

Matthäikirchplatz 6. **Map** 5 C5.
☎ 20 90 55 55. **Ⓢ** & **Ⓤ**
Potsdamer Platz or **Ⓤ** Mendelssohn-Bartoldy-Park. **🚌** 129, 148, 200, 348. **Exhibitions** 10am–6pm Tue–Fri, 11am–6pm Sat–Sun. 🖼 🖰 ♿ 🅿
🎥 🍴 🚫

THE PRINT COLLECTIONS of galleries in the former East and West Berlin were united in 1994 in this building located in the Kulturforum. These displays originate from a collection started by the Great Elector in 1652, which has been open to the public since 1831. Despite wartime losses it has an imposing breadth and can boast around 2,000 engraver's plates, over 520,000 prints and at least 80,000 drawings and watercolours.

Edvard Munch's *Girl on a Beach*, a coloured lithograph

Unfortunately, only a small fraction of these delicate treasures can be even briefly exposed to daylight. Therefore the museum does not have a permanent exhibition, only galleries with temporary displays of selected works. For those with a special interest, items in storage can be viewed in the studio gallery by prior arrangement.

The collection includes work from every renowned artist from the Middle Ages to contemporary times. Well represented is the work of Botticelli (including illustrations for Dante's *Divine Comedy*), Dürer, Rembrandt and the Dutch Masters, Watteau, Goya, Daumier, and painters of the Brücke art movement.

Kunstbibliothek ❻

ART LIBRARY

Matthäikirchplatz 6. **Map** 5 C5.
☎ 20 90 55 55. **Ⓢ** & **Ⓤ** Potsdamer Platz or **Ⓤ** Mendelssohn-Bartoldy-Park. **🚌** 129, 148, 200, 348.
Exhibits 10am–6pm Tue–Fri, 11am–6pm Sat, Sun. **Library** 2–8pm Mon, 9am–8pm Tue–Fri. 🖼

THE KUNSTBIBLIOTHEK is not only a library with a wide range of publications about the arts, it is also a museum with a huge collection of posters, advertisements and an array of other forms of design. Worth seeing is a display on the history of fashion, as well as a vast collection of items of architectural interest. The latter includes around 30,000 original plans and drawings by architects such as Johann Balthasar Neumann, Erich Mendelssohn and Paul Wallot.

The exhibitions can be seen in the reading and studio rooms, although parts of the collection are also exhibited in the library's own galleries.

St-Matthäus-Kirche ❼

ST MATTHEW'S CHURCH

Matthäikirchplatz. **Map** 5 C5. **☎**
262 12 02. **Ⓢ** & **Ⓤ** Potsdamer Platz or **Ⓤ** Mendelssohn-Bartholdy-Park. **🚌** 129, 148, 200, 348. **⏲** noon–6pm Tue–Sun, and for services.

ST MATTHEW'S CHURCH once stood in the centre of a small square surrounded by buildings. After bomb damage in World War II, the structure was restored, making it the focal point of the Kulturforum. The church was originally built between 1844 and 1846 to a design by Friedrich August Stüler and Hermann Wentzel in a style based on Italian Romanesque temples.

Each of the three naves is covered by a separate two-tier roof, while the eastern end of the church is closed by a semi-circular apse. The exterior of the church is covered in a two-tone brick façade arranged in yellow and red lines. Ironically, this picturesque church with its slender tower now creates quite an exotic element among the many ultramodern and sometimes extravagant buildings of the Kulturforum complex.

The colourful exterior of the St-Matthäus-Kirche

Kunstgewerbemuseum ❹

THE MUSEUM OF Arts and Crafts holds a rich collection embracing many genres of craft and decorative art, from the early Middle Ages to the modern day. Goldwork is especially well represented, as are items made from other metals

Meissen porcelain figure

during the Middle Ages. Among the most valuable exhibits is a collection of medieval goldwork from the church treasuries of Enger near Herford, and the Guelph treasury from Brunswick. The museum also takes great pride in its collection of late-Gothic and Renaissance silver from the civic treasury in the town of Lüneberg. There are also fine examples of Italian majolica, and 18th- and 19th-century German, French and Italian glass, porcelain and furniture.

★ Domed Reliquary (1175–80)
From the Guelph treasury in Brunswick, the figures in this temple-shaped reliquary are made from walrus ivory.

Main entrance

Minneteppich (c.1430)
The theme of this famous tapestry is courtly love. Amorous couples, accompanied by mythical creatures, converse on topics such as infidelity, their words extending along the banners they hold.

★ Goblet (c.1480)
This glass Gothic goblet was made in Venice and is decorated with scenes from the lives of Adam and Eve.

Lüneburg Lion (1540)
From the civic treasury in Lüneburg, this gold-plated silver jug in the form of a lion was crafted in the workshop of Joachim Worm.

Basement

VISITORS' CHECKLIST

Matthäikirchplatz. **Map** 5 C5.
20 90 55 55. (S) Potsdamer
Platz. (U) Potsdamer Platz or
Mendelssohn-Bartholdy-Park.
129, 148, 200 341, 348.
10am–6pm Tue–Fri,
11am–6pm Sat & Sun.
Tue after Easter, Whitsun,
24, 25 & 31 Dec.

Candelabra (1900)
This striking Art Nouveau candelabra made from silver, ivory and onyx is the work of Belgian artists Egide Rombaux and Frans Hoosemans.

Wedding Dress (c.1780)
Made from brocade, with a lace collar and cuffs, this Rococo wedding dress belonged to Eleonor Schuster from Breslau (now Wrocław).

★ Harlequin Group (c.1740)
These highly decorative, comic porcelain characters from Meißen are just one of the treasures from the cabinets of curiosities and Baroque collections to be found on the second floor.

Second floor

First floor

Ground floor

KEY

- Middle Ages
- Renaissance
- Baroque
- Neo-Classical, Art Nouveau
- 20th-century
- Temporary exhibitions

GALLERY GUIDE
The entrance to the museum is on the first floor, where there is also an information gallery. In the basement is an exhibition of contemporary design, on the ground floor are exhibits from the Middle Ages and the Renaissance, and on the second floor are handicrafts from the Renaissance through to Art Nouveau.

STAR EXHIBITS

★ **Domed Reliquary**

★ **Goblet**

★ **Harlequin Group**

Exploring the Kunstgewerbemuseum

OPENED IN 1867, the Museum of Arts and Crafts was the first of its kind in Germany. It was housed initially in the Martin-Gropius-Bau *(see p140)*, then, from 1919 to 1939 it occupied the Stadtschloss *(see p74)*, and in 1940 it was moved to Schloss Charlottenburg *(see pp160–61)*. The current building, designed by Rolf Gutbrod especially to house the collection, was built between 1978 and 1985. A part of the collection is also now on show in the Schloss Köpenick *(see p175)*.

Pendant of the suffering of Christ

MIDDLE AGES

A LARGE PART OF this collection is devoted to sacred art, much of it originating from church treasuries. A fine 8th-century reliquary in the shape of a burse (the container used in the Roman Catholic mass to hold the white linen cloth on which the bread and the wine are placed), comes from the treasury of a church in Enger in Westphalia. More reliquaries, many in the form of crosses, date from the 11th and 12th centuries. Two of the most interesting are the Heinrichskreuz, a gift to the cathedral in Basel from the Roman Emperor Heinrich II, and the Welfenkreuz, which comes from the Guelph treasury in Brunswick. Also from the latter comes a beautiful domed reliquary in the form of a small temple, and a portable altarpiece decorated with enamelwork, produced around 1150 by the craftsman Eilbertus of Cologne.

Exhibits from the Gothic period (12th to 16th centuries) include the stunning reliquary of St George of Elbing, made around 1480. Also fascinating are examples of secular art from this period, including caskets, vessels, a mirror, a knight's amulet and the renowned Minneteppich. This tapestry depicts a number of love scenes, and is designed to hang on the wall above a seat as a decorative means of keeping out draughts.

11th-century reliquary cross

RENAISSANCE

THE ARTS AND CRAFTS of the Renaissance period are well represented here. Especially valuable is a collection of Italian majolica, a type of pottery glazed in bright metallic oxides, imported into Tuscany from Majorca in the 15th century. Majolica workshops flourished during the 16th century, and many, including those of Faenza, Cafaggiolo and Urbino, are on show here.

Other interesting exhibits in this section are the 15th- and 16th-century Venetian glass, porcelain decorated with enamel work from Limoges in central France, and fine furniture and tapestry collections.

The highlight of the collection is a set of 32 magnificent, richly decorated goblets, bowls and jugs from the civic treasury at Lüneburg in northern Germany, acquired by the museum in 1874. Made of gold-plated silver, the set is the work of the skilled metalworkers of the town; some take the form of lions. Also notable are the works of the Nürnberg master craftsmen, above all the renowned Wenzel Jamnitzer and his nephew Christoph Jamnitzer.

As a result of the 16th-century fashion for *Kunstkammern*, or curiosity cabinets, the collection also includes rare examples of naturalistic and exotic creations from other cultures, as well as some unusual technical equipment. Look out for a few pieces from the Pommersche Kunstschrank (curio cabinet), made for a 16th-century Pomeranian prince, Phillip II, as well as a display of 17th-century clocks and scientific instruments.

BAROQUE

TREASURES FROM the Baroque period include an exquisite collection of German and Bohemian glass. A few of the pieces are made from so-called "ruby glass", a technique that was pioneered by Johann Kunckel in the second half of the 17th century.

A varied and rich collection of 18th-century ceramics includes some German faïence work, with amusingly decorated jugs and tankards. The porcelain display begins with a series of Böttger ceramics, the result of some of the very first European

16th-century tapestry entitled *The Triumph of Love*

Desk-board (c.1610–17) from the Pommersche Kunstschrank

experiments in porcelain production, undertaken by Johann Friedrich Böttger with the assistance of Ehrenfried Walther von Tschirnhaus.

Among some of the finest works from a variety of European factories, the porcelain from the Meißen factory is particularly well represented, with several pieces by one of the most famous Meißen modellers and designers, Johann Joachim Kändler.

Also on show is a fascinating selection of artifacts from the Königliche Porzellan-Manufaktur (Royal Porcelain Factory) in Berlin (see p133) which is well-known for its porcelain pieces depicting views of the city.

The collection of porcelain is complemented by a display of silver dishes produced in European work-shops at the same period.

NEO-CLASSICAL REVIVAL AND ART NOUVEAU

A COMPREHENSIVE collection of late-18th and early-19th century Neo-Classical artifacts includes porcelain from some of the most famous European and Russian factories, French and German silver, as well as comprehensive exhibitions of glassware and furniture.

The Revival movement in central European art and

crafts took place during the second half of the 19th century and is well represented here. A high standard of craftsmanship is seen in the sophisticated Viennese glass and jewellery. The collection also includes furniture made from papier-mâché. This interesting technique was first applied to furniture in England around 1850 and involves a wooden or wire frame which is covered in layers of paste and paper. Decorative techniques include painting and inlaying with mother-of-pearl.

The Secessionist and Art Nouveau movements of the 1890s and 1900s are represented by various artists including Henri van der Velde and Eugène Gaillard. Many pieces were acquired at the

Baroque clock by Johann Gottlieb Graupner (1739)

various World Fairs that occurred at this time. Of note are the frosted glass vases by French artist Emile Gallé, and pieces by the American Louis Comfort Tiffany, creator of the Favrile style of iridescent stained glass. Also displayed are pieces by the legendary René Lalique, including jewellery and glassware.

An interesting diversion is offered by two entertaining pieces of furniture, both dating from 1885, by the Italian designer, Carlo Bugatti. Taking inspiration from Native American, Islamic and Far Eastern art, Bugatti made unique and spectacular use of rare woods and delicate inlays.

THE 20TH CENTURY

T HE YEARS BETWEEN the two World Wars were a time of mixed trends in the decorative arts. On the one hand the traditions of the 19th-century Historical movement were continued, while on the other many artists were developing a completely new perspective on both form and decoration.

Art Nouveau vase, Emile Gallé (1900)

This part of the museum includes pieces that embody both approaches, but the strongest emphasis is placed on the innovative Art Deco style. Notable examples include a small porcelain tea service by Gertrud Kant, and a silver coffee set decorated with inlaid ebony, designed by Jean Puiforcat.

The museum's unique 20th-century collection has been continually updated since 1945, aiming to document developments in 20th- and 21st-century decorative arts. On display are a wide range of ceramics, furniture by well-known designers, and a variety of items in daily use.

Gemäldegalerie ●

THE GEMÄLDEGALERIE collection is exceptional in the consistently high quality of its paintings. Unlike those in many other collections, they were chosen by specialists who, from the beginning of the 19th century, systematically acquired pictures to ensure that all the major European schools of painting were represented. Originally part of the Altes Museum collection *(see p75)*, the paintings achieved independent status in 1904 when they were moved to what is now the Bodemuseum *(see p79)*. After the division of Berlin in 1945, part of the collection was kept in the Bodemuseum, while the majority ended up in the Dahlem Museum *(see pp178–9)*. Following reunification, with the building of a new home as part of the Kulturforum development, this unique set of paintings has finally been united again.

Woman in a Bonnet by Rogier van der Weyden

★ Cupid Victorious (1602)
Inspired by Virgil's Omnia vincit Amor, Caravaggio depicted a playful god, trampling over the symbols of Culture, Fame, Knowledge and Power.

Madonna with Child (c.1477)
A frequent subject of Sandro Botticelli, the Madonna and Child depicted here are surrounded by singing angels holding lilies, symbolizing purity.

Circular lobby leading to the galleries

Birth of Christ (c.1480)
This beautiful religious painting is one of the few surviving paintings on panels by Martin Schongauer.

Portrait of Hieronymus Holzschuher (1529)
Albrecht Dürer painted this affectionate portrait of his friend, who was the mayor of Nuremberg.

Main entrance

The Glass of Wine
(c.1658–61)
Jan Vermeer's carefully composed picture of a young woman drinking wine with a young man gently hints at the relationship developing between them.

VISITORS' CHECKLIST

Matthäikirchplatz 8.
Map 5 C5. 20 90 55 55.
& Potsdamer Platz.
Mendelssohn-Bartholdy-Park.
129, 148, 200, 348.
10am–6pm Tue–Sun (to 10pm Thu). first Tue after Easter and Whitsun, 1 May, 24, 25 & 31 Dec.

Love in the French Theatre
This picture has a companion piece called Love in the Italian Theatre *(see p21).* Both are the work of French painter, Jean-Antoine Watteau.

★ Portrait of Hendrickje Stoffels (1656–7)
This portrait of Rembrandt's lover, Hendrickje Stoffels, is typical in that the painter focuses on the subject and ignores the background.

KEY

- 13th–16th-century German painting
- 14th–16th-century Dutch and French painting
- 17th-century Flemish and Dutch painting
- 18th-century French, English and German painting
- 17th–18th-century Italian painting, 17th-century German, French and Spanish painting
- 13th–16th-century Italian painting
- 16th–18th-century miniatures
- Digital gallery
- Non-exhibition space

GALLERY GUIDE
The main gallery contains over 900 masterpieces grouped according to their country of origin and period. The educational gallery on the lower floor houses 13th–18th-century European paintings and another digital gallery.

★ Dutch Proverbs (1559)
Pieter Bruegel managed to illustrate more than 100 proverbs in this painting.

STAR EXHIBITS

★ Cupid Victorious

★ Portrait of Hendrickje Stoffels

★ Dutch Proverbs

Visiting the Gemäldegalerie

THE GEMÄLDEGALERIE'S MODERN building was designed by Heinz Hilmer and Christoph Sattler and its exhibition space offers a superb environment in which to view the paintings. The pictures are gently lit by the diffused daylight that streams in from above, while the walls are covered in light-absorbing fabric. The vast hall which occupies the centre of the building allows the visitor to take a break from sightseeing at any time. The hall, with a futuristic sculpture by Walter de Maria set in a water-filled pool, provides an ideal setting for a few moments of quiet contemplation and rest.

Frans Hals' portrait, *Malle Babbe* or *Crazy Babette* (c.1629–30)

Hans Holbein's *Portrait of Georg Gisze* (1532)

GERMAN PAINTING

GERMAN PAINTINGS are exhibited in several areas of the gallery. The first group comprises art from the 13th–16th centuries. A fine body of religious paintings and altar-pieces contains a historic 13th-century rectangular altarpiece from Westphalia. Other religious artifacts include the side panels of the 15th-century *Wurzach Altar*, ascribed to Hans Multscher, which vividly depict the torment of Christ and the life of the Virgin Mary. A real rarity is the *Nativity* by Martin Schongauer. Often thought of primarily as an engraver, he was one of the most significant painters of the late 15th century but few of his paintings have survived.

Another artist known for his engravings as well as paintings, Albrecht Dürer was a major figure in Renaissance art in northern Europe. His works displayed here include *Madonna with the Siskin*, painted in 1506 while he was visiting Italy, and two later portraits of Nürnberg patriarchs. There are also exhibits by Hans Süss von Kulmbach, Hans Baldung Grien and Albrecht Altdorfer. Among the many works by Lucas Cranach the Elder is the delightful *Fountain of Youth*, from which old women emerge young and beautiful, while men regain their youth through amorous liaisons with the women. Another excellent painting in this collection is a portrait of the Danzig merchant Georg Gisze, painted by Hans Holbein the Younger at a time when both men were living in London. 17th- and 18th-century paintings, including the works of Adam Elsheimer and Johann Heinrich Tischbein, are on show elsewhere.

DUTCH AND FLEMISH PAINTING

THE GALLERY WITH Dutch and Flemish paintings begins with the captivating canvases of Jan van Eyck. In addition to his precise portraits, you can see here the celebrated *Madonna in a Church*. The high quality of paintings is maintained with the works of Petrus Christus and Rogier van der Weyden. Among the pictures by Hugo van der Goes, the most prized is *The Adoration of the Magi*, once the centre panel of a triptych.

The collection has four paintings by Hans Memling, and also the small *Madonna with Child* painted by one of his pupils, Michel Sittow. There is a large group of paintings by Gerard David, Jan Gossaert and Joos van Cleve. Try to keep an eye out for a modest picture by Hieronymus Bosch called *St John on Patmos*. One of the most outstanding paintings of the collection is Pieter Bruegel the Elder's *Dutch Proverbs*. However, in order to fully appreciate the mastery and humour in this work, make sure you use the accompanying board which explains all the one hundred or so proverbs illustrated here.

Within the large collection of excellent Flemish paintings you can marvel at the Baroque vitality and texture evident in the canvases of friends and

Salomon van Ruysdael's *Riders and Cattle* (1656)

sometime collaborators Petrus Paulus Rubens, Jacob Jordaens, Jan Brueghel the Elder and Frans Snyders. The exceptional portraits of Anton van Dyck, who painted complex, psychologically revealing studies, are indicative of the artist at the height of his powers.

The gallery of 17th-century Dutch paintings probably holds the richest collection in the museum. Included among these are the portraits by Frans Hals, which perfectly illustrate his enormous artistic talents. Excellent examples of his varied work are the vigorous *Malle Babbe* (*c.1629–30*) – a portrait of the "crazy Babette" of Haarlem.

In fact, all the most famous Dutch painters are represented here but, of course, the works of Jan Vermeer and the master, Rembrandt, attract the greatest amount of interest. The works of Rembrandt include the paintings *Samson and Delilah*, *Susanna and the Two Elders*, and *Joseph and the Wife of Potiphar*. It is also worth taking time to view the *Man in the Golden Helmet*, a sad yet noble painting originally attributed to Rembrandt. Carbon dating has shown it to be the work of members of his studio. It is a magnificent tribute to his skill as a teacher.

Titian's *Venus with the Organ Player* (1550–52)

beginning of the 15th century, and the *Madonna with Child*, dating from c.1410, is one of the oldest preserved works of art painted on a canvas. One of the most valuable French works is by Jean Fouquet, entitled *Étienne Chevalier with Saint Stephen*. Comprising half of the *Diptych of Melun* this is one of Fouquet's few non-miniature paintings.

Nicolas Poussin, the mainspring of the French Classical tradition, and Claude Lorrain, famous for his idealized landscapes, represent 17th-century French painting. Eighteenth-century painting is strongly represented by the canvases of Jean-Antoine Watteau, Jean Baptiste Siméon Chardin and François Boucher.

Two areas in which this collection is less complete are Spanish and English painting. Nevertheless, there is a portrait by Diego Velázquez which is worth seeing, while the English pictures include good portraits by rivals Sir Joshua Reynolds and Thomas Gainsborough.

Jean Baptiste Siméon Chardin's *The Draughtsman* (1737)

FRENCH, ENGLISH AND SPANISH PAINTING

THE COLLECTION OF French art can be found in various parts of the gallery. Paintings of the 15th and 16th century are exhibited alongside Dutch paintings of that era. The oldest works date from the

Sir Joshua Reynolds' *Portrait of Lady Sunderlin* (1786)

ITALIAN PAINTING

THE COLLECTION of Italian paintings is fairly comprehensive. There are exemplary works by 14th-century masters, including *Laying the Body to Rest in the Grave* by Giotto and parts of *Scenes from the Life of St Humilitas* by Pietro Lorenzetti. Paintings by Piero della Francesca, Fra Angelico, Masaccio, Andrea del Verrocchio, Sandro Botticelli, and Antonio del Pollaiuolo all represent the 15th century. In this collection you will also find later works by Raphael, including the *Madonna di Casa Colonna*, and the *Madonna di Terranuova*, painted after Raphael's arrival in Florence around 1505. There is also a collection of works by the Venetian Renaissance painter, Giovanni Bellini.

Indeed, the Venetian school in general is well represented: *Portrait of a Young Man* by Giorgione is a vibrant and colourful study; there is also Titian's *Venus and the Organ Player* and Tintoretto's *Virgin and the Child Adored by Saints Mark and Luke*. It is worth comparing Caravaggio's *Cupid Victorious*, whose provocative and distinctly human sexuality contrasts with the spiritual orthodoxy of *Heavenly and Earthly Love*, by Giovanni Baglione. Similar in style, the two paintings convey opposing ideologies. Cardinal Giustiani, whose brother owned Caravaggio's controversial canvas, commissioned the latter painting. Works by Giovanni Battista Tiepolo, Francesco Guardi and Antonio Canaletto represent the art of 18th-century Venice.

Karl Schmidt-Rottluff's *Farm in Daugart* (1910), Neue Nationalgalerie

Neue Nationalgalerie ❾

NEW NATIONAL GALLERY

Potsdamer Strasse 50. **Map** 5 C5.
⒞ 20 90 55 55. **Ⓤ** & **Ⓢ** Potsdamer Platz or **Ⓤ** Mendelssohn-Bartholdy-Park. 🚌 129, 148, 200, 341, 348.
⬜ 10am–6pm Tue–Fri (to 10pm Thu), 11am–6pm Sat & Sun. 🎦 ♿

THE MAGNIFICENT collection of modern art housed in the Neue Nationalgalerie has a troubled history. The core of the collection consisted of 262 paintings that belonged to banker JHW Wagener. In the late 1860s, when Wagener died, he bequeathed them to Crown Prince William, who housed them in the National-galerie on Museum Island.

However, in 1937, a Nazi programme of cultural cleansing meant that many of the works in the collection, which had grown to include paintings by Monet, Manet and Renoir, were confiscated.

After World War II the Berlin municipal authority decided to rebuild the collection and authorized the construction of a suitable building in West Berlin to house it. A commission was given to the elder statesman of modern architecture, the 75-year-old Mies van der Rohe. The result was the first museum in what would later become known as the Kulturforum. The new national gallery is a striking, minimalist building with a flat steel roof over a glass hall, which appears to float in mid-air supported only by six slender interior struts. The permanent collection is in the basement of the museum, while the spacious ground-level glass hall plays host to temporary exhibitions.

The collection of the Neue Nationalgalerie comprises largely 20th-century art, but begins with artists of the late 19th century, such as Edvard Munch, Ferdinand Hodler and Oskar Kokoschka. German movements, such as Die Brücke, are well represented, with pieces by Ernst Ludwig Kirchner (notably his *Potsdamer Platz*) and Karl Schmidt-Rottluff.

As well as the Bauhaus movement, represented by Paul Klee and Wassily Kandinsky, the gallery shows works by exponents of a crass realism, such as Otto Dix and Georg Grosz. The most celebrated artists of other European countries are also included in the collection – Pablo Picasso, Ferdinand Léger, and the Surrealists Giorgio de Chirico, Salvador Dalí, René Magritte and Max Ernst. Post-World War II art is represented by the works of Barnett Newman and Frank Stella, among many others. The sculpture garden houses a variety of important works, both figurative and abstract.

Following reunification, a number of new works have been added to the collection. The most recent of these are displayed in the Hamburger Bahnhof branch *(see pp110–11)* of the museum.

Potsdamer Platz ❿

See pp128–131.

Shell-Haus ⓫

Reichpietschufer 60. **Map** 11 C1.
Ⓤ Mendelssohn-Bartholdy-Park.
🚌 129, 341.

THIS IS UNDOUBTEDLY a gem for lovers of the architecture developed during the period between World Wars I and II. This modernist office block was designed by Emil Fahren-kamp. Built from 1930 to 1931, it was one of the first buildings in Berlin to use a steel-frame construction.

The most eye-catching wing extends along Landwehrkanal with a zig-zag elevation; from a height of five storeys it climbs upwards in a series of steps, finishing up ten storeys high.

Damaged during World War II, Shell-Haus went through several stages of restoration and several incarnations, including as headquarters of the German navy and as a military hospital. Beautiful proportions and original design place the structure among the finest of Berlin's buildings of its era.

The impressive exterior of the Shell-Haus office building

The German State Naval Office, now part of the Bendlerblock complex

Bendlerblock (Gedenkstätte Deutscher Widerstand) ⓬

Stauffenbergstrasse 13–14. **Map** 5 B5, 5 C5. ⟦ 26 99 50 00. Ⓤ Mendelssohn-Bartholdy-Park. 🚌 129, 341. ⏰ 9am–6pm Mon–Fri (to 8pm Thu), 10am–6pm Sat & Sun. ⬤ 1 Jan, 24, 25 & 31 Dec. 🈯

THE COLLECTION of buildings known as the Bendler-block was originally built during the Third Reich as an extension to the German State Naval Offices. During World War II these buildings were the headquarters of the Wehrmacht (German Army). It was here that a group of officers planned their famous and ultimately unsuccessful assassination attempt on Hitler on 20 July 1944. When the attempt led by Claus Schenk von Stauffenberg failed, he and his fellow conspirators were quickly rounded up and arrested. The death sentences on these men were passed at the Plötzensee prison (see

p186). General Ludwig Beck was forced to commit suicide, while Stauffenberg, Friedrich Olbricht, Werner von Haeften and Ritter Mertz von Quirnheim were shot in the Bendlerblock courtyard.

A monument commem-orating this event, designed by Richard Scheibe in 1953, stands where the executions were carried out. On the upper floor of the building there is an exhibition documenting the history of the German anti-Nazi movements.

Villa von der Heydt ⓭

Von-der-Heydt-Strasse 18. **Map** 11 B1. Ⓤ Nollendorfplatz. 🚌 100, 129, 187, 341.

THIS FINE VILLA, built in a late-Neo-Classical style, is one of the few surviving reminders that the southern side of the Tiergarten was one of the most expensive and beautiful residential areas of Berlin.

Designed by Hermann Ende and GA Linke, the villa was built from 1860 to 1862. The neatly manicured gardens and railings around the villa are adorned with busts of Christian Daniel Rauch and Alexander von Humboldt. The statues, by Reinhold Begas, originally lined the Avenue of Triumph in the Tiergarten before being moved here. After restoration in 1967, the villa became the headquarters of one of the most influential cultural bodies, the Stiftung Preussischer Kulturbesitz (Foundation of Prussian Cultural Heritage).

The captivating, streamlined buildings of the Bauhaus-Archiv

Bauhaus-Archiv ⓮

Klingelhöferstrasse 14. **Map** 11 A1. ⟦ 254 00 20. Ⓤ Nollendorfplatz. 🚌 100, 129, 187, 341. ⏰ 10am–5pm Wed–Mon. 🈯 ♿ 🏛 🛈 🍸

THE BAUHAUS school of art, started by Walter Gropius in 1919, was one of the most influential art institutions of the 20th century. The belief of the Bauhaus group was that art and technology should combine in harmonious unity.

Originally based in Weimar, and from 1925 in Dessau, this school provided inspiration for numerous artists and architects. Staff and students included Mies van der Rohe, Paul Klee, Wassily Kandinsky, Theo van Doesburg and László Moholy-Nagy. The school moved to Berlin in 1932, but was closed down by the Nazis in 1933.

After the war, the Bauhaus-Archiv was relocated to Darmstadt. In 1964 Walter Gropius designed a building to house the collection, but it was never realized. The archive was moved to Berlin in 1971 and the design had to be adapted to the new site. Because the maestro was no longer alive, the project was taken over by Alexander Cvijanovic. The gleaming white building with its distinctive glass-panelled gables was built between 1976 and 1979 and houses the archive, library and exhibition halls for temporary displays.

Neo-Classical façade of the elegant Villa von der Heydt

Potsdamer Platz ⓪

To EXPERIENCE THE vibrant energy of the new Berlin, there is no better place to visit than Potsdamer Platz. During the Roaring Twenties it was Europe's busiest plaza and a bustling entertainment centre, but during World War II it was bombed into a mountain of rubble. After the war, the square was left as a derelict wide open space, a no-man's-land beside the Berlin Wall. With reunification, the square was redeveloped by various international business concerns, such as DaimlerChrysler and Sony, and became Berlin's largest building project. Today, a phoenix has risen from the ashes. Berlin's old hub is once again a dynamic centre, a jewel of modern architecture created by architects such as Renzo Piano, Helmut Jahn and Arata Isozaki.

View of modern-day Potsdamer Platz

Beisheim Center

Lenné-, Bellevue- and Ebertstrasse

Otto Beisheim, the founder and owner of the Metro retail chain, and one of Europe's wealthiest entrepreneurs, has created a glass and steel monument on Potsdamer Platz – the Beisheim Center. On its completion in 2004, the two elegant high-rise towers on the northern edge of the square will encompass several de luxe apartments. The largest was sold for around $5 million, to an American émigrée returning to her home city, and is probably Berlin's most expensive apartment. The center will also incorporate a luxurious Ritz-Carlton and an elegant Marriott hotel.

The building was designed by the Berlin architectural team Hilmer, Sattler & Albrecht, although parts of the building were also created by architect David Chipperfield. The sandstone appearance of the small 19-floor skyscrapers, with receding façades on the upper levels, is meant to be a modern reinterpretation of New York's Rockefeller Center.

Filmmuseum Berlin

Potsdamer Strasse 2 (at Sony Center). 🛈 30 09 030. ⏰ 10am–6pm Tue–Sun, 10am–8pm Thu. 🌐 🚫 📷

In a city once famous for its world-class film industry, the new film museum takes visitors backstage to Hollywood and the historic UFA (Universal Film AG) film studios.

Located in the Sony Center and run by the Freunde der Deutschen Kinemathek, a non-profit-making association for film-lovers, the museum chronicles the development of cinema from the first silent movie hits to the latest science-fiction productions. However, the main focus is on German films from the glorious UFA days in the 1920s, when Germany's leading film company produced one smash hit after another at the Babelsberg studios (see p205). Films such as *The Cabinet of Dr Caligari*, directed by Friedrich Wilhelm Murnau (1888–1931), or *M* and *Metropolis* by Fritz Lang (1890–1976) are presented with costumes, set sketches, original scripts, models and photos. The Nazi era, when film making became a propaganda machine, is particularly interesting, and the museum documents the life and work of the actor Kurt Gerron, who died in Auschwitz, as well as other exhibits relating to the uses of propaganda in film.

One of the treasure-troves of the museum is the collection of personal effects of the Berlin-born diva Marlene Dietrich (1901–1992). The exhibition presents her gowns, personal correspondence and complete luggage set. A unique item is a minute cigarette case, given to her as a gift by the director Josef von Sternberg (1894–1969), bearing the inscription: "To Marlene Dietrich, woman, mother and actress as there never was one before". Also on display are personal possessions from German film and television stars such as Heinz Rühmann (1902–1994) and Hans Albers (1891–1960).

The museum features a range of exhibitions with changing themes and special film programmes.

Façade of the Filmmuseum Berlin

Arkaden, one of Berlin's favourite shopping centres

Potsdamer Platz Arkaden

Alte Potsdamer Str. 7. [C] 25 59 270.
[O] 9:30am–8pm Mon–Fri, 9am–4pm
Sat. **CinemaxX** Potsdamer Str. 5.
[C] Programme info: 25 92 21 11;
reservations: (0180) 524 63 62 99. [✉]

This entertainment and
shopping complex is hugely
popular with visitors. Spread
over three floors, the building
includes around 140 shops,
restaurants and boutiques. The
basement houses a food court
with many budget eateries
offering regional specialities
from all over Germany, as
well as several grocery shops.

Berlin's largest cinema, the
CinemaxX, is nearby. With
19 screens it can accommodate
up to 3,500 filmgoers. Current
Hollywood blockbusters and
foreign-language films are
shown regularly.

Stella Musical Theater Berlin

Marlene-Dietrich-Platz 1. [C] (018 0)
544 44. [O] 8pm daily. [✉] **Spielbank
Berlin** Marlene-Dietrich-Platz 1.
[C] 25 59 90. [O] 2pm–3am daily. [✉] .

Situated in a square dedicated
to the famous actress Marlene
Dietrich, Berlin's largest
musical stage is housed in

the modern Stella Musical
Theater, designed by Renzo
Piano as part of the
DaimlerChrysler Quartier (see
pp130–1). For a long time it
has shown the German version
of the Broadway hit musical
Cats. Other crowd-pulling
musicals are planned over the
next few years.

The exclusive Adagio
nightclub is located in the
basement of this building and
Berlin's most popular casino,
Spielbank Berlin, can also
be found here. As well as
offering roulette and Black
Jack, an entire floor is given
over to a wide variety of slot
machines.

A large blue,
bubble-like
sculpture –
Balloon Flower
by the
American
artist Jeff
Koons,
adorns the
square in front
of the building.

Balloon Flower by
Jeff Koons

The theatre
complex is also the main
forum for the Berlinale,
Berlin's world-renowned film
festival held throughout the
city each February (see p51).

HISTORIC POTSDAMER PLATZ

Potsdamer Platz first evolved from a green park in 1831 and was named after one of the city's
gates, the Potsdamer Tor, located to the east of today's square. Thanks to a new railway station
of the same name, where the city's first ever train made its maiden journey in 1838, the
square developed into a major traffic hub at the intersection of Potsdamer Strasse and other
thoroughfares. Later an underground train line, along with a total of 31 tram and bus lines,
added to the traffic chaos here. At the beginning of the 20th century it became the centre of
Berlin's celebrated nightlife, with legendary, huge entertainment venues such as Haus Vaterland
and the Café Josty (a meeting place for famous artists including author Theodor Fontane
and painter Adolph von Menzel),
as well as several luxury hotels.
Germany's first radio trans-
mission was broadcast in 1923 at
the Vox Haus. The square was
almost destroyed by Allied
bombardments during the final
Battle of Berlin in April 1945. It
became a vast open space in the
shadow of the Berlin Wall where
Western tourists, standing on high
observation platforms, could peek
over the wall. The empty square
featured in Wim Wenders' 1987
hit film, Wings of Desire.

Development commenced in
1992, and Potsdamer Platz rose to
become Europe's largest
construction site where a total of
$25 billion has been invested.

Bustling Potsdamer Platz in the 1930s

Sony Center

Potsdamer Strasse 2. ☐ 24 hrs.

The Sony Center, designed by the German-American architect Helmut Jahn, is Berlin's most exciting new architectural complex. Built between 1996 and 2000, the glitzy steel and glass construction covers a breathtaking 4,013 sq m (43,195 sq ft).

The piazza at the heart of the Center has become one of Berlin's most popular attractions. Set under a soaring tent-like roof, it is dominated by a pool with constantly changing fountains where the water sprays high above the pool, then falls back to rise again in a different location. The light and airy piazza is surrounded by the offices of Sony's European headquarters, as well as apartment complexes, several restaurants, cafés and shops including the Sony style store. There is also the Cinestar *(see pp264–5)*, a huge multiplex cinema with eight different screens, in addition to the Filmmuseum Berlin *(see p128)*. At the rear of the building is the blue-domed IMAX cinema which shows nature and science films on imposing 360° screens.

Inside the Sony Center is the small but magnificent **Kaisersaal**, a historic architectural gem that is set behind a glass façade. This dining hall, now home to the fledgling Kaisersaal gourmet restaurant, was once part of the Grand Hotel Esplanade. The epitome of luxury in pre-war Berlin, it was almost

Interior of the cupola of the Sony Center, designed by Helmut Jahn

destroyed during World War II. When the site was sold to Sony by the City of Berlin in the early 1990s, the Berlin magistrate stipulated that the Kaisersaal, stairways, bathrooms and several other smaller rooms should be restored and integrated into the Sony Center. The historic ensemble originally stood some 46 m (150 ft) away and was carefully moved on air cushions to its present location in 1996. The fully restored Kaisersaal is dominated by a portrait of Kaiser Wilhelm II, the last German emperor, whose frequent visits to the original hotel gave this hall its name, although he never actually dined in this particular room.

Replica traffic lights, DaimlerChrysler Quartier

DaimlerChrysler Quartier

Around Alte Potsdamer Strasse.
Panorama Punkt observation platform Potsdamer Platz 1.
☎ 25 29 43 72. ☐ 11am–7:30pm Tue–Sun. 🅿

This vast complex was built between 1993 and 1998 and comprises 19 modern buildings, all designed in different styles according to an overall plan by architects Renzo Piano and Christoph Kohlbecker. The buildings form a long, narrow column of modern architectural jewels leading south from Potsdamer Platz all the way down to the Landwehr Canal.

Standing on either side of Alte Potsdamer Strasse, the red-brick high-rise block and its sister building opposite mark the entrance to this city quarter, and were designed by Berlin architect Werner Kollhoff. The western skyscraper is topped by a 96-m (315-ft) high observation platform called **Panorama Punkt** (Panorama Point). It offers a breathtaking view which can be reached via Europe's fastest elevator.

The green traffic-light tower in front of the DaimlerChrysler Quartier is a replica of the first automatic traffic light in Berlin, which was erected on the same spot in 1924. In

The glass façade of the Kaisersaal, part of the Sony Center

prewar days, Potsdamer Platz was an intricate crossing of several major streets and avenues, making it Europe's busiest traffic junction at the time.

At the southern end of this complex is yet another high-rise tower block, the **Debis-Haus** (formerly the Daimler-Chrysler software subsidiary). This 90-m (295-ft) high, 22 floor, yellow and green skyscraper is topped by a striking green cube and was designed by Renzo Piano and Hans Kollhoff *(see p43)*. A captivating sculpture by Jean Tinguely, entitled *Meta-Maxi*, adorns its soaring atrium. The sculpture is powered by 16 engines and symbolizes the constant movement of time.

Various works of art were commissioned for this complex and these can be seen throughout the public areas.

The red-brick office block of the DaimlerChrysler House

Leipziger Platz

Leipziger Platz, a small square just east of Potsdamer Platz, is currently undergoing major reconstruction. Completion of this historic site is planned for 2005. The original octagonal but rather bland square was created between 1732 and 1734 and later renamed Leipziger Platz in commemoration of the Battle of Leipzig in 1813 (the first decisive defeat of Napoleon). In the 19th century, the architects Karl-Friedrich Schinkel (1781–1841) and Peter Joseph Lenné (1879–1866) transformed the square into an architectural gem with beautifully landscaped gardens, surrounded by some of the most elegant city palaces and mansions in the whole of Berlin.

At the beginning of the 20th century the modern buildings, most notably the Kaufhaus Wertheim by Alfred Messel (1853–1909) built in 1905, made Leipziger Platz one of the major, and more fashionable, shopping districts in pre-war Berlin.

Unfortunately, there are no historic remnants left. The new buildings will have a modern look but will be restricted to a maximum height of only 35 m (115 ft), the same height as the original buildings. They will house various shops and restaurants, the Canadian Embassy and further international company headquarters.

Weinhaus Huth

Alte Potsdamer Strasse 5.
☏ 25 94 14 20. ◯ 11am–6pm daily. **Sammlung DaimlerChrysler Contemporary** ◯ as *Weinhaus Huth.*
✍ 6pm daily.

The only historic building on Potsdamer Platz to escape destruction in World War II was the grey limestone building of the Weinhaus Huth. Originally a restaurant and wine shop, it was one of the first buildings in Berlin to be erected with a steel frame, intended to support the weight of the wine. It was designed by architects Conrad Heidenreich and Paul Michel in 1912. After the war, it stood alone on the vast

Rauschenberg's sculpture *Riding Bikes*, with Weinhaus Huth in the background

eroded square. Today however, the offices of the famous car manufacturers DaimlerChrysler are located here, along with the Diekmann im Weinhaus Huth restaurant, a small café and Hardy's, an upmarket wine shop.

Weinhaus Huth is also home to the **Sammlung DaimlerChrysler Contemporary**, a small exhibition featuring the latest additions to the corporation's collection of 20th-century art – mostly abstract and geometric paintings by German and international artists.

The best view of the building is from its south side where a jubilant, bright light installation by Robert Rauschenberg called *Riding Bikes* can be found.

The historic Weinhaus Huth on Leipziger Platz

Diplomaten-viertel ⓯

DIPLOMATIC QUARTER

Map 4 F5, 5 A5, B5, C5.
Ⓤ *Nollendorfplatz.* 🚌 *100, 129, 187, 341.*

Although a number of consulates existed in the Tiergarten area as early as 1918, the establishment of a diplomatic district along the southern edge of the Tiergarten, between Stauffenbergstrasse and Lichtensteinallee, did not take place until the period of Hitler's Third Reich between 1933 and 1945. During the years 1938 to 1943 large embassies representing the Axis Powers, Italy and Japan, were built here.

Despite the fact that these monumental buildings were designed by a number of different architects, the Fascist interpretation of Neo-Classicism and the influence of Albert Speer as head architect meant that the group was homogenous, if bleak. Many of the buildings did not survive World War II bombing.

A new diplomatic area has now emerged along Tiergartenstrasse. The Austrian embassy designed by Hans Hollein stands at the junction of Stauffenbergstrasse, next door to the embassies of Turkey and the Republic of South Africa. At Tiergartenstrasse Nos. 21–3 the pre-World War II Italian embassy still stands, while next door is a copy of the first Japanese embassy. Between Klingelhöferstrasse and Rauchstrasse stands an imposing complex of five embassies. Completed in 1999, these represent Norway, Sweden, Denmark, Finland and Iceland.

Tiergarten ⓰

Map 4 E4, 5 A3, 6 D3. Ⓢ *Tiergarten or Bellevue.* 🚌 *100, 187, 200, 341.*

This is the largest park in Berlin. Situated at the geographical centre of the city it occupies a surface area of more than 200 ha (495 acres). Once a forest used as

One of many tranquil areas within the Tiergarten

the Elector's hunting reserve, it was transformed into a landscaped park by Peter Joseph Lenné in the 1830s. A half-kilometre Triumphal Avenue was built in the eastern section of the park at the end of the 19th century, lined with statues of the country's rulers and statesmen.

World War II inflicted huge damage on the Tiergarten, including the destruction of the Triumphal Avenue, many of whose surviving monuments can now be seen in the Lapidarium *(see p144)*. Replanting, however, has now restored the Tiergarten which is a favourite meeting place for Berliners. Its avenues are now lined with statues of figures such as Johann Wolfgang von Goethe and Richard Wagner.

By the lake known as Neuer See and the Landwehrkanal are memorials to the murdered leaders of the Spartacus movement, Karl Liebknecht and Rosa Luxemburg *(see p26)*. Also worth finding is a collection of gas lamps, displayed near the Tiergarten S-Bahn station.

Grosser Stern ⓱

GREAT STAR

Map 5 A4. Ⓢ *Bellevue.* 🚌 *100, 187, 341.*

This vast roundabout at the centre of the Tiergarten has five large roads leading off it in the shape of a star. At its centre is the enormous Siegessäule (Triumphal Column). Surrounding it are various monuments brought over from the nearby Reichstag

building *(see pp134–5)* during the late 1930s. At the same period the Strasse des 17 Juni was widened to twice its size, the square surrounding the roundabout was enlarged and much of the existing statuary removed.

In the northern section of the square stands a vast bronze monument to the first German Chancellor, Otto von Bismarck (1815–98). Around it stand allegorical figures, the work of late-19th-century sculptor Reinhold Begas. Other statues represent various national heroes including Field Marshal Helmuth von Moltke (1800–91), chief of the Prussian general staff between the years 1858 and 1888, who won the Franco-German war.

Monument to Otto von Bismarck at the Grosser Stern

Siegessäule ⓲

TRIUMPHAL COLUMN

Grosser Stern. **Map** 5 A4. 📞 *391 29 61.* Ⓢ *Bellevue.* 🚌 *100, 187, 341.* ⏰ *Apr–Oct: 9:30am–6:30pm daily; Nov–Mar: 9:30am–5:30pm daily.*

The triumphal column is based on a design by Johann Heinrich Strack, and was built to commemorate victory in the Prusso-Danish war of 1864. After further Prussian victories in wars against Austria (1866) and France (1871), a gilded figure by Friedrich Drake representing Victory, known as the "Goldelse", was added to the top. The monument originally stood in front of the Reichstag building, but was moved to its present location by the Nazi government in 1938. The base is decorated with bas-reliefs commemorating battles, while higher up the column a mosaic frieze by Anton von Werner depicts the founding of the German Empire in 1871. An observation terrace at the top of the monument offers magnificent vistas over Berlin.

Siegessäule (Triumphal Column)

Hansaviertel ⓳

Map 4 E3, E4, F3. Ⓢ *Bellevue.*
🚌 *123, 341.* **Akademie der Künste**
Hanseatenweg 10. ☎ *39 07 60.*
⭕ *11am–8pm Tue–Sun.* 📷

T HIS AREA TO the west of Schloss Bellevue is home to some of the most interesting modern architecture in Berlin, built for the 1957 Internationale Bauausstellung (International Architectural Exhibition). Taking on a World War II bomb site, prominent architects from around the world designed 45 projects, of which 36 were realized, to create a varied residential development set in an environment of lush greenery. The list of distinguished architects involved in the project included Walter Gropius (Händelallee Nos. 3–9), Alvar Aalto (Klopstockstrasse Nos. 30–32) and Oskar Niemeyer (Altonaer Strasse Nos. 4–14). The development also includes a school, a commercial services building and two churches.

In 1960, a new headquarters for the **Akademie der Künste** (Academy of Arts) was built at Hanseatenweg No. 10. Designed by Werner Düttmann, the academy has a concert hall, an exhibition area, archives and a library. In front of the main entrance is a magnificent piece, *Reclining Figure*, by eminent British sculptor Henry Moore.

KÖNIGLICHE PORZELLAN-MANUFAKTUR

Established in 1763, the Königliche Porzellan-Manufaktur (Royal Porcelain Factory) was soon producing items of the highest artistic quality, competing with the products of the older Meissen factory in Saxony. The Berlin factory is particularly renowned for its Neo-Classical urns and plates decorated with views of the city. Large collections of porcelain with the markings KPM can be seen at the Ephraim-Palais *(see p 91)*, in the Kunstgewerbemuseum *(see pp118–21)* and at the Belvedere within the grounds of Schloss Charlottenburg *(see pp160–61)*. It is also worth visiting the factory, located at Wegelystrasse 1, which is still producing porcelain, and includes a sales gallery and exhibition hall.

Neo-Classical vase with a view of the Gendarmenmarkt

Schloss Bellevue ⓴

BELLEVUE PALACE

Spreeweg 1. **Map** 5 A3. Ⓢ *Bellevue.*
🚌 *100, 187.* ⭕ *to the public.*

T HIS CAPTIVATING palace with its dazzlingly white Neo-Classical façade is now the official residence of the German Federal President. Built in 1786 to a design by Philipp Daniel Boumann for the Prussian Prince August Ferdinand, the palace served as a royal residence until 1861. In 1935 it was refurbished to house a Museum of German Ethnology. Refurbished again in 1938, it became a hotel for guests of the Nazi government.

Following bomb damage during World War II, the palace was carefully restored to its former glory, with the oval ballroom rebuilt to a design by Carl Gotthard Langhans. The palace is set within an attractive park laid out to the original late-18th-century design, though unfortunately the picturesque garden pavilions did not survive World War II.

Imposing façade of Schloss Bellevue, now the official Berlin residence of the German President

Haus der Kulturen der Welt or "pregnant oyster" as it is also known

Haus der Kulturen der Welt ㉑

HOUSE OF WORLD CULTURE

John-Foster-Dulles-Allee 10.
Map 5 C3. 39 78 70.
Unter den Linden. 100.
Exhibitions *noon–8pm Tue–Sun.*

THIS FORMER congress hall's squat structure and parabolic roof has given rise to its affectionate nickname "the pregnant oyster". Built between 1956 and 1957 to a design by the American architect Hugh Stubbins, it was intended as the American entry in the international architecture competition "Interbau 1957", (from which the Hansaviertel apartment blocks originated). It soon became a symbol of freedom and modernity in West Berlin during the Cold War, particularly when compared to the GDR-era monumental buildings of Karl-Marx-Allee in East Berlin *(see pp172–3)*. However, its concept outran current technologies and the roof failed to withstand the test of time, as the building partially collapsed in 1980.

After reconstruction it was re-opened in 1989, with a change of purpose. It is now used to bring world cultures to a wider German audience, and stages various events and performances to this effect. It is known for its jazz festivals in particular *(see pp48–51)*.

Standing nearby is the black tower of the Carillon built in 1987 to commemorate the 750th anniversary of Berlin. Suspended in the tower is the largest carillon in Europe, comprising 67 bells. Daily at noon and 6pm, the bells give a brief computer-controlled concert.

Regierungsviertel ㉒

GOVERNMENT DISTRICT

Map 6 D2, E2. Unter den Linden. 100, 248.

THIS BOLD CONCEPT for a new government district in keeping with a 21st-century capital was the winning design in a competition held in 1992. Construction of the complex began in 1997 and was completed in 2003. Axel Schultes and Charlotte Frank's grand design proposed a rectangular site cutting across the meander of the Spree river just north of the Reichstag.

While many of the buildings have been designed by other architects, their plans fitting within the overall concept, Schultes and Frank designed the Bundeskanzleramt, situated opposite the Riechstag, which is the official residence of the German Chancellor.

The offices – Alsenblock and Luisenblock – are the work of Stephan Braunfels, as is the office Dorotheenblöcke, built by a consortium of five architects. The whole project will be complemented by an ultra-modern, integrated transport system which will include a road tunnel under the Tiergarten and a vast subterranean railway station – Berlin Hauptbahnhof. The architects responsible for the station project are Mainhard von Gerkan, Oswald Mathias Ungers and Max Dudler.

Reichstag ㉓

Platz der Republik. **Map** 6 D3, E3.
Unter den Linden. 100, 248.
227 32 152. **Dome** *8am–midnight daily.* **Assembly Hall**
by appointment only. *noon Tue, 10am Sat (in English).* *1 Jan, 24, 26 & 31 Dec.*

BUILT TO HOUSE the German Parliament, the Reichstag was intended as a symbol of national unity and to showcase the aspirations of the new German Empire, declared in 1871. The Neo-Renaissance design by Paul Wallot captured the prevailing spirit of German optimism. Constructed between the years 1884 and 1894 it was funded by money paid by the French as wartime reparations.

On 23 December 1916, the inscription *"Dem Deutschen Volke"* ("To the German People") was added to the façade. The Reichstag became a potent symbol to the German populace; this power would be exploited in the years to come.

In 1918 Philipp Scheidemann declared the formation of the

The Reichstag spectacularly wrapped up in 1995 by artist Christo

The Reichstag crowned by a dome designed by Sir Norman Foster

Weimar Republic from the building. The next time the world heard about the Reichstag was on the night of 28 February 1933, when a fire destroyed the main hall. The Communists were blamed, accelerating a political witch-hunt driven by the Nazis, who subsequently came to power.

With the onset of World War II, the building was not rebuilt. Yet its significance resonated beyond Germany, as shown by the photograph of the Soviet flag flying from the Reichstag in May 1945, which became a symbol of the German defeat.

Rebuilding work undertaken between 1957 and 1972 removed the dome and most of the ornamentation on the façades. As well as providing a meeting-place for the lower house of the German Bundestag (Parliament), the Reichstag also made a spec-tacular backdrop for huge festivals and rock concerts, much to the annoyance of the East German authorities.

On 2 December 1990, the Reichstag was the first meeting-place of a newly-elected Bundestag following German reunification. On 23 June 1995 the artist Christo and his wife Jeanne-Claude wrapped the Reichstag in glistening fabric – an artistic statement that lasted for two weeks.

The latest rebuilding project was undertaken between 1995 and 1999 to a design by Sir Norman Foster that transforms the Reichstag into a modern meeting hall crowned with an elliptical dome with a viewing gallery. The first parliamentary meeting in the new building took place on 19 April 1999.

Sowjetisches Ehrenmal ㉔
MONUMENT TO SOVIET SOLDIERS

Strasse des 17 Juni. **Map** 6 D3.
Ⓢ Unter den Linden. 🚌 100, 248.

THIS HUGE monument near the Brandenburg Gate was unveiled on 7 November 1945, on the anniversary of the start of the October Revolution in Russia. Flanked by the first two tanks into the city, the monument commemorates over 300,000 Soviet soldiers who perished in the battle for Berlin at the end of World War II. The vast column was made from marble taken from the headquarters of the Chancellor of the Third Reich, when it was being dismantled. The column was designed by Nicolai Sergiejev, while the imposing figure on top, a soldier cast in bronze, is the work of Lew Kerbel. This monument is also a cemetery for around 2,500 Soviet casualties. Following the partition of Berlin, the site ended up in the British sector, but formed a kind of non-territorial enclave to which Soviet soldiers posted to East Berlin had access.

The sculpture of a Soviet soldier atop the Sowjetisches Ehrenmal

BERLIN'S BRIDGES

Despite wartime damage, Berlin's bridges are still well worth seeing. The Spree river and the city's canals have some exemplary architecture on their banks, while many of the bridges were designed and decorated by famous architects and sculptors. Probably the most renowned bridge is the Schlossbrücke designed by Karl Friedrich Schinkel (see p74). Further south along the Kupfergrabenkanal, the Schleusenbrücke dates from c.1914, and is decorated with reliefs of the early history of the city's bridges and sluices. The next bridge, heading south, is the Jungfernbrücke dating from 1798, which is the last drawbridge in Berlin. The next bridge along is the Gertraudenbrücke (see p85). Where Friedrichstrasse crosses the Spree river is the Weiden-dammer Brücke, originally built in 1695-7 and subsequently rebuilt in 1923, with an eagle motif decorating its balustrade. On the Spree near the Regierungsviertel is the magnificent Moltkebrücke (1886–91). The bridge is guarded by a huge griffin wielding a shield adorned with the Prussian eagle, while cherubs dressed in a military fashion hold up lamps. On the arches of the bridges are portraits of leaders designed by Karl Begas.

Ornamental feature of a bear on the Liebknechtbrücke

KREUZBERG

THE AREA COVERED in this chapter is only a part of the suburb of the same name. The evolution of Kreuzberg began in the late 19th century when it was a working-class area. After World War II unrepaired buildings were abandoned by those who could afford to move, leaving a population of artists, foreigners, the unemployed and members of a variety of sub-cultures.

Detail from the Martin-Gropius-Bau façade

Kreuzberg is now an area of contrasts, with luxury apartments next to dilapidated buildings. Some parts of Kreuzberg are mainly Turkish, while others are inhabited by affluent young professionals. The district's attractions are its wealth of restaurants and Turkish bazaars, as well as an interesting selection of nightclubs, cinemas, theatres and galleries.

SIGHTS AT A GLANCE

Museums
Berlin-Museum ❺
Checkpoint Charlie ❹
Deutsches Technikmuseum Berlin ❾
Jüdisches Museum ❻
Lapidarium ❽
Martin-Gropius-Bau ❷
Topographie des Terrors ❸

Historic Buildings
Anhalter Bahnhof ❶
Flughafen Tempelhof ⓭
Riehmers Hofgarten ⓫

Squares, Parks and Cemeteries
Friedhöfe vor dem Halleschen Tor ❿
Mehringplatz ❼
Viktoriapark ⓬

GETTING THERE

U-Bahn line 6, with stations at Kochstrasse, Halleches Tor, Mehringdamm and Platz der Luftbrücke, crosses the area from north to south, while U-Bahn lines 1, 7 and 15 run east to west.

KEY

▨	Street-by-Street map *See pp138–9*
Ⓤ	U-Bahn station
Ⓢ	S-Bahn station
🚏	Bus stop
Ⓟ	Parking

◁ **Old machinery displayed at the Deutsches Technikmuseum**

Street-by-Street: Mehringplatz and Friedrichstrasse

THE AREAS NORTH OF Mehringplatz are the oldest sections of Kreuzberg. Mehringplatz, initially called Rondell, together with the Oktogon (Leipziger Platz) and the Quarré (Pariser Platz), were laid out in 1734 as part of the enlargement of Friedrichstadt. World War II totally changed the character of this area. It is now full of modern developments such as the Friedrichstadt Passagen – a huge complex of shops, apartments, offices, galleries and restaurants. Only a few buildings recall the earlier splendour of this district.

★ **Checkpoint Charlie**
This sign marks the place of the notorious border crossing between East and West Berlin ❹

Topographie des Terrors
A shocking exhibition detailing Nazi crimes is housed within the former Gestapo and SS headquarters ❸

Martin-Gropius-Bau
This interesting, multi-coloured Neo-Renaissance building was once home to the Kunstgewerbe-museum (see pp118–21) ❷

Deutsches Technikmuseum ◄

0 metres   150
0 yards   150

STAR SIGHTS

★ **Checkpoint Charlie**

★ **Jüdisches Museum**

Haus am Checkpoint Charlie
Butterflies on a piece of the Berlin Wall mark the entrance to this museum.

Berlin-Museum
The monogram of King Friedrich Wilhelm I decorates the balcony of this former courtroom, now home to the Jewish Museum's café and temporary exhibitions on German-Jewish history ❺

LOCATOR MAP
See Street Finder maps 12 & 13

Märkisches Museum

★ **Jüdisches Museum**
Windows made to resemble cracks create a striking effect in the metallic facing of this new building by architect Daniel Libeskind ❻

KOCHSTRASSE

CHARLOTTENSTRASSE

MARKGRAFENSTRASSE

BESSELSTRASSE

RICHSTRASSE

ANZ-KLUHS-STRASSE

Mehringplatz
The former Rondell was known for many years as Belle-Alliance-Platz. Completely destroyed during World War II, it was rebuilt by Hans Scharoun, who followed the original design ❼

KEY

– – – Suggested route

Anhalter Bahnhof ❶

Askanischer Platz 6–7. **Map** 12 E1.
Ⓢ *Anhalter Bahnhof.* 🚌 *129,
248, 341.*

ONLY A TINY FRAGMENT now
remains of Anhalter
Bahnhof (Hitchhiker Station),
once Berlin's largest and
Europe's second largest
railway station.

The hugely ambitious
structure was designed by
Franz Schwechten and con-
structed in 1880. The station
was intended to be the largest
and most elegant in Europe
in order to impress official
visitors to the capital of the
German Empire. Some of
the most famous people to
alight at Anhalter Bahnhof
were the Italian king Umberto,
who was welcomed by Kaiser
Wilhelm II himself, and the
Russian tsar Nicholas. From
here trains travelled to
Dresden, Vienna, Rome and
Athens. The station was
taken out of public use
in 1943 after its roof was
destroyed by Allied bombing.

Despite attempts to preserve
the building, the station was
pulled down in 1960. Only
the front portico remains,
crowned by still-damaged
sculptures and the hole that
housed a large electric clock,
as well as fragments
of its once glorious façade.

Martin-Gropius-Bau ❷

Stresemannstrasse 110. **Map** 12 E1.
📞 *25 48 60.* ⏰ *10am–8pm
Wed–Mon.* Ⓢ & Ⓤ *Potsdamer Platz.*
🚌 *129, 248, 341.*

THE INNOVATIVE Martin-
Gropius-Bau was
originally built to fulfil the
requirements of an arts
and crafts museum. It was
designed by Martin Gropius
with the participation of
Heino Schmieden and
constructed in 1881. The
building is in a style
reminiscent of an Italian
Renaissance palace, with a
magnificent glazed interior
courtyard, an impressive
atrium and unusual, richly

Exhibition documenting Nazi crimes at the Topographie des Terrors

decorated elevations. Located
between the windows are
the crests of German cities,
and within the friezes are
reliefs illustrating the
different arts and crafts. In
the plaques between the
windows of the top storey
are beautiful mosaics
containing allegorical figures
representing the cultures of
different eras and countries.

From 1922 Martin-Gropius-
Bau accommodated the
Museum of Ethnology, but
after World War II the
building was abandoned and
left in ruins. Although plans
for an inner-city motorway
threatened it until the 1970s,
a reconstruction programme
eventually commenced in
1981, led by architects
Winnetou Kampmann and
Ute Westroem. This was
followed in 1999 by a
further refurbishment, and
since then the building has
housed a changing series of
exhibitions on art, photography
and architecture.

**Allegorical mosaic on display in
the Martin-Gropius-Bau**

Topographie des Terrors ❸

Stresemannstrasse 110 (entrance on
Niederkirchner Strasse). **Map** 6 F5,
12 F1. 📞 *25 48 67 03.* Ⓢ &
Ⓤ *Potsdamer Platz.* Ⓤ *Potsdamer
Platz.* 🚌 *129, 248, 341.*
⏰ *May–Sep: 10am–8pm daily;
Oct–Apr: 10am–6pm daily.* 📷

DURING the Third Reich
Prinz-Albrecht-Strasse
was probably the most
frightening address in Berlin.
In 1934, three of the most
terrifying Nazi political
departments had their head-
quarters in a block between
Stresemann-, Wilhelm-,
Anhalter-, and Prinz-Albrecht-
Strasse (now Niederkirchner
Strasse), making this area
the government district of
National Socialist Germany.

The Neo-Classical Prinz-
Albrecht palace at Wilhelmstrasse No. 102 became the
headquarters of Reinhard
Heydrich and the Third
Reich's security service (SD).
The arts and crafts school
at Prinz-Albrecht-Strasse
No. 8 was occupied by
the head of the Gestapo,
Heinrich Müller, while the
Hotel Prinz Albrecht at
No. 9 became the head-
quarters of the Schutzstaffel
or SS, with Heinrich
Himmler in command. It
was from the buildings
in this area that decisions
about the Germanization of
the occupied territories were
made, as well as plans on the
genocide of European Jews.

After World War II, the buildings were pulled down. In 1987, however, in cellars that were once torture cells, an exhibition was mounted that documented Nazi crimes. A new museum building, designed by Peter Zumthor, has been under construction on the site since 1998.

A preserved section of the Berlin wall runs alongside the grounds of the Topographie des Terrors at Niederkirchner Strasse.

Checkpoint Charlie ④

Friedrichstrasse 43–45. **Map** 7 A5.
📞 253 72 50. 🇺 Kochstrasse.
🚌 129. **Haus am Checkpoint Charlie** ⏰ 9am–10pm daily. 🚹

A ALPHA, B Bravo, C Charlie. Not many people remember that the name of this notorious border crossing between the American and Soviet sectors stemmed from the word that signifies the letter C in the international phonetic alphabet.

Between 1961 and 1990, Checkpoint Charlie was the only crossing point for foreigners between East and West Berlin. During that time, it represented a symbol of both freedom and separation for the many East Germans trying to escape from the DDR's Communist regime.

Little remains of the former crossing point, which was witness to a number of dramatic events during the Cold War, including a tense two-day standoff between Russian and American tanks in 1961.

In 1990, the checkpoint was formally closed with a ceremony, which was attended by the foreign ministers of the US, Great Britain, France and the Soviet Union.

Today, there are no longer any gates, barriers or barbed wire; instead there is a replica checkpoint booth, complete with sand bags and the famous, huge

The replica booth at the former Checkpoint Charlie

sign on the old Western side that reads "You are leaving the American Sector".

Also on Friedrichstrasse are two large photographs of an American and a Russian soldier, that form part of a well-known series by the Berlin photographer Frank Thiel. His portraits of four Allied soldiers commemorate the departure of the Allies.

One of the original watchtowers is worth visiting at the museum nearby – **Haus am Checkpoint Charlie**. The museum's rich collection details Cold War border conflicts, and the construction of the Berlin Wall. Of interest are the exhibits connected with the escape attempts of East Germans to the West. The ingenuity and bravery of these escapees is astonishing, using devices such as secret compartments built into cars, and specially constructed suitcases.

A separate exhibition illustrates the peaceful campaigns carried out in the name of democracy in a number of totalitarian countries.

Berlin-Museum ⑤

Lindenstrasse 14. **Map** 13 A2.
🇺 Hallesches Tor or Kochstrasse.
🚌 143, 240, 248. ⏰ 10am–10pm Mon, 10am–8pm Tue–Sun. ⚫ Jewish hols and 24 Dec.

D ESIGNED BY architect Philipp Gerlach, this was one of the first buildings in the new section of the enlarged Friedrichstadt. The Baroque façade dates from the time of King Friedrich Wilhelm I (1713–40). The main features are the front balconied portal and the triangular pediment with the Prussian crest and the allegorical figures of Justice and Prudence. Inside the building, within the hallway leading to the left wing, is an integral Baroque portal that came originally from the Palais Danckelmann, which was built in 1690 and designed by Johann Arnold Nering.

The building suffered severe damage during World War II, but it was restored and the Baroque façade preserved.

The erection of the Berlin Wall prevented West Berliners from visiting one of their favourite museums, the Märkisches Museum *(see p84)*. Therefore, between 1963 and 1969, the interior of the Berlin-Museum building was redesigned by architect Günther Hönow in order to accommodate an interesting collection of artifacts, maps and urban designs that illustrated the history of the city from its beginnings to 1945.

Today, it is part of the Jüdisches Museum Berlin *(see pp142-3)*, housing the museum café as well as temporary exhibitions.

Plaque adorning a window of the Berlin-Museum

Jüdisches Museum Berlin 6

THE JEWISH MUSEUM designed by Daniel Libeskind, a Polish-Jewish architect based in the United States, is an exciting and imaginative example of late 20th-century architecture. The plan, shape, style, and interior and exterior arrangement of the building are part of a complicated philosophical programme to illustrate the history and culture of Germany's Jewish community, and the repercussions of the Holocaust. The exhibition has gathered together many artifacts, such as books and photographs, to bring the memories and stories of Jewish life alive. The long, narrow galleries with slanting floors and sharp zig-zagging turns are designed to evoke the feeling of loss and dislocation. These are interspersed by "voids" that represent the vacuum left behind by the destruction of Jewish life.

★ **Moses Mendelssohn's Glasses**
These glasses are on show in the section entitled "Moses Mendelssohn and the Enlightenment", which details the philosopher's fight for religious tolerance in a time when Jews possessed no civil rights.

"Darwinian" (1904)
This caricature, published in the magazine Schlemiel, *shows the evolution of a Jewish Hanukkah light into a Christian Christmas tree, implying that the wish of many Jews was to assimilate with Germans.*

Rural Jews and Court Jews

At the Heart of the Family

Same Responsibilities – Same Rights?

STAR SIGHTS

★ **Moses Mendelssohn's Glasses**

★ **Daniel Libeskind's Design**

★ **Garden of Exile and Emigration**

MUSEUM GUIDE

Entrance to the museum is via an underground path from the former Berlin-Museum. Stairs lead up to the start of the exhibition which is divided into 14 sections, taking visitors through German Jewish history and culture from early history, through the Middle Ages and up to the present day.

VISITORS' CHECKLIST

Lindenstrasse 9–14. **Map** 13 A2.
🄲 25 99 33 00. 🅄 *Hallesches Tor or Kochstrasse.* 🚌 143, 240, 248. ◐ *10am–10pm Mon, 10am–8pm Tue–Sun.* ● *Jewish hols and 24 Dec.* 🖼 🖼 *in German: 11am, 2pm (English too), 3pm Sat & Sun.* 🅆 www.jmberlin.de

Entrance to
exhibition via
underground
tunnel

German Jews and
Jewish Germans

Persecution –
Resistance –
Extermination

Exit

East and
West

★ **Daniel Libeskind's Design**
The extraordinary zinc-clad, jagged structure of the museum is likened to a deconstructed Star of David, and attracted over 350,000 visitors to the museum in the two years before the exhibitions were installed.

Electric Iron AEG
An iron made by one of Germany's largest electrical companies, founded by Emil Rathenau, forms part of the collection celebrating the dominant position of Jews in trade and industry in Berlin throughout the late 19th and early 20th centuries.

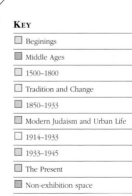

KEY

☐ Beginings
☐ Middle Ages
☐ 1500–1800
☐ Tradition and Change
☐ 1850–1933
☐ Modern Judaism and Urban Life
☐ 1914–1933
☐ 1933–1945
☐ The Present
☐ Non-exhibition space

★ **Garden of Exile and Emigration**
Comprising 49 tilted pillars to represent the foundation of the state of Israel in 1948 plus one for Berlin, the garden also symbolizes the forced exile of Germany's Jews.

A representation of Peace, by Albert Wolff, in Mehringplatz

Mehringplatz **7**

Map 13 A2. **U** *Mehringplatz.*
🚌 *248, 341.*

MEHRINGPLATZ WAS planned in the 1830s, when the boundaries of the city were extended. Its original name was Rondell, meaning round-about. This was an appropriate name as Wilhelmstrasse, Friedrichstrasse and Linden-strasse all converged here.

Mehringplatz was the work of Philipp Gerlach then, in the 1840s, Peter Joseph Lenné designed the decoration of the square. At the centre is the Column of Peace, designed by Christian Gottlieb Cantian, commemorating the Wars of Liberation in 1815. The column is crowned by the figure of Victory by Christian Daniel Rauch. Two sculptures were added in the 1870s: *Peace* by Albert Wolff; and *Clio* (the Muse of History) by Ferdinand Hartzer. In the 19th and early 20th centuries the area was fashionable and populated with politicians, diplomats and aristocrats. The current buildings date from the 1970s.

Lapidarium **8**

Hallesches Ufer 78. **Map** 12 E2.
📞 *25 48 63 05.* **◯** *by appointment only.* **U** *Mendelssohn-Bartholdy-Park.*

THIS INTERESTING building, decorated with an enchanting Oriental-style chimney, was once Berlin's pumping station. It was built from 1873 to 1876 and designed by Hermann Blankenstein. The original steam pumps have

survived to this day and can be seen during a visit. The Lapidarium contains numerous sculptures, some of which have been replaced by copies for conservation purposes. Virtually all the sculptures that once decorated the Avenue of Victory in the Tiergarten, known as "Puppenallee", are housed here. These majestic statues of celebrated warriors and rulers stand side by side in their robes and weapons, only slightly diminished by the loss of many heads, arms and other body parts.

Deutsches Technikmuseum Berlin **9**

Trebbiner Strasse 9. **Map** 12 E2.
📞 *90 25 40.* **U** *Gleisdreieck.*
🚌 *129, 341.* **◯** *9am–5:30pm Tue–Fri, 10am–6pm Sat–Sun.* **♿** **📷**

THE TECHNICAL MUSEUM was first established in 1982 with the intention of grouping more than 100 smaller, specialized collections under one roof. The current collection is arranged on the site of the former trade hall, the size of which allows many of the museum's exhibits, such as locomotives, aircraft, boats, water towers and storerooms, to be displayed full-size and in their original condition.

Of particular interest in the collection are the dozens of locomotives and railway carriages from different eras as well as the vintage cars. There are also exhibitions dedicated to flying, the history of paper manufacture, printing, weaving,

electro-technology and computer technology. There are also two windmills, a brewery and an old forge. The section called Spectrum is especially popular with children as it allows them to conduct "hands-on" experiments.

Friedhöfe vor dem Halleschen Tor **10**

Mehringdamm, Blücher-, Baruther & Zossener Strasse. **Map** 13 A3.
U *Mehringdamm.* **🚌** *140, 341.*
◯ *10am–5pm daily.*

BEYOND THE CITY WALLS, next to the Hallesches Tor, four neighbouring cemeteries were established in 1735. A number of famous people are buried here. Among the beautiful gravestones are the greatest of Berlin's artists, including the composer Felix Mendelssohn-Bartholdy, architects Georg Wenzeslaus von Knobelsdorff, David Gilly and Carl Ferdinand Langhans, portraitist Antoine Pesne and the writer, artist and composer ETA Hoffmann.

Riehmers Hofgarten **11**

Yorckstr. 83–86, Grossbeerenstr. 56–57 & Hagelberger Strasse 9–12. **Map** 12 F4.
U *Mehringdamm.* **🚌** *119, 140.*

RIEHMERS HOFGARTEN is the name given to the 20 or so exquisite houses arranged around a picturesque garden in the area bordered by the

Headstone in the picturesque Friedhöfe vor dem Halleschen Tor

Renaissance-style façade in Riehmers Hofgarten

streets Yorck-, Hagelberger and Grossbeerenstrasse. These houses were built between 1881 and 1892 to the detailed designs of Wilhelm Riehmer and Otto Mrosk. These respected architects created this unique group of houses, not only designing intricate, Renaissance-style façades but also giving equal splendour to the elevations overlooking the courtyard garden. The streets of Riehmers Hofgarten have been carefully restored and Yorckstrasse also has quite a few cafés. Next to Riehmers Hofgarten is the church of St Bonifaz, which was designed by Max Hasak. Adjacent to the church is a similar complex of houses built in an impressive Neo-Gothic style.

To experience the authentic atmosphere of old Kreuzberg, you need to go no further than Bergmannstrasse. Here, entire districts of 19th-century houses have been restored to their original state. The atmosphere is further enhanced by antique streetlamps, a pedestrianized street, and bars and galleries. This is also true for Marheinekeplatz, where there is a lively covered market.

Viktoriapark ⑫

Map 12 E4, E5, F5. **U** *Platz der Luftbrücke.* 🚌 *104, 140.*

THIS RAMBLING PARK, with several artificial waterfalls, short trails and a small hill, was designed by Hermann Machtig and built between 1884 and 1894. The Neo-Gothic Memorial to the Wars of Liberation at the summit of the hill is the work of Karl Friedrich Schinkel, created

between 1817 and 1821. The monument commemorates the Prussian victory against Napoleon's army in the Wars of Liberation. The cast-iron tower is well ornamented. In the niches of the lower section are 12 allegorical figures by Christian Daniel Rauch, Friedrich Tieck and Ludwig Wichmann. Each figure symbolizes a battle and is linked to a historic figure – either a military leader or a member of the royal family.

Flughafen Tempelhof ⑬

Platz der Luftbrücke. **Plan** 12 F5. **U** *Platz der Luftbrücke.* 🚌 *104, 119, 184, 341.*

SITUATED BEYOND Kreuzberg, the Tempelhof airport was once Germany's largest. Built in 1923, the structure was enlarged during the Third Reich. The building is typical of Third Reich architecture, even though the eagles that decorate the buildings predate the Nazis. The additions to the original structure were designed by Ernst Sagebiel and completed in 1939.

In 1951, a monument was added in front of the airport. Designed by Edward Ludwig, it commemorates the airlifts of the Berlin Blockade. The three spikes on the top symbolize the air corridors used by Allied planes. The names of those who lost their lives during the Blockade appear on the plinth.

THE BERLIN BLOCKADE (1948–9)

On 24 June 1948, as a result of rising tensions between East Germany and West Berlin, Soviet authorities blockaded all the roads leading to West Berlin. In order to ensure food and fuel for the residents, US General Lucius Clay ordered that provisions be flown into the city. British and American planes made a total of 212,612 flights, transporting almost 2.3 million tons of goods, among which were parts of a power station. In April 1949, at the height of the airlifts, planes were landing every 63 seconds. The blockade ended in May, 1949. Although the airlifts were successful, there were casualties: 70 airmen and 8 ground crew lost their lives.

Allied plane bringing supplies during the Berlin Airlift

AROUND KURFÜRSTENDAMM

THE EASTERN AREA of the Charlottenburg region, around the boulevard known as Kurfürstendamm, was developed in the 19th century. Luxurious buildings were constructed along Kurfürstendamm (the Ku'damm), while the areas of Breitscheidplatz and Wittenbergplatz became replete with hotels and department stores. After World War II, with the old centre (Mitte) situated in East Berlin,

Sculpture from the Jüdisches Gemeindehaus

Charlottenburg became the centre of West Berlin. Traces of wartime destruction were removed very quickly and this area was transformed into the heart of West Berlin, and dozens of new company headquarters and trade centres were built. The situation changed after the reunification of Berlin, and although many tourists concentrate on Mitte, the heart of the city continues to beat around Kurfürstendamm.

SIGHTS AT A GLANCE

Museums
Käthe-Kollwitz-Museum **9**

Streets and Squares
Fasanenstrasse **8**
Kurfürstendamm **4**
Savignyplatz **10**
Tauentzien-
   strasse **13**

Parks
Zoologischer
   Garten **1**

Historic Buildings
Europa-Center **2**
Jüdisches Gemeindehaus **7**
KaDeWe **14**
Kaiser-Wilhelm-Gedächtnis-
   Kirche pp152–3 **3**
Ludwig-Erhard-Haus **5**
Technische Universität **12**
Theater des Westens **6**
Universität der Künste **11**

KEY

⬜	Street-by-Street map *pp148–9*
🚆	Railway station
Ⓢ	S-Bahn station
Ⓤ	U-Bahn station
🚌	Bus station
🅿	Parking

GETTING THERE
S-Bahn lines 3, 5, 7, 9 and 75 go to Savigny-platz and Zoologischer Garten. U-Bahn lines 2, 9 and 15 also traverse the area. Next to Zoo station is a large bus terminal.

0 metres   400

0 metres   400

◁ **Mosaic depicting a standard-bearer inside the Kaiser-Wilhelm-Gedächtniskirche**

Street-by-Street: Breitscheidplatz and Ku'damm

T HE AREA SURROUNDING the eastern end of the Ku'damm, especially Tauentzienstrasse and Breitscheidplatz, is the centre of the former West Berlin. Thirty years ago this ultramodern district, full of department stores and office blocks, attracted visitors from all over the world. Today, although the area still retains its unique atmosphere, it is becoming overshadowed by Potsdamer Platz and the arcades of Friedrichstrasse. However, nowhere else in Berlin is there a place so full of life as Breitscheidplatz, a department store with such style as KaDeWe, or streets as refined as Fasanenstrasse.

Kant-Dreieck
This building, containing only right angles, was designed by Josef Paul Kleihues. The "sail" on the roof makes it instantly recognizable.

Jüdisches Gemeindehaus
Some of the remaining fragments of the old synagogue have been incorporated into the façade of this building ❼

Literaturhaus
contains a charming café and a good bookshop.

Käthe-Kollwitz-Museum
The museum is housed in one of the charming villas on Fasanenstrasse ❾

Fasanenstrasse
This tranquil street features some of the most expensive shops in Berlin ❽

Ku'damm
A stroll along the Ku'damm is a stroll into the heart of Berlin, and an essential part of any visit to the city ❹

STAR SIGHTS

★ **Kaiser-Wilhelm-Gedächtniskirche**

★ **Zoologischer Garten**

KEY

 — — Suggested route

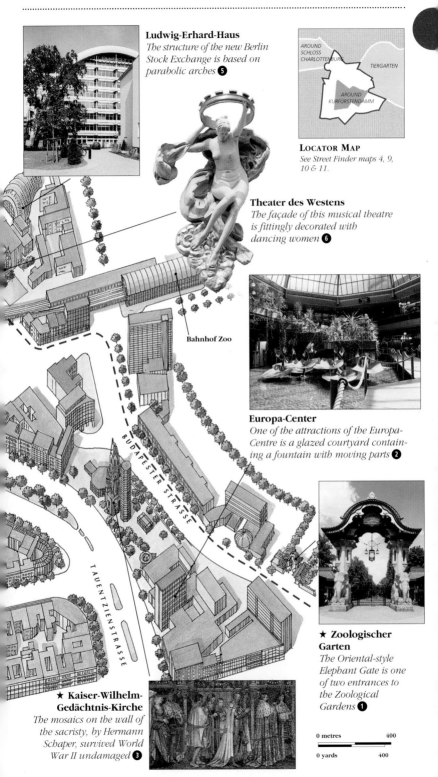

Ludwig-Erhard-Haus
The structure of the new Berlin Stock Exchange is based on parabolic arches ❺

LOCATOR MAP
See Street Finder maps 4, 9, 10 & 11.

Theater des Westens
The façade of this musical theatre is fittingly decorated with dancing women ❻

Bahnhof Zoo

Europa-Center
One of the attractions of the Europa-Centre is a glazed courtyard containing a fountain with moving parts ❷

★ **Zoologischer Garten**
The Oriental-style Elephant Gate is one of two entrances to the Zoological Gardens ❶

★ **Kaiser-Wilhelm-Gedächtnis-Kirche**
The mosaics on the wall of the sacristy, by Hermann Schaper, survived World War II undamaged ❸

0 metres	400
0 yards	400

one of the largest in Europe, contains sharks, piranhas and unusual animals from coral reefs. There is also a huge terrarium with an overgrown jungle that is home to a group of crocodiles. Some of the best-loved animals at the zoo are the giant pandas – Bao-Bao and Yan-Yan.

Bao-Bao, one of the star attractions at the Zoologischer Garten

Zoologischer Garten ❶

ZOOLOGICAL GARDEN

Hardenbergplatz 8 or Budapester Strasse 34. **Map** 4 E5, 10 E1. *25 40 10.* Ⓢ & Ⓤ *Zoologischer Garten.* 🚌 *100, 109, 110, 145, 146, 149, 200, 204, 245, 249, X-10, X-34.* ◯ *Apr–Sep: 9am–6:30pm daily; Oct: 9am–6pm daily; Nov–Mar: 9am–5pm daily.* 📷

THE ZOOLOGICAL garden is one of Berlin's greatest attractions. It is part of the Tiergarten and dates from 1844, which makes this zoo one of the oldest in Germany. You can enter from Hardenberg-platz through the Lion's Gate, and from Budapester Strasse through the decorative Oriental-style Elephant Gate.

The zoo offers a number of attractions, including the monkey house, which contains a family of gorillas, and a darkened pavilion for nocturnal animals. The hippopotamus pool has a glazed wall that enables visitors to observe these enormous animals underwater. The aquarium,

Europa-Center ❷

Breitscheidplatz. **Map** 10 E1. Ⓢ & Ⓤ *Zoologischer Garten.* 🚌 *100, 109, 119, 146, 200, 219, X-9.*

THE EUROPA-CENTER stands on the site of the legendary Romanisches Café, a famous meeting place for Dada artists in the 1920s. The current building was established in 1965, and since that time it has been one of the largest complexes of its type in Germany. Designed by Helmut Hentrich and Hubert Petsch-nigg, the Europa-Center is a group of low-rise buildings housing a trade centre, numerous restaurants and pubs, a vast multiplex cinema and a casino. The edifice of the deluxe Palace Hotel *(see p226)* has been incorporated into the centre, as well as a 22-storey office block.

There are more than 100 shops to browse in as well as some amusing fountains. One of these is the "Flow of Time Clock", designed by Bernard Gitton. Seconds, minutes and hours are measured in vials and spheres of green liquid. The Europa-Center also houses the political cabaret *Die Stachelschweine* and Berlin's largest tourist information centre *(see pp278–9).*

A fountain representing Earth, outside the Europa-Center

Kaiser-Wilhelm-Ged-ächtnis-Kirche ❸

See pp152–3.

One of many outdoor cafés on the Ku'damm

Kurfürstendamm ❹

Map 9 A2, B2, C3, 10 D1. Ⓤ *Kurfürstendamm.* 🚌 *109, 119, 129, 219.*

THIS IS UNDOUBTEDLY one of the most elegant streets in Berlin. The wide avenue was established in the 1880s on the site of a former track that led to the Grunewald forest. It was quickly populated with imposing buildings and grand hotels. In the 20 years between World Wars I and II, the Ku'damm (as it is popularly called) was renowned for its great cafés, visited by famous writers, directors and painters.

After World War II, the damaged houses were replaced with modern buildings, but this did not change the char-acter of the finest street in West Berlin. Elegant shops and cafés with pretty summer gardens continue to attract a chic crowd. A cup of coffee in the corner café in the Kempinski Hotel Bristol should not be missed.

Ludwig-Erhard-Haus ❺

Fasanenstrasse 83–84. **Map** 4 D5. Ⓢ & Ⓤ *Zoologischer Garten.* 🚌 *145, 149, 245, X-9, X-34.*

THIS INNOVATIVE new building houses the headquarters of the Berlin stock exchange as well as a trade and industry centre. Completed in 1998, Ludwig-Erhard-Haus is the creation of British architect Nicholas Grimshaw and has been compared to the skin of an armadillo, a giant skeleton and the ribbing of a shell.

The main structure of the building is composed of 15 elliptical arches, which extend above the roof and through the glass walls of the building. For this reason the entire interior space is completely free of any supports or columns. This allows for freedom and flexibility in the subdivision of the interior.

A system of temperature-sensitive glass Venetian blinds, or louvres, ensures the climate inside the building remains constant. On a windy day, when the sun clouds over, the entire edifice begins to flicker and glisten like a fluttering fish with the movement of the louvres.

Theater des Westens ❻

Kantstrasse 9–12. **Map** 10 D1.
🚇 *(0180) 599 89 99.* Ⓢ & Ⓤ *Zoologischer Garten.* 🚌 *149, X-34.*

THE THEATER DES WESTENS, one of the most picturesque of all Berlin's theatres, was built in 1896 to a design by Bernhard Sehring. The composition of its façade links Neo-Classical elements with Palladian and Art Nouveau details. The interior of the theatre has been designed in a splendid Neo-Baroque style, while the back and the sections that houses the stage have been rebuilt

The façade of the Theater des Westens on Kantstrasse

within a Neo-Gothic structure, incorporating the decorative elements of a chess set.

From its very beginning the theatre catered for lighter forms of musical entertainment. Operettas and vaudeville were staged here, followed by reviews, musicals, and cabaret. Some of the world's greatest stars have appeared on the stage here, including Josephine Baker, who performed her famous banana dance in 1926. Near the theatre is the renowned Delphi cinema and popular jazz club Quasimodo.

Jüdisches Gemeindehaus ❼

JEWISH COMMUNITY HOUSE

Fasanenstrasse 79/80. **Map** 10 D1.
Ⓤ *Uhlandstrasse or Kurfürstendamm.*
🚌 *109, 119, 129, 149, 219, X-10, X-34.*

THE JEWISH COMMUNITY has its headquarters in this building, constructed on the site of a synagogue that was burned down during *Kristallnacht* on 9 November 1938 *(see p27)*. The original synagogue was designed by Ehenfried Hessel in a Romanesque-Byzantine style and built in 1912. The ruins of the synagogue were removed only in the mid-1950s. The new building,

The entrance of the Jüdisches Gemeindehaus

designed by Dieter Knoblauch and Heinz Heise, was constructed in 1959. The only reminders of the splendour of the former synagogue are the portal at the entrance to the building and some decorative fragments on the façade.

Inside there are offices, a school, a kosher restaurant called Arche Noah and a prayer room covered by three glazed domes. At the rear there is a courtyard with a place of remembrance. There is also an emotive statue at the front of the building, depicting a broken scroll of the Torah (the holy book of Jewish Law).

GERMAN CINEMA

The 1920s were a boom time for the arts, and German cinema gained prominence throughout the world with the rise of Expressionism. The opening of the UFA film studios in 1919 in Babelsberg *(see p205)* was a milestone in the development of German cinema. The studios became the heart of the film industry and rivalled Hollywood as a centre for innovation. Many

Marlene Dietrich in the well-known film *The Blue Angel*

famous films were produced here, including the Expressionist masterpiece *The Cabinet of Dr Caligari* (1920) by Robert Wiene, Ernst Lubitsch's *Madame Dubarry* (1919) with Pola Negri and *Nosferatu* (1922) by Friedrich Murnau. Other films released by the studios were Fritz Lang's *Doctor Mabuse* (1922) and his futuristic film *Metropolis* (1927). In April 1930, the studios premiered Josef von Sternberg's *The Blue Angel* featuring the young Marlene Dietrich in the lead role. After Hitler came to power many directors and actors left Germany.

Kaiser-Wilhelm-Gedächtnis-Kirche ❸

THIS CHURCH-MONUMENT is one of Berlin's most famous landmarks, surrounded by a lively crowd of street traders, buskers and beggars. The vast Neo-Romanesque church was designed by Franz Schwechten. It was consecrated in 1895 but was destroyed by bombs in 1943. After World War II the ruins were removed, leaving only the massive front tower at the base of which the Gedenkhalle (Memorial Hall) is situated. This hall documents the history of the church and contains some of the original ceiling mosaics, marble reliefs and liturgical objects from the church. In 1961, Egon Eiermann designed a new octagonal church in blue glass and a new freestanding bell tower.

Kaiser's Mosaic
Kaiser Heinrich I is depicted here in this elaborate mosaic, sitting on his throne.

Bell Tower
The new hexagonal bell tower stands on the site of the former main nave of the destroyed church.

Rose window

Mosaic Decoration
Original mosaics remain on the arches and the walls near the staircase. These feature the Dukes of Prussia among the other decorative elements.

Main Altar
The vast figure of Christ on the Cross is the work of Karl Hemmeter.

Walls of reinforced concrete and blue-coloured glass form a dense grid.

Tower Ruins
The damaged roof of the former church has become one of the best-known symbols of Berlin.

VISITORS' CHECKLIST

Breitscheidplatz. **Map** 10 D1.
[218 50 23. **S** & **U**
Zoologischer Garten or **U**
Kurfürstendamm. **[bus]** 100, 119,
129, 146, 200, 219, X-9. **[ ]**
Church 9am–7pm daily.
Gedenkhalle 10am–4pm Mon–
Sat. **[ ]** 10am & 6pm Sun. In
English, Jun–Aug: 9am Sun. **[ ]**

Tower Clock
The tower is decorated with a clock based on a Classical design.

★ **Mosaic of the Hohenzollerns**
The mosaic of the Hohenzollerns is in the vestibule. The family is led by Queen Luise and the centre is dominated by Kaiser Wilhelm I.

Orthodox Cross
This cross was a gift from the Russian Orthodox bishops from Volokolamsk and Yuryev, given in memory of the victims of Nazism.

Figure of Christ
This vast sculpture by Hermann Schaper once decorated the church altar. It survived World War II damage.

Main entrance

★ **Coventry Crucifix**
This modest cross was fashioned from nails found in the ashes of Coventry Cathedral, England. The Cathedral was destroyed during German bombing raids in 1940.

STAR SIGHTS

★ **Mosaic of the Hohenzollerns**

★ **Coventry Crucifix**

Fasanenstrasse – one of the most elegant streets in Berlin

Fasanenstrasse ❽

Map 9 C2, 10 D1, 10 D3.
U *Uhlandstrasse.* 🚌 *109, 119, 129, 219, 249, X-10.*

THE DISCREET CHARM of Fasanenstrasse, particularly between Lietzenburger Strasse and Kurfürstendamm, has attracted the most exclusive designer shops in the world. Well maintained buildings, *fin-de-siècle* villas set in tranquil gardens and elegant shop windows of jewellers, art galleries and fashion shops will all entice you to take an after-noon stroll along this street.

It is worth seeing the villas at No. 23–5, which are called the Wintergarten-Ensemble. The first one, No. 23, dates from 1889. Tucked away in a garden, the villa is home to the Literaturhaus, which organizes interesting exhibi-tions and readings. It has an excellent café that extends into a conservatory. At No. 24 is the Käthe-Kollwitz museum, and No. 25, built in 1892 by Hans Grisebach, accommodates an auction house and art gallery.

Käthe-Kollwitz-Museum ❾

Fasanenstrasse 24. Map 9 C2.
📞 *882 52 10.* **U** *Uhlandstrasse or Kurfürstendamm.* 🚌 *109, 119, 129, 219, 249, X-10.* 🕐 *11am–6pm Wed–Mon* 👥 🎧

THIS SMALL private museum provides a unique oppor-tunity to become acquainted with the work of Käthe Kollwitz (1867–1945). Born in

Königsberg, the artist settled in Berlin where she married a doctor who worked in Prenz-lauer Berg, a working-class district *(see p170)*. Her drawings and sculptures portrayed the social problems of the poor, as well as human tragedy and suffering. She frequently took up the theme of motherhood and war after losing a son and grandson in World Wars I and II.

The museum exhibits her work, including sculptures, posters and drawings, as well as letters and photographs.

Mother and Child, **from the Käthe-Kollwitz-Museum**

Savignyplatz ❿

Map 9 C1. **S** *Savignyplatz.* 🚌 *149.*

SAVIGNYPLATZ is enclosed on the south side by the arcade of a railway viaduct, which appears in the film *Cabaret* by Bob Fosse. During the day the square does not look interesting – there are no remarkable historic buildings,

only carefully tended green-ery and flower beds. However, the area around the square truly comes alive at night. The dozens of cafés and restau-rants fill up, while in summer the entire edge of the square and neighbouring streets turn into one big garden filled with tables and umbrellas. People come from outlying districts to visit popular restaurants and cafés such as Zwiebelfisch, Dicke Wirtin, or XII Apostel *(see p240)*. The arcades in the viaduct contain many cafés and bars. One section of the arcades has been taken up by the Bücher-bogen bookshop *(see p254)*.

Universität der Künste ⓫
UNIVERSITY OF THE ARTS

Hardenbergstrasse 32–33 and Fasanenstrasse 1b. Map 4 D5.
S *Zoologischer Garten or* **U** *Ernst-Reuter-Platz.* 🚌 *145, 245, X-9.*

THE UNIVERSITÄT der Künste was originally called Preussische Akademie der Künste, which was established in 1696. It continued a long tradition of teaching artists in Berlin and has been headed by well-known figures includ-ing Johann Gottfried Schadow and Anton von Werner. As a result of a number of reforms between 1875 and 1882, the Academy was divided into two separate colleges. A complex of buildings was erected for them on Harden-bergstrasse and Fasanen-strasse. The Neo-Baroque buildings were constructed between 1897 and 1902 to a design by Heinrich Keyser and Karl von Grossheim.

After World War II, only two large buildings, both with decorative façades, survived. On the Hardenbergstrasse side was the Hochschule für Bildende Künste (College for Fine Art), while on the Fasanenstrasse side was the Hochschule für Musik und Darstellende Kunst (College for Music and Performing Arts). Unfortunately, the concert hall did not survive. A new one was built in 1955, designed by Paul Baumgarten.

Bas-relief sculpture on the façade of the Hochschule der Künste

A small *fin-de-siècle* building that looks like a castle, at Hardenbergstrasse No. 36, is a college for religious music which belongs to this group of college buildings.

Technische Universität ⓬

TECHNICAL UNIVERSITY

Strasse des 17 Juni 135. **Map** 3 C4. Ⓤ *Ernst-Reuter-Platz.* 🚌 145, 245, X-9.

THE VAST AREA that lies to the east of Ernst-Reuter-Platz along the Strasse des 17 Juni is occupied by the buildings of the Technische Universität. Officially called Technische Hochschule Berlin (TUB), it was established in 1879 after the unification of the School of Crafts and the renowned Bauakademie. From its inception the Technische Universität had five different departments, which were all housed, from 1884, in a Neo-Renaissance building designed by Richard Lucae, Friedrich Hitzig and Julius Raschdorff. After World War II, the ruined front wing was rebuilt as a flat block without any divisions, while the rear wings and three internal courtyards retained their original appearance.

It is worth continuing along Strasse des 17 Juni towards the colonnade of the Charlottenburger Tor (or gate), dating from 1908. The colonnade is ornamented with the figures of Friedrich and Sophie Charlotte holding a model of Schloss Charlottenburg *(see pp160–1)* in their hands. Beyond the gate and to the right, on the island, is an unusual green building with a gigantic pink pipe. This is the centre that monitors water currents and caters to the needs of seagoing vessels.

Tauentzienstrasse ⓭

Map 10 E1. Ⓤ *Wittenbergplatz.* 🚌 119, 129, 146, 219.

THIS IS ONE OF THE most important streets for trade and commerce in this part of Berlin. The shops are not as expensive or as elegant as on Kurfürstendamm – but they attract more visitors for this reason. One of the highlights of the street is the unusual façade of the department store Peek & Clopenburg. Designed by Gottfried Böhm, the walls of the building are covered with transparent, gently slanting and undulating "aprons".

Other highlights include the central bed of colourful flowers as well as an interesting sculpture entitled *Berlin*. Created by Brigitte and Martin Matschinsky-Denninghoff, the sculpture was erected near Marburger Strasse in 1987 on the occasion of the 750th anniversary of Berlin.

KaDeWe ⓮

Tauentzienstrasse 21–24. **Map** 10 E2. Ⓤ *Wittenbergplatz.* 🚌 119, 129, 146, 185, 219. ⏰ 9:30am–8pm Mon–Fri, 9am–4pm Sat.

KAUFHAUS DES Westens, or KaDeWe, as it is popularly known, is the largest department store in Europe. It was built in 1907 to a design by Emil Schaudt, but it has been extended several times from the original building. From the very beginning KaDeWe was Berlin's most exclusive department store with a comprehensive collection of goods for sale and with a slogan that ran "In our shop a customer is a king, and the King is a customer".

After World War II, KaDeWe effectively became the symbol of the economic success of West Berlin. You can buy everything here, however, the main attraction must be the gourmet's paradise, with the largest collection of foodstuffs in the whole of Europe. Here there are exotic fruits and vegetables, live fish and seafood, 100 varieties of tea, more than 2,400 wines and a host of other gastronomic delights. KaDeWe also has a restaurant, the Wintergarten.

The sculpture *Berlin*, symbolizing the former divided Berlin

AROUND SCHLOSS CHARLOTTENBURG

THE AREA SURROUNDING Schloss Charlottenburg is one of the most enchanting regions of the city, full of greenery and attractive buildings dating from the end of the 19th century. Originally a small settlement called Lützow, it was only when Elector Friedrich III (later King Friedrich I) built his wife's summer retreat here at the end of the 17th century *(see p19)* that this town attained significance. Initially called Schloss Lietzenburg, the palace was renamed Schloss Charlottenburg after the death of Queen Sophie Charlotte. By the 18th century Charlottenburg had become a town, and was for many years an independent administration, inhabited by wealthy people living in elegant villas. It became officially part of Berlin in 1920, and despite World War II and the ensuing division of the city, the central section of this area has kept its historic character.

Urn at Schloss Charlottenburg

SIGHTS AT A GLANCE

Museums
Ägyptisches Museum **9**
Bröhan-Museum **11**
Hohenzollern-Museum **3**
Museum für Vor-
    und Frühgeschichte **5**
Sammlung Berggruen **10**

Historic Buildings
Belvedere **8**
Luisenkirche **13**
Mausoleum **7**

Neuer Pavillon
    (Schinkel-Pavillon) **4**
Schloss Charlottenburg
    pp160–61 **1**
Schlossstrasse Villas **12**

Parks and Gardens
Schlosspark **6**

GETTING THERE
The best routes to the palace are bus 109, 110, 145, X-21 and X-26; U-Bahn 7 to Richard-Wagner-Platz, U-Bahn 2 or 12 to Sophie-Charlotte-Platz or S-Bahn 45 or 46 to Westend station.

Monuments
Reiterdenkmal des Grossen
    Kurfürsten **2**

KEY
	Street-by-Street map *pp158–9*
U	U-Bahn station
	Bus terminus
P	Parking

0 metres   600
0 yards   600

◁ **The façade of Schloss Charlottenburg, originally the summer residence of Elector Friedrich III**

Street-by Street: Around the Schloss

THE PARK SURROUNDING the former royal summer residence in Charlottenburg is one of the most picturesque places in Berlin. Visitors are drawn here by the meticulous post-war rebuilding of this luxury Baroque complex and outlying structures, whose marvellous interiors were once home to Prussian nobles. The wings of the palace and its pavilions house interesting exhibitions. After a stroll in the beautiful park, you can take refreshment in the Kleine Orangerie.

Detail from the main gate

★ **Schloss Charlottenburg**
The central section of the palace is called Nering-Eosanderbau, in honour of the architects who designed the building ❶

Museum für Vor- und Frühgeschichte
The museum is housed in a pavilion which served formerly as the court theatre, designed by Carl Gotthard Langhans ❺

Monument to the Great Elector
The momument to the Great Elector was funded by his son King Friedrich I and designed by Andreas Schlüter ❷

Kleine Orangerie

Hohenzollern-Museum
This museum is planned for the new wing of the palace and will house a selection of precious items from the royal collection ❸

KEY
– – – Suggested route

Mausoleum
In the Neo-Classical mausoleum built for Queen Luise, members of the royal family are laid to rest ❼

LOCATOR MAP
See Street Finder map 2.

Belvedere
In 1960 Karl Bobeck created the group of statues that surmount the Belvedere, in imitation of the original figures which were designed by Johann Eckstein ❽

Palace Park
A French-style park, laid-out in a geometric pattern, extends behind the palace ❻

★ **Neuer Pavillon**
In front of the western elevation of this pavilion are two granite columns (1840), topped by statues of Victory, the work of Christian Daniel Rauch ❹

0 metres   150

0 yards   150

STAR SIGHTS

★ **Schloss Charlottenburg**

★ **Neuer Pavillon**

Schloss Charlottenburg ❶

THE PALACE IN CHARLOTTENBURG was intended as a summer home for Sophie Charlotte, Elector Friedrich III's wife. Construction began in 1695 to a design by Johann Arnold Nering. Between 1701 and 1713 Johann Eosander von Göthe enlarged the palace, crowning it with a cupola and adding the orangery wing. Subsequent extensions were undertaken by Frederick the Great (Friedrich II), who added the east wing, designed by Georg Wenzeslaus von Knobelsdorff, between 1740 and 1746. Restored to its former elegance following World War II, its collection of richly decorated interiors is unequalled in Berlin.

GALLERY GUIDE
The ground floor of the main building must be visited by guided tour. The upper floor and the Neuer Flügel, containing Oriental porcelain and Rococo paintings, can be visited independently.

First floor

Ground floor

★ **Porzellankabinett**
This exquisite mirrored gallery has walls lined from top to bottom with a fine display of Japanese and Chinese porcelain.

Schlosskapelle
Only the pulpit in the court chapel is original to the palace. All the remaining furniture and fittings, including the splendid royal box, are reconstructions.

Main entrance

Façade
The central section of the palace is the oldest part of the building, and is the work of Johann Arnold Nering.

Cupola
The palace's tall, Baroque cupola completes the perspective from Schlossstrasse.

Fortuna
A new sculpture by Richard Scheibe crowns the palace, replacing the original statue destroyed during World War II.

VISITORS' CHECKLIST

Luisenplatz. **Map** 2 E2.
Altes Schloss (Nering-Eosanderbau) (32 09 12 75.
U *Richard-Wagner-Platz &
Sophie-Charlotte- Platz.*
S *Westend.* 109, 145, 210,
X-21. ☐ *9am–5pm Tue–Fri,
10am–5pm Sat & Sun.*
compulsory on ground floor only.
Neuer Flügel (Knobels-dorff-Flügel) (32 09 12 02.
☐ *10am–6pm Tue–Fri,
11am–6pm Sat & Sun.*

KEY

☐ Official reception rooms

☐ Apartments of Sophie-Charlotte

☐ Neuer Flügel or Knobelsdorff-Flügel exhibition space

☐ Friedrich Wilhelm II's summer apartments

☐ Mecklenburg apartments

☐ Apartments of Friedrich Wilhelm IV

☐ Friedrich Wilhelm II's winter apartments

☐ Frederick the Great's apartments

Eichengalerie
This long gallery, lined with huge oil paintings and decorated with oak-panelling, was completed in 1713.

Weisser Saal

Goldene
Galerie

Neuer Flügel
The new wing holds the elegant apartments and exquisite furniture of Frederick the Great.

Entrance to
Neuer Flügel

STAR SIGHTS

★ **Porzellankabinett**

★ **Gersaint's Shop Sign**

★ **Gersaint's Shop Sign** (1720)
An avid collector of French painting, Frederick the Great bought this and seven other fine canvases by Antoine Watteau for his collection.

CD Friedrich's *Moonrise over the Sea* now in the Alte Nationalgalerie (*p78*)

Reiterdenkmal des Grossen Kurfürsten ❷

MONUMENT TO THE GREAT ELECTOR

Luisenplatz. **Map** 2 E2. 🇺 *Richard-Wagner-Platz & Sophie-Charlotte-Platz.* Ⓢ *Westend.* 🚌 *109, 145, 210, X-21.*

T HE STATUE OF THE Great Elector (Friedrich Wilhelm) is the finest in Berlin and was paid for by his son, Elector Friedrich III (later King Friedrich I). Designed by Andreas Schlüter to be cast in one piece, the statue was started in 1696 but not finished until 1703. It was initially erected near the former Berlin palace, by Lange Brücke (now called Rathausbrücke). The statue was moved to safety during World War II but ironically, on the return journey, the barge transporting the monument sank in the port of Tegel.
    In 1949 the statue was retrieved intact from the water and erected in the courtyard of Schloss Charlottenburg. However, it lacked the original base which was left behind in East Berlin, so a copy was commissioned. The original base finally ended up in the Bodemuseum topped with a replica of the statue.
    The statue portrays the Great Elector as a warrior in ancient armour (albeit wearing a 17th-century wig) mounted on horseback, triumphant over the figures of prisoners of war around the base. The base itself is decorated with

patriotic reliefs of allegorical scenes. One scene depicts the kingdom surrounded by figures representing History, Peace and the Spree river; another shows the kingdom protected by embodiments of Faith, Bravery (in the form of Mucius Scaevola) and Strength (represented by Hercules).

Hohenzollern-Museum ❸

Luisenplatz (Schloss Charlotten-burg–Neuer Flügel). **Map** 2 E2. 🇨 *20 90 55 55.* 🇺 *Richard-Wagner-Platz & Sophie-Charlotte-Platz.* Ⓢ *Westend.* 🚌 *109, 145, 210.* ⭘ *until 2005 for the installation of the new collection.*

B UILT BETWEEN 1740 and 1746, the new wing of Schloss Charlottenburg used to house the popular Galerie der Romantik. The main part of this collection of Romantic paintings has now been

returned to the Alte National-galerie *(see p78).* The rest have been moved to the Neuer Pavillon. In its place, a new museum that will bring together precious items from the Hohenzollern family collection, including paintings, craft objects and furniture, is due to open in 2005.

Neuer Pavillon (Schinkel-Pavillon) ❹

Luisenplatz (Schlosspark Charlottenburg). **Map** 2 F2. 🇨 *32 09 11.* 🇺 *Richard-Wagner-Platz & Sophie-Charlotte-Platz.* Ⓢ *Westend.* 🚌 *109, 210, X-21.* ⭘ *10am–5pm Tue–Sun.* 🅰

T HIS CHARMING Neo-Classical pavillon, with its clean lines and first-floor balcony, was built for Friedrich Wilhelm III and his second wife, Princess Auguste von Liegnitz. During a visit to Naples, the king stayed in the Villa Reale del Chiamonte and was so impressed that he commissioned Karl Friedrich Schinkel to build him something similar. The pavilion was completed for the king's birthday on 3 August 1825. Schinkel designed a two-storey structure with a central stair-case and ranged the rooms around it in perfect symmetry. Pillared galleries, on the first floor, added variety to the eastern and western elevations. A cast iron balcony runs around the entire structure.
    The display inside the pavilion reveals the original splendour and atmosphere of

The Neuer Pavillon which was modelled on a Neapolitan villa

the aristocratic interiors, enhanced with pictures and sculptures of the period. The prize picture is a renowned panorama of Berlin dated 1834, painted by Eduard Gärtner from the roof of the Friedrichs-werdersche Kirche *(see p63)*.

The painting collection has recently been enhanced through the addition of works from the old Galerie der Romantik. These include landscapes by Casper David Friedrich. You can also admire the paintings of Karl Friedrich Schinkel, who was not only a great architect but also a fine painter of fabulous architectural fantasies.

**Urn (c.800 BC) from the Museum
für Vor- und Frühgeschichte**

Museum für Vor- und Frühgeschichte ❺

**MUSEUM OF PRE- AND
EARLY HISTORY**

Luisenplatz (Schloss Charlotten-burg–Theater). **Map** 2 E2. 🞁 *20 90 55 55.* Ⓤ *Richard-Wagner-Platz & Sophie-Charlotte-Platz.* Ⓢ *Westend.* 🚍 *109, 145, 210, X-21.* 🞅 *10am–6pm Tue–Fri, 11am–6pm Sat & Sun.* 🖼 🖼 ♿

O RIGINALLY USED as the court theatre, this Neo-Classical pavilion was designed by Carl Gotthard Langhans and added to the orangery wing of Schloss Charlottenburg between 1787 and 1791. It now holds a museum that documents the development of early cultures and civilizations. The evolution of mankind from prehistoric times, through the Stone Age, Bronze Age and Iron Age up to medieval times is portrayed by means of dioramas, skulls (real and imitation) and a

large display of pottery, tools, weapons and artifacts. A similar wealth of archaeological finds charts the growth of Celtic, Germanic, Slavic, Baltic and even Sumerian civilizations.

The museum's best display is a magnificent collection from the ancient city of Troy, donated in 1881 by Heinrich Schliemann. The collection contains an array of tools and pottery on the second floor, and a spectacular collection of gold jewellery known as "The Treasure of Priam". Some of the exhibits are replicas, the originals having disappeared after World War II. Many origi-nals, however, are now in the Pushkin Museum, Moscow.

Schlosspark ❻

PALACE PARK

Luisenplatz (Schloss Charlottenburg). **Map** 2 D1. Ⓤ *Richard-Wagner-Platz & Sophie-Charlotte-Platz.* Ⓢ *Westend.* 🚍 *109, 145, 210, X-21.*

T HIS EXTENSIVE royal park surrounding Schloss Charlottenburg *(see pp160–61)*, criss-crossed with tidy gravel paths, is a favourite place for Berliners to stroll at the weekend. The park is largely the result of reconstruction work carried out after World War II, when 18th-century prints were used to help reconstruct the varied layout of the original grounds. Immediately behind Schloss Charlottenburg is a French-style Baroque garden, made to a strict geometrical design with a vibrant patchwork of flower beds, carefully trimmed shrubs and ornate fountains adorned with replicas of antique sculp-tures. Further away from the

palace, beyond the curved carp lake, is a less formal English-style landscaped park, the original layout of which was created between 1819 and 1828 under the direction of the renowned royal gar-dener, Peter Joseph Lenné.

Mausoleum ❼

Luisenplatz (Schlosspark Charlotten-burg) **Map** 2 D2. 🞁 *32 09 11.* Ⓤ *Richard-Wagner-Platz & Sophie-Charlotte-Platz.* Ⓢ *Westend.* 🚍 *109, 145, 210.* 🞅 *Apr–Oct: 10am–noon 1–5pm Tue–Sun.* 🖼

Q UEEN LUISE, the beloved wife of Friedrich Wilhelm III, was laid to rest in this dignified, modest building, set among the trees in Schloss-park. The mausoleum was designed by Karl Friedrich Schinkel, in the style of a Doric portico-fronted temple.

In the original design, the queen's sarcophagus was housed in the crypt while the tombstone (actually a ceno-taph sculpted by Christian Daniel Rauch) stood in the centre of the mausoleum. After the death of Friedrich Wilhelm in 1840, the mausoleum was refurbished; an apse added and the queen's tomb moved to one side, leaving room for her husband's tomb, also designed by Rauch. The second wife of the king, Princess Auguste von Liegnitz, was also buried in the crypt of the mausoleum, but without a tombstone.

Between the years 1890 and 1894, the tombs of Kaiser Wilhelm I and his wife, Auguste von Sachsen-Weimar, were added to the crypt. Both monuments are the work of Erdmann Encke.

French-style garden in the Schloss Charlottenburg park

The Belvedere's Baroque flourishes and clean Neo-Classical lines

Belvedere ❽

Spandauer Damm (Schlosspark
Charlottenburg). **Map** 2 E1.
(32 09 11. **U** Richard-Wagner-
Platz & Sophie-Charlotte-Platz.
Ⓢ Westend. 🚌 109, 145, 210, X-21.
◯ Apr–Oct: 10am–5pm Tue–Sun;
Nov–Mar: noon–4pm Tue–Fri, noon–
5pm Sat & Sun. ♿

THE BELVEDERE IS a summer-
house in the Schlosspark
which served as a tea pavilion
for Friedrich Wilhelm II and,
in times of war, as a watchtower. It dates from 1788 and
was designed by Carl Gotthard
Langhans. The architect mixed
Baroque and Neo-Classical
elements, giving the building
an oval central structure with
four straight-sided annexes.
The building is crowned by
a low dome topped with a
sculpture of three cherubs
dragging a basket of flowers.
  Ruined during World War II,
the summer-house was reconstructed between 1956 and
1960 and adapted to serve as
exhibition space. The exhibition is a large collection of
porcelain from the Berlin Königliche Porzellan-Manufaktur
(Royal Porcelain Workshop),
which has pieces from the
Rococo period up to late
Biedermeier, including some
outstanding individual items.

Ägyptisches Museum ❾

EGYPTIAN MUSEUM

Schlossstrasse 70. **Map** 2 E3.
(20 90 55 55. **U** Richard-Wagner-
Platz & Sophie-Charlotte-Platz.
Ⓢ Westend. 🚌 109, 145, 210,
X-21. ◯ 10am–6pm Tue–Sun.

THE TWO PAVILIONS on either
side of Schlossstrasse were
intended as officers' barracks
for the Kings's Garde du Corps.
Built between the years 1851
and 1859 by Friedrich August
Stüler, they were inspired by
a design by King Friedrich
Wilhelm IV. The eastern
pavilion joins the stable
block and now houses the
collection of the Egyptian
Museum. Numerous
sculptures, sarcophagi,
murals and architectural
fragments of various
eras are on display,
including the Berlin
Green Head, a 4th-
century BC head
carved from green
stone. The greatest
attraction, however,
is the fascinating
collection from the
19th century
archaeological
digs by Richard
Lepsius and

Ludwig Borchardt in Tell el-
Amarna. This was the capital
of Egypt during the era of the
reign of Amenhotep IV, a
Pharaoh in the 14th century
BC, also called Akhenaten.
He revolutionized Egyptian
religion, introducing the cult
of the god Aton, and also
brought about a radical change
in the basic principles of repre-
sentative arts. In a break from
previous traditions he and his
wife, Nefertiti, are depicted
with broad hips and swollen
stomachs. While the Pharaoh is
plainly depicted, the queen's
face is beautiful, as can be
seen from the other
representations in the museum.
The most renowned is the
delicate, long-necked Nefertiti
Bust, carved from limestone
and carefully painted. This
delightful exhibit was
discovered in 1912 in the
workshop of the ancient
Egyptian sculptor Thutmosis.

Sammlung Berggruen ❿

Schlossstrasse 1. **Map** 2 E3.
(20 90 55 55. **U** Richard-
Wagner-Platz & Sophie-Charlotte-
Platz. **Ⓢ** Westend. 🚌 109, 145,
210, X-21. ◯ 10am–6pm Tue–Sun.

HEINZ BERGGRUEN assembled
this tasteful collection of
art dating from the late 19th
and first half of the 20th century. Born and educated in
Berlin, he emigrated to the US
in 1936, spent most of his life
in Paris, but finally
entrusted his collection
to the city of his birth.
The museum opened
in 1996, in what was
once the west pavilion
of the barracks using
space freed up by
moving the Antiken-
sammlung to Museum
Island (see p75). The
exhibition halls were
modified according to
the designs of Hilmer
and Sattler, who also
designed the layout of
the Gemäldegalerie.
The Sammlung

**Figure from Ägyptisches
Museum (c.660 BC)**

Pablo Picasso's *Woman in a Hat* (1939), Sammlung Berggruen

Berggruen is particularly well-known for its large collection of quality paintings, drawings and gouaches by Pablo Picasso. In addition to these, the museum displays more than 20 works by Paul Klee and paintings by other major artists from that time. The exhibition is supplemented by some excellent sculptures, particularly those of Henri Laurens and Alberto Giacometti.

Bröhan-Museum ⓫

Schlossstrasse 1a. **Map** 2 E3.
[C] *32 69 06 00.* [U] *Richard-Wagner-Platz & Sophie-Charlotte-Platz.*
ⓢ *Westend.* 🚌 *109, 145, 210, X-21.*
◯ *10am–6pm Tue–Sun.* ● *24 & 31 Dec.* 📷

L OCATED IN A late-Neo-Classical building which, like the Sammlung Berggruen, was formerly used as army barracks, is this small but interesting museum. The collection of decorative arts was amassed by Karl H Bröhan, who from 1966 collected works of art from the Art Nouveau (Jugendstil or Secessionist) and Art Deco styles. The paintings of the artists particularly connected with the Berlin Secessionist movement, such as Karl Hagermeister and Hans Baluschek, are especially well represented. Alongside the paintings there are fine examples of other media and crafts: furniture, ceramics, glassware, silverwork and textiles.

Art Deco vase, Brohan-Museum

THE GREAT ELECTOR (1620–88)

The Elector Friedrich Wilhelm was one of the most famous rulers of the Hohenzollern dynasty. He inherited the position of Elector of Brandenburg in 1640. Brandenburg-Prussia, founded in 1618, was subject to the Polish crown. One of his first duties was to rebuild the region after the devastation of the 30 Years' War *(see p19)* and in 1660 he wrested the territory from Poland. During the course of his reign, Berlin became a powerful city. Rich families from all over Europe, fleeing persecution in their own land, chose to settle in Berlin – wealthy Dutch merchants, Huguenots from France and Jews from Vienna following the Edict of Potsdam (1685).

Each of the main halls features an individual artist, but often using an array of artistic media. There is also a display of furniture by Hector Guimard, Eugène Gaillard, Henri van de Velde and Joseph Hoffmann, glasswork by Emile Gallé, and porcelain from the best European manufacturers.

Schlossstrasse Villas ⓬

Schlossstrasse 65–67. **Map** 2 E3.
[U] *Sophie-Charlotte-Platz.* 🚌 *210.*

M OST OF THE historic villas and buildings that once graced Schlossstrasse no longer exist. However, careful restoration of a few villas enables the visitor to get a feel for what the atmosphere must have been like at the end of the 19th century. It is worth taking a stroll down Schlossstrasse to look at three of the renovated villas — No. 65, No. 66 and especially No. 67. The latter villa was built in 1873, in a Neo-Classical style to a design by G Töbelmann. After World War II, the building was refurbished to return it to its former splendour. The front garden, however, a characteristic of the area, was only returned to its original state in 1986, when several villas had their gardens restored.

If you continue the walk down the nearby Schustehrusstrasse, there is an interesting school building at No. 39–43 linked to the Villa Oppenheim since the end of the 19th century. In the same area another school building on Nithackstrasse has survived. Built between 1913 and 1914, its sides are covered in pretty terracotta decorations.

Luisenkirche ⓭

LUISE CHURCH

Gierkeplatz. **Map** 2 F3. [C] *341 90 61.* [U] *Richard-Wagner-Platz & Sophie-Charlotte-Platz.* 🚌 *109, 145, X-9.* ◯ *during Sunday service (10 & 11:30am).*

T HIS SMALL CHURCH has undergone a series of re-designs and refurbishments in its lifetime. The original plans by Philipp Gerlach were first adapted by Martin Böhme, before the church was built (1713–16). Its Baroque styling was removed in the next course of rebuilding, undertaken by Karl Friedrich Schinkel from 1823 to 1826, when the church was renamed in memory of Queen Luise, who died in 1810. The most recent refurbishment took place after the church suffered major damage during World War II.

The shape of the church is based on a traditional Greek cross, with a tower at the front. The interior fixtures and fittings are not the originals, and the elegant stained-glass windows were only made in 1956.

FURTHER AFIELD

ERLIN IS AN EXTENSIVE city with a totally unique character, shaped by its history. Up until 1920 the actual city of Berlin consisted only of the districts which now comprise mainly Mitte, Tiergarten, Wedding, Prenzlauer Berg, Friedrichshain and Kreuzberg. It was surrounded by satellite towns and villages, which for many years had been evolving independently. Each of these had its own administrative centre, parish church, and individual architecture.

Coat of Arms on the Oberbaumbrücke

In 1920, as part of great administrative reforms, seven towns were incorporated into Berlin, along with 59 communes, and 27 country estates. This reform effected the creation of an entirely new city occupying around 900 sq km (348 sq miles), with a population that had expanded to 3.8 million.

In this way the range of the metropolis extended to small towns with medieval origins, such as Spandau.

Private estates and palaces, such as Britz and Niederschönhausen, were absorbed into Berlin. So were many old villages, such as Marienfelde with its 13th-century church. Suburban housing developments full of luxury villas were also incorporated.

Over the last hundred years the faces of many of these places have changed. Modern housing developments have arisen together with industrial centres, although the character of individual areas has remained intact. Thanks to this diversity, a stay in Berlin is like visiting many cities simultaneously. A short journey by S-Bahn enables you to travel from a metropolitan city centre of the 21st century to the vast forests of the Grunewald or the beach at Wannsee. You can explore everything from Dahlem's tranquil streets lined with villas to Spandau with its Renaissance citadel and vast Gothic church of St Nicholas.

MAP OF GREATER BERLIN

See pp186–7

See pp168–9

See pp184–5

See pp170–71

See pp172–3

See pp182–3

See pp178–9

See pp174–5

See pp176–7

See pp180–81

KEY

▪ Central Berlin	▬ Autobahn (motorway)	▬ Railway line
▫ Outskirts of Berlin	▬ Main road	0 kilometres 3
✈ Airport	▭ Minor road	0 miles 3

◁ **The Funkturm or radio tower in Berlin's western outskirts, illuminated at night** *(see p183)*

Northeast Berlin

I N THE NORTHEAST of Berlin, but still within the Mitte district, a fragment of the Berlin Wall has survived; this has been earmarked as a place of remembrance. Further east extends Prenzlauer Berg *(see pp170–71)*, currently the most fashionable area for alternative youth culture. In the southern part of Pankow is the Baroque palace of Niederschönhausen. From here it is also worth setting off to see the Weissensee district, which has one of the largest Jewish cemeteries in Europe.

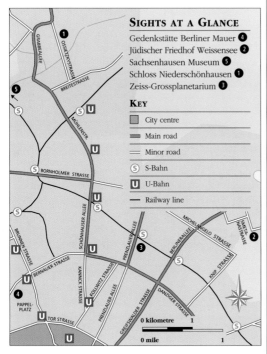

SIGHTS AT A GLANCE

Gedenkstätte Berliner Mauer ❹
Jüdischer Friedhof Weissensee ❷
Sachsenhausen Museum ❺
Schloss Niederschönhausen ❶
Zeiss-Grossplanetarium ❸

KEY

▨	City centre
▬	Main road
─	Minor road
Ⓢ	S-Bahn
Ⓤ	U-Bahn
─	Railway line

0 kilometre 1
0 mile 1

Schloss Nieder-schönhausen ❶

Ossietzkystrasse Ⓢ *Pankow.* 🚋 *52.*
🚌 *107, 155, 250, 255, X-33.*
Schloss ⬛ *closed to public.* **Park**
⬛ *8am–8pm daily.*

T HIS PALACE, located in an extensive and picturesque park, belonged to the von Dohna family during the 17th century. Ownership of the estate passed to the Elector Friedrich III in 1691, for whom Johann Arnold Nering designed the palace. In 1704 it was extended to a design by Johann Friedrich Eosander von Göthe, who added side wings. The palace was home to Queen Christine, estranged wife of Frederick the Great, between 1740 and 1797. In 1763 further extensive refurbishment was undertaken by architect Johann Boumann.

A section of the garden elevation of Schloss Niederschönhausen

The property remained in the hands of the Prussian royal family for the next hundred years. Among those who resided here were Princess Auguste von Liegnitz, following the death of her husband, King Friedrich Wilhelm III.

After World War II the rebuilt palace was occupied by the president of the German Democratic Republic, Wilhelm Pieck. In 1990 Round Table discussions were held here and the treaty to reunify Germany was signed here on 3 October that year.

Make time for a stroll through the vast park, which has kept the character bestowed by Peter Joseph Lenné in the 1820s.

Jüdischer Friedhof Weissensee ❷

Herbert-Baum-Strasse 45. ⬛ *925 08 33.* ⬛ *8am–4pm (5pm in winter) Sun–Thu, 8am–3pm Fri.* Ⓢ *Greifswalder Strasse, then* 🚋 *2, 3, 4, 13, 23, 24.*

T HIS EXTENSIVE Jewish cemetery is the final resting place for more than 115,000 Berliners, many of whom were victims of Nazi persecution. The cemetery was established in 1880 according to a design by Hugo Licht.

By the main entrance is a place of remembrance for the victims of the Holocaust, with plaques bearing the names of the concentration camps. Buried here are renowned figures from Berlin's Jewish cultural and commercial past. Among others here rest the publisher Samuel Fischer and the restaurateur Berthold Kempinski.

Some tombstones are outstanding works of art, such as that of the Panowsky family, designed by Ludwig Hoffmann, or the Cubist tombstone of Albert Mendel, designed by Walter Gropius.

In 1999 Weissensee cemetery was desecrated in an act of anti-Semitic vandalism. More than 100 headstones were kicked over and some were smeared with swastikas.

Silvery dome of the Zeiss-Grossplanetarium

Zeiss-Gross-planetarium ❸

Prenzlauer Allee 80 (Ernst-Thälmann-Park) 42 18 45 12; 42 18 45 16 (reservations). Prenzlauer Allee, then 1. call for details.

THE SILVERY DOME visible from afar is the huge planetarium, built in the grounds of a park dedicated to the memory of the inter-war communist leader Ernst Thälmann, who died at Buchenwald concentration camp. The foyer of the planetarium houses an exhibition of optical equipment and various accessories produced by the renowned factory of Carl-Zeiss-Jena.

Gedenkstätte Berliner Mauer ❹

Bernauer Strasse 111. Nordbahnhof. Bernauer Strasse. 147, 245. **Wall Documentation Center** 464 10 30. 10am–5pm Wed–Sun. 11am & 2pm Sat & Sun.

ON THE NIGHT between 12 and 13 August 1961 the East German authorities decided to close the border around the western sectors of Berlin. Initially the Berlin Wall (die Mauer) consisted simply of rolls of barbed wire. However, these were soon replaced by a 4-m (13-ft) wall safeguarded by a second wall made from reinforced concrete. This second wall was topped with a thick pipe to prevent people from reaching the top of the Wall with their fingers.

Along the Wall ran what was known as a "death zone", an area controlled by guards with dogs. Where the border passed close to houses, the inhabitants were relocated, while windows on to the "western" street were bricked up. Along the border with West Berlin there were 293 watch towers and 57 bunkers. Later, there were alarms, too.

On 9 November 1989, with the help of Soviet leader Mikhail Gorbachev, the Berlin Wall was finally breached. Dismantling it took much longer, however, with more than a million tons of rubble to be removed.

Only small fragments of the Wall have survived. One of these, along Bernauer Strasse between Acker- and Bergstrasse, is now an official place of remembrance.

During the Wall's 28-year existence, about 5,000 people managed to escape into West Berlin; a total of 192 people were killed by the Eastern border guards while attempting to do so.

Sachsenhausen Museum ❺

Strasse der Nationen 22, Oranienburg. 03301/2000. Oranienburg, then 804. Apr–Sep: 8:30am–6pm Tue–Sun; Oct–Mar: 8:30am–4:30pm Tue–Sun. W www.sachsenhausen.brandenburg.de

BUILT BY THE NAZIS in 1936, the concentration camp at Sachsenhausen was liberated in 1945 by the Russians. Up to 200,000 people were incarcerated in this camp during its nine-year existence. However, when the Soviet Army entered Sachsenhausen, there were only 3,000 inmates in the camp, mostly women and sick people.

The iron gate at the entrance bears a sign that reads "Arbeit macht frei" ("Work will set you free"), and indeed, many early prisoners were released upon demonstrating that they had learned how to be "good German citizens". By 1939, however, fewer prisoners were being released. It is estimated that over 30,000 people died in the camp, killed by hunger, disease or mass extermination.

Sachsenhausen is now a museum. Each area of the camp hosts a relevant exhibit – for example, the one in the former infirmary focuses on medicine and racism under the Nazi regime. Other exhibits illustrate the daily life of the prisoners, or the way Sachsenhausen worked as a Soviet Special Camp between 1945 and 1950, when it housed Nazi functionaries and political undesirables.

Former entrance to the Sachsenhausen Prison Camp

Prenzlauer Berg

Once one of the most impoverished and densely populated working-class districts of Berlin, the 19th-century tenement houses in Prenzlauer Berg are now occupied by students, young families, artists and an increasing number of West Berliners looking for more affordable apartments. Even during communist times, this area was known for its independent art and nightlife scene which still thrives today around Kollwitzplatz, along the beautifully restored Husemannstrasse and the Kastanienallee, and in former factories in the vicinity.

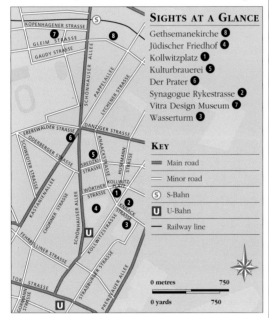

Sights at a Glance

Gethsemanekirche **8**
Jüdischer Friedhof **4**
Kollwitzplatz **1**
Kulturbrauerei **5**
Der Prater **6**
Synagogue Rykestrasse **2**
Vitra Design Museum **7**
Wasserturm **3**

Key

━━━ Main road
─── Minor road
Ⓢ S-Bahn
Ⓤ U-Bahn
─── Railway line

0 metres 750
0 yards 750

Kollwitzplatz **1**

Ⓤ *Senefelderplatz.*

This green square is named after the German painter and sculptress Käthe Kollwitz (1867–1945), who once lived nearby. It was here that the socially engaged artist observed and painted the daily hardships of the working-class people living in overcrowded tenements. One of her sculptures stands on the square which is now the major nightlife hub of the district, with numerous trendy bars, restaurants and shops that extend into the surrounding streets, primarily along Kollwitzstrasse. Käthe Kollwitz's work can be seen at the Käthe-Kollwitz-Museum (*see p154*).

Synagogue Rykestrasse **2**

Rykestrasse 53. **℃** *44 25 931 or 88 02 80 by appointment only.* Ⓤ *Senefelderplatz.*

This small synagogue is one of the few reminders of old Jewish life in Berlin, and one of the few in Germany left almost intact during the Nazi terror regime. Built in 1904, the red-brick synagogue has a basilica-like nave with three aisles and certain Moorish features. Thanks to the fact that it was built inside a huge tenement area, Nazi SA troops did not set it on fire during the "*Kristallnacht*" pogrom on 9 November 1938, when hundreds of other synagogues were razed to the ground. Despite being hit by bombs during World War II, the synagogue has been restored to its old glory and can be visited by appointment.

Wasserturm **3**

Knaackstrasse/Belforter Strasse.
Ⓤ *Senefelderplatz.*

The unofficial symbol of the district is a 30 m (98 ft) high water tower, standing high on the former mill hill in the heart of Prenzlauer Berg. It was here that some of the windmills, once typical in Prenzlauer Berg, turned and ground grain, providing flour for the city's population. The distinctive brick water tower was built in 1874 by Wilhelm Vollhering and served as a water reservoir for the country's first running water system. Later, the tower was transformed into an apartment complex. In the 1930s, the basement served as a *wildes Konzentrationslager*, a make-shift jail, where Nazi SA troops held and tortured Communist opponents. This dark period is commemorated by a plaque.

The giant Wasserturm looming high in Knaackstrasse

Jüdischer Friedhof **4**

Schönhauser Allee 23–25. **℃** *925 08 33.* Ⓤ *Senefelderplatz.* ◯ *8am–4pm Mon–Thu, 8am–1pm Fri.* ● *day before Jewish holidays after 1pm and Jewish holidays.*

This small Jewish cemetery is hidden behind thick walls on Schönhauser Allee, but the serene atmosphere, with tall trees and thick

Gravestones in the peaceful Jüdischer Friedhof

undergrowth between the gravestones, is a welcome oasis for many visitors. The cemetery was laid out in 1827, even though the oldest gravestone dates back to the 14th century. It served as Berlin's second largest Jewish cemetery after the Jüdischer Friedhof Weissensee *(see p168)*. Among the many prominent Berliners resting here are the painter Max Liebermann (1847–1935), the composer and musical director of the Staatsoper Unter den Linden; Giacomo Meyerbeer (1791–1864); and the author David Friedländer (1750–1834).

Kulturbrauerei ❺

Schönhauser Allee 36–39. ☎ *44 31 51 00.* Ⓤ *Eberswalder Strasse.* 🚃 *50, 53.* **Sammlung Industrielle Gestaltung** ◯ *Varies for each exhibition. Telephone to check.*

THIS VAST Neo-Gothic, industrial red and yellow brick building is the former Schultheiss brewery, Berlin's most famous brewery, built by Franz Schwechten in 1889–1892. Now housing the Kulturbrauerei, the vast complex with several courtyards has been revived as a cultural and entertainment centre with theatres, restaurants and cafés, a cinema, as well as artists' ateliers. Inside the Kulturbrauerei, the **Sammlung Industrielle Gestaltung** (Collection of Industrial Design) features changing exhibitions on East German industrial product designs.

Der Prater ❻

Kastanienallee 7–9. ☎ *24 06 55.* Ⓤ *Eberswalder Strasse.* 🚃 *50, 53.*

DER PRATER HAS been one of Berlin's best known entertainment institutions for more than a century. The building, along with its quiet courtyard, was constructed in the 1840s and later became the city's largest beer garden *(see p249)*. It now not only houses a restaurant, but also stages a wide variety of pop, rock and folk concerts.

Vitra Design Museum ❼

Kopenhagener Strasse 58. ☎ *47 37 770.* Ⓢ *Schönhauser Allee.* ◯ *11am–8pm Tue–Sun, 11am–10pm Fri.* 📷 ✔

THIS STYLISH DESIGN museum is tucked away in a red-brick industrial power plant, designed by Hans Heinrich Müller in 1925. It presents changing exhibitions on international design, lifestyle, fashion, product design and architecture. Many of the exhibitions feature unique furniture. Past exhibitions have showcased works by Charles and Ray Eames, Cartier, Verner Panton, Issey Miyake and the style and designs of pop artists in the 1970s. The museum is a subsidiary of the famous Vitra Design Museum in Weil am Rhein, which is one of the world's leading design museums.

Kulturbrauerei tower

Gethsemanekirche ❽

Stargader Strasse 77. ☎ *44 57 745.* Ⓤ & Ⓢ *Schönhauser Allee.* ♦ *11am Sun.*

THE QUAINT LITTLE area surrounding this Neo-Gothic red-brick church is one of the most intact original communities to be found anywhere in Berlin. The neighbourhood is dominated by the Protestant Gethsemanekirche, which dates back to 1890. The church was one of several built on the order of Emperor Wilhelm II, who wanted to increase religious worship among the mostly Social Democratic working-classes living in Prenzlauer Berg and other areas. The building was designed by August Orth (1828–1911), one of the period's most important architects of churches and railway stations.

The Protestant community here is proud to have pioneered civil rights move- ments, and hosted political Anti-Nazi rallies from 1933–45. The congregation also questioned the socialist regime after World War II, while the church itself served as an assembly hall for peaceful opponents in October 1989. On 2 October that year, the praying crowd was brutally attacked by the East German secret service police, marking the start of the Communist regime's demise.

Today, the square is surrounded by beautiful restored buildings, housing many sidewalk restaurants,

Entrance to the red-brick Gethsemanekirche

Friedrichshain and Treptow

BOTH THESE DISTRICTS are situated to the southeast of Mitte and provide excellent opportunities for walks amid some spectacular remnants of Berlin's most recent history. Visitors can see the official face of the German Democratic Republic, as shown in the Socialist Realist architecture of Karl-Marx-Allee, and the Soviet ideals of nationalism in the huge monument to the Red Army in Treptower Park. A sharp contrast is provided by stark reminders of a less glorious past – the Berlin Wall, East Side Gallery and the grim watchtower on the border.

The park has undergone frequent redesigns in its history including, during World War II, the construction of two large bunkers. After the war, the site was covered with a mound of earth.

Between the years 1969 and 1973 a sports and games area was established in the park, although there is still plenty of room for leisurely strolls.

Fragment of Socialist Realist decoration from Karl-Marx-Allee

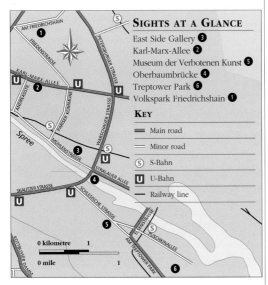

SIGHTS AT A GLANCE

East Side Gallery **3**
Karl-Marx-Allee **2**
Museum der Verbotenen Kunst **5**
Oberbaumbrücke **4**
Treptower Park **6**
Volkspark Friedrichshain **1**

KEY

▬▬▬	Main road
──	Minor road
Ⓢ	S-Bahn
Ⓤ	U-Bahn
──	Railway line

0 kilometre   1

0 mile   1

Volkspark Friedrichshain **1**

Am Friedrichshain/Friedenstrasse.
Map 8 F1. 🚌 142, 200, 348.

THIS EXTENSIVE PARK complex of Friedrichshain, with its picturesque nooks and crannies, was one of Berlin's first public parks. It was laid out in the 1840s on the basis of a design by Peter Joseph Lenné, with the idea of creating an alternative Tiergarten for the inhabitants of the eastern districts of the city.

The greatest attraction of the park is the Fountain of Fairy Tales – Märchenbrunnen by Ludwig Hoffmann, built from 1902 until 1913. It is a spectacular feature, in a Neo-Baroque style with fountain pools made from Tivoli stone, decorated with small statues of turtles and

other animals. The fountain is surrounded by well-known characters from the fairy tales by the Brothers Grimm.

Neo-Baroque Märchenbrunnen in Volkspark Friedrichshain

Karl-Marx-Allee **2**

Map 8 F3. Ⓤ *Strausberger Platz or Weberwiese.*

THE SECTION OF Karl-Marx-Allee between Strausberger Platz and Frankfurter Tor is effectively a huge open-air museum of Socialist Realist architecture. The route to the the east, leading on to Poland and Moscow, was named Stalinallee in 1949 and chosen as the site for the construction showpiece of the new German Democratic Republic. The avenue was widened to 90 m (300 ft) and in the course of the next ten years, huge residential tower blocks and a row of shops were built on it. The designers, led by Hermann Henselmann, succeeded in combining three sets of architectural guidelines. They used the style known in the Soviet Union as "pastry chef" according to the precept: "nationalistic in form but socialist in content", and linked the whole work to Berlin's own traditions. Hence there are motifs taken from famous Berlin architects Schinkel and Gontard, as well as from the renowned Meissen porcelain.

The buildings on this street, renamed Karl-Marx-Allee in 1961, are now considered historic monuments. The buildings have been cleaned up and the crumbling details are gradually being restored.

East Side Gallery ❸

Mühlenstrasse. Ⓢ & Ⓤ *Warschauer Strasse.* Ⓢ *Hauptbahnhof.* 🚌 *142.*

SINCE 1990, this 1300-m (one mile) section of the Berlin Wall, running along Mühlenstrasse between Hauptbahnhof and Oberbaumbrücke, has been known as the East Side Gallery. A huge collection of graffiti is on display here, comprising the work of 118 different artists from 21 countries. This expansive display was organized by the Scottish artist Chris MacLean.

Oberbaumbrücke ❹

Ⓢ & Ⓤ *Warschauer Strasse* Ⓤ *Schlesisches Tor.* 🚌 *265.*

THIS PRETTY BRIDGE crossing the Spree river was built from 1894 to 1896 to a design by Otto Stahn. It is actually made from reinforced concrete, but the arches are covered with red brick. The most decorative element of the bridge is a Neo-Gothic arcade which supports a line of the U-Bahn. The central arch of the bridge is marked by a pair of crenellated Neo-Gothic towers.

The bridge was not open to traffic for 12 or so years prior to reunification, as it linked districts from opposing sides of the Berlin Wall. Only pedestrians with the relevant documents were able to use this bridge. After reunification and renovation, it was returned to full working order.

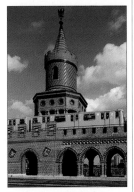

The picturesque Neo-Gothic archway of Oberbaumbrücke

Museum der Verbotenen Kunst ❺

MUSEUM OF FORBIDDEN ARTS

Im Schlesischen Busch (Puschkinallee/ Schlesische Strasse). 📞 *532 00 09.* Ⓤ *Schlesisches Tor.* Ⓢ *Treptower Park.* 🚌 *265.* **Park** ☐ *Apr–Oct: noon–6pm Sat, Sun.*

IN A NEGLECTED PARK near the former Berlin Wall stands the only remaining watchtower in the border control system that divided East and West Berlin.

The upper floor has been preserved as it was during the Cold War years, when it was used by border guards to monitor the Wall. While it is possible to visit the park, you will need to telephone ahead to find out when the tower is open to the public.

Museum der Verbotenen Kunst in the last remaining watchtower

Treptower Park ❻

Archenhold-Sternwarte, Alt-Treptow 1. Ⓢ *Treptower Park.* 🚌 *166, 167, 265.* **Archenhold Sternwarte** 📞 *53 48 080.* 🗓 *2–4:30pm Wed–Sun.*

THE VAST PARK in Treptow was laid out in the 1860s on the initiative and design of Johann Gustav Meyer. In 1919 it was where revolutionaries Karl Liebknecht, Wilhelm Pieck and Rosa Luxemburg assembled 150,000-strong group of striking workers.

The park, however, is best known for the colossal monument to the Red Army. Built between 1946 and 1949, it stands on the grave of 5,000

Gigantic wreath commemorating the Red Army in Treptower Park

Soviet soldiers killed in the battle for Berlin in 1945. The gateway is marked by a vast granite sculpture of a grieving Russian Motherland surrounded by statues of Red Army soldiers. This leads to the mausoleum, topped by an 11-m (35-ft) high figure of a soldier rescuing a child and resting his mighty sword on a smashed swastika. The whole scheme was the work of architect Jakow Białopolski and sculptor Jewgien Wuczeticz.

In the farthest section of the park it is worth going to see the astronomical observatory, **Archenhold Sternwarte**, built for a decorative arts exhibition held here in 1896. Given a permanent site here in 1909, the observatory was used by Albert Einstein for a lecture on the Theory of Relativity in 1915. It is also home to the longest refracting telescope in the world (21-m or 70-ft), and a small planetarium.

Beyond Treptower Park lies another park, Plänterwald, while the Spree river provides an ideal place for a riverside stroll or maybe a trip in one of the rowing or pedal boats.

At the beginning of the 19th century, Berliners flocked to the banks of the Spree to enjoy themselves at the weekend. However, from the many dance halls and restaurants, only one historic building has remained – Zenner. This can trace its history back as far as the 17th century.

The small Insel der Jugend can be reached via the Abtei-brücke, an ornamental bridge built by French prisoners of war in 1916. The island was once home to an abbey, but it now houses a fashionable arts complex and nightclub.

Southeast Berlin

A N EXPEDITION to Berlin's furthest corners, Lichtenberg and Hohenschönhausen, provides an occasion to visit shocking museums documenting the work of the German Democratic Republic's security services (Stasi). However, you can just as easily stroll through the zoological garden in the park at the Baroque Schloss Friedrichsfelde or enjoy a leisurely break in Köpenick, which has retained the atmosphere of a small town.

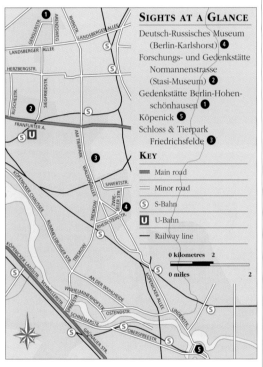

SIGHTS AT A GLANCE

Deutsch-Russisches Museum
(Berlin-Karlshorst) ❹
Forschungs- und Gedenkstätte
Normannenstrasse
(Stasi-Museum) ❷
Gedenkstätte Berlin-Hohen-
schönhausen ❶
Köpenick ❺
Schloss & Tierpark
Friedrichsfelde ❸

KEY

━━━ Main road

──── Minor road

Ⓢ S-Bahn

Ⓤ U-Bahn

━━━ Railway line

0 kilometres   2

0 miles   2

Gedenkstätte Berlin-Hohen-schönhausen ❶

Genslerstrasse 66. **C** 982 42 19.
Ⓢ Landsberger Allee, then 🚋 6, 7,
17. 🚌 256. ◯ 9am–6pm daily.
📷 (in German) 11am, 1pm daily
(also 3pm Sat & Sun).

T HIS MUSEUM was established in 1995 within the former custody building of the Stasi – the dreaded security service of the GDR. The custody building was part of a huge complex built in 1938. In May 1945 the occupying Russian authorities created a special transit camp here, in which they interned war criminals

who were subsequently transported to Siberia. Shortly thereafter they started to bring anyone under political suspicion to the camp. During this time more than 20,000 people passed through here.

From 1946 this group of buildings was refashioned into the custody area for the KGB (Soviet Secret Service), and in 1951 it was given over for the use of the Stasi.

During a visit to the complex you can see prisoners' cells and interrogation rooms, two of which have no windows and are lined with rubber. Housed in the cellars was the "submarine" – a series of cells without daylight for the most "dangerous" suspects.

Forschungs-und Gedenkstätte Normannenstrasse (Stasi-Museum) ❷

Ruschestrasse 103 (Haus 1).
C 553 68 54. Ⓤ Magdalenen-
strasse. ◯ 11am–6pm Mon–Fri,
2–6pm Sat & Sun. 📷

U NDER THE GERMAN Demo-cratic Republic, this huge complex of buildings at Ruschestrasse housed the Ministry of the Interior. It was here that the infamous Stasi (GDR secret service) had its headquarters. The Stasi's "achievements" in infiltrating its own community were with-out equal in the Eastern bloc.

Since 1990 one of the build-ings has housed a museum that displays photographs and documents depicting the activities of the Stasi. You can see a model of the head-quarters, and equipment used for bugging and spying on citizens suspected of holding an unfavourable view of the political regime. You can also walk around the office of in-famous Stasi chief Erich Mielke. A "big-brother"-like figure, Mielke's legacy of suffering still lives on in the memory of millions of German citizens.

Stasi chief Erich Mielke's office at the Stasi Museum

Schloss & Tierpark Friedrichsfelde ❸

Am Tierpark 125. Ⓤ Tierpark.
🚌 296, 396. **Schloss** ◯ Apr–Sep:
10am–6pm Wed–Sun; Oct–Mar:
10am–5pm Wed–Sun. **Tierpark**
C 51 53 10. ◯ 9am–6pm daily (or
until dusk in winter). 📷

T HIS CHARMING Baroque palace was built for the Dutchman Benjamin von Raule around 1695, to a

The façade of Schloss Friedrichsfelde

design by Johann Arnold Nering. Under successive owners, it underwent major renovations. In 1719 it was redesigned by Martin Heinrich Böhme, and again in 1786 this time to designs by Peter Biron. It was this renovation which gave the residence its current appearance.

The well-balanced structure, typical of the style during the transition from Baroque to Neo-Classical, was extensively restored in the 1970s. It now houses a museum of interiors, and is chiefly furnished with 18th- and 19th-century pieces. The palace's park was re-designed into the zoological garden of East Berlin in 1957.

Deutsch-Russisches Museum (Berlin-Karlshorst) ❹

Zwieseler Strasse 4/Rheinsteinstrasse
🚗 50 15 08 10. Ⓢ Karlshorst.
🚋 26, 27, 28. 🚌 396. ⏰ 10am–6pm Tue–Sun.

THIS BUILDING was erected in the 1930s as the casino of the Wehrmacht (armed services of the Third Reich). It was here on the night of 8 May 1945 that Hitler's successor Grossadmiral Karl Dönitz, Field Marshal Wilhelm Keitel, Admiral Hans Georg von Friedeburg and General Hans-Jürgen Stumpff signed the unconditional surrender of Germany's armed forces. You can visit the renowned hall in which the surrender was signed, the office of Marshal Zhukov, and see an exhibition documenting the history of World War II.

Köpenick ❺

Kunstgewerbemuseum Ⓢ Spindlersfeld, then 🚋 167, 169 or Ⓢ Köpenick, then 🚋 169, 360, 369. 🚋 60, 61, 62, 63, 68. ⬤ for renovation until mid-2004.

KÖPENICK IS MUCH older than Berlin. Already in the 9th century AD this island contained a fortified settlement called Kopanica. It was inhabited by Slavs from the Łaba river region, which in the 12th century was ruled by Duke Jaksa, who was waging a war against the Ascanian Albrecht the Bear over Brandenburg *(see p17)*. From the late 12th century Köpenick belonged to the Margrave of Brandenburg, also an Ascanian. In about 1240 a castle was built, around which a town began to evolve, though over the years it lost out in importance to Berlin. Craftsmen settled here, and after 1685 a large colony of Huguenots also settled here.

Part of the town hall's Neo-Gothic façade

A reconstructed drawing room dating from 1548 in Köpenick's Kunstgewerbemuseum

In the 19th century Köpenick recreated itself as an industrial town. Despite wartime devastation it has retained its historic character. There are no longer any 13th-century churches, which in the years 1838 to 1841 were replaced by buildings in the style of Schinkel, nevertheless it is worth strolling around the old town. By the old market square and the neighbouring streets, such as Alt Köpenick and Grünstrasse, modest houses have survived which recall the 18th century, next to buildings from the end of the 19th century.

At Alt Köpenick No. 21 is a vast brick town hall built in the style of the Brandenburg Neo-Renaissance between the years 1901 and 1904 by Hans Schütte and Hugo Kinzer. It was here on 16 October 1906 that a famous swindle took place. Wilhelm Voigt dressed himself in a Prussian officer's uniform and proceeded to arrest the mayor and then fraudulently empty everything from the city treasury. This incident became the inspiration for a comedy, *The Captain from Köpenick* by Carl Zuckmayer, which is still popular.

Köpenick's greatest attraction is a magnificent palace on the island in the southern part of town. It was built between 1677 and 1681 for the heir to the throne Friedrich (later King Friedrich I), to a design by the Dutch architect Rutger van Langfeld. The three-storey Baroque building that resulted was extended to a design by Johann Arnold Nering, but until 1693 only part of the extension was completed: the chapel, entrance gate and a small gallery wing.

In 2004 the **Kunstgewerbemuseum** *(see pp118–21)* will open a series of Renaissance and Baroque rooms in the Köpenick palace. This collection will also include magnificent furniture.

Southwest Berlin

A N EXCURSION TO BRITZ provides a chance to visit one of the few surviving manor houses in the suburbs of Berlin, Schloss Britz. In Schöneberg you can see the town hall from which President Kennedy gave his famous speech, and visit the grave of Berlin-born actress and singer, Marlene Dietrich. The Botanical Gardens are great for those who enjoy a stroll through cultivated and wild gardens, but you should allow at least half a day.

Neo-Classical Königskolonnaden, gateway to the Kleistpark

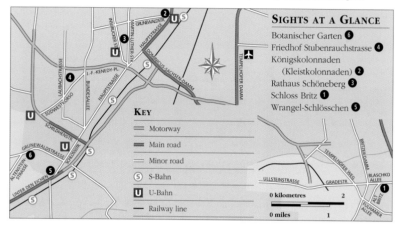

SIGHTS AT A GLANCE

Botanischer Garten **6**
Friedhof Stubenrauchstrasse **4**
Königskolonnaden
   (Kleistkolonnaden) **2**
Rathaus Schöneberg **3**
Schloss Britz **1**
Wrangel-Schlösschen **5**

KEY

═══	Motorway
▬▬	Main road
──	Minor road
Ⓢ	S-Bahn
Ⓤ	U-Bahn
──	Railway line

0 kilometres 2
0 miles 1

Schloss Britz **1**

Alt-Britz 73. [60 97 92 30.
Ⓤ *Parchimer Allee.* ▬ *144, 174, 181.*
◯ *2–6pm Wed.* ✔ *compulsory.*

O RIGINALLY A small manor house built in 1706 for Sigismund von Erlach, Schloss Britz was extended to its current size between 1880 and 1883 to a design by Carl Busse. It is a one-storey palace with a modest Neo-Classical aspect adorned with Baroque statues at the front and a tower on the garden side. As well as housing a permanent museum, the building is often used as a venue for concerts and temporary exhibitions.

The palace displays furnishings from the *Gründerzeit* – the years after the founding of the German Empire in 1871. The 19th-century interiors are excellent but it is also worth strolling through the park, where there is a bust of one of the former owners, Rüdiger von Ilgen. This statue once stood on the Avenue of Triumph in the Tiergarten.

Next to the palace is a housing estate called Hufeisen-siedlung (Horseshoe Colony), built in the late 1920s to a design by Bruno Taut and Bruno Schneidereit. The architects' aim was to create spacious and affordable housing for Berliners.

Schloss Britz's Neo-Classical façade

Königskolonnaden (Kleistkolonnaden) **2**

Potsdamer Strasse **Map** 11 B4.
Ⓤ *Kleistpark.* ▬ *148, 187, 348.*

A SHORT WALK north of U-Bahn Kleistpark, the unremarkable architecture of Potsdamer Strasse suddenly transforms dramatically. Leading to the park, the elegant sandstone Königskolonnaden captivates the passer-by with its Baroque ornamental sculptures. The royal colonnade, designed by Carl von Gontard and built between 1777 and 1780, once graced the route from Königs-strasse to Alexanderplatz. In 1910, to protect it from traffic, it was moved to this new site.

The huge Kammergericht at the far boundary of the park was built between 1909 and 1913 to a design by Carl Vohl, Rudolf Mönnich and Paul Thömer. The site of the notorious Nazi Volksgericht or "People's Court", it was also used to try members of the failed July 1944 Bomb Plot against Hitler (*see p127*).

Rathaus Schöneberg ❸

SCHÖNEBERG TOWN HALL

John-F-Kennedy-Platz.
Ⓤ *Rathaus Schöneberg.*

THE GIGANTIC BUILDING with a tower is the Schöneberg town hall, built between 1911 and 1914. From 1948 to 1990 it was used as the main town hall of West Berlin. Here, on 26 June 1963, the US President John F Kennedy gave his famous speech. More than 300,000 Berliners assembled to hear the young president say "*Ich bin ein Berliner*" – "I am a Berliner", intended as an expression of solidarity from the democratic world to a city defending its right to freedom.

While Kennedy's meaning was undoubtedly clear, pedants were quick to point out that, strictly speaking, he said "I am a small doughnut".

Rathaus Schöneberg – the site of President Kennedy's speech

Friedhof Stuben-rauchstrasse ❹

STUBENRAUCHSTRASSE CEMETERY

Stubenrauchstrasse/Südwestkorso.
Ⓢ & Ⓤ *Bundesplatz.* 🚌 *348.*

THIS SMALL CEMETERY in the shadow of a motorway achieved renown in 1993 as the burial place of Marlene Dietrich, who died on 6 May. Born Maria Magdalena von Losch in 1901, she grew up at Leberstrasse No. 65 in Schöneberg. For a few years she struggled to make a career as an actress, playing small parts.

The pleasantly cultivated spaces of the Botanischer Garten

In 1929 she was discovered in Berlin by Hollywood director Josef von Sternberg who was filming *The Blue Angel*, based on Heinrich Mann's novel *Professor Unrat*. The ensuing role of Lola took Marlene to the height of fame. She sang only once more in Berlin, giving a concert at the Titania-Palast in 1960. Although she died in Paris, she was laid to rest in the city of her birth.

Wrangel-Schlösschen ❺

Schlossstrasse 48. 📞 *63 210.*
Ⓤ *Rathaus Steglitz.* 🚌 *148, 170, 185, 277, 280, 283, 285.*

THIS COMPACT Neo-Classical palace derives its name from Field Marshal Wrangel, the building's mid-19th century owner. However, the house was built much earlier, in 1804, following a design by Heinrich Gentz. The simplicity and clarity of its details make it a prime example of early Neo-Classical architecture. It currently houses the cultural centre for the district of Steglitz.

Botanischer Garten ❻

BOTANICAL GARDEN

Unter den Eichen 5–10 & Königin-Luise-Strasse 6–8. 📞 *83 85 01 00.*
Ⓤ *Dahlem-Dorf.* Ⓢ *Botanischer Garten.* 🚌 *101, 148.* ◻ Mar & Oct: 9am–6pm daily; Apr & Aug: 9am–8pm daily; May–Jul: 9am–9pm daily; Nov–Jan: 9am–4pm daily; Feb & Sep: 9am–7pm daily. **Museum** ◻ 10am–6pm daily. 🎫

THE BOTANICAL GARDEN is one of the most beautiful places in Berlin. The expansive park was created towards the end of the 19th century and has a romantic character with gentle hills and picturesque lakes. Of particular interest is the 19th-century palm house, designed by Alfred Koerner. The new greenhouses were built from 1984 to 1987 to a design by Engelbert Kremser. The most popular plants are the exotic species such as the orchids and cacti. By the entrance on the Königin-Luise-Platz side is the Botanisches Museum, home to an excellent collection of plant specimens.

COUNTRY CHURCHES

The establishment of Greater Berlin in 1920 swallowed up nearly 60 villages, some of which were older than the city itself. Now they have evolved into large residential estates, and many of the parish churches (more than 50) have survived. The most treasured, dating from the 13th century, can be seen in the south of Berlin, for instance in Britz by Backbergstrasse, Buckow (Alt-Buckow) or in Mariendorf (Alt Mariendorf). The oldest church, dating from the 13th century, has survived in Marienfelde (Alt Marienfelde).

St Anna's in Dahlem   Wittenau   Marienfelde

Dahlem

DAHLEM IS FIRST MENTIONED in 1275 and it remained a small village surrounded by private estates until the 19th century. Retaining its Gothic parish church and its manor house, Dahlem was transformed into an affluent, tranquil city suburb with grand villas and a clutch of museums, designed by Bruno Paul, at the beginning of the 20th century. The district was confirmed as a major cultural and educational centre after World War II with the establishment of the Freie Universität and the completion of the museum complex. The Botanischer Garten also sits on the borders of Dahlem *(see p177).*

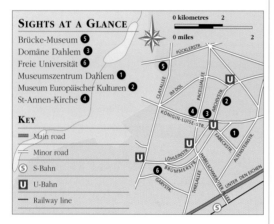

SIGHTS AT A GLANCE

Brücke-Museum **5**
Domäne Dahlem **3**
Freie Universität **6**
Museumszentrum Dahlem **1**
Museum Europäischer Kulturen **2**
St-Annen-Kirche **4**

KEY

— Main road
— Minor road
Ⓢ S-Bahn
Ⓤ U-Bahn
— Railway line

0 kilometres 2
0 miles 2

Museumszentrum Dahlem **1**

Lansstrasse 8. **⚹** 20 90 55 55.
Ⓤ *Dahlem Dorf.* 🚌 *110, 183, X-11, X-83.* **Museum für Indische Kunst, Museum für Ostasiatische Kunst, Ethnologisches Museum** (formerly Museum für Völkerkunde), **Museum für Kunst Afrikas & Nordamerika Ausstellung** ◯ *10am–6pm Tue–Fri, 11am–6pm Sat & Sun.* ▨

DAHLEM'S FIRST museums were built between 1914 and 1923. After World War II, with many of Berlin's collections fragmented, a large miscellany of art and artifacts was put on display here. In the 1960s the museums were extended considerably: the new Museumszentrum was created to rival East Berlin's Museum Island. Reunification in 1990 meant the collections could be reunited and reorganized. Paintings were moved to the Kulturforum *(see pp122–5)*, and sculptures to the Bode-museum *(see p79)*. Five

museums are now housed at Dahlem: the Ethnologisches Museum (Museum of Ethnology); the Museum für Indische Kunst (Museum of Indian Art); the Museum für Ostasiatische Kunst (Museum of Far Eastern Art); the Museum für Kunst Afrikas (Museum for African Art) and

Japanese woodcut from the Museum für Ostasiatische Kunst

the more recent Nordamerika Ausstellung (Exhibition of Native North American Cultures).

Highlights from the collections include bronzes from Benin at the Museum of African Art, gold Inca jewellery at the Museum of Ethnology, and Japanese woodcuts and Buddhist cave paintings from Chinese Turkestan at the Museum of Far Eastern Art. Opened in 1999, the Exhibition of Native North American Cultures includes a collection of 600 ceremonial objects.

An East Prussian carpet from the Museum Europäischer Kulturen

Museum Europä-ischer Kulturen **2**

MUSEUM OF EUROPEAN CULTURE

Im Winkel 6. **⚹** 83 90 12 87.
Ⓤ *Dahlem Dorf.* 🚌 *110, 183, X-11, X-83.* ◯ *10am–6pm Tue–Fri, 11am–6pm Sat & Sun.* ▨

THIS ETHNOGRAPHIC museum specializes in European folk art and culture, documenting the daily life of its inhabitants. It hosts long-running but temporary exhibitions, often in conjunction with museums from other European countries. Among the exhibits you can expect to see are earthenware items, costumes, jewellery, toys and tools.

Domäne Dahlem **3**

DAHLEM CITY FARM

Königin-Luise-Str. 49. **⚹** 24 00 20.
Ⓤ *Dahlem Dorf.* 🚌 *110, 183, X-11, X-83.* ◯ *10am–6pm Tue–Sun.* ▨
(museum only).

DOMÄNE DAHLEM, a manor house and farming estate, is a rare oasis of country life in the Berlin suburbs. The Baroque house was built for Cuno Johann von Wilmersdorff

The combined museum and working farm of Domäne Dahlem

around 1680 and still retains its original character. Part of the Stadtmuseum Berlin (Museum of the City of Berlin), the manor house boasts period interiors, while the 19th-century farm buildings hold a collection of agricultural tools. Also on show is a large and varied collection of beehives.

Domäne Dahlem is a farm and a museum with a garden, workshops and farm animals. Festivals and markets are held here with demonstrations of rural crafts and skills – you can learn how to shoe a horse or milk a cow, or, if you prefer, you can just relax with a glass of cold beer.

Gothic St-Annen-Kirche dating back to the 14th century

St-Annen-Kirche ❹

Königin-Luise-Strasse/Pacelliallee. 834 20 25. **U** Dahlem Dorf. 110, 183, X-11. 9am–6pm daily.

AT THE CENTRE of a small leafy cemetery stands the Gothic 14th-century St-Annen-

Kirche. The church was built initially with a plain roof. The chancel was completed in the 15th century, the vaulting in the 17th century and the tower was added in the 18th century.

Inside the church, 14th-century wall paintings depict scenes from the life of St Anna, alongside items of ecclesiastical furnishings. These include a 15th-century painting called *The Crucifixion*, 11 late-Gothic figures of saints and a 17th-century Baroque pulpit.

Brücke-Museum ❺

Bussardsteig 9. 831 20 29. 115, X-10. 11am–5pm Wed–Mon.

ONE OF THE MORE interesting museums dedicated to 20th-century art is hidden away on a leafy, tranquil street lined with picturesque villas. The elegant Functionalist building was built by Werner Düttmann in 1966 to 1967. The museum houses a collection of German Expressionist painting linked to the artistic group known as Die Brücke, which originated in Dresden in 1905 and was based in Berlin from 1910. The members of this group included Karl Schmidt-Rottluff, Emil Nolde, Max Pechstein, Ernst Ludwig Kirchner and Erich Heckel. The collection is based on almost 80 works by Schmidt-Rottluff bequeathed to the town in 1964. The collection quickly grew, thanks to donations and acquisitions. In addition to displaying other works of art contemporary to Die Brücke (which was disbanded in 1913), there are also some paintings from the later creative periods of these artists, as well as works of other closely associated artists.

Nearby, at Käuzchensteig No. 8, lie the foundation's headquarters, established in the former studio of the sculptor Bernhard Heliger. The garden, which borders the Brücke-Museum, has a display of his metal sculptures.

A Bernhard Heliger sculpture outside the Brücke-Museum

Freie Universität ❻

Henry-Ford-Bau Garystrasse 35–39. **U** Thielplatz. 111.

THE FREE UNIVERSITY was established on 4 December 1948 on the initiative of a group of academics and activists, led by Ernst Reuter. This was a reaction to the restrictions introduced at the Humboldt-Universität in the Soviet sector and further evidence of the competition between the two halves of the city. The new university was initially located in rented buildings. It was only thanks to the American Ford Foundation that the university's Henry-Ford-Bau, housing the rector's office, the auditorium and the library, was built. Designed by Franz Heinrich Sobotka and Gustav Müller, and built from 1951 to 1954, the building is distinguished by its fine proportions.

Henry-Ford-Bau, the rector's office and library at the Freie Universität

Zehlendorf

WITH NEARLY HALF of Zehlendorf covered by forests, lakes and rivers, the region has a quiet, rustic atmosphere that belies the fact that it is a mere 20 minutes away from the hustle and bustle of a huge metropolis. The area is dotted with picture-postcard villas and small settlements where life carries on at an unchanging, slow pace. It is worth taking a walk *(see pp208–211)* to see the stunning lakeside summer residences and royal parks, Pfaueninsel and Klein Glienicke, which are located in the furthest corner of this district.

Reconstructed medieval settlement at the Museumdorf Düppel

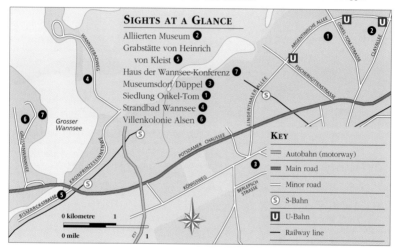

SIGHTS AT A GLANCE

Alliierten Museum **2**
Grabstätte von Heinrich von Kleist **5**
Haus der Wannsee-Konferenz **7**
Museumsdorf Düppel **3**
Siedlung Onkel-Tom **1**
Strandbad Wannsee **4**
Villenkolonie Alsen **6**

Grosser Wannsee

KEY

═══	Autobahn (motorway)
▬▬▬	Main road
───	Minor road
Ⓢ	S-Bahn
🅄	U-Bahn
━━━	Railway line

0 kilometre   1
0 mile   1

Siedlung Onkel-Tom **1**

Argentinische Allee. 🅄 *Onkel-Toms-Hütte.*

THIS HOUSING ESTATE, known as "Uncle Tom's Estate", represents one of the most interesting urban architectural achievements of the Weimar Republic. It was built from 1926 to 1932, to a design by

The Siedlung (estate) Onkel-Tom, built between 1926 and 1932

Bruno Taut, Hugo Häring and Otto Rudolf Salvisberg. Their primary intention was to solve the city's housing shortage by building large developments that were both pleasant to live in and fairly inexpensive. This project in Zehlendorf was the realization of the English concept of garden cities. The result is an enormous housing estate comprising single- and multiple-family houses. It is set in lush greenery on the borders of Grunewald and accommodates nearly 15,000 people.

Alliierten Museum **2**

Clayallee 135. 🄲 *818 19 90.* Ⓢ *Zehlendorf, then* 🚌 *115, X-10.* 🅄 *Oskar-Helene-Heim.* 🕐 *10am–6pm Thu–Tue.* 📷 *by appointment.*

IN THE HEART of the former US military sector of Berlin is the Allied Museum, which combines exhibition space with open-air grounds. A fascinating exhibition of everyday objects, military memorabilia, photographs and films explains life during the Cold War and the story of Berlin and its inhabitants between 1945 and 1994.

Museumsdorf Düppel **3**

Clauerstrasse 11. 🄲 *802 66 71.* Ⓢ *Mexikoplatz or* 🅄 *Krumme Lanke, then* 🚌 *211, 629.* 🕐 *Easter–15 Oct: 3–7pm Thu, 10am–5pm Sun.* 📷

A VISIT TO THE Museumsdorf Düppel takes the visitor on a trip back in time. A reconstruction of a medieval village has been made on the site of a 13th-century settlement, discovered in the 1940s. It is a living village surrounded by still cultivated gardens and fields, where traditional breeds of pigs and sheep are raised in the sheds and pigsties.

On Sundays the village puts on displays of traditional

crafts. Here you can see how primitive saucepans and tools were fashioned; how wool was spun, dyed and woven; and how baskets were made.

Strandbad Wannsee ❹

Wannseebadweg. ⑤ *Nikolassee.* 🚌 *218.*

THE VAST PICTURESQUE lake of Wannsee, situated on the edge of Grunewald, is a principal destination for Berliners who are looking for some kind of recreation. Here you can take part in water sports, enjoy a lake cruise, bathe, or simply enjoy relaxing on the shore. The most developed part is the southeastern corner of the lake. Here, near S-Bahn Wannsee, there are yachting marinas and harbours, while further north is one of the largest inland beaches in Europe – Strandbad Wannsee. It has been in use since the beginning of the 20th century, and was developed between 1929 and 1930 by the construction of a complex of changing rooms, shops and cafés on top of man-made terraces.

On sunny summer days, sun-worshippers completely cover the sandy shore, while the lake is filled with yachts and windsurfers. It is also quite pleasant to take a walk around Schwanenwerder island. It has many elegant villas, one of which, Inselstrasse No. 24/26, was built for Axel Springer, the German newspaper publisher.

Boarding point for lake cruises on the Wannsee

Grabstätte von Heinrich von Kleist ❺
GRAVE OF HEINRICH VON KLEIST

Bismarckstrasse (near No. 3). ⑤ *Wannsee.* 🚌 *114, 116, 211, 216, 316, 318.*

A NARROW STREET running from Königstrasse at the viaduct of the S-Bahn Wannsee leads to the spot where the playwright Heinrich von Kleist committed suicide. On 21 November 1811 he shot his companion Henriette Vogel and then turned the pistol on himself. They are both buried here. A stone marks the location of their grave, on which flowers are left by well-wishers.

Villenkolonie Alsen ❻

Am Grossen Wannsee. ⑤ *Wannsee,* then 🚌 *114.*

THIS CLUTCH OF VILLAS forms a delightful holiday resort – the oldest of its kind in Berlin. The villas are thought to be the most beautiful, not just because of their picturesque lakeside location, but also because of the quality of their architecture.

Strolling along Am Grossen Wannsee, it is worth looking at the villa at No. 39/41, known as Haus Springer. It was designed by Alfred Messel in 1901 and is covered with shingles which reflect contemporary American designs.

Haunting sculptures in front of Haus der Wannsee-Konferenz

At No. 42 stands a villa that was designed by Paul Baumgarten in 1909 for the painter Max Liebermann, who spent many summers here painting.

Haus der Wannsee-Konferenz ❼

Am Grossen Wannsee 56/58. ☎ *805 00 10.* ⑤ *Wannsee, then* 🚌 *114.* ⏰ *10am–6pm daily.*

THIS IS ONE OF THE most beautiful of the luxury Alsen holiday villas, and yet the most abhorrent. Designed by Paul Baumgarten between 1914 and 1915, it is in the style of a small Neo-Baroque palace with an elegant portico. In 1940 the villa was sold to the Nazi SS. On 20 January 1942, a meeting took place between Richard Heydrich and 14 other officers from the secret service and the SS, among them Adolf Eichmann. It was then that the decision was taken about "the final solution on the question of Jews". Their plans for the outright extermination of 11 million Jews embraced the whole of Europe, including Great Britain and neutral countries.

Since 1992 this has been a museum and place of remembrance. An exhibition depicts the history of the Holocaust with some shocking documents and photographs from the ghettos and extermination camps. For security reasons, the gate to the villa is always locked, and to enter the park you have to announce yourself through the intercom.

Western Berlin

WEST OF CHARLOTTENBURG, beyond the city ring road, stretches an area notable for its striking Funkturm (Radio Tower) and Internationales Congress Centrum, as well as a number of large exhibition centres. After World War II, a residential estate of villas was built here, one of which belonged to the sculptor Georg Kolbe and now houses a museum of his works. A radio station has its recording studios in a very large building nearby; its plain, almost boring looking façade hides one of Berlin's most beautiful art deco interiors.

The futuristic exterior of the Internationales Congress Centrum

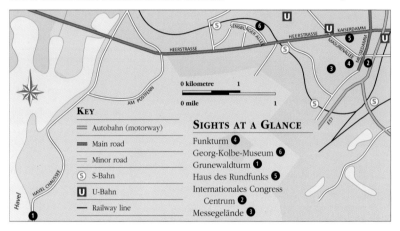

KEY

═══	Autobahn (motorway)
▬▬	Main road
═══	Minor road
Ⓢ	S-Bahn
Ⓤ	U-Bahn
───	Railway line

SIGHTS AT A GLANCE

Funkturm ❹
Georg-Kolbe-Museum ❻
Grunewaldturm ❶
Haus des Rundfunks ❺
Internationales Congress
  Centrum ❷
Messegelände ❸

Grunewaldturm ❶

Havelchaussee. ▨ 218.

THE NEO-GOTHIC tower built on a hill at the edge of the Havel river is one of the most prominent features of the area. This type of tower became popular in Germany during the 19th century as a way of commemorating important events or people. The Grune-waldturm was built in 1899 on the centenary of the birth of Wilhelm I. After 1871, he was the first Emperor of the Second Reich, and the tower was initially named "Kaiser-Wilhelm-Turm". The 56-m (185-ft) tower was designed by Franz Schwechten and is made of red brick with plaster details. The tower is made all the more striking by the green background provided by the surrounding leafy trees.

Currently used as an observation tower, the view from the top of this structure is well worth climbing the 204 steps for. There is a popular restaurant in the base of the tower and above, in the domed hall, is a marble statue of the Emperor that was designed by Ludwig Mansel.

The impressive red-brick Neo-Gothic Grunewaldturm

Internationales Congress Centrum ❷

Messedamm 19. Ⓢ Witzleben. Ⓤ Kaiserdamm. ▨ 104, 149, 218, X-34, X-49.

THIS SILVER FUTURISTIC struc-ture stands on a peninsula of land, surrounded on two sides by a continuous stream of fast moving cars. The Internationales Congress Centrum (ICC) marked yet another stage in the rivalry between East and West Berlin – it was built in reply to the East's Palast der Republik.

Constructed between 1973 and 1979, to a design by Ralf Schüler and Ursulina Schüler-Witte, the building is a mass of angular aluminium shapes that disguise its well thought-out construction. The con-ference area is separate from the concert halls, for good sound-proofing. One of the most modern buildings of its type in the world, it has a state-of-the-art electronic security system and an advanced means of co-ordinating and directing the several thousand people who come here to attend various meetings and conferences. More than 80 rooms and halls enable the venue to host a variety of events, from rock concerts for up to 5,000 spectators to a small artistic workshop or seminar. The building also has a roof garden, where you can rest during intervals. In front of the main entrance stands *Alexander the Great in front of Ekbatana*, by French sculptor Jean Ipoustéguy (born 1920).

Monumental façade of the Ehren-halle part of the Messegelände

Messegelände ❸

Hammarskjöldplatz. Ⓢ *Witzleben.* Ⓤ *Kaiserdamm.* 🚌 *104, 149, 204, 219.*

THE PAVILIONS of the vast exhibition and trade halls which lie south of Hammarsk-jöldplatz cover more than 160,000 sq m (1,700,000 sq ft). Many of the international events organized here, including the food and agricultural fair Grüne Woche, are among the largest events of their kind in Europe. Even so, the exhibition areas are constantly enlarged and updated.

The original exhibition halls on this site were built before World War I, but nothing of these buildings remains. The oldest part is the Funkturm and the group of pavilions which surround it. The huge building at the front – Ehren-halle – was built in 1936 to a design by Richard Ermisch, and is one of the few surviving buildings in Berlin designed in a Fascist architectural style.

The straight motorway that lies at the rear of the halls, in the direction of Nikolassee, is the famous Avus, the first German autobahn, built in 1921. It was adapted for motor racing, and became Germany's first car-racing track. It was here that the world speed record was broken before World War II. Now it forms part of the autobahn system.

Funkturm ❹

Hammarskjöldplatz. 📞 *30 38 0.* Ⓢ *Witzleben.* Ⓤ *Kaiserdamm.* 🚌 *104, 139, 149, 218, X-21.* **Observation Terrace** ⬜ *10am–11pm Tue–Sun, 11am–9pm Mon.*

THE RADIO TOWER, resembling Paris' Eiffel tower, has become one of Berlin's most recognizable landmarks. Built in 1924 to a design by Heinrich Straumer, it rises 150 m (500 ft) into the air. It now operates as both an air-traffic control tower and a radio mast. Visitors can enjoy views from the observation terrace at 125 m (400 ft), or dine at the Funkturm's lofty restaurant at 55 m (180 ft).

Haus des Rundfunks ❺

Masurenallee 8–14. Ⓢ *Witzleben.* Ⓤ *Theodor-Heuss-Platz.* 🚌 *104, 149, 218, X-34, X-49.*

THIS BUILDING'S depressing, flat, brick-covered façade hides an interior of startling beauty. The huge edifice was constructed as a radio station between 1929 and 1931 to a design by Hans Poelzig. The building has a triangular shape, with three studio wings radiating from the central five-storey hall. The impressive Art Deco interiors, which are spectacularly lit from above, are enhanced by geometrically-patterned rows of balconies and large, pendulous,

Clean, geometric shapes in the Art Deco lobby, Haus des Rundfunks

octagonal lamps. They represent one of the finest architectural achievements of this era in Berlin.

From the studio concert hall, concerts are often broadcast on radio SFB.

Fountain in the garden of the sculptor Georg Kolbe's villa

Georg-Kolbe-Museum ❻

Sensburger Allee 25. 📞 *304 21 44.* Ⓢ *Heerstrasse.* 🚌 *149, X-34, X-49.* ⬜ *10am–5pm Tue–Sun.*

ONE OF THE MOST renowned German sculptors, Georg Kolbe (1877–1947) bequeathed the house in which he lived and worked almost his entire life to the city of Berlin. The villa was built by the Swiss architect, Ernst Reutsch, between 1928 and 1929 in a Functionalist style. Extended a few years later by the architect Paul Lindner, it was given an old-fashioned styling with rooms that open onto a large hall. Kolbe also left the city 180 of his sculptures, as well as his own art collection, which includes works by the Expressionist painter Ernst Ludwig Kirchner and the sculptor Wilhelm Lehmbruck. Visiting here is not only a rare chance to get to know Kolbe's works but also an opportunity to see his house and workshop, which display the tools and various devices for lifting a heavy or large sculpture.

Northwest Berlin

A VISIT TO THIS PART of the city provides a chance to see the grandeur of the Olympia-Stadion, which was inspired by the monumental architecture of ancient Rome. Nearby stands the monolithic Le Corbusier Haus, once regarded as the model for future housing. The historic town of Spandau has some pretty medieval streets and a well-preserved Renaissance citadel. A number of original timber-framed houses remain and are well worth seeing, along with the Gothic St-Nikolai-Kirche.

500 two-storey apartments with integral services, such as a post office, shops, a sports hall and nursery school. The structure fell short of Le Corbusier's aspirations as financial pressure meant the estate lacked some service elements; in addition, structural alterations changed the building's proportions from the original plans.

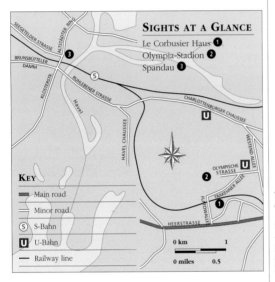

SIGHTS AT A GLANCE

Le Corbusier Haus ❶
Olympia-Stadion ❷
Spandau ❸

KEY

- Main road
- Minor road
- ⑤ S-Bahn
- Ⓤ U-Bahn
- Railway line

0 km   1

0 miles   0.5

Two sculptures of athletes decorating the Olympia-Stadion

Olympia-Stadion ❷

Olympischer Platz. **[** 301 11 00.
⑤ & Ⓤ *Olympia-Stadion.* 🚌 218.
Exhibition 🕙 10am–6pm Wed, Sun.

Le Corbusier Haus ❶

Reichssportfeldstrasse 16.
⑤ *Olympia-Stadion.* 🚌 218.

T HIS APARTMENT building by Le Corbusier, on a hill near the site of the Olympia-Stadion, was this architect's entry to the 1957 Interbau Exhibition *(see p133)*. Following World War II,

there was a housing shortage all over Europe, especially in the bomb-damaged cities. Le Corbusier's innovative design for what he called a *Unité d'Habitation* was his attempt to create fully self-sufficient housing estates in answer to this problem. He built three of these complexes, the most famous being in Marseilles. For his Berlin design, Le Corbusier wanted to build over

T HE OLYMPIA-STADION, or Reichssportfeld, as it was originally known, was built for the 1936 Olympic Games in Berlin. It was designed by Werner March in the Nazi architectural style and was inspired by the architecture of ancient Rome. The Olympia-Stadion was immortalized in the dramatic final scenes of István Szabó's classic film *Mephisto.* To the west of the stadium lie the Maifeld and the Waldbühne. The former is an enormous assembly-ground surrounded by grand-stands and fronted by the Glockenturm, a 77-m (250-ft) tower, while the latter is an open-air amphitheatre. To the north are swimming pools and sports grounds. This complex provided the infrastructure for the Berlin Olympics.

The Olympia-Stadion is currently being renovated. A small exhibition showcases the stadium's history.

Le Corbusier Haus, by the renowned French architect

Interior of the Gothic St-Nikolai-Kirche in Spandau

Spandau ❸

Zitadelle Spandau Am Juliusturm.
📞 354 94 42 00. Ⓤ *Zitadelle.*
🕐 *9am–5pm Tue–Fri, 10am–5pm Sat & Sun.* 🎫

S PANDAU IS ONE of the oldest towns within the area of greater Berlin, and it has managed to retain a distinct character for itself. Evidence of the earliest settlement dates back to the 8th century, although the town of Spandau was only granted a charter in 1232. The area was spared the worst of the World War II bombing, so there are still some interesting sights to visit.

The heart of the town is a network of medieval streets with a picturesque market square and a number of original timber-framed houses; in the north of Spandau sections of town wall still stand, dating from the 15th century. In the centre of town is the magnificent Gothic St-Nikolai-Kirche dating from the 15th century. The church holds many valuable ecclesiastical furnishings, such as a splendid Renaissance stone altar from the end of the 16th century, a Baroque pulpit from around 1700 which came from a royal palace in Potsdam, a Gothic baptismal font and many epitaphs.

Crowned black Prussian eagle

A castle was first built on the site of the Zitadelle Spandau (citadel) in the 12th century, but today only the 36-m (120-ft) Juliusturm (tower) remains. In 1560 the building of a fort was begun here, to a design by Francesco Chiaramella da Gandino. It took 30 years to bring to completion, however, and most of the work was supervised by architect Rochus Guerrini, Graf zu Lynar. Though the citadel had a jail, Rudolf Hess, Spandau's most infamous resident, was incarcerated a short distance away in a military prison after the 1946 Nuremberg trials. In 1987 the former deputy leader of the Nazi party died, and the prison was torn down.

The Hohenzollern coat of arms above the main gate of the citadel

ZITADELLE SPANDAU

This magnificent and perfectly proportioned 16th-century citadel stands at the confluence of the Spree and Havel rivers. Both the main citadel and its various 19th-century additions are still in excellent condition. The "Iron Chancellor", Otto von Bismarck *(see p22),* moved the gold treasure of the Reichskriegs-schatz (Imperial War Fund) here in 1874, where it remained until 1919. The citadel now holds museums of local history, and an observation terrace on the crenellated Juliusturm (tower).

KEY

Bastion Kronprinz ①
Bastion Brandenburg ②
Palace ③
Main gate ④

Bastion König ⑤
Bastion Königin ⑥
Juliusturm ⑦
Ravelin Schweinekopf ⑧

Northern Berlin

BEYOND THE TIERGARTEN lie the AEG-Turbinenhalle, designed by Peter Behrens, and the Gedenkstätte Plötzensee, a sombre memorial to those executed for their supposed crimes against the Third Reich. Further north past the airport, the Tegel area contains the picturesque Schloss Tegel and the IBA-Viertel, an unusually colourful, modern housing estate designed by a team of architects. It is worth taking a cruise boat to Tegel and linking together sight-seeing in this area and a visit to Spandau with a relaxing voyage along the Havel river.

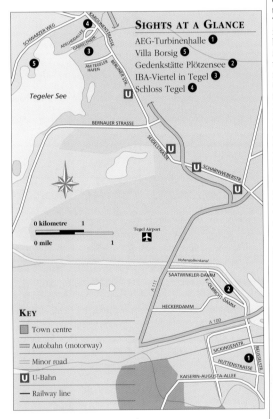

SIGHTS AT A GLANCE

AEG-Turbinenhalle ❶
Villa Borsig ❺
Gedenkstätte Plötzensee ❷
IBA-Viertel in Tegel ❸
Schloss Tegel ❹

Tegeler See

KEY

- ▨ Town centre
- ━ Autobahn (motorway)
- ━ Minor road
- 🆄 U-Bahn
- ━ Railway line

0 kilometre 1
0 mile 1

Gedenkstätte Plötzensee ❷

PLÖTZENSEE MEMORIAL

Hüttigpfad. 📞 344 32 26.
🆄 Jakob-Kaiser-Platz, then 🚌 123.
🕐 Mar–Oct: 9am–5pm; Nov–Feb: 9am–4pm.

A NARROW street leads from Saatwinkler Damm to the site where nearly 2,500 people convicted of crimes against the Third Reich were hanged. The Gedenkstätte Plötzensee is a simple memorial in a brick hut, which still has the iron hooks from which the victims were suspended. The main figures in the unsuccessful assassination attempt against Hitler, on July 20 1944, were executed in Bendlerblock *(see p127)*, although the remainder of the conspirators were killed here. Count Helmut James von Moltke, one of the leaders of the German resistance movement, was also executed here. The count organized the Kreisauer Kreis – a political movement which gathered together and united German opposition to Hitler and the Third Reich.

Memorial to concentration camp victims at Gedenkstätte Plötzensee

IBA-Viertel in Tegel ❸

Karolinenstrasse & Am Tegeler Hafen.
🆄 Alt Tegel.

THE DEVELOPMENT around the southern edge of the port of Tegel is an essential stop for lovers of modern, and

AEG-Turbinen-halle ❶

Huttenstrasse 12–16. 🆄 *Turmstrasse,* *then* 🚌 227.

THIS BUILDING IS one of the most important textbook examples of modern architecture dating from the beginning of the 20th century. It was commissioned by the electronics company, AEG, in 1909 and designed by Peter Behrens in conjunction with

Karl Bernhardt. It was among the earliest structures not to incorporate any element, decorative or otherwise, that reflected previous architectural styles. A huge hangar of a building, it has enormous windows and stretches 123 m (400 ft) down Berlichingenstrasse. The principal design imperative for this structure was to maintain a streamlined profile, while making no effort to disguise the materials used in its construction.

The elegant Neo-Classical façade of Schloss Tegel

particularly post-modern, architecture. This complex developed out of the IBA (Internationale Baustellung) building exhibition in 1987. Over 30 architects were involved in this project, although the main designers were Charles Moore, John Ruble and Buzz Yudell. Within this complex stands the Humboldt-Bibliothek, which draws on Neo-Classical themes. In 1997 a monument was established to the eminent scientists Wilhelm and Alexander von Humboldt in front of this library.

Running the length of Am Tegeler Hafen street is a large housing estate where each unit has been designed by a different architect. As a result, each one has its own colour scheme, and reflects a distinct style. For instance, at No. 8, the house by Stanley Tigerman recalls a style popular in Hanseatic architecture, while the red house at No. 10, designed by Paolo Portoghesi, looks as though it has been cracked lengthwise in two.

To the north, the IBA-Viertel estate borders another modern building, the Hotel Sorat, carefully built around the remaining section of an old windmill that was once part of the Humboldt estate.

Schloss Tegel ❹

Adelheidallee 19–21. **📞** 434 31 56. **U** Alt Tegel. **🚌** 124, 133, 222. **🗓** May–Sep: Mon. **📷** compulsory (10am, 11am, 3pm, 4pm Mon).

Sᴄʜʟᴏss ᴛᴇɢᴇʟ is one of the most interesting palace complexes in Berlin. In the 16th century there was already a manor house on this site, which in the second half of the 17th century was rebuilt into a hunting lodge for the Elector Friedrich Wilhelm. In 1766 the ownership of the property passed to the Humboldt family, and between the years 1820 and 1824, Karl Friedrich Schinkel thoroughly rebuilt the palace, giving it its current style.

There are tiled bas-reliefs decorating the elevations on the top floor of the towers. These were designed by Christian Daniel Rauch and depict the ancient wind gods. Some of Schinkel's marvellous interiors have survived, along with several items from what was once a large collection of antique sculptures. The palace is still private property, owned by descendants of the Humboldt family, but guided tours are offered on Mondays.

It is also worth visiting the park. On its western limits lies the Humboldt family tomb designed by Schinkel and decorated with a copy of a splendid sculpture by Bertel Thorwaldsen; the original piece stands inside the palace.

Villa Borsig ❺

Reiherwerder. **U** Alt Tegel. **🚌** 124, 133, 222, 224, then a 15-minute walk.

Tʜɪs ᴠɪʟʟᴀ sɪᴛs on a peninsula which cuts into the Tegeler See and is reminiscent of Schloss Sanssouci in Potsdam. It was built much later, however, between 1911 and 1913. It was designed by Alfred Salinger and Eugen Schmohl, for the Borsig family, one of the wealthiest industrialist families in Berlin. This villa is particularly picturesque when observed from the lake, so it is worth looking out for it while cruising in a boat.

The Villa Borsig façade viewed from the garden

KARL FRIEDRICH SCHINKEL (1781–1841)

Schinkel was one of the most renowned German architects; even today his work forms an essential element of the architectural landscape of Berlin. He graduated from the Berlin Bauakademie, and for many years held a high-profile position in the Prussian Building Ministry. He was equally skilled in producing both Neo-Classical and Neo-Gothic designs. In Berlin and Potsdam he designed a few dozen buildings – palaces, civic buildings and churches, many of which still stand today. He also excelled at painting and even designed scenery for the opera house on Unter den Linden, among others. You can admire his paintings in the Galerie der Romantik in Schloss Charlottenburg. Schinkel's creativity had a truly enormous influence on the next generation of architects working in Prussia.

GREATER
BERLIN

POTSDAM

POTSDAM IS AN independent city bordering Berlin. It is also the capital of Brandenburg, with almost 140,000 inhabitants. The first historical reference to Potsdam dates from AD 993. The town blossomed in the 1600s, during the era of the Great Elector *(see p18)*, and then again during the 18th century. Potsdam suffered very badly during World War II, particularly on the nights of 14 and 15 April 1945, when the Allies bombed the town's centre. Today, despite its

Sculpture from Park Sanssouci

wartime losses, Potsdam is one of the most interesting cities in Germany. Tourists flock to see the royal Park Sanssouci and palaces such as the Marmorpalais and Schloss Cecilienhof. It is also worth strolling around Neuer Garten and the historic area around the Rathaus. The Russian colony of Alexandrowka, the Holländisches Viertel, the film studios of Babelsberg and Babelsberg park *(see pp210–211)* also rate among the attractions of Potsdam.

SIGHTS AT A GLANCE

Historic Buildings
Altes Rathaus ㉑
Bildergalerie ⑪
Chinesisches Teehaus ⑥
Communs ③
Historische Mühle ⑫
Marmorpalais ⑯
Neue Kammern ⑨
Neues Palais pp194–5 ①
Orangerie ⑦
Römische Bäder ⑤
Schloss Cecilienhof ⑮
Schloss Charlottenhof ④
Schloss Sanssouci pp200–1 ⑩

Wasserwerk Sanssouci ㉔

Historic Areas
Alexandrowka ⑬
Holländisches Viertel ⑰

Churches
Französische Kirche ⑲
Friedenskirche ⑧
Nikolaikirche ⑳
Peter und Paul Kirche ⑱

Parks and Theme Parks
Filmpark Babelsberg ㉖

Neuer Garten ⑭
Park Sanssouci ②
Telegrafenberg ㉕

Museums
Marstall (Filmmuseum) ㉒
Potsdam-Museum ㉓

KEY

	Street-by-Street map *pp192–3*
P	Parking
🚉	Railway station

0 metres   750
0 yards   750

GETTING THERE

S-Bahn 7 goes to Potsdam from Berlin. From Potsdam station, bus 606 goes to Neues Palais and trams 94, 96 and X-98 go to the centre of town. Bus 695 travels between Park Sanssouci and Neuer Garten.

◁ **Colonnaded cloister at the Friedenskirche**

Street-by-Street: Park Sanssouci

THE ENORMOUS Park Sanssouci, occupying an area of 287 hectares, is among the most beautiful palace complexes in Europe. The first building to be constructed was Schloss Sanssouci, the summer palace of Frederick the Great. It was built on the site of an orchard in 1747. Over the years, Park Sanssouci was expanded considerably and enriched by the addition of other palaces and pavilions. Allow yourself at least a whole day to enjoy the park fully.

Flower-filled urn, Park Sanssouci

Communs
This house for the palace staff has an unusually elegant character, and is situated next to a pretty courtyard ❸

★ **Neues Palais**
This monumental building of the New Palace, constructed between 1763 and 1769, is crowned by a massive dome ❶

Römische Bäder
The Roman baths include a mock-Renaissance villa and a suite of Roman-style rooms ❺

0 metres		200
0 yards		200

STAR SIGHTS

★ **Neues Palais**

★ **Schloss Sanssouci**

Schloss Charlottenhof
This Neo-Classical palace gained its name from Charlotte von Gentzkow, the former owner of the land on which the palace was built ❹

Park Sanssouci
The extensive parkland is made up of several gardens. The one near the Orangerie is called the Lustgarten (pleasure garden) **2**

Orangerie
This Neo-Renaissance palace, the largest in the park, was built in the mid-19th century to house foreign royalty and guests **7**

Neue Kammern
This Rococo pavilion was once the orangerie of the Sanssouci Palace, but was rebuilt as a guest house **9**

★ Schloss Sanssouci
A beautifully terraced vineyard creates a grand approach to Schloss Sanssouci, the oldest building in the complex **10**

Bildergalerie
Built between 1755 and 1764, this pavilion houses an art gallery. It is Germany's oldest purpose-built museum building **11**

Chinesisches Teehaus
The small Rococo-style Chinese Tea House features an exhibition of exquisite Oriental porcelain **6**

Friedenskirche
The Neo-Romanesque Church of Peace is modelled on the Basilica of San Clemente in Rome **8**

Neues Palais ●

Cabinet from the study

THIS IMPOSING BAROQUE PALACE, on the main avenue in Park Sanssouci, was built at the request of Frederick the Great. The initial plans were prepared in 1750 by Georg Wenzeslaus von Knobelsdorff. However, construction only began in 1763, after the Seven Years' War *(see p19)*, to a design by Johann Gottfried Büring, Jean Laurent Le Geay and Carl von Gontard. The result was a vast two-storey building, decorated with hundreds of sculptures and more than 200 richly adorned rooms, which together make up one of Germany's most beautiful palaces.

Façade
The entrance to the Neues Palais is through the gate on the western façade. The imposing gate is flanked by stone sentry boxes.

The Schlosstheater
was completed in 1768, and designed by JC Hoppenhaupt.

Study
This Rococo-style study was part of Frederick the Great's personal apartment.

Upper Gallery
The Rococo interior, with a beautiful inlaid floor, is decorated with Italian paintings.

STAR FEATURES

★ **Marmorsaal**

★ **Grottensaal**

Figures on the Dome
The Neues Palais is crowned by a dome with a gilded royal crown. The crown is carried by a sculpture of three nymphs.

Bas-reliefs
on the triangular tympanum depict figures from Greek mythology, including Minerva, the Muses and Pegasus.

VISITORS' CHECKLIST

Am Neuen Palais.
(0331) 969 42 55. 606, 695. Apr–Oct: 9am–5pm Sat–Thu; Nov–Mar: 9am–4pm Sat–Thu (guided only).

★ Marmorsaal
This vast ballroom features walls inlaid with marble and a beautiful fresco on the ceiling. The gallery was used by the orchestra.

Main entrance

Commode
This Rococo commode was designed by JF Spindler in c.1765. It is located in the Red Room in the Duke's Apartments.

Upper Vestibule
This elegant room was designed by Carl von Gontard. The walls are covered with Silesian marble and the ceiling depicts Venus and the Graces.

★ Grottensaal
The walls of this unusual grotto-style room are lined with semi-precious stones, coral and shells as well as man-made stalactites.

Park Sanssouci ❷

Schopenhauerstrasse/ Zur Historischen Mühle. 🚌 *612, 614, 695.*

THIS VAST PARK, covering some 287 ha (700 acres), was established in 1725 on the site of an orchard. However, it was only transformed into an enormous landscaped park when construction work began on Schloss Sanssouci *(see pp200–1)*. Today, the park is made up of smaller gardens dating from different eras, each of which has been maintained in the original style. At the foot of Schloss Sanssouci is the oldest section of the park, containing the Dutch garden, a number of fountains and the French-style Lustgarten (pleasure garden), with a symmetrical layout and lovely rose beds. Surrounding Friedenskirche is the Marlygarten, created in the mid-19th century by Ludwig Persius.

The eastern part of the park is called the Rehgarten, a beautifully landscaped park in the English style, designed by Peter Joseph Lenné, and established on the site of former hunting grounds. This park extends right up to the Neues Palais. To the south, surrounding the small palace,

extends the Charlottenhof Park, also designed by Lenné. In the northern section of the park, next to the Orangerie, is the Nordischer Garten and the Paradiesgarten.

The range of different garden styles makes a simple stroll through this park particularly pleasant. There are also a large number of sculptures, columns, obelisks and grottoes for the visitor to explore. The perspectives that suddenly open up across the park, and the picturesque groupings of trees, are also beautiful.

Communs ❸

Am Neuen Palais. 🚌 *606, 695.*

THIS AREA OF the park consists of a pair of two-storey pavilions linked by a semi-circular colonnade. They are unusually elegant buildings considering they were used for servants' quarters and the palace kitchens. However, they also served to screen from view the cultivated fields that extended past the park from the palace.

The Communs were built between 1766 and 1769 by Carl von Gontard, to a design by Jean Laurent Le Geay. The

Elegant façade of the Communs, the servants' quarters

buildings are enclosed by an elegant courtyard reflected in the style of the buildings. The kitchen was in the south pavilion, linked to the palace by an underground passageway, and the north pavilion accommodated the servants of the king's guests. Today, the rectors' offices of the University of Potsdam are located here in the Communs.

Schloss Charlottenhof ❹

CHARLOTTENHOF PALACE

Geschwister-Scholl-Strasse (Park Charlottenhof). 📞 *(0331) 969 42 28.* 🚌 *605, 606, 610, X-5.* 🚋 *94, 96, X-98.* ⏰ *15 May–15 Oct: 10am–5pm Tue–Sun.*

THIS SMALL Neo-Classical palace is located in the southern extension of Park Sanssouci, Park Charlottenhof. It was designed by Karl Friedrich Schinkel in 1829 for the heir to the throne, later King Friedrich Wilhelm IV. This small one-storey building was built in the style of a Roman villa. The rear of the palace has a portico that opens out onto the garden terrace.

Some of the wall paintings which were made in the so-called Pompeiian style, designed by Schinkel, are still in place. The most interesting part of the interior is the blue-and-white-striped Humboldt Room, also called the Tent Room due to its resemblance to a tent. The palace is surrounded by a picturesque landscaped park designed by Peter Joseph Lenné.

One of the many sculptures on display in Park Sanssouci

Römische Bäder ❺
ROMAN BATHS

Lenné-Strasse (Park Charlottenhof).
☎ *(0331) 969 42 24*. 🚌 *606*.
🚊 *94, 96, X-98*. ⬜ *15 May–15 Oct: 10am–5pm Tue–Sun.*

THIS PICTURESQUE group of pavilions, situated by the edge of a lake, forms the Roman Baths, which actually served as accommodation for the king's guests. It was designed by Karl Friedrich Schinkel, with the involvement of Ludwig Persius, between 1829 and 1840. At the front is the gardener's house, which is adjacent to an asymmetrical low tower in the style of an Italian Renaissance villa. In the background, to the left, extends the former bathing pavilion, which is currently used for temporary exhibitions. All of the pavilions are arranged around an internal garden planted with a multi-coloured carpet of shrubs. A closer look will reveal that many of these colourful plants are actually vegetables.

Spring of water, Römische Bäder

Chinesisches Teehaus ❻
CHINESE TEAHOUSE

Ökonomieweg (Rehgarten). ☎ *(0331) 969 42 22*. 🚌 *606*. 🚊 *94, 96, X-98*. ⬜ *15 May–15 Oct: 10am–5pm Tue–Sun.*

THE LUSTROUS, GILDED pavilion that can be seen glistening from a distance is the Chinese Teahouse. Chinese art was

The Chinesisches Teehaus, now housing a collection of porcelain

popular during the Rococo period – people wore Chinese silk, rooms were wallpapered with Chinese designs, furniture was lacquered, drinks were served in Chinese porcelain, and Chinese pavilions were built in gardens.

The Chinesisches Teehaus was built in Park Sanssouci between 1754 and 1756 to a design by Johann Gottfried Büring. It is circular in shape with a centrally located main hall surrounded by three studies. Between each of these are pretty *trompe l'oeil* porticos. Ornaments, together with gilded figures of Chinese gentlemen and ladies, surround the pavilion. Originally the Chinesisches Teehaus served as a tea room and a summer dining room. Today, it houses a collection of porcelain.

Orangerie ❼

Maulbeerallee (Nordischer Garten).
☎ *(0331) 96 94 280*. 🚌 *695*.
⬜ *15 May–15 Oct: 10am–5pm Tue–Sun.* **Observation terrace** *1 Apr–14 May: 10am–5pm Sat–Sun; 15 May–15 Oct: 10am–5pm Tue–Sun.*

TOWERING ABOVE the park is the Orangerie, designed in the Italian Renaissance style and crowned by a colonnade. The Orangerie was built to house guests, not plants. It was constructed between 1851 and 1860 by Friedrich August Stüler, on the initiative and direction of Friedrich Wilhelm IV. The final design was partly based on the plans of Ludwig Persius. It served as a guest residence for the

king's sister and her husband Tsar Nicholas I. The rooms were grouped around the Raphael Hall, which was based on the Regia Hall in the Vatican and decorated with copies of the works of Italian artist Raphael. It is also worth climbing up to the observation terrace, from where the view extends over Potsdam.

Friedenskirche ❽

Allee nach Sanssouci (Marlygarten).
☎ *(0331) 97 40 09*. 🚌 *692, 695.* 🚊 *94, 96, X-98*. ⬜ *May–Oct: 10am–6pm daily; Nov–Apr: 10am–noon Sun.*

CLOSE TO SCHLOSS Sanssouci is Friedenskirche, or the Church of Peace. The foundation stone was laid by King Friedrich Wilhelm IV in 1845 and the church was completed in 1848. Designed by Ludwig Persius, Friedrich August Stüler and Ludwig Hesse, the church is based on San Clemente in Rome.

Inside, the vaulted ceiling of the apse is almost completely covered by an enchanting 12th-century mosaic depicting the figure of Christ as a judge. This Byzantine mosaic was originally located in the church of San Capriano on the island of Murano in Venice, Italy. Next to the church is a colonnaded atrium and a mausoleum containing the tombs of Friedrich Wilhelm I, Friedrich Wilhelm IV and Kaiser Friedrich III.

Long flight of stairs leading to the Renaissance-style Orangerie

Neue Kammern 9

NEW CHAMBERS

Zur Historischen Mühle (Lustgarten).
📞 *(0331) 969 42 06.* 🚌 *612, 614, 695.* 🕐 *mid-May–mid-Oct: 10am–5pm Tue–Sun; Apr–mid-May: 10am–5pm Sat–Sun.* 🎟️ 📷

T HE NEUE KAMMERN contains residential apartments. It is the mirror image of the Bildergalerie and was originally built as an orangery in 1747 to a design by Georg Wenzeslaus von Knobelsdorff. In 1777 Frederick the Great (Friedrich II) ordered the building to be remodelled as guest accommodation. The architect, Georg Christian Unger, left the elegant Baroque exterior of the orangery largely untouched and instead concentrated on converting the interior. As well as the sumptuous guest suites, the new design included four elegant halls. The best of these is the Ovidsaal, with its rich reliefs and marble floors. The interior décor has been maintained in Frederick's Rococo style. The building also houses a collection of Meissen figurines.

Schloss Sanssouci 10

See pp200–201.

Detail of Caravaggio's *Doubting Thomas*, in the Bildergalerie

Bildergalerie 11

Zur Historischen Mühle. 📞 *(0331) 969 42 02.* 🚌 *612, 614, 695.* 🕐 *mid-May–mid-Oct: 10am–5pm Tue–Sun.* 📷

T HE PICTURE GALLERY housed in the building adjacent to Schloss Sanssouci is the first purpose-built gallery in Germany. It was constructed between 1755 and 1764 to a design by JG Büring. The garden elevation reveals an allegorical tableau representing Art, Education and Crafts, while busts of renowned artists have been placed in the windows.
The gallery contains an exhibition of Baroque paintings once owned by Frederick the Great, although part of the collection can be found in the Gemäldegalerie *(see pp122–5).* Highlights include Caravaggio's *Doubting Thomas* and Guido Reni's *Cleopatra's Death*, as well as a number of canvases by Rubens and van Dyck.

Historische Mühle 12

HISTORIC WINDMILL

Zur Historischen Mühle. 📞 *(0331) 969 42 84.* 🚌 *612, 614, 695.* 🕐 *Apr–Oct: 10am–6pm daily; Nov–Mar: 10am–4pm Sat & Sun.* 📷

A MILL HAS BEEN located here since the early 18th century, although this is actually a reconstruction, dating from 1993. According to local legend, the old windmill was so noisy that Frederick the Great ordered it to be dismantled. However, a court upheld the miller's cause and the mill stayed. In 1790 a new windmill was built in its place, which lasted until 1945. The mill currently houses a museum of mechanical windmills.

Alexandrowka 13

Russische Kolonie Allee/ Puschkinallee. 🚇 *90, 92, 95, X-91.* 🚌 *604, 609, 650, 692, 697.*

A TRIP TO Alexandrowka takes the visitor into the world of Pushkin's stories. Wooden houses made from logs,

A Russian-style wooden house in the settlement of Alexandrowka

decorated with carved motifs and set in their own gardens, create a very pretty residential estate. Although they appear to be picturebook, traditional Russian houses, they were constructed in 1826 under the direction of a German military architect called Captain Snethlage. What is interesting is that the estate was created for the singers of a Russian choir. The choir was set up in 1812 to entertain the troops and was recruited from over 500 Russian prisoners of war, who had fought with Napoleon. In 1815, when the Prussians and the Russians joined forces, the choir was retained by Friedrich Wilhelm III.

Peter Joseph Lenné was responsible for the overall appearance of the estate, and it was named Alexandrowka after the Tsarina, the Prussian Princess Charlotte. It is based on the shape of the cross of St Andrew inscribed within an oval. In all, 12 houses were built here, as well as an outhouse which now contains a small museum. Some of the dwellings are still owned by the descendants of the choir. To the north of this estate stands the Russian Orthodox church of Alexander Nevski (1829).

Schloss Cecilienhof, summer residence of the Hohenzollern family

layout was created by Peter Joseph Lenné in 1816. It is a Romantic park ornamented with numerous pavilions and sculptures. The charming Marmorpalais stands beside the lake, while the northern section contains the early 20th-century Schloss Cecilienhof. Elsewhere you can see the red and green gardeners' houses, the pyramid-shaped ice house and a Neo-Gothic library pavilion completed in 1794.

Schloss Cecilienhof **⑮**

Am Neuen Garten. ☎ (0331) 969 42 44. 🚌 695. ⏰ Apr–Oct: 9am–5pm; Nov–Mar: 9am–4pm Tue–Sun.

THE CECILIENHOF residence played a brief but important part in history because it was here that the 1945 Potsdam

Conference took place. Built between 1914 and 1917, the palace is the most recent of the Hohenzollern dynasty buildings and was designed by Paul Schultze-Naumburg in the style of an English country manor. It is a sprawling, asymmetrical building with wooden beams making a pretty herringbone pattern on its walls. The gatehouse passageways leading to the courtyards are decorated with Baroque reliefs.

The palace was the Hohenzollern family residence after they lost the crown; the family remained in Potsdam until February 1945. It now functions as a first-class hotel and restaurant, where history lovers can relax amid carefully tended shrubbery. Most of the historic furnishings used during the famous Potsdam conference are on display.

Orange growing in the Neuer Garten's Marmorpalais

Neuer Garten **⑭**
NEW GARDEN

Am Neuen Garten. 🚌 695.

RUNNING ALONG the edge of Heiliger See, on what was once the site of palace vineyards, is a park laid out between 1787 and 1791. It was landscaped originally by Johann August Eyserbeck on the instructions of Friedrich Wilhelm II, while the current

THE POTSDAM CONFERENCE OF 1945

On 17 July 1945 the heads of government for Great Britain (Winston Churchill, later represented by Clement Attlee), the United States (Harry Truman) and the Soviet Union (Joseph Stalin) met in Schloss Cecilienhof to confirm the decisions made earlier that year at Yalta. The aim of both conferences was to resolve the problems arising at the end of World War II. They decided to abolish the Nazi Party, to limit the size of the German militia and monitor it indefinitely, and also to punish war criminals and establish reparations. They also revised the German borders and arranged the resettlement of Germans from Poland. The conference played a major part in establishing the political balance of power in Europe, which continued for the next 45 years.

Attlee, Truman and Stalin at Cecilienhof

Schloss Sanssouci ⑩

THE NAME SANSSOUCI is French for "without a care" and gives a good indication of the flamboyant character of this enchanting Rococo palace, built in 1745. The original sketches, made by Friedrich II (Frederick the Great) himself, were finalized by Georg Wenzeslaus von Knobelsdorff. The glorious interiors were designed by Knobelsdorff and Johann August Nahl. The king clearly loved this palace, as his final wishes were that he should be buried here, near the tomb of his Italian greyhounds. He was actually interred in the Garnisonkirche, Potsdam, but his final wishes were carried out in 1991.

Bacchanalian Figures
The carved male and female bacchanalian figures on the pilasters are the work of Friedrich Christian Glume.

The colonnade frames the view of the artificial ruins on the hill.

The wings were added to the building between 1841 and 1842.

Voltaire Room
This room, located in the Damenflügel (Ladies' wing), is decorated with naturalistic carvings of birds, flowers and fruit.

Domed Roof
The oxidized green dome covers the Marmorsaal. It is decorated with Baroque sculptures.

Marmorsaal
The imposing marble hall is decorated with pairs of columns made from Carrara marble. Frederick the Great wanted this room to be loosely based on the Pantheon in Rome.

STAR SIGHTS

- ★ **Fêtes Galantes by Antoine Watteau**

- ★ **Konzertzimmer**

Arbour
The palace design is completed by picturesque arbours and pergolas decorated with sun motifs.

VISITORS' CHECKLIST

Zur Historischen Mühle.
📞 (0331) 969 41 90. 🚌 612, 614, 650, 695. 🚊 94, 96, X-98.
🕐 1 Apr–31 Oct: 9am–5pm Tue–Sun; 1 Nov–31 Mar: 9am–4pm Tue–Sun. **Damen-flügel** 15 May–15 Oct: 10am–5pm Sat–Sun. 🎦 📷 compulsory.

★ Fêtes Galantes (c. 1715)
The real jewels in the palace are the enchanting paintings by Antoine Watteau. He was one of Frederick the Great's favourite artists.

Weimar Urn (1785)
This Neo-Classical urn from the Berlin company KPM (see p133) is a copy of the original urn, which was presented to the Duchess of Weimar.

★ Konzertzimmer
The walls of the salon are decorated with paintings by Antoine Pesne, based on Greek mythology.

Bibliothek
The library of Frederick the Great contains about 2,100 books. The walls are lined with cedar panelling to create a contemplative atmosphere.

Marmorpalais 🔟
MARBLE PALACE

Am Ufer des Heiligen Sees (Neuer Garten). ((0331) 969 42 46. 🚌 612, 614, 650, 695. ⭕ 1 Apr–31 Oct: 10am–5pm Tue–Sun; 1 Nov–31 Mar: 10am–4pm Sat–Sun.

THE MARMORPALAIS is situated on the edge of the lake in Neuer Garten (see p199), a park northeast of the centre of Potsdam. This small palace is a beautiful example of early Neo-Classical architecture. The palace owes its name to its façade, which is lined with Silesian marble.

The square main body of the palace was the initiative of King Friedrich Wilhelm II. The original building was completed in 1791 to a design by Carl von Gontard, under the direction of Carl Gotthard Langhans. The single-storey building had small rooms around a central staircase, but this turned out to be too small, and in 1797 it was extended. An extra floor and two projecting wings were added. This gave the Marmorpalais the character of a Palladian villa.

The main part of the palace contains Neo-Classical furnishings from the late 1700s, including furniture from the workshops of Roentgen and porcelain from Wedgwood, the English firm. The interiors of the wings date from slightly later, from the 1840s. The concert hall in the right hand wing is particularly beautiful. King Friedrich Wilhelm II died in this palace in 1797.

Neo-Classical Marmorpalais, with its inlaid marble façade

The historic Dutch district known as the Holländisches Viertel

Holländisches Viertel 🔟
DUTCH QUARTER

Friedrich-Ebert-/Kurfürsten-/Hebbel-/ Gutenbergstr. 🚌 138, 604, 606, 638, 639, 692, 695. 🚊 92, 95, X-91.

JUST AS AMAZING as the Russian district of Alexandrowka (see pp198–9) is this Dutch district. The area is popular with tourists, with numerous shops, galleries, cafés and beer cellars, especially along the central Mittelstrasse.

Dutch workers, invited by Friedrich Wilhelm I, arrived in Potsdam at the beginning of the 18th century. Between 1733 and 1742 a settlement was built for them, comprising 134 gabled houses arranged in four groups, according to plans by Johann Boumann the Elder. They were built from small red bricks, and finished with stone and plaster details. These houses are typically three-storey, with picturesque roofs and gables.

Peter und Paul Kirche 🔟

Bassinplatz. ((0331) 230 79 90. 🚌 618, 750, 780. 🚊 90, 92, 93, 96, X-91, X-98. ⭕ 11am–5pm Tue–Sat. ✝ 10am & 7pm Sun.

THIS 19TH-CENTURY church was the first large Catholic church built in Potsdam, at the initiative of Friedrich Wilhelm IV. The first designs came from Friedrich August Stüler, but the final version is the work of Wilhelm Salzenberg. The church was built in 1870, in the shape of a Neo-

Romanesque cross. Its slender tower is a copy of the campanile of San Zeno Maggiore in Verona, Italy. Inside are three beautiful paintings by Antoine Pesne.

The colonnaded portico of the Französische Kirche

Französische Kirche 🔟
FRENCH CHURCH

Bassinplatz. ((0331) 29 12 19. 🚌 618, 750, 780. 🚊 90, 92, 93, 96, X-91, X-98. ⭕ noon–5pm daily.

THIS CHURCH, reminiscent of the Pantheon in Rome, was built especially for the Hugenots in 1752. Following their expulsion from France, they were given the option of settling in Prussia in 1685 (see p19). Those who settled in Potsdam initially benefited from the hospitality of other churches, then eventually the Französische Kirche was built for them. It was designed by Johann Boumann the Elder in the shape of an ellipse. The front elevation is supported by a grand columned portico. The side niches, which are the entrances of the church, are decorated with the allegorical figures of Faith and Knowledge. The interior dates from the 1830s and is based on designs by Karl Friedrich Schinkel.

Nikolaikirche ⑳

Am Alten Markt. ☎ (0331) 29 16 82. 🚌 604, 609, 692. 🚊 90, 92, 93, 96, X-90, X-91, X-98. ⏰ 2–5pm Mon, 10am–5pm Tue–Sat, 11:30am–5pm Sun.

THIS IMPOSING church, built in a late Neo-Classical style, is the most beautiful church in Potsdam. It was designed in 1830 by Karl Friedrich Schinkel and the building work was overseen by Ludwig Persius. The main body of the church is based on a square cross, with a semicircular presbytery.

It was decided only in the 1840s to crown the church with a vast dome, supported on a colonnaded tambour (wall supporting a dome). Schinkel had envisaged this from the beginning of the project, but it was not included in the orders of the king. Initially it was thought that the dome would be supported by a wooden structure, though ultimately it was built using iron between 1843 and 1848, according to a design by Persius and Friedrich August Stüler. The interior decoration and the furnishings of the church date back to the 1850s, and in the main area of the church they were based on the earlier designs by Schinkel.

In front of the church stands an obelisk built between 1753

and 1755 to a design by Georg Wenzeslaus von Knobelsdorff. Initially it was decorated by medallions depicting portraits of Prussian rulers, but during the post-World War II restorations, they were replaced with portraits of renowned Prussian architects.

Altes Rathaus ㉑
OLD TOWN HALL

Am Alten Markt. 🚌 604, 609, 692, 694. 🚊 90, 92, 93, 96, X-90, X-91, X-98.

THIS ELEGANT, colonnaded building, located on the eastern side of Alter Markt, is the old town hall. Designed by Johann Boumann the Elder, it was built in 1753 on the site of an earlier building that served a similar purpose. The uppermost storey, which features an ornamental attic roof, is decorated with the crest of Potsdam and allegorical sculptures. At the summit of the small tower are two gilded figures

Atlas at Altes Rathaus

of Atlas, each carrying a globe of the earth. The Altes Rathaus is currently used as a cultural centre. The interior of the neighbouring mid-18th century building was also refurbished, and a glassed-in passageway was built, linking the two buildings.

The Potsdam Royal Palace was located at one time on the west side of Alter Markt. It was a massive two-storey building with three wings. There was also an elegant courtyard and a superb gateway crowned by a tower. The palace was built in 1662 on the site of a former castle, on the initiative of the Great Elector. Over the following years the palace was greatly enlarged and modernized for members of the royal family, including Frederick the Great (Friedrich II). After a bombing raid in 1945 the palace remained in ruins for many years, but the East German Government decided finally to pull down the remains in 1960. A temporary theatre now occupies the site.

Nikolaikirche's imposing exterior, with its green, weathered dome

---

POTSDAM TOWN GATES

The city of Potsdam was enclosed by a wall in 1722. This wall did not serve a defensive purpose – it was supposed to contain criminals and stop soldiers deserting. When the borders of the town were extended in 1733, new districts were also enclosed by the wall. There was a total of five city gates, of which three have survived. Jägertor has survived in its original condition and dates from 1733. Featuring solid, wide pillars, the gate is crowned with a group of sculptures depicting hunting dogs attacking a deer. Nauener Tor was redesigned in 1755 by Johann Gottfried Büring and, interestingly, it is one of the earliest examples of Neo-Gothic design occurring outside Great Britain. The most imposing of the gates is the Brandenburger Tor. It was rebuilt in 1770 in a Neo-Classical style to commemorate victory in the Seven Years' War (see p19). The designers, Gontard and Unger, gave it the appearance of an ancient triumphal arch. At the very top is a number of different groups of sculptures. These include figures from Greek mythology, such as Hercules and Mars.

Nauener Tor   **Jägertor**   **Brandenburger Tor**

Stately building of the Marstall (Filmmuseum)

Marstall (Filmmuseum) ㉒

Alter Markt. ☏ 27 18 10. ⏰ 10am–6pm daily. 🚌 601, 603, 692, 694. 🚊 90, 92, 93, 96, X-91, X-98.

THIS BAROQUE PAVILION, once used as a royal stables, hence the name Marstall, is the only remaining building of a former royal residence. It was first established in 1714 by refashioning the orangery built by Johann Nering in 1685. In 1746 it was extended and refashioned once more, according to a design by the architect GW von Knobelsdorff. It suffered extensive damage in World War II and in 1977, after major restoration, it was converted to a film museum. As well as temporary exhibitions, this museum documents the history and work of the Babelsberg studios, Germany's earliest film studios. Exhibits include old projectors, cameras and other equipment as well as props used in some of the most famous German films.

Potsdam-Museum ㉓

Breite Strasse 8–12. ☏ 289 66 00. ⏰ 10am–5pm Tue–Sun. 🚌 695, X-5.

THE POTSDAM-MUSEUM'S collection embraces natural science and historical exhibits equally, including a display illustrating the geography and nature of the Havel river basin. In the main building, the history of Potsdam is documented up until 1900 and the exhibition continues in two smaller buildings, called the Hiller-Brandt's Häuser (houses). These were built in

1769 by Georg Christian Unger and were a deliberate copy of Inigo Jones's Banqueting House on Whitehall, London.

Cherubs decorating the façade of the Potsdam-Museum

Wasserwerk Sanssouci ㉔

Breite Strasse. ☏ (0331) 969 42 01. ⏰ 15 May–15 October: 10am–5pm Sat–Sun. 🚌 606. 🚊 94, 96, X-98.

ALTHOUGH POTSDAM once boasted a Russian and a Dutch community, the remarkable mosque was not built to serve the needs of an Islamic community. Rather, it was built to disguise the special steam pump that serviced the fountains in Park Sanssouci. This Moorish-style building, with its slender minaret and Oriental dome, was designed by Ludwig Persius in 1842. The dome does not serve any useful purpose, although within the minaret there is a huge chimney. While visiting the mosque you can see the preserved steam-powered machinery manufactured by the Borsig company.

Telegrafenberg ㉕

Albert-Einstein-Strasse. Ⓢ Potsdam Hauptbahnhof. **Einsteinturm** 🎟 (0331) 29 17 41. ⏰ by appointment only. 🎫 compulsory.

THE BUILDINGS on the Telegrafenberg are considered to be some of the best 20th-century structures in the world and attract many admirers of modern architecture. The hill received its current name in 1832, when an optical telegraph station linking Berlin and Koblenz was built here. In the late 19th century, various educational institutes were located here, including the Institute of Astrophysics, for which the complex of buildings in yellow brick was built.

The meandering avenues lead to a picturesque clearing where the small Einsteinturm (Einstein's Tower) breaks through the surrounding trees. Specially designed to observe the solar system, the tower was intended to provide information that would support Einstein's Theory of Relativity. It was built in 1920 by Erich Mendelsohn and is regarded as one of the finest architectural examples of German Expressionism. Its fantastical appearance was intended to show what could be achieved with reinforced concrete. However, the costs of the complicated form limited the use of concrete, and above the first storey the building is made from brickwork covered in plaster.

Moorish Wasserwerk Sanssouci, complete with minaret

Filmpark Babelsberg 🔞

THIS AMAZING theme park was laid out on the site of the film studios where Germany's first films were produced in 1912. From 1917 the studio belonged to Universum-Film-AG (UFA), which produced some of the most renowned films of the silent era, such as *Metropolis* *(see p151)*. Nazi propaganda films were also made here. The studio is still operational today, although part of the complex is open to visitors. Expect to see the sets from old films, special effects at work and stuntmen in action.

VISITORS' CHECKLIST

August-Bebel Strasse 26–53 (entrance in Grossbeeren Strasse). 📞 *(0331) 721 27 50.* 🚌 690, 696. Ⓢ *Griebnitzsee.* ⏱ *mid-Mar–early Nov: 10am–6pm daily.* 🅿 🅆 www.filmpark.de

Sandmann
Sandmann is a character from an animated television series. Sandmann has entertained children in East Germany from 1959 to the present day.

Simulator ride

World of Horrors
You can take a spine-chilling stroll through a world of haunted houses, eerie graveyards and ghostly figures.

Submarine (U-Boot "Boomer")

Panama – Janosch's Dreamland
A short boat trip will take you through the enchanting world of the children's illustrator Janosch in the company of Little Tiger and Little Bear.

Adventure Restaurant
This is in a medieval castle made for the film Prinz Eisenherz *(Prince Valiant).*

Main entrance

Stuntshow
at the Vulkan gives the Babelsberg stunt crew the chance to impress and thrill in a spectacular daily show.

THREE GUIDED WALKS

BERLIN IS FULL of enchanting parks, gardens, lakes and interesting monuments, and one of the best ways to enjoy them is by going on a guided walk. The three walks suggested in this chapter provide for relaxation far from the hustle and bustle of the city centre. The first takes you onto the picturesque Pfaueninsel (Peacock Island), which at the end of the 18th century was refashioned into a romantic English-style park with garden pavilions and an enchanting little palace. After visiting the island you can pay a short visit to Nikolskoe – a Russian-style *dacha* (country house) built for the future Tsar Nicholas I and his wife, the daughter of King Friedrich Wilhelm III. The second walk begins in Berlin and takes you first through the grounds of the Klein

Statue at Klein Glienicke

Glienicke Park, which was laid out in the 1820s for Prince Karl of Prussia. This route continues across the former border between East and West Germany, in an area which is now part of Potsdam. There you can visit the Romantic-era park of Babelsberg, and the Neo-Gothic palace designed for Prince Wilhelm by Karl Friedrich Schinkel. The third walk, around the forest called Grunewald, takes you initially through a deluxe villa resort of the late 19th century, and then along forest paths to the Grunewaldsee. On the shores of this lake stands an enchanting hunting lodge. From there you can continue walking to the Brücke-Museum. Because each of these three walks leads you across unpaved paths, remember to wear comfortable shoes.

GREATER BERLIN

Grunewald
(see pp212–13)

Pfaueninsel
and Nikolskoe
(see pp208–9)

Havel

Grosser
Wannsee

KÖNIGSTRASSE

POTSDAMER CHAUSEE

UNTER DEN EICHEN

Klein Glienicke
and Babelsberg
(see pp210–11)

KEY

..... Walking route

═══ Autobahn (motorway)

▬ Major road

═ Minor road

— Railway line

0 kilometres 2

0 miles 2

◁ **A picturesque corner of the Neo-Gothic Babelsberg palace**

Pfaueninsel and Nikolskoe

Statue at the small palace

T HIS WALK takes you around Pfaueninsel (Peacock Island). This picturesque park, now a nature reserve, was laid out in 1795 according to a design by Johann August Eyserbeck. Its final form, which you see today, is the work of the renowned landscape architect Peter Joseph Lenné. This pleasant, relaxing walk allows you to explore several interesting sights, and to encounter the peacocks for which the island is named. Afterwards you can have refreshments at the lakeside, or head straight to Nikolskoe, the location of one of Berlin's finest restaurants.

James's Well, deliberately built to resemble a picturesque ruin

One of the colourful peacocks on Pfaueninsel (Peacock Island)

Around Pfaueninsel

At the jetty ① you board a small passenger ferry which takes you to the island in a few minutes. After disembarking, follow the path which leads to the left. It continues along the edge of the island, gently uphill to the Castellan's House ② and further on to the Swiss House, dating from 1830, in which the gardener lived. Continue along the path to the extensive clearing with a picturesque flower garden, beyond which is the small romantic palace of Schloss Pfaueninsel ③. Dating from 1794, it was designed by

The Neo-Gothic Schloss Pfaueninsel designed by Johann Brendel

Johann Gottlieb Brendel for Friedrich Wilhelm II and his mistress Wilhelmine Encke (the future Countess Lichtenau). The palace was built of wood, with a façade (hidden away) fashioned in the form of a ruined medieval castle. The façade was visible from Neuer Garten in Potsdam. The cast-iron bridge which links the towers was built in 1807. During the summer months you can go inside the palace to see its furnishings from the 18th and 19th centuries.

After leaving the palace follow the path that leads along the edge, passing by the kitchen pavilion ④ on the left, which is set amid greenery. At the next junction turn gently right into the depths of the island. You will pass by the James's Well ⑤ which was built to resemble an ancient ruin, and cross a meadow heading towards a small wood which contains the Kavalierhaus ⑥. This building was used to provide the

royal household with accommodation. At the front of the house, Karl Friedrich Schinkel installed an authentic façade from a late Gothic house brought over from Danzig (now Gdansk) in Poland. From here you proceed further in the same

KEY

••• Suggested route

– – Ferry route

⚓ Ferry boarding point

0 metres   200

0 yards   200

direction, and emerge again in a large clearing. To the left you can marvel at the Parschenkessel bay ⑦ in the distance, surrounded by dead trees on which cormorants nest. Take the path on the left to the Neo-Gothic Dairy ⑧

Guests on the terrace of the Blockhaus Nikolskoe in summer

mausoleum in Schlosspark Charlottenburg *(see p163)* in 1829. The path leads further along the edge of the lake, while on the right side among the trees you pass the stone commemorating Johannes Kunckel, an alchemist who lived on Pfaueninsel in the 17th century. In his quest to uncover how to make gold he, in fact, discovered a method of producing ruby-coloured glass. Carry on further through the forest, passing the Gothic Bridge ⑪, and then take the path to the right up towards the hill of the Aviary ⑫, home to multi-coloured parrots and pheasants. From here you continue towards the tall column of a Fountain ⑬ designed by Martin Friedrich Rabe in 1824. Next, walk onward to the jetty, passing the market gardens with their hothouses on the way.

From the Jetty to Nikolskoe
Once you've taken the little ferry back to the mainland, head off to the right, going

Havel

and the Dutch House ⑨. This was a cow shed and dates from 1802, while the Dairy is an artificial ruin of a medieval abbey dating from 1795. From here take the path along the edge of the lake heading south; you can marvel at the wonderful views. To the right by the edge of the forest you can see Luisentempel ⑩ in the form of a Greek temple. Its sandstone portico at the front was moved to the island from the

TIPS FOR WALKERS

Beginning of the walk: the jetty for the ferry to Pfaueninsel.
Length: 4.4 km (2.7 miles).
Duration: 2.5–3 hours.
Getting there: bus 216 or 316 from S-Bahn Wannsee; or ferry from Wannsee or Potsdam.
Stops: There are no cafés or restaurants on Pfaueninsel itself. By the jetty on the mainland is "Wirtshaus zur Pfaueninsel", a little place to eat with a summer beer garden. In Nikolskoe is a restaurant with a terrace called "Blockhaus Nikolskoe".

south. When you come to the fork take the left hand path leading gently uphill. This leads to the church of Saints Peter and Paul ⑭, which rises above a large terrace from where there are pretty views of Pfaueninsel. The church was built between the years 1834 and 1837, according to a design by Friedrich August Stüler. The small, orderly, body of the church is fronted by a tower crowned by an onion-shaped dome, which reflects Russian Orthodox sacral architecture. This links to the adjacent Blockhaus "Nikolskoe" ⑮, a Russian-style wooden *dacha* (country house), built in 1819 by the architect Snethlage, who created the Alexandrowka estate in Potsdam. The *dacha* was a present from King Friedrich Wilhelm III to his daughter and son-in-law, the future Tsar Nicholas I. Following a fire in 1985 the *dacha* was reconstructed, and it currently houses a restaurant. Nearby you will find a bus-stop where you can catch buses back to the S-Bahn Wannsee.

The little ferry on the Havel river which takes passengers to Pfaueninsel

Klein Glienicke and Babelsberg

A griffin in Klein Glienicke

THIS GUIDED WALK takes you through an area covered by two interesting palace-park complexes – Klein Glienicke and Babelsberg. They were built originally for members of the royal family during the mid-19th century. The buildings of Klein Glienicke were designed by Schinkel, Persius and von Arnim in a Neo-Classical style. Peter Joseph Lenné created the charming park in which they are located. Babelsberg has a more romantic park that was completed by Hermann von Pückler-Muskau. It is maintained in a completely different style, with regal Neo-Gothic pavilions.

Mosaic from the Klosterhof in the gardens of Klein Glienicke

Around Klein Glienicke

The walk begins by the main gate leading into the park. The southern section of the park has the feel of an Italianate Arcadian garden. Soon on the left you will see the Stibadium ①, a roofed pavilion designed by Ludwig Persius. Nearby you can marvel at the imposing Fountain of Lions ②, decorated with gilded figures of these royal beasts. The fountain stands on the axis of the palace ③ which was built in 1825, according to a design

The reconstructed Gothic Gerichts-laube (arcaded courthouse)

by Karl Friedrich Schinkel for Prince Karl of Prussia. During summer weekends you can visit the palace between 10am and 5pm. Beyond the symmetrical, Neo-Classical building extends an irregular cluster of buildings, grouped around a courtyard with a veranda, which include a pergola and staff cottages. You pass by the palace and approach the Coach House ④, designed by Schinkel but refurbished several times. This now houses the Coach House restaurant *(see p243)*.

Beyond the Coach House you can see the orangery and greenhouses built by Persius. A path leads in the direction of the lake, but on the way it is worth diverting to the right to the Klosterhof ⑥, a mock monastery with pavilions, also by Persius. In the walls of these buildings are numerous Byzantine and Romanesque architectural elements from Italy. Further to the north extends a second "wild" section of the park created to resemble an alpine and Carpathian landscape, with man-made waterfalls, planks

for crossing the water, and hunting lodges. You can return in the direction of the lake and go up to the Casino ⑦, which once contained guest apartments. From here a path extending along the lake takes you to the Grosse Neugierde ⑧, a circular pavilion with a roof supported by Doric columns, based on the Athenian monument to Lysikrates from the 4th century BC. From here there are beautiful views across the Havel river and Glienicker Brücke ⑨, known paradoxically as the bridge of unity under the East German contain original Roman and Byzantine fragments.

From Klein Glienicke to Babelsberg

On leaving the park you cross to the other side of Potsdamer Chaussee and proceed along Mövenstrasse, passing the massive building of the Jagd-schloss Glienicke ⑪ on the right. Located on the site of an earlier hunting lodge, its Neo-Mannerist appearance is the result of a massive rebuilding process undertaken in 1889 by Albert Geyer, on behalf of Prince Friedrich Leopold. It now houses an international meeting centre as well as an academy of folk art. Passing the Jagdschloss you turn right into Waldmüller-strasse, then right again into Lankestrasse, which leads you to the bridge linking Glienicke with Babelsberg.

Around Schloss Babelsberg

From the bridge you head right towards the engine house ⑫, designed by Persius to look like a medieval castle with a tall tower covering the chimney. From here you head towards Schloss Babelsberg ⑬, designed by Karl Friedrich Schinkel for the future Kaiser Wilhelm I of Germany. The palace was built between 1833 and 1835 in a Neo-Gothic style and shows the influence of English architecture on Schinkel. This beautiful, irregular building with many

Babelsberg's Neo-Gothic Flatow-turm dating from 1853 to 1856

towers and bay windows is one of Schinkel's greatest works. Visitors can go inside.

From here, take the path leading along the edge of the Havel to the so-called Kleines Schloss ⑭. Another Neo-Gothic palace, although much smaller in scale, this was where ladies of the court once resided. It now houses a café.

From here you proceed further to the edge of the lake, taking the left branch to the Neo-Gothic stable ⑮, and further to the Gerichtslaube (Gothic arcaded courthouse) ⑯ which was moved here from Berlin. The final sight on this walk is the Flatowturm ⑰, a Neo-Gothic tower dating from 1853 to 1856, from which there are marvellous views of the surrounding area. From here follow the path to the park exit at Grenzstrasse. Turning left, you reach the bus stop for the No. 690 and No. 691 which go to S-Bahn Babelsberg station.

regime. The border with West Berlin ran across this bridge, where the exchange of spies was conducted during the Cold War. You return via a path along the wall of the main gate, passing the Kleine Neugierde ⑩, a pavilion serving as a tea room. This was built in the form of an ancient temple, and its walls

| 0 metres | 300 |
| 0 yards | 300 |

KEY

• • • Suggested route

⚓ Ferry boarding point

The Neo-Gothic Schloss Babelsberg, designed by KF Schinkel

TIPS FOR WALKERS

Beginning of the walk: bus stop at Klein Glienicke. *Length:* 4.2 km (2.6 miles). *Duration:* 3 hours. *Getting there:* bus 116 from S-Bahn station Wannsee or ferry from Wannsee or Potsdam. *Stops:* Café at Park Babelsberg; Coach House at Klein Glienicke. *Schloss Babelsberg* ⬜ but no regular times due to restoration work. ☎ (0331) 969 42 50 for latest information.

Grunewald

THIS WALK leads initially through one of Berlin's most elegant residential areas, established in 1889. Once the haunt of politicians, wealthy industrialists, renowned artists and academics, some villas now serve as the headquarters of academic institutes. This walk continues through the forest to a small hunting lodge with an interesting art collection, and ends at the edge of the Grunewald in a residential estate of elegant villas, home of the Brücke-Museum.

The elegant villa at Winklerstrasse No. 11

From Bahnhof Grunewald to Hagenstrasse

From the S-Bahn Grunewald station follow the signs to "Grunewald (Ort)". Be sure to take a close look at the station itself ① – this picturesque wooden framed building was built in 1899. The station has a dark past, though, as Berlin's Jews were transported from here to the concentration camps. From the square in front of the station go along Winklerstrasse, which turns left. Along the way you will pass stunningly beautiful villas. The Neo-Classical house at No. 15, dating from 1899, was home to architect Ewald Becher ②. Not much further on the same side of the road, at No. 11, is a villa dating from 1906 ③. It was designed by Hermann Muthesius, who transplanted onto German soil the style of English rustic building. On the right at No. 12 is Villa Maren, dating from 1897, an example of a Neo-Renaissance building in the style of an Italian palazzo with *sgraffito* decorations ④. The villa at No. 8–10,

dating from 1902, boasts costly stone elevations, which fan out richly with decorations in the German Renaissance style ⑤. By this villa turn right into Hasensprung, which leads across the bridge decorated with running hares, dividing Dianasee from Königssee. You reach Königsallee and turn left before immediately turning right into Lassenstrasse, and then right again into Bismarckstrasse, which leads to a small square where you can marvel at the picturesque Neo-Gothic Grunewald-Kirche ⑥. From here go left into Furtwänglerstrasse, where it is worth looking at the villa at No. 15, a beautiful example of a southern German country house ⑦. Next turn right into Hubertusbader Strasse, where at No. 25 an interesting villa has survived with Neo-Classical motifs ⑧, which is the work of Arnold Hartmann dating from 1896. He is also responsible for the villa at No. 23

Rose window, Grunewald-Kirche

Seebergsteig, featuring fantastic elevations decorated with Secessionist motifs ⑨. From here continue along Hubertusbader Strasse to Hagenstrasse.

From Hagenstrasse to the Brücke-Museum

You cut through Hagenstrasse and continue further, straight into Wildpfad, where you turn left in Waldmeisterstrasse, which leads along the fence of the grounds of private clubs. Turn right into Eichhörnchensteig, which gradually becomes surrounded by forest and changes from being a

KEY

···· Suggested route

Ⓢ S-Bahn

road into a forest path. Once past the grounds of the private clubs, follow a road which goes gently to the right, and down to the edge of the picturesque Grunewaldsee. Turn left and continue along its edge to Jagdschloss Grunewald ⑩. This is one of the oldest civic buildings to survive in Berlin. It was built for the Elector Joachim II in 1542, and around 1700 it was rebuilt in a Baroque style. Through the gate you enter a courtyard enclosed on three sides with household buildings. In the small palace is Berlin's only surviving Renaissance hall. It houses a collection of paintings, with canvases by Rubens and van Dyck among others. In the east wing is the small Waldmuseum, with illustrations that depict forest life. Following a recent fire, which destroyed the roof and other parts of the building, Jagdschloss will reopen by 2005.

From the palace you proceed further along the edge to Forsthaus Paulsborn ⑪. This picturesque building was constructed in 1905, according to a design by Friedrich Wilhelm Göhre (see p243). The entire building is maintained in the style of a hunting lodge with decorations that reflect hunting themes. During the summer the garden is filled with tables, where you can

The household buildings in the hunting lodge in Grunewald

Detail from Toni-Lessler-Strasse No. 23

enjoy a tasty meal and have a rest, following the walk.

From Paulsborn you return to Jagdschloss Grunewald; at the crossroads you should take the central avenue signposted "Wilmersdorf". This leads through the forest and emerges on Pücklerstrasse. Passing modern deluxe villas you continue straight on, and then turn right into Fohlenweg, then turn right again into Bussardsteig, at the end of which is the Brücke-Museum (see p179) ⑫. It is also worth looking at the exhibition of sculptures by Bernhard Heliger arranged in the garden surrounding the villa at Käuzchensteig No. 8. From here you continue to Clayallee where buses on the No. 115 route operate.

Restaurant in the Forsthaus Paulsborn near Jagdschloss Grunewald

---

TIPS FOR WALKERS

Beginning of the walk:
Grunewald S-Bahn station.
Distance: 3 km (1.8 miles).
Duration: 2.5–3 hours.
Getting there: S-Bahn line 3 or 7; U-Bahn Oskar-Helene-Heim; Bus 115. **Museum:** Jagdschloss Grunewald. 🕿 813 35 97. ⬤ for restoration work. It is currently planned to reopen in late 2004 or 2005. **Stops:** There are numerous cafés and restaurants in the Grunewald residential area. Near Jagdschloss Grunewald there is a very good restaurant, Forsthaus Paulsborn.

TRAVELLERS' NEEDS

WHERE TO STAY

BERLIN HAS A good selection of hotels to suit any budget. Many of the expensive hotels belong to well-known international chains, but you can also find reasonably priced rooms in and around the centre. There are good-quality mid-range hotels in eastern Berlin, where many new hotels have been built recently. There is no lack of luxurious hotels in eastern Berlin, either, particularly around Unter den Linden. Many of the more affordable hotels in the western part of Berlin require urgent repairs. The area around Grunewald is an oasis of peace that will guarantee a good rest. From the numerous hotels in Berlin, this section highlights some of the best; these have been categorized according to location and price. Details about each of the hotels can be found on pages 220–29. Information about alternative ways of spending a night can be found on pages 218–19.

Reception area in the Sorat Art'otel *(see p226)*

WHERE TO LOOK

THERE ARE A FEW areas in Berlin with large concentrations of hotels. In each area there is usually at least one luxury hotel as well as several more affordable places. In Charlottenburg, around Kurfürstendamm and Tauentzienstrasse, are well-known hotels, such as the Kempinski, Savoy, Palace Berlin and the Steigenberger. Bear in mind that this part of Berlin was severely damaged during World War II and the majority of these hotels occupy modern buildings; hotels in old buildings, like the Brandenburger Hof, are a rarity. Inexpensive hotels and pensions can be found in the side streets off the main road, but ask to see the rooms before you decide. Good hotels are also situated in the east part of Charlottenburg, around Lützowufer.

There have been changes in recent years to hotels in the former East Berlin. These hotels have been privatized and the majority of them have been refurbished extensively. In addition, many new hotels have been built. The Adlon, Hilton and Grand, situated in the western part of Mitte around Unter den Linden, are the most luxurious. In the eastern part of this area, around Marx-Engels-Forum and Alexanderplatz, the hotels are more reasonably priced and offer good-quality rooms.

Grunewald is an oasis of peace far from the bustle of Berlin. There is the luxurious Ritz hotel, as well as cosy pensions and little hotels, some of them operating from 19th-century villas and palaces.

If you want to be certain of finding a room and you don't mind staying outside the centre of Berlin, you should head for Neukölln. Here, close to Treptower Park, is the recently opened Estrel – the largest hotel in Germany.

HOTEL PRICES

THE PRICE OF a hotel room in Berlin does not alter much with the season. However, major events and trade fairs do push up prices. Many more luxurious hotels offer weekend discounts and often, if you just turn up without a reservation, you can find yourself a good deal. If you intend to stay for an extended period of time, it is worth trying to negotiate a better rate.

HIDDEN EXTRAS

IN GERMANY, taxes are included in hotel room rates, but like anywhere else, you are expected to tip for any additional services, such as bringing luggage to the room or booking a theatre ticket. Hotels from the Dorint chain are an exception: they provide a range of services (such as free bicycle hire) at no additional cost.

Swimming pool at the Grand Hotel Esplanade *(see p222)*

Café at the Berlin Hilton *(see p220)*

There is no hard and fast rule about breakfast: it is best to ask if it is included in the price when making a reservation.

The majority of Berlin hotels have their own parking spaces, but sometimes their rates are exorbitant. Ask about telephone charges before using the phone in your room and check the exchange rates and the commission for cashing travellers' cheques before using this service. Items from the minibar and paid-television channels can also turn out to be surprisingly costly.

FACILITIES

THERE IS NO standardized system of categorizing hotels by stars in Germany, although the price of a room usually reflects the quality. Small hotels usually include breakfast in the price of the room – they will probably not have a restaurant and their services are limited. If you choose to stay for a longer period, an Aparthotel might be an option to consider. This type of accommodation is an apartment, complete with a fully equipped kitchen.

HOW TO BOOK

YOU CAN BOOK A ROOM in Berlin by mail, telephone or fax, and some rooms can also be booked through the Internet. If you prefer, you can use the city's tourist service **Berlin Tourismus Marketing** *(see p219)*, which can be contacted via the internet or by telephone or fax. This company can make

your booking in hotels throughout Berlin. When making a reservation, however, be prepared to give your credit card details.

If you are already in Berlin and would like to find a comfortable room, your best option is to go to one of the large tourist information bureaux. Some of the best of these are situated in the **Europa-Center**, at the **Brandenburg Gate**, and at **Alexanderplatz** *(see p219)*.

PRIVATE ROOMS

BED & BREAKFAST-style accommodation is not particularly popular in Berlin, although this kind of service can be found in some of the residential districts far from the city centre. You can obtain information about them from tourist information bureaux and the other organizations whose numbers are listed in the Directory *(see p219)*.

Conference room in the Villa Kastania *(see p228)*

KEY TO SYMBOLS

The hotels listed on pages 220–29 are grouped according to area and price category. To help you make your choice, the following symbols summarize the facilities offered at each hotel.

📷 Most rooms with bath or shower
1️⃣ Single-room rate
🏠 Family room: room for more than two people, or extra bed available
24 24-hour room service
TV Television in most of the rooms
🚭 Non-smoking rooms available
🏞 Rooms with a view
🖥 Air conditioning in all rooms
🏋 Gymnasium
🏊 Swimming pool
💼 Business facilities: information service, fax machine, desk and conference or meeting room
🧒 Facilities for children, including cots and, sometimes, babysitting
♿ Wheelchair access
🛗 Elevator
P Hotel parking available
🌳 Garden or terrace
🍸 Hotel bar
🍴 Restaurant
ℹ Tourist information
💳 Credit Cards accepted:
   AE American Express
   DC Diners Club
   MC MasterCard/ Access
   V VISA
   JCB Japan Credit Bureau

Price categories are for a double room with a bathroom or shower, including breakfast (usually), service charges and 16 per cent VAT (in euros)

€ under €80
€€ €81–€130
€€€ €131–€180
€€€€ €181–€230
€€€€€ over €230

The luxurious lounge at the Kempinski Hotel *(see p226)*

TRAVELLING WITH CHILDREN

TRAVELLING WITH CHILDREN in Berlin should not present a problem. A cot can be requested in most hotels, and there is usually no extra charge for having a small child in the room, although an extra bed for an older child may sometimes incur a cost. In better hotels, a reliable babysitter can be obtained at a few hours' notice. In hotel restaurants, high chairs for children are standard.

Elegant hallway in the Four Seasons Hotel *(see p220)*

DISABLED TRAVELLERS

NEARLY ALL TOP-QUALITY and luxury hotels are able to accommodate disabled travellers – at least one entrance will have wheelchair access and some rooms will have specially-adapted bathrooms. Unfortunately, the situation in mid-range and lower standard hotels is not as promising; special equipment is a rarity and in many cases these hotels are not situated on the ground floor. In very old buildings, there may not be an elevator. The **Hotel Mondial** *(see p225)*, located near Kurfürstendamm, is recommended for disabled travellers. It has many facilities for wheelchair users in all its public rooms and has as many as 22 bedrooms equipped for people with special needs.

DEPOSITS

IN MANY BERLIN HOTELS, a deposit may be requested either when reserving the room or upon checking in at the hotel. A credit card number is the most common way to secure a room over the telephone. If you do not have one, however, be prepared to use cash to pay about 20 to 40 per cent of the price for one night's stay. The amount you pay as a deposit should always be credited to the final bill. In some smaller hotels or pensions, don't be surprised if you are asked to pay for your first night's accommodation in full when you arrive.

YOUTH HOSTELS

IT IS EASY to find inexpensive accommodation in Berlin at a youth hostel. The **DJH (Deutsches Jugendherbergs-werk)**, an organization that belongs to the International Youth Hostels Association, gives discounts to all its members. Membership is usually inexpensive and if you are not a member, you will have to join to stay at a hostel. The DJH has hostels in different locations throughout Berlin. There are also several independent youth hostels as well as hotels for students in Berlin that do not belong to any organization.

The type of accommodation offered usually consists of dormitory-style rooms containing bunk beds. There is often a communal bathroom on each floor and a kitchen is usually also available for cooking your own meals. Most youth hostels have a dining room where breakfast and a hot evening meal are served. Some youth hostels are closed during the day, allowing no access to the rooms; confirm this in advance.

CAMPING

CAMPING IS a popular pastime throughout Germany, and the **Deutscher Camping Club** has a lot of information about campsites in and around Berlin. This organization also

Illuminated façade of the Westin Grand *(see p220)*

provides information about other independently run campsites in Berlin.

Campsites are open usually from the beginning of April until the end of October. There are two exceptions: the Berlin-Kladow in Spandau and the Am Krossinsee in Köpenick, which are open year round. The majority of people that choose to stay at campsites are young, particularly during the Oktoberfest *(see p50)* and the weekend in July when the famous Love Parade takes place *(see p49)*. During these times campsites can be very busy and noisy.

Spacious suite at the Hotel Palace *(see p226)*

Organized Youth Groups

BERLIN has a large base of accommodation for organized youth groups. Most of these consist of hostel-style accommodation, situated on the outskirts of the city, often in green belt areas. They were established not only for the purpose of school trips to Berlin but also for children from West Berlin; until the unification of Germany in 1990, it was difficult for youth groups to organize trips to the country-side so they had to opt for trips to the Grunewald instead. Information about availability and reservations is offered by **Berlin Tourismus Marketing** and by larger tourist information centres, such as the one in the Europa-Center.

DIRECTORY

INFORMATION AND BOOKING

Berlin Tourismus Marketing
Am Karlsbad 11, Berlin.
Map 12 D1.
[C] *25 00 25.*
[W] www.berlin.de

Tourist Information
Europa-Center,
Budapester Strasse 45.
Map 10 E1.
[O] *8:30am–8:30pm Mon–Sat, 10am–6:30pm Sun.*

Alexanderplatz
Tourist Info Café at
Fernsehturm. **Map** 7 C3.
[O] *10am–6pm daily.*

Also at: Europa-Center,
Panoramastrasse 1a.
[O] *10am–6pm daily.*

Brandenburg Gate
Pariser Platz.
Map 6 E3, 15 A3.
[O] *9:30am–6pm daily.*

Infopoint KaDeWe
Kaufhaus des Westens,
Tauentzienstrasse 21–24.
Map 10 F2.
[O] *Mon–Fri 9:30am–8pm, 9am–4pm Sat.*

Potsdam Information
Friedrich-Ebert-Strasse 5.
[C] *(0331) 275 58 0.*
[FAX] *(0331) 275 58 99.*
[W] www.potsdam.de

CAMPING

Deutscher Camping Club
Kladower Damm 207-13,
14089 Berlin.
Map 10 E3, 10 F3.
[C] *218 60 71.*
[O] *10:30am–6:30pm Mon, 8am–3pm Wed, 8am–1:30pm Fri.*

DCC-Campingplatz Berlin-Kladow (Spandau)
Krampnitzer Weg 111–117
14089 Berlin.
[C] *365 27 97.*
[FAX] *365 12 45.*

YOUTH HOSTELS

DJH (Deutsches Jugendherbergs-werk)
Tempelhofer Ufer 32
10963 Berlin.
Map 12 E2.
[C] *264 95 20.*
[FAX] *262 04 37.*

Jugendgästehaus
Kluckstrasse 3
10785 Berlin.
Map 11 C1.
[C] *25 79 98 08.*
[FAX] *265 03 83.*

Jugendherberge Ernst Reuter
Hermsdorfer Damm 48–50
13467 Berlin.
[C] *404 16 10.*
[FAX] *404 59 72.*

Jugendgästehaus Am Wannsee
Badeweg 1,
14129 Berlin.
[C] *803 20 34.*
[FAX] *803 59 08.*

DISABLED TRAVELLERS

Berliner Behinderten-verband
Jägerstrasse 63d
10117 Berlin-Mitte.
[C] *204 38 47.*

Behinderten-beauftragter des Landes Berlin
Oranienstrasse 106
10997 Berlin.
[C] *90 28 29 17.*

BED & BREAKFAST

Bed & Breakfast in Berlin
[C] *746 14 46.*
[FAX] *44 05 05 83.*

Coming Home
[C] *21 79 800.*
[FAX] *21 79 80 21*
[W] www.coming-home.org

Erste Mitwohn-zentrale
Sybelstrasse 53.
10629 Berlin-Charlottenburg.
Map 9 A2.
[C] *324 30 31.*
[FAX] *324 99 77.*

Fine and mine
Neue Schönhauser Str. 20
10178 Berlin.
Map 7 C2.
[C] *23 55 120.*
[FAX] *23 55 12 12.*
[@] office@fineandmine.de

Wohnwitz
Holsteinische Strasse 55.
10717 Berlin-Wilmersdorf.
Map 9 C4, 9 C5.
[C] *861 82 22.*
[FAX] *861 82 72.*

Choosing a Hotel

THE CHOICE OF HOTELS selected in this guide is based on quality of accommodation and service as well as location. The list of hotels covers all the areas and price categories with additional information to help you choose a hotel that best meets your needs. Hotels within the same price category are listed alphabetically.

	Credit Cards	Number of Rooms	Fitness Facilities	Air Conditioning	Parking
AROUND UNTER DEN LINDEN					
MADISON FRIEDRICHSTRASSE €€€	AE DC MC V JCB	83	▦		▦
DAS DORINT HOTEL AM GENDARMENMARKT €€€€	AE DC MC V	92	▦	●	▦
MARITIM proARTE HOTEL BERLIN €€€€	AE DC MC V JCB	403	▦	●	▦
BERLIN HILTON €€€€€	AE DC MC V JCB	589	▦	●	▦
FOUR SEASONS HOTEL €€€€€	AE DC MC V JCB	204	▦	●	▦
HOTEL ADLON €€€€€	AE DC MC V JCB	336	▦	●	▦
WESTIN GRAND €€€€€	AE DC MC V JCB	358	▦	●	▦

MADISON FRIEDRICHSTRASSE €€€
Friedrichstrasse 185–190, 10117 Berlin. **Map** 6 F4, 15 C4. ℂ 202 920. FAX 20 29 29 20.
W www.madison-berlin.de.
This hotel offers only suites, the price of which depends upon the size and the duration of stay. The hotel offers many services, including car and bicycle rental, shopping, clothes repair and CD players in all rooms. It pays to stay here for at least a week but, even on a per-night basis, the prices are much lower than in many other hotels.

DAS DORINT HOTEL AM GENDARMENMARKT €€€€
Charlottenstrasse 50–52, 10117 Berlin. **Map** 7 A4, 16 D4. ℂ 203 750. FAX 20 37 51 00.
W www.dorint.de @ bergen@dorint.com
Very nice, cosy hotel located near the Gendarmenmarkt, not far from Unter den Linden and Friedrichstrasse. Guests can expect well-furnished rooms and good service.

MARITIM proARTE HOTEL BERLIN €€€€
Friedrichstrasse 151, 10117 Berlin. **Map** 6 F3, 15 C2. ℂ 20 33 5. FAX 20 33 42 09.
W www.maritim.de @ info.lopa@maritim.de
Although this hotel aims to attract mainly conference business, its central location and excellent facilities make it one of the most attractive hotels in Berlin. It is an ultra-modern building, with furnishings and art displays to match. Its luxurious rooms are divided into three categories and have marble and granite bathrooms.

BERLIN HILTON €€€€€
Mohrenstrasse 30, 10117 Berlin. **Map** 7 A4, 16 D4. ℂ 20 23 0. FAX 20 23 42 69.
W www.hilton.com @ sales_berlin@hilton.com
This hotel is near the Gendarmenmarkt. There are spectacular views of the Konzerthaus and two churches from the rooms at the front of the building. The bedrooms are wonderfully furnished and spacious, and there are two splendid restaurants.

FOUR SEASONS HOTEL €€€€€
Charlottenstrasse 49, 10117 Berlin. **Map** 7 A4, 16 D3. ℂ 20 33 8. FAX 20 33 61 66.
W www.fourseasons.com @ reservation.ber@fourseasons.com
This hotel is ranked as one of the three best hotels in Berlin. Situated near the Gendarmenmarkt, it is a modern building with an impressive façade. The interiors will astonish with the opulence of their Neo-Baroque objects and magnificent flower arrangements. The hotel offers luxurious rooms in three categories and impeccable service. Excellent light cuisine is served in the restaurant.

HOTEL ADLON €€€€€
Unter den Linden 77, 10117 Berlin. **Map** 6 E3, 15 A3. ℂ 22 61 0. FAX 22 61 22 22.
W www.hotel-adlon.de @ adlon@Kempinski.com
This deluxe hotel located near the Brandenburg Gate opened in 1997 and continues the traditions of its illustrious predecessor, which was bombed during World War II. Marble, leather and exotic woods line the interior. The hotel has excellent service and also offers special rooms for people with allergies, cordless telephone handsets, and soundproofed walls and windows in all rooms.

WESTIN GRAND €€€€€
Friedrichstrasse 158–164, 10117 Berlin. **Map** 6 F3, 15 C3. ℂ 20 27 0. FAX 20 27 33 62.
W www.westin.com/berlin
A lavish hotel built at the end of the 19th century in Empire and Secessionist styles. The main hall is particularly impressive, with a huge atrium and a breathtaking staircase. It has a good location, close to most historic sites.

Price categories are for a double room per night, including all taxes:

€ under €80
€€ €81–€130
€€€ €131–€180
€€€€ €181–€230
€€€€€ over €230

CREDIT CARDS
Indicates which credit cards are accepted: AE American Express; DC Diners Club; MC MasterCard/Access; V Visa; JCB Japan Credit Bureau.

FITNESS FACILITIES
Gym and/or fitness facilities are available.

AIR CONDITIONING
All rooms are air-conditioned.

PARKING
The hotel has its own car park, garage or parking spaces. These may not be on the same premises.

	CREDIT CARDS	NUMBER OF ROOMS	FITNESS FACILITIES	AIR CONDITIONING	PARKING

MUSEUM ISLAND

ART'OTEL BERLIN MITTE €€

Wallstrasse 70–73, 10179 Berlin. **Map** 7 C4. 240 620. **FAX** 240 62 222.
www.artotel.de info@artotel.de
Overlooking the Spree river, this hotel is reasonably priced and one of the most popular places in Mitte. Inside, it is modern with simple and elegant furniture. In summer there is a café on a riverboat tied to the bank of the river.

| AE DC MC V JCB | 109 | ■ | ● | ■ |

DeragHotel GROSSER KURFÜRST €€€

Neue Ross Strasse 11–12, 10179 Berlin. **Map** 7 C4. 246 000. **FAX** 24 60 03 00.
www.deraghotels.de grosserkurfuerst@deraghotels.de
A good middle-range hotel, with modern facilities and a convenient location close to the U-Bahn station Märkisches Museum. The hotel's services include free public transport or bicycle hire.

| AE DC MC V | 144 | ■ | | |

EAST OF THE CENTRE

ALEXANDER PLAZA BERLIN €€€

Rosenstrasse 1, 10187 Berlin. **Map** 7 B2, 16 F1. 240 010. **FAX** 240 01 777.
www.hotel-alexander-plaza.de info@hotel-alexander-plaza.de
This top-quality hotel, opened in 1997, is located near the S-Bahn station Hackescher Markt. Rooms are large, comfortable and full of light, with soundproof windows.

| AE DC MC V | 92 | ■ | ● | ■ |

PARK INN HOTEL BERLIN €€€

Alexanderplatz, 10178 Berlin. **Map** 8 D2. 23 89 0. **FAX** 23 89 43 05.
www.parkinn.com
This 37-storey building was constructed under the GDR and, despite modernization, has an ugly exterior. However, it has an elegant hall, a conference area, a good restaurant and a casino.

| AE DC MC V JCB | 1006 | ■ | | ■ |

NORTH OF THE CENTRE

BOARDINGHOUSE BERLIN €€

Mulackstrasse 1, 10119 Berlin. **Map** 7 C1. 283 88 488. **FAX** 283 88 489.
www.boardinghouse-berlin.com info@boardinghouse-mitte.com
The EKOS Boardinghouse consists of single and double apartments. These must be rented for a minimum of two nights. Breakfast is included, but you have your own kitchen. Ideal for a longer stay.

| AE DC MC V | 21 | | | ■ |

MÄRKISCHER HOF €€

Linienstrasse 133, 10115 Berlin. **Map** 6 F1. 282 71 55. **FAX** 282 43 31.
www.maerkischer-hof-berlin.de service@maerkischer-hof-berlin.de
A small, cosy hotel with a family atmosphere. The building dates from the 19th century, but the rooms have recently been redecorated. They are of a surprisingly high standard considering their low prices.

| MC V | 20 | | | ■ |

HACKESCHER MARKT €€€

Grosse Präsidentenstrasse 8, 10178 Berlin. **Map** 7 B2, 16 F1. 280 030. **FAX** 280 03 111.
info@hackescher-markt.com
Built in 1998, this charming hotel has an excellent location opposite Hackesche Höfe. The rooms are elegantly furnished and its bar, Mags, has an excellent wine list.

| AE DC MC V | 31 | | | ■ |

HOTEL ALBRECHTSHOF €€€

Albrechtstrasse 8, 10117 Berlin. **Map** 6 F2, 15 B1. 308 860. **FAX** 308 86 100.
www.hotel-albrechtshof.de albrechtshof-hotel@t-online.de
This charming hotel is situated near the Spree river, in a modernized early 19th-century building. It offers not only a bar, restaurant and banqueting hall, but a chapel. Weekend discounts.

| AE DC MC V JCB | 107 | | | ■ |

For key to symbols *see p217*

	CREDIT CARDS	**NUMBER OF ROOMS**	**FITNESS FACILITIES**	**AIR CONDITIONING**	**PARKING**

Price categories are for a double room per night, including all taxes:

€ under €80
€€ €81–€130
€€€ €131–€180
€€€€ €181–€230
€€€€€ over €230

CREDIT CARDS
Indicates which credit cards are accepted: AE American Express; DC Diners Club; MC MasterCard/Access; V Visa; JCB Japan Credit Bureau.

FITNESS FACILITIES
Gym and/or fitness facilities are available.

AIR CONDITIONING
All rooms are air-conditioned.

PARKING
The hotel has its own car park, garage or parking spaces. These may not be on the same premises.

TIERGARTEN

BLUE BAND HOTEL BERLIN €€€
Lützowplatz 17, 10785 Berlin. **Map** 11 A1. **(** 26 05 27 00. **FAX** 260 52 716.
W www.blueband.de **@** hotel-berlin@blueband.de
Although one of the largest hotels in Berlin, it is not overwhelming thanks to its welcoming service and good organization. There is a good chance of finding a vacant room, even without a reservation. Rooms are bright, spacious and classically decorated.

Credit Cards: AE DC MC V JCB | Number of Rooms: 701 | Fitness Facilities: ■ | Air Conditioning: ● | Parking: ■

HOTEL HAMBURG €€€
Landgrafenstrasse 4, 10787 Berlin. **Map** 11 A1. **(** 264 770. **FAX** 262 93 94.
W www.hoham.de **@** hoham@t-online.de
Located in the southern part of the Tiergarten district, this hotel was redecorated in 1994, but the elegant rooms, in all shades of warm red, are a bit on the small side.

Credit Cards: AE DC MC V JCB | Number of Rooms: 191 | Parking: ■

DORINT SCHWEIZERHOF BERLIN €€€€
Budapester Strasse 25, 10787 Berlin. **Map** 10 F1. **(** 26 96 0. **FAX** 269 61 000.
W www.dorint.com
This luxurious hotel opened in 1999. It sports an elegant, sand-finished façade and offers beautifully furnished rooms, two restaurants, a ballroom and a conference centre.

Credit Cards: AE DC MC V | Number of Rooms: 384 | Fitness Facilities: ■ | Air Conditioning: ● | Parking: ■

GRAND HOTEL ESPLANADE BERLIN €€€€
Lützowufer 15, 10785 Berlin. **Map** 11 A1. **(** 254 780. **FAX** 254 78 82 22.
W www.esplanade.de **@** info@esplanade.de
A modern, lavish establishment overlooking the Landwehrkanal, the hotel has well-furnished rooms that attract prominent guests. Harry's New York Bar is famous and the Harlekin restaurant is one of the city's best.

Credit Cards: AE DC MC V JCB | Number of Rooms: 386 | Fitness Facilities: ■ | Air Conditioning: ● | Parking: ■

GRAND HYATT BERLIN €€€€€
Marlene-Dietrich-Platz 2, 10785 Berlin. **Map** 6. **(** 25 53 12 34. **FAX** 25 53 12 35.
W www.hyatt.com **@** berlin@hyatt.de
One of the most modern and splendid hotels in Berlin, the Hyatt is close to the Potsdamer Platz and the Kulturforum *(see pp114–15)*. It has a sushi bar, a bistro, a restaurant and a quiet café.

Credit Cards: AE DC MC V JCB | Number of Rooms: 342 | Fitness Facilities: ■ | Air Conditioning: ● | Parking: ■

INTER-CONTINENTAL BERLIN €€€€€
Budapester Strasse 2, 10787 Berlin. **Map** 10 F1. **(** 26 02 0. **FAX** 26 02 26 00.
W www.interconti.com **@** berlin@interconti.com
This newly renovated hotel is situated on the outskirts of the Zoologischer Garten *(see p150)*. The massive building is hard to miss, with a glass dome covering its main lobby. The hotel offers large rooms in several categories. A swimming pool and a rejuvenating salon provide the chance for tired guests to relax.

Credit Cards: AE DC MC V JCB | Number of Rooms: 587 | Fitness Facilities: ■ | Air Conditioning: ● | Parking: ■

KREUZBERG

HOTEL AM ANHALTER BAHNHOF €
Stresemannstrasse 36, 10963 Berlin. **Map** 12 E1. **(** 251 03 42. **FAX** 251 48 97.
W www.hotel-anhalter-bahnhof.de **@** Hotel-AAB@t-online.de
This small and friendly hotel is situated in an old apartment block. Its low prices only apply to rooms without bathrooms; expect to pay more for an en suite bathroom. The more expensive rooms face on to a courtyard.

Credit Cards: MC V | Number of Rooms: 35 | Parking: ■

HOTEL TRANSIT €
Hagelberger Strasse 53–54, 10965 Berlin. **Map** 12 F4. **(** 789 04 70. **FAX** 789 04 777.
W www.hotel-transit.de **@** welcome@hotel-transit.de
A small, inexpensive hotel in the west part of Viktoriapark. Don't expect luxury, but there is easy access to the town centre.

Credit Cards: AE MC V | Number of Rooms: 49

JUGENDGÄSTEHAUS DER DSJ

€

Franz-Künstler-Strasse 10, 10969 Berlin. **Map** 13 B2. [615 10 07. FAX 61 40 11 50.
W www.gaestehaus.berlin.de
This pleasant, if large, youth hostel is excellently located in the central part of Kreuzberg. The rooms do not have bathrooms, but there are shower rooms on the corridors. The cheapest rate is for a bed in a dormitory.

MC
V
JCB

124

HOTEL ANTARES

€€

Stresemannstrasse 97, 10963 Berlin. **Map** 12 E1. [254 160. FAX 25 41 62 22.
W www.hotel-antares.com @ reservierung@hotel-antares.com
This modern hotel is close to Martin-Gropius-Bau (see p140) and Potsdamer Platz. If offers both economy and business-class rooms. It is worth enquiring about special weekend rates.

AE
DC
MC
V
JCB

85

HOTEL RIEHMERS HOFGARTEN

€€

Yorckstrasse 83, 10 965 Berlin. **Map** 12 F4. [78 09 88 00. FAX 78 09 88 08.
W www.hotel-riehmers-hofgarten.de
This beautiful building is part of a Gothic red-brick complex in Kreuzberg and dates from the late 19th century. Rooms are comfortable and elegant. The best rooms overlook the courtyard.

AE
MC
V

21

RELEXA HOTEL STUTTGARTER HOF

€€€

Anhalter Strasse 9, 10963 Berlin. **Map** 12 F1. [264 830. FAX 264 83 900.
W www.relexa-hotels.de @ berlin@relexa-hotels.de
This is a top-quality hotel dating back to 1907. Situated behind Potsdamer Platz, the hotel has good-sized rooms, a restaurant called La Fenêtre and a charming, green courtyard.

AE
DC
MC
V

110

AROUND KURFÜRSTENDAMM

HOTEL PENSION FUNK

€

Fasanenstrasse 69, 10719 Berlin. **Map** 10 D2. [882 71 93. FAX 883 33 29.
W www.hotel-pensionfunk.de @ berlin@hotel-pensionfunk.de
This small, charming hotel is on one of Berlin's finest streets. The building dates from the late 19th century and was once the home of film star Asta Nielsen. Many of the original features are still in place. (most).

MC
V

14

BEST WESTERN HOTEL BOULEVARD AM KURFÜRSTENDAMM

€€

Kurfürstendamm 12, 10719 Berlin. **Map** 10 D1. [884 250. FAX 884 25 450.
W www.hotel-boulevard.com @ info@hotel-boulevard.com
Although this well-located hotel lacks a restaurant, it is made up for by the number of places to eat in the area. During the summer, there is a very charming garden café on the roof.

AE
DC
MC
V

57

BLUE BAND BERLIN MARK HOTEL

€€

Meinekestrasse 18–19, 10719 Berlin. **Map** 10 D2. [88 00 28 04.
W www.markhotel.de @ info@markhotel.de
The pleasant rooms in this comfortable three-star hotel are lightly furnished. Sixteen of the rooms have a higher standard of decoration and facilities for business travellers.

AE
DC
MC
V
JCB

233

BLUE BAND BERLIN PLAZA HOTEL

€€

Knesebeckstrasse 63, 10719 Berlin. **Map** 9 C2. [884 13 444. FAX 884 13 754.
W www.plazahotel.de @ reservations.hotel-plaza@blueband.de
Besides its proximity to Kurfürstendamm and functional, bright rooms, the hotel offers good food at its restaurant, called Knese, which is famous for its Berlin dishes. It is well worth enquiring about their special weekend rates.

AE
DC
MC
V
JCB

131

HOTEL ASKANISCHER HOF

€€

Kurfürstendamm 53, 10707 Berlin. **Map** 9 B2. [881 80 33. FAX 881 72 06.
W www.askanischer-hof.de @ info@askanischer-hof.de
One of the few hotels that survived World War II. The interior is decorated in the style of the 1920s and the rooms are cosy and comfortable. Authors Franz Kafka and Arthur Miller used to stay here.

AE
DC
MC
V
JCB

16

HOTEL ASTORIA

€€

Fasanenstrasse 2, 10623 Berlin. **Map** 4 D5. [312 40 67. FAX 312 50 27.
W www.hotelastoria.de @ astoriahotel@t-online.de
Managed by the same family for three generations, this intimate hotel occupies a 19th-century building. The rooms are comfortable and the lack of a restaurant is made up for by the hotel's proximity to Savignyplatz.

AE
DC
MC
V
JCB

32

For key to symbols see p217

Price categories are for a double room per night, including all taxes:

€ under €80
€€ €81–€130
€€€ €131–€180
€€€€ €181–€230
€€€€€ over €230

CREDIT CARDS
Indicates which credit cards are accepted: AE American Express; DC Diners Club; MC MasterCard/Access; V Visa; JCB Japan Credit Bureau.

FITNESS FACILITIES
Gym and/or fitness facilities are available.

AIR CONDITIONING
All rooms are air-conditioned.

PARKING
The hotel has its own car park, garage or parking spaces. These may not be on the same premises.

	CREDIT CARDS	NUMBER OF ROOMS	FITNESS FACILITIES	AIR CONDITIONING	PARKING
HOTEL BERLINER HOF €€ Tauentzienstrasse 8, 10789 Berlin. **Map** 10 E1. 254 950. FAX 262 30 65. www.berliner-hof.com info@berliner-hof.com Situated near the Europa-Center, this is a small guesthouse-type hotel. Rooms on the Tauentzienstrasse side have soundproofed windows, but if you like to sleep with the window open, ask for a room at the back. All rooms were redecorated in 1998 and are large and light.	AE DC MC V	76	▦		
HOTEL GATES €€ Knesebeckstrasse 8–9, 10623 Berlin. **Map** 3 C5. 311 060. FAX 312 20 60. www.hotel-gates.com info@hotel-gates.com Offering varying prices and standards, this hotel has equipped some rooms with a private bathroom, minibar and television.	AE DC MC V JCB	71			
HOTEL PENSION AUGUSTA €€ Fasanenstrasse 22, 10719 Berlin. **Map** 10 D1. 883 50 28. FAX 882 47 79. www.hotel-augusta.de info@hotel-augusta.de This relatively inexpensive guesthouse is located in the very heart of Berlin. As it is based in a 19th-century building, the rooms are spacious and quiet. Some rooms lack en suite bathrooms and so are much cheaper. There is no hotel restaurant, but there are many good places to eat nearby.	AE MC V JCB	32			
HOTEL PENSION DITTBERNER €€ Wielandstrasse 26, 10707 Berlin. **Map** 3 B5. 881 64 85. FAX 885 40 46. One of the charming old-style *hotelpensionen* that were once typical for Berlin. This is the place to stay if you are looking for personal, if somewhat disorganized, service in a 19th-century setting. Rooms are large, although the furniture looks a bit used. The prime location off Kurfürstendamm and the flair of old Berlin more than make up for this.		22			
IMPERATOR €€ Meinekestrasse 5, 10719 Berlin-Charlottenburg. **Map** 10 D2. 881 41 81. FAX 885 19 19. Just a stone's throw away from the Kurfürstendamm, this comfortable hotel is a regular favourite with artists and others who appreciate the individual atmosphere it offers. The late 19th-century building, set in an exclusive street, recalls a more prosperous time.		11			▦
KU'DAMM 101 €€ Kurfurstendamm 101, 10711 Berlin. 520 05 50. 520 055 555. www.kudamm101.com info@kudamm101.com Behind the minimalist-looking façade, the Ku'Damm 101 is a new and stylish hotel for the international traveller, with interior design inspired by Le Corbusier. There are high-tech communication facilities in every room and a breakfast room with panoramic views.	AE DC MC V	171	●		▦
PROPELLER ISLAND CITY LODGE €€ Albrecht-Achilles Strasse 58, 10709 Berlin-Wilmersdorf. 891 90 16. FAX 892 87 21. www.propeller-island.de Situated in a 19th-century apartment block in one of the quiet streets off Kurfürstendamm, this hotel is known as an art hotel. Each room is differently and often outrageously themed – with real works of art – full of fantasy and flair. An ideal place for those looking for a memorable stay.		32			
REMTER €€ Marburger Strasse 17, 10789 Berlin. **Map** 10 E1. 23 50 88 0. FAX 213 86 12. hotel-remter@t-online.de This is a pleasant, quiet hotel, and is well located for tourists – it is close to the historic landmark Kaiser-Wilhelm-Gedächtniskirche. Although the prices for its rooms are not the cheapest in Berlin, the Remter is one of the best-value hotels in this central location.	AE DC MC V	31			▦

ALSTERHOF €€€ | AE DC V | 200

Augsburger Strasse 5, 10789 Berlin. **Map** 10 E2. (212 420. FAX 218 39 49.

W www.alsterhof.com @ info@alsterhof.com

This hotel is recommended for non-smokers, who can have a special non-smoking bedroom and dine in a non-smoking breakfast room. During the summer, coffee is served under a pretty chestnut tree in an inner courtyard.

BLEIBTREU HOTEL €€€ | AE DC MC V JCB | 60

Bleibtreustrasse 31, 10707 Berlin. **Map** 9 B2. (884 740. FAX 884 74 444.

W www.bleibtreu.com @ info@bleibtreu.com

This hotel occupies a restored 19th-century building located on a quiet street. The sophisticated interiors will appeal to guests who appreciate natural materials. The restaurant serves mainly organic food from farms outside Berlin.

BLUE BAND BERLIN EXCELSIOR HOTEL €€€ | AE DC MC V JCB | 317

Hardenbergstrasse 14, 10623 Berlin. **Map** 4 D5. (315 522. FAX 31 55 10 02

W www.blueband.de @ reservations.hotel-excelsior@blueband.de

This is a good-quality hotel next to the famous Ludwig-Erhard-Haus (*see p150*). It offers helpful service and good food. Children under 14 can stay for free.

CONCEPT HOTEL €€€ | AE DC MC V JCB | 153

Grolmanstrasse 41–43, 10623 Berlin. **Map** 9 C1. (884 260. FAX 884 26 500.

W www.concept-hotel.com @ info@concept-hotel.com

This welcoming hotel is situated in a quiet street. The building itself is modern and some of its rooms have extra-long beds for taller guests. There is a roof terrace and during summer, dinner is served in the inner courtyard.

CROWNE PLAZA BERLIN CITY CENTRE €€€ | AE DC MC V | 423

Nürnberger Strasse 65, 10787 Berlin. **Map** 10 E2. (210 070. FAX 213 20 09.

W www.cp-berlin.com @ info@crowneplaza.de

This luxurious hotel is located near Kaiser-Wilhelm-Gedächtniskirche and Tauentzienstrasse. It has a swimming pool, a good restaurant, large rooms and a pleasant atmosphere. It offers special weekend rates combined with sightseeing tours.

HECKER'S HOTEL €€€ | AE DC MC V JCB | 71

Grolmanstrasse 35, 10623 Berlin. **Map** 9 C1. (889 000. FAX 88 90 260.

W www.heckers-hotel.com @ info@heckers-hotel.com

Situated in the very heart of town, this low-key, private hotel caters not only for its guests' needs but tries for a more individual approach.

HOTEL AMBASSADOR BERLIN €€€ | AE DC MC V | 199

Bayreuther Strasse 42–3, 10787 Berlin. **Map** 10 F1. (219 020. FAX 219 02 380.

W www.sorat-hotels.com @ ambassador-Berlin@sorat-hotels.com

This high-standard hotel is in a quiet street near Wittenbergplatz. Its rooms are comfortable, traditionally furnished and have soundproofed windows.

HOTEL AVANTGARDE €€€ | AE DC MC V JCB | 27

Kurfürstendamm 15, 10719 Berlin. **Map** 10 D1. (884 83 30. FAX 882 40 11.

W www.hotel-avantgarde.com @ info@hotel-avantgarde.com

Occupying the upper floors of a Neo-Baroque building, this hotel offers large rooms with soundproofed windows and decorative stucco ceilings. There is a Mövenpick restaurant on the ground floor.

HOTEL MONDIAL €€€ | AE DC MC V | 75

Kurfürstendamm 47, 10707 Berlin. **Map** 9 B2. (884 110. FAX 8841 11 50.

W www.hotel-mondial.com @ hotel-mondial@t-online.de

Wonderfully located near George-Grosz-Platz, this hotel is very pleasant, offering a high standard of service. It is well equipped for the disabled.

HOTEL RESIDENZ BERLIN €€€ | AE DC MC V | 81

Meinekestrasse 9, 10719 Berlin. **Map** 10 D2. (884 430. FAX 882 47 26.

W www.hotel-residenz.com @ info@hotel-residenz.com

A recently restored 19th-century building, this pleasant establishment is in a side street close to Kurfürstendamm.

Price categories are for a double room per night, including all taxes: € under €80 €€ €81–€130 €€€ €131–€180 €€€€ €181–€230 €€€€€ over €230	**CREDIT CARDS** Indicates which credit cards are accepted: AE American Express; DC Diners Club; MC MasterCard/Access; V Visa; JCB Japan Credit Bureau. **FITNESS FACILITIES** Gym and/or fitness facilities are available. **AIR CONDITIONING** All rooms are air-conditioned. **PARKING** The hotel has its own car park, garage or parking spaces. These may not be on the same premises.

	CREDIT CARDS	NUMBER OF ROOMS	FITNESS FACILITIES	AIR CONDITIONING	PARKING
SORAT ART'OTEL BERLIN €€€ Joachimstaler Strasse 29, 10719 Berlin. **Map** 10 D2. 884 470. **FAX** 88 447 700. www.sorat-hotels.com art-hotel@sorat-hotels.com The Sorat Art'otel can be easily recognized from a distance by the figure of a discus-thrower on the façade. Its interiors are boldly designed in a colourful, ultra-modern style. Whatever guests might think of the decor, they are impressed by the service.	AE DC MC V JCB	133	●		▦
HOTEL BRANDENBURGER HOF €€€€ Eislebener Strasse 14, 10789 Berlin. **Map** 10 E2. 214 050. **FAX** 214 05 100. www.brandenburger-hof.com info@brandenburger-hof.com An intimate family atmosphere, impeccable service and quiet, luxurious rooms make this one of the most desirable hotels in Berlin. This enchanting building has been carefully restored.	AE DC MC V JCB	82			▦
SAVOY HOTEL €€€€ Fasanenstrasse 9–10, 10623 Berlin. **Map** 10 D1. 31 10 30. **FAX** 311 03 333. www.hotel-savoy.com info@hotel-savoy.com One of the most beautiful hotels in Berlin, the Savoy's comfortable rooms and friendly atmosphere attract an exclusive clientele. The suites on the sixth floor offer good views. Facilities include: babysitting, theatre ticket service and Berlin's first cigar bar.	AE DC MC V JCB	125	▦	●	▦
HOTEL PALACE BERLIN €€€€€ Budapester Strasse 45, 10789 Berlin. **Map** 10 E1. 25 02 0. **FAX** 2502 1161. www.palace.de hotel@palace.de The uninspiring shape of the building hides its charming interior, which is full of discreet elegance. The hotel, which has just added one of Berlin's most elegant spas to its facilities, is distinguished by the intimate atmosphere.	AE DC MC V JCB	282	▦	●	▦
HOTEL STEIGENBERGER BERLIN €€€€€ Los-Angeles-Platz 1, 10789 Berlin. **Map** 10 E2. 212 70. **FAX** 212 71 17. www.steigenberger.de berlin@steigenberger.de With a very good location, this hotel offers cosy rooms and several categories of apartments. The hotel's facilities include a swimming pool, sauna, massage, a pleasant bar and good Berlin cuisine in the hotel restaurant, Berliner Stube.	AE DC MC V JCB	397	▦	●	▦
KEMPINSKI HOTEL BRISTOL BERLIN €€€€€ Kurfürstendamm 27, 10719 Berlin. **Map** 10 D1. 884 340. **FAX** 883 60 75. www.kempinskiberlin.de reservations.bristol@kempinski.com One of Berlin's most famous hotels, the Kempinski was redecorated in the 1990s and has a classic interior. Its luxurious rooms are very comfortable, and 18 rooms have wheelchair access. The famous restaurant Kempinski-Grill serves international cuisine.	AE DC MC V JCB	301	▦	●	▦

AROUND SCHLOSS CHARLOTTENBURG

	CREDIT CARDS	NUMBER OF ROOMS	FITNESS FACILITIES	AIR CONDITIONING	PARKING
HOTEL AN DER OPER €€ Bismarckstrasse 100, 10625 Berlin. **Map** 3 A4. 315 830. **FAX** 315 83 109. www.hotel-an-der-oper.de info@hotel-an-der-oper.de Located near the opera house in Charlottenburg. Although some rooms overlook the noisy Bismarckstrasse, windows have been soundproofed. There is a non-smoking breakfast room.	AE DC MC V JCB	48			▦
SCHLOSSPARKHOTEL €€€ Heubnerweg 2a, 14059 Berlin. **Map** 2 D2. 326 90 30. **FAX** 326 90 36 00. www.schlossparkhotel.de schlossparkhotel@t-online.de Schlossparkhotel is a very pleasant, small hotel near the beautiful gardens of Schlosspark Charlottenburg. The S-Bahn Westend is nearby. Request a room with a balcony overlooking the garden.	DC MC V JCB	39	▦		▦

FURTHER AFIELD

DIE FABRIK
€ · 45

Schlesische Strasse 18, 10997 Berlin-Kreuzberg. **C** *611 71 16.* **FAX** *618 29 74.*
W www.diefabrik.com **@** info@diefabrik.com
Set in an old factory building, this youth hostel-type hotel offers shared bathrooms and simple furnishings, but its easy-going atmosphere appeals to all. Single, double and cheap dormitory rooms available. 1

HOTELPENSION ALPINA
€ · DC MC V · 17

Trabener Strasse 3, 14193 Berlin-Wilmersdorf. **C** *891 35 17.* **FAX** *893 53 42.*
The Alpina is similar to the Hotel Belvedere *(see p228)* – unsurprising, since it is owned by the same people. The rooms are decorated in an old-fashioned style and only some of them have en suite bathrooms. TV

ARTEMISIA
€€ · DC MC V · 12

Brandenburgische Strasse 18, 10707 Berlin-Wilmersdorf. **C** *873 89 05.* **FAX** *861 86 53.*
W www.artemisia-berlin.com **@** info@artemisia-berlin.com
Artemisia caters exclusively for women and is often visited by business travellers. Men are allowed into the conference room. Some of the rooms share bathrooms. The hotel's breakfast room has a delightful terrace.

DORINT AM MÜGGELSEE
€€ · AE DC MC V · 176

Am Grossen Müggelsee, 12559 Berlin. **C** *65 88 20.* **FAX** *65 88 22 63.*
W www.dorint-berlin.de **@** hotel@dorint-berlin.de
This first-class hotel is far from the hustle and bustle of the city. Tucked away in the greenery on the Müggelsee in Köpenick, it is perfect for a relaxed stay.

EAST-SIDE HOTEL
€€ · AE MC V · 36

Mühlenstrasse 6, 10243 Berlin-Friedrichshain. Map 8 F5. **C** *29 38 33.* **FAX** *293 83 55.*
W www.eastsidecityhotel.de **@** info@eastsidecityhotel.de
The East-Side Hotel is located opposite the East-Side-Gallery *(see p173)*. It has big, bright rooms with modern facilities, spacious bathrooms and a family atmosphere.

ESTREL HOTEL & CONVENTION CENTER
€€ · AE DC MC V · 1125

Sonnenallee 225, 12057 Berlin-Neukölln. Map 14 F5. **C** *68 31 0.* **FAX** *68 31 23 45.*
W www.estrel.com **@** reservierung@estrel.com
Opened in 1994, Estrel hotel was originally designed to house major conferences, but it is also popular among tourists. Conveniently linked by S-Bahn to the town centre, it offers so many rooms that you will always find one vacant.

FORSTHAUS AN DER HUBERTUSBRÜCKE
€€ · AE MC V · 20

Stölpchenweg 45, 14109 Berlin-Wannsee. **C** *805 86 80.* **FAX** *80 58 68 100.*
W www. concordehotel.de **@** forthaus@concorde-hotels.de
Ideal for those looking for rest after a day of sightseeing, this relaxing hotel is situated in green surroundings. Staying here allows you to forget that you are only 20 minutes away from the centre of Berlin.

FORSTHAUS PAULSBORN
€€ · AE DC V · 10

Am Grunewaldsee/Hüttenweg 90, 14193 Berlin-Grunewald. **C** *818 19 10.*
FAX *81 81 91 50.* **W** www.forsthaus-paulsborn.de **@** paulsborn@t-online.de
The peaceful location, deep in the Grunewald, means that the hotel is better suited to visitors with cars. Stained-glass windows and a fireplace in the lobby add character to this stylish former hunting lodge.

HOLIDAY INN BERLIN CITY CENTER EAST
€€ · AE DC MC V JCB · 122

Prenzlauer Allee 169, 10409 Berlin-Prenzlauer Berg. **C** *446 610.* **FAX** *44 66 16 61.*
W www.hi-berlin.com **@** info@hi-berlin.com
Situated in the fashionable Prenzlauer district, this modern art hotel has good public transport on its doorstep. The rooms are well equipped and clean, and there is a hand-signed print by the Spanish artist Gustavo in every room.

HOTEL AHORN
€€ · DC MC V JCB · 28

Schlüterstrasse 40, 10707 Berlin-Charlottenburg. Map 9 B2. **C** *881 43 44.*
FAX *88 71 98 71.* **W** www.hotel-ahorn.com **@** info@hotel-ahorn.com
This pleasant guesthouse-style hotel has a prime location only a few steps away from Kurfürstendamm. As well as double and triple rooms, apartments with kitchens are available for longer stays.

For key to symbols *see p217*

Price categories are for a double room per night, including all taxes:

€ under €80
€€ €81–€130
€€€ €131–€180
€€€€ €181–€230
€€€€€ over €230

CREDIT CARDS
Indicates which credit cards are accepted: AE American Express; DC Diners Club; MC MasterCard/Access; V Visa; JCB Japan Credit Bureau.

FITNESS FACILITIES
Gym and/or fitness facilities are available.

AIR CONDITIONING
All rooms are air-conditioned.

PARKING
The hotel has its own car park, garage or parking spaces. These may not be on the same premises.

	CREDIT CARDS	NUMBER OF ROOMS	FITNESS FACILITIES	AIR CONDITIONING	PARKING
HOTEL BELVEDERE €€ Seebergsteig 4, 14193 Berlin-Wilmersdorf. **(** 82 60 010. **FAX** 82 60 01 63. Located in a quiet street in the district of Grunewald, this charming villa is surrounded by a garden. The atmosphere is homely. Those who like crystal chandeliers and old-fashioned wallpaper will feel at home here. 1 TV Y	AE DC MC V	18			▦
HOTEL PENSION WITTELSBACH €€ Wittelsbacher Strasse 22, 10707 Berlin-Wilmersdorf. **(** 864 98 40. **FAX** 862 15 32. W www.hotel-pension-wittelsbach.de A pleasant pension in a 19th-century building. Ideal for families with small children – one floor is dedicated to them. There are plenty of toys and nursery rooms are decorated in the style of the "Wild West". Guests can rent almost everything required to cater for children. ▦ 1 ▦ TV Y ▦ ▦ ▦ ▦ Y	AE MC V JCB	31			▦
HOTEL RHEINSBERG AM SEE €€ Finsterwalder Strasse 64, 13435 Berlin-Reinickendorf. **(** 402 10 02. **FAX** 403 50 57. W www.hotel-rheinsberg.com @ info@hotel-rheinsberg.com If you place more value on peace, picturesque surroundings overlooking a lake and comfortable, reasonably priced rooms than on proximity to the town centre, then this hotel will meet your needs. The building's amusing shape makes it an unusual place to stay. ▦ 1 ▦ TV ▦ ▦ ▦ ▦ ▦ ▦ ▦	DC MC V	81	▦		
IBIS BERLIN-MESSE €€ Messedamm 10, 14057 Berlin-Charlottenburg. **Map** 1 C5. **(** 303 930. **FAX** 301 95 36. W www.accor-hotels.de @ h0357@accor-hotels.com Visitors to the frequent trade fairs held in this area of the city only have to cross the street to reach this hotel. It has been newly refurbished and the hotel chain has a good reputation. It is located next door to the Funkturm, which has the best view of Berlin. ▦ 1 TV ▦ ▦ Y	AE DC V JCB	168	●		
IBIS BERLIN MITTE €€ Prenzlauer Allee 4, 10405 Berlin-Mitte. **Map** 8 D1. **(** 443 330. **FAX** 44 33 31 11. W www.accor-hotels.de One of the three Berlin hotels belonging to this chain, the Ibis hotel is situated in Mitte, close to Alexanderplatz. Modern rooms (which are slightly small), pleasant service and relatively low prices make it a popular place. The nearby petrol station has a 24-hour shop. ▦ 1 TV ▦ ▦ ▦ Y ▦	AE DC MC V JCB	198			▦
JURINE €€ Schwedter Strasse 15, 10119 Berlin-Mitte. **(** 443 29 90. **FAX** 44 32 99 99. W www.hotel-jurine.de @ mail@hotel-jurine.de This small hotel is located in a side street near Senefelderplatz, in the centre of Prenzlauer Berg. The nearby U-Bahn station gives easy access to the town centre. The recently redecorated rooms are of a high standard and there is a hotel garden. ▦ 1 TV ▦ ▦ ▦ ▦ ▦ Y	AE DC MC V	53			
VILLA KASTANIA €€ Kastanienallee 20, 14052 Berlin-Charlottenburg. **Map** 1 A5. **(** 300 00 20. **FAX** 30 00 02 10. W www.villakastania.com @ info@villakastania.com A pleasant, intimate establishment with a high standard of service. It is located in a quiet street, a few minutes by foot from Messegelände (complex of trade fair halls) and with excellent links to the centre. All rooms have balconies and standard rooms have kitchenettes. ▦ 1 ▦ TV Y ▦ ▦ ▦ ▦ ▦ ▦	AE MC V JCB	43	▦		▦
VILLA TOSCANA €€ Bahnhofstrasse 19, 12207 Berlin-Steglitz. **(** 76 89 270. **FAX** 773 44 88. W www.villa-toscana.de This quiet hotel is situated in an Italian-style villa, dating from the late 19th century. It's more convenient for tourists who have their own transport as the hotel is far from the centre and from any S- and U-Bahn stations. The rooms are well furnished and the marble bathrooms are elegant. ▦ 1 TV Y Y	AE DC MC V JCB	16			▦

Best Western Kanthotel Berlin
€€€
Kantstrasse 111, 10627 Berlin-Charlottenburg. **Map** 9 A1. 323 020. FAX 324 09 52.
www.kanthotel.com info@kanthotel.com
This good-quality hotel is located near to Charlottenburg railway station.
There are special facilities for business travellers, and non-smoking rooms
are available. The hotel offers services, such as babysitting and laundry.
There are many places to eat close by.

	AE	70		
	DC			
	V			
	JCB			

Hotel Luisenhof
€€€
Köpenicker Strasse 92, 10179 Berlin-Mitte. **Map** 8 D5. 241 59 06. FAX 279 29 83.
www.luisenhof.de info@luisenhof.de
Situated near the Märkisches Museum, this hotel occupies the oldest
building (1882) in this part of Berlin. Extensive restoration in 1993 created
a charming, small hotel with nice rooms and a pleasant restaurant in the
cellar.

	AE	27		
	DC			
	MC			
	V			
	JCB			

Hotel Seehof Berlin
€€€
Lietzenseeufer 11, 14057 Berlin-Charlottenburg. **Map** 2 D5. 32 00 20. FAX 32 00 22 51.
www.hotel-seehof-berlin.de info@hotel-seehof-berlin.de
This is an amazing, modern hotel only 10 minutes on foot from Messegelände (the complex of trade fair halls). The modern structure does
not reveal the stylish interiors and large rooms. Its Restaurant Au Lac is
one of the best in Berlin.

	AE	75	■	●	■
	MC				
	V				
	JCB				

SORAT Hotel Humboldt-Mühle Berlin
€€€
An der Mühle 5–9, 13507 Berlin-Reinickendorf. 439 040. FAX 43 90 44 44.
www.sorat-hotels.com humboldt-muehle@sorat-hotels.com
Located near Tegel airport, Sorat occupies a former grain mill. The interior's
modern style uses light-coloured woods and old architectural elements.
Because of its history, dishes in the breakfast bar and restaurant contain
wholemeal grains.

	AE	120	■	●	■
	DC				
	MC				
	V				
	JCB				

SORAT Hotel Spree-Bogen Berlin
€€€
Alt-Moabit 99, 10559 Berlin-Tiergarten. **Map** 4 F1. 399 200. FAX 399 20 999.
www.sorat-hotels.com spree-bogen@sorat-hotels.com
Beautifully located on the bank of the Spree river, the hotel is surrounded
by modern tower blocks close to the Tiergarten. The building was an old
dairy. The best rooms have views of the river and the hotel has its own yacht
for trips along the river.

	AE	220	■	●	■
	DC				
	MC				
	V				

Regent Schlosshotel, Berlin
€€€€€
Brahmsstrasse 10, 14193 Berlin-Wilmersdorf. 895 840. FAX 895 84 801.
www.regenthotels.com schlosshotelberlin@regenthotels.com
This exclusive hotel was formerly a palace, built in 1912 for Walter von
Pannwitz, the Kaiser's personal lawyer. The contemporary interiors were
created by Karl Lagerfeld. There is a breathtaking lobby with a magnificent
coffered ceiling and decorative woodcarving. The restaurant, Vivaldi *(see
p243)*, has a good reputation.

	AE	54	■		■
	DC				
	MC				
	V				
	JCB				

GREATER BERLIN

Art'otel Potsdam
€€
Zeppelinstrasse 136, 14471 Potsdam. (0331) 98 15 0. FAX (0331) 98 15 555.
www.artotel.de potsdam@artotel.de
Part of this luxurious hotel on the bank of the Havel river occupies an old
19th-century granary where rooms have beautiful ceilings with restored
beams and designer furniture. The best feature of rooms in the modern
wing is their balconies overlooking the Havel.

	AE	123	■	●	■
	DC				
	MC				
	V				

NH Voltaire
€€
Friedrich-Ebert-Strasse 88, 14467 Potsdam. (0331) 23 17 0. FAX (0331) 23 17 100.
www.nh-hotels.com
This is a top-quality hotel in the centre of town. Comfortably furnished
rooms have individual colour schemes. The modern part of the building is
joined to a converted Baroque palace.

	AE	143	■		
	DC				
	MC				
	V				

Relaxa Schlosshotel Cecilienhof
€€€€
Am Neuen Garten, Potsdam. (0331) 37 05 0. FAX (0331) 29 24 98.
www.relaxa-hotel.de potsdam-cecilienhof@relaxa-hotel.de
A treat for history lovers. The hotel occupies most of the Cecilienhof
palace. In the evening, when the daytrippers have left, hotel guests can
take a stroll in the gardens or a boat trip on the lake.

	AE	41		
	DC			
	MC			
	V			
	JCB			

For key to symbols *see p217*

RESTAURANTS, CAFÉS AND BARS

IVEN THAT BERLIN is so cosmopolitan, you will find a wider range of restaurants here than in any other city in Germany. This includes Indian, Greek, Chinese, Thai and Turkish as well as Alsatian and Cambodian. Recently, new places have been opened by famous chefs, which maintain high European standards of international-style cuisine. There are also plenty of restaurants specializing in local dishes: the food can be a little heavy, but it is usually very tasty and

Shield of the Forst-haus Paulsborn restaurant

served in large portions. Wherever you are in Berlin, you won't have to travel far to find somewhere to eat – every area has its own cluster of restaurants, cafés and bars, covering a range of styles and prices. Some of the best places are listed on pages 236–43. These have been chosen for their delicious food and/or good value. The listings on pages 244–9 should help those who would like a bite to eat but want the more relaxed setting of a café or bar.

The elegant interior of Margaux (see p237)

WHERE TO GO

ALTHOUGH GOOD restaurants and cafés can be found all over Berlin, some of the best gourmet restaurants tend to be located in exclusive hotels, including **Die Quadriga** in the Branden-burger Hof (see p241) or **First Floor** in the Hotel Palace Berlin (see p241). Alternatively, good restaurants, such as **Bamberger Reiter** (see p243), can also be found on quiet streets.

The largest concentrations of restaurants are in a number of well-known districts. In the former West Berlin, for example, the most famous restaurants are clustered around Savignyplatz. Good places to eat in the centre can be found in and around

Oranienburger Strasse. One of the recent top spots in Berlin that is popular with young people is Prenzlauer Berg, near Kollwitzplatz.

Despite all the changes that have taken place in the eastern part of Berlin over the past few years, restaurants in Kreuzberg (particularly along Oranienstrasse) are among the busiest in the city. The places in these areas are all consistently good and offer a wide choice in style and price.

WHAT TO EAT

IN THE MORNING, nearly all eateries, including those in most hotels, will offer a sub-stantial breakfast. This usually consists of eggs, ham or cold cuts and different kinds of cheese. On Sundays some places also serve a German

buffet-style brunch (breakfast combined with lunch) until 2pm. At lunchtime, one can easily find an elaborate salad or a bowl of steaming soup almost anywhere. In addition many restaurants may also offer their standard menus with slightly reduced prices.

The options for an evening meal are practically unlimited. In a restaurant serving local food one can have, for example, a tasty pork knuckle or potato soup (see pp232–3). Lovers of Italian cuisine can easily find a good pizzeria or an Italian restaurant that serves sophisticated regional Italian dishes. Fans of Oriental food can choose between many Asian national cuisines, a great variety of which are situated along Prenzlauer Berg and around Savignyplatz. In addition, Berlin also has very good

Outside Oxymoron (see p237), in the Hackesche Höfe

Outside Dressler Unter den Linden *(see p236)*

Mexican restaurants, particularly around Oranienburger Strasse and in Kreuzberg, and the food served at Greek restaurants is usually quite good and very inexpensive. Vegetarians can easily find something suitable at almost every restaurant; however places that offer a significant choice of meat-free dishes are specially marked in the restaurant listings *(see pp236–43)*.

Prices and Tipping

Menus, showing meals and their prices, are usually on display outside restaurants and cafés. The price of meals can vary a great deal. It is possible to eat a three course meal, without alcohol, for €15, but in the centre of Berlin the price rises to €20–€25. In a top-notch establishment the cost of a meal can be over €80. The price of alcohol varies as well, but the most popular and cheapest drink is beer. Although prices include service and tax, many Germans will round up the bill. In more expensive restaurants a 10 per cent tip is customary.

Eating Hours

In general, cafés open at 9am and restaurants at noon; the latter sometimes also close between 3 and 6pm. However, there are a lot of places that stay open very late, sometimes until 2 or 3am. Some of the most expensive and best restaurants are only open in the evening and are sometimes closed on one day during the week as well.

Booking

In the most up-market restaurants, reservations are almost certainly required – in popular places it is advisable to book well in advance. For the majority of good restaurants it is necessary to book only for Friday or Saturday evenings, when all restaurants are at their busiest. If you do not have a reservation, look for a street or square with a large concentration of restaurants – there is bound to be an empty table among these.

Disabled Diners

In order to avoid any problems in advance, you should discuss wheelchair access when booking. Bear in mind, however, that even if a dining room may be accessible on the ground floor, the toilets may be up or down stairs or through a narrow corridor.

Children

Casual restaurants usually welcome children, though this may not be the case in more upmarket establishments. Those that do cater for children may provide high chairs as well as light dishes, particularly during lunchtime. Some places will offer a separate children's menu with small portions. Children are also allowed in pubs and bars.

Reading the Menu

Menus are written out, in many places, in German and English, although some restaurants will provide menus in French as well. If you find yourself in a casual restaurant or bar, where the menu is perhaps handwritten, you can ask a waiter for help. Apart from the standard menu many restaurants will sometimes also offer a menu of the day containing seasonal dishes or the chef's specials, which are always worth considering.

The stylish Ana e Bruno (see p242)

Smoking

Smoking is allowed everywhere in Berlin – except in some fast-food places. There are special non-smoking rooms in some restaurants, but this is a rarity. To avoid a smoky meal, sit near a door or window, or look for a restaurant with high ceilings.

Inside First Floor, near the Kurfürstendamm *(see p241)*

What to Eat in Berlin

Loaf of Berlin bread

Berlin cuisine is richly varied but its many wonderful and tasty dishes are often overshadowed by German food's reputation as rich and stodgy. Concentrating on fresh ingredients from local forests and lakes, Berlin chefs create excellent seasonal cuisine, including particularly delicious wild mushrooms *(Pfifferlingen)*, crayfish, and river fish such as eel, which is often cooked with a green sauce *(Aal grün)*. You can always rely on finding excellent potato soup *(Kartoffelsuppe)*, while veal or pork knuckle with cabbage is also popular.

Berlin Breads
A wide range of excellent breads, rolls and pretzels is available in Berlin every day.

Käsestange

Brezel

Mohn-
brötchen

Zander mit Radieschenpfann-kuchen *is sautéed fillets of pike-perch served with delicate pancakes stuffed with radishes.*

Zander

Radish-stuffed pancakes

Forelle mit Spargel, *or fresh trout from the Wannsee, is often filleted and served with delicate green asparagus.*

Kalb mit Petersilienmousse, *slices of stewed veal with a light parsley mousse, is accompanied by* Spätzle *(German noodles) and herb dumplings.*

Wilde Pilze in Aspik *is carefully chosen wild mushrooms covered in aromatic aspic, which makes an elegant seasonal starter.*

Geräucherte Barbe mit Kartoffelpuffern *is slices of smoked barbel (a carp-like fish) served with crispy grated-potato pancakes.*

Rote Bete mit Schlagsahne, *a beetroot soup, is blended with cream and served with highly-flavoured meatballs.*

Kartoffelsuppe, *or creamy potato soup, is flavoured with marjoram, and served with slices of pork sausage.*

Brotsuppe, *made of brown bread and enriched with cream, is served with crisp bacon pieces and croûtons.*

Entenbraten mit Kraut, *a traditional dish, is roast duck served in an aromatic sauce with new potatoes and slowly braised spring cabbage.*

Ochsenschwanz mit Lendenfilet, *or stuffed oxtail, is simmered slowly in wine and served with rare sirloin steak and spring vegetables.*

Eisbein mit Kraut und Erbsenpüree *is a braised pork knuckle on a bed of cabbage cooked in champagne with puréed peas.*

Hühnerfrikassee mit Languste
This tasty fricassée of chicken is served with crayfish and squares of flaky pastry.

Crayfish

Gefüllte Forelle, *wild trout from the river Havel, is stuffed and served with a salad of mixed leaves and mushrooms.*

Fried chicken

Flaky pastry

BERLIN DESSERTS

The classic Berlin dessert is *Rote Grütze*, a compôte of mixed berries served with vanilla sauce. A simpler dessert is the famous *Pfann-Kuchen* or doughnut.

Savarin mit Blaubeeren und Minzsorbet *is sponge-cake soaked in syrup and served with blueberries and refreshing mint sorbet.*

Pfann-Kuchen mit Holundersorbet, *are mini* Berliner *doughnuts filled with plum mousse and served with elderflower sorbet, sliced pears and a fruit coulis.*

CURRYWURST

One of the most popular of Berlin snacks is the *Curry-wurst.* Invented in the city and sold on every street corner, a *Currywurst* is a spicy sausage served in a bread roll with a curried tomato sauce.

What to Drink in Berlin

I N BERLIN, AS THROUGHOUT the rest of Germany, beer
is the most widely drunk alcoholic beverage.
There are no productive vineyards around Berlin,
but wines from the Rhine and Mosel regions are
always popular. As an *aperitif*, or with pork dishes,
Berliners often enjoy a shot of rye vodka *(Korn)*,
sometimes flavoured with herbs. With dessert, a
glass of herbal liqueur often fits the bill.

Engelhardt brewery logo

Pilsner beers from Berlin breweries

LAGER *(PILSNER)*

B ERLINERS DRINK BEER on every occasion, and
Germany's many beers are some of the best
and purest in the world. Some of the best-known
Berlin breweries are Schultheiss, Berliner Kindl,
Berliner Pils and Engelhardt, but beers brewed in
other parts of Germany are just as popular.
Although beer is available in all sorts of venues
and *"Ein Bier bitte"* can be heard in pubs, cafés
and restaurants, it is worth experiencing the atmosphere of an old-fashioned beerhouse, or *Kneipe*.
The most highly esteemed beer is
draught beer, drawn from the cask
(vom Fass) and poured slowly into
tall glasses. Pouring in a thin trickle is
essential to achieve a thick head of
foam, and a good barman will take
a few minutes to fill your glass.
Berliners drink mostly lager *(Pils)*,
but other beers are also popular.

A *Brezel* makes a good
snack with beer

OTHER BEERS

I N ADDITION TO the usual light, Pilsner-type beers,
Berlin's breweries, many of them small and independent, also make a number of more adventurous
brews. Dark, sweetish beer, known as *Schwarzbier*
or black beer, is becoming more and more popular
and has rather more than the standard four per cent
alcohol. *Weizenbier* is made from wheat rather than
barley, and is usually served in half-litre (one pint)
glasses wth a slice of lemon. Another unusual drink
is *Bock*, an especially strong beer made with barley.
Maibock is a special version, available only in May.

Strong, dark
Bock beer

Berliner Weisse,
a light malted-
wheat beer

Berliner Weisse
with raspberry and
woodruff cordials

BERLINER WEISSE MIT SCHUSS

A BERLIN SPECIALITY, called *Berliner Weisse
mit Schuss*, is a light, newly-fermented
wheat beer that continues fermenting in
the bottle. On its own, it is not very
palatable as it is rather watery and sour,
but when mixed with raspberry cordial it
becomes fruity and delicious. Mixing with
sweet woodruff syrup gives it a vivid green
colour and a slightly medicinal flavour.
Berliner Weisse mit Schuss is served in
large wine glasses with a straw, and makes
a very refreshing drink, particularly
popular during the hot summer months.

WINE

N O WINE IS PRODUCED around Berlin as the climate here is too cold for vines, but a variety of wines from Germany's southern and western regions are available in Berlin. The most famous are the white wines, particularly those made from Riesling grapes. Most expensive are those from the Rheingau region. The northern climate dictates that most German wines are white, but lovers of red wine can try the Rhine Assmanshausen Spät-burgunder, made from Pinot Noir grapes. Although there is no regional system of classification like the French *Appellation d'Origine Contrôlée*, a national quality control system divides German wines into three categories: *Tafelwein* or table wine is the most basic; next comes *Qualitätswein*, and the highest is *Qualitätswein mit Prädikat*, which includes wines made from specially selected grapes. *Trocken* means dry, *halbtrocken* means medium dry and *süss* means sweet. You can also find some very good sparkling wines known as *Sekts*.

A prize-winning bottle of German red wine

Riesling from Schloss Vollrads

OTHER ALCOHOLIC BEVERAGES

V ODKA IS OFTEN DRUNK with more substantial meals, particularly those based on pork. Especially recommended is one of the rye vodkas, such as *Weizendoppelkorn*, that are popular in Berlin. Many establishments also serve brandies, known generically as *Weinbrand*. In addition, various digestive liqueurs and vodkas flavoured with plant extracts are quite popular, particularly *Kümmerling*, *Jägermeister* and, a Berlin favourite, *Kaulzzdorferkräuter Likör*. In many restaurants you will come across a speciality honey liqueur from east Prussia known as *Bärenfang*. More of an acquired taste is *Goldwasser* from Danzig, a traditional herbal liqueur containing flakes of gold leaf. It is made according to a secret 16th-century German recipe.

Weizendoppel-korn rye vodka

Herbal digestive liqueur

Bitter-sweet Jägermeister liqueur

NON-ALCOHOLIC COLD DRINKS

A LTHOUGH BERLIN TAP WATER is safe to drink, it is not usually served with restaurant meals. If you want water you should order a bottle of mineral water *(Mineralwasser)* adding *"ohne Kohlen-Säure"* if you prefer still water. A wide variety of canned sparkling soft drinks, ubiquitous across Europe and the US, are popular in Berlin. Fruit juices are also widely drunk and a wide selection is available in every restaurant and café. Another popular soft drink is *Apfelschorle*, apple juice mixed in equal proportions with sparkling mineral water.

Apfelschorle

Peppermint and camomile, two widely available herbal teas

COFFEE AND TEA

C OFFEE IS VERY POPULAR in Berlin and is served in a variety of ways. The most usual is filter coffee, served by the cup or the pot, generally with condensed milk and sugar. If you prefer something stronger and more aromatic you should go for an espresso. It is also easy to enjoy a good cup of tea in Berlin, herbal or otherwise. Germans drink a lot of herbal teas, two of the most common being peppermint *(Pfefferminz-tee)* and camomile *(Kamillentee)*. If you want a cup of non-herbal tea, you can make a point of ordering *Schwarzen Tee*. If you want milk with your tea, then ask for *Tee mit Milch*.

Choosing a Restaurant

T HE RESTAURANTS in this guide have been selected because of
their good value, good food and attractive interiors. The
chart below lists restaurants in Berlin by area, and the entries
are alphabetical within each price category. The type of
cuisine is listed in brackets by each restaurant. For information
on cafés and bars, see pages 244–249.

	CREDIT CARDS	TABLES OUTSIDE	VEGETARIAN DISHES	GOOD WINE LIST
AROUND UNTER DEN LINDEN				
XII APOSTEL (ITALIAN) € Georgenstrasse 2 (S-Bahnbögen 177–180). **Map** 7 A2, 16 D2. ⚏ *201 02 22.* Picturesquely situated in the old arcade of an S-Bahn railway bridge, this restaurant offers popular Italian cuisine. During the week, from midday to 4pm, all pizzas are half price. ♫ ☐ *11am–1am Sun–Thu, 11am–2am Fri, Sat.*			●	
BORCHARDT (INTERNATIONAL) €€€ Französische Strasse 47. **Map** 6 F4, 15 C3. ⚏ *20 38 71 10.* One of the few restaurants in Berlin with its original interior, including marble columns, mosaics and patterned floors in the Wilhelmine style. Prices are reasonable and the food is very good. Borchardt is favoured by German politicians. ❦ ☐ *11:30am–1am.*	AE DC MC V		●	■
MÖWE (INTERNATIONAL) €€€ Am Festungsgraben 1. **Map** 7 A3, 16 E2. ⚏ *20 61 05 40.* Situated inside the Palais am Festungsgraben *(see p69)*, Möwe serves good-quality German cuisine in its lighter form. The elegant interior is furnished with comfortable, soft sofas. ❦ ♫ ☐ *6-11:30pm Tue–Sat.*	AE DC V	■	●	■
SCHINKEL-KLAUSE IM OPERNPALAIS (GERMAN AND INTERNATIONAL) €€€ Unter den Linden 5. **Map** 7 A3, 16 E3. ⚏ *20 26 84 50.* Situated in the basement of the Prinzessinnenpalais *(see p63)*, this is a good place to dine before or after going to the opera next door. It offers a high standard of German and international dishes. ❦ ☐ *11am–midnight daily.*	AE DC MC V		●	■
BOCCA DI BACCO (ITALIAN) €€€€ Friedrichstrasse 167-8. **Map** 15 C3, 5 F3. ⚏ *20 67 28 28.* Berlin's finest Italian restaurant follows its own motto "to be the ambassador of good taste". It offers a simple elegant setting, with selected artworks on the walls, and floor to ceiling glass onto Friedrichstrasse. The menu consists of the most exquisite classical Italian dishes. A haunt of movie stars. ❦ ☐ *noon–midnight Mon–Sat, 6pm–midnight Sun.*	AE MC V		●	
SEASONS (GERMAN AND INTERNATIONAL) €€€€ Charlottenstrasse 49. **Map** 7 A4, 16 D3. ⚏ *20 33 63 63.* This restaurant is based in the exclusive Four Seasons Hotel. Wood- panelled rooms are lit by chandeliers, candles and the glow from the fireplace. Seasons is an ideal place for a romantic evening and for sampling light meals of international cuisine. The restaurant also offers low-cholesterol dishes and a full vegetarian selection, as well as a non-smoking area. Prices are lower for lunch. ❦ ☐ *6:30–11:30am,* *noon–2pm & 6–11:30pm daily.*	AE DC MC V		●	■
DRESSLER (GERMAN AND FRENCH) €€€€€ Unter den Linden 39. **Map** 6 E4, 15 A3. ⚏ *204 44 22.* Dressler is the perfect setting for a quick dinner before or after a visit to the nearby theatres or opera houses. This brasserie-like restaurant serves traditional German and French cuisine in an Art Deco-designed, yet cosy, dining hall. In season, Dressler has some of the city's best seafood, including lobster and a selection of oysters. In winter, try their hearty German fare, such as oven-roasted duck with red cabbage and dumplings. ❦ ☐ *8am–midnight daily.*	AE DC MC V JCB	■	●	■
LORENZ-ADLON-GOURMET (FRENCH) €€€€€ Unter den Linden 77. **Map** 6 E4, 15 A3. ⚏ *22 61 19 60.* This establishment is worthy of the hotel in which it is located, the Adlon. From the day it opened, this restaurant has been rated among the best in Berlin. Under the guidance of its chefs, Lorenz-Adlon-Gourmet has managed to maintain its place among the ten best restaurants in the city. ❦ ☐ *7pm–midnight Tue–Sat.*	AE DC MC V		●	■

Price categories for a three-course meal per person, including tax and service but not alcohol: € up to €18 €€ €19–€25 €€€ €26–€36 €€€€ €37–€51 €€€€€ over €51	**CREDIT CARDS** Indicates which credit cards are accepted: AE American Express; DC Diners Club; MC Master Card/Access; V Visa; JCB Japan Credit Bureau. **TABLES OUTSIDE** Weather permitting, meals can be served outside. **VEGETARIAN DISHES** The restaurant offers a good selection of meat-free and vegetarian dishes. **GOOD WINE LIST** Denotes a wide selection of good wines.	CREDIT CARDS	TABLES OUTSIDE	VEGETARIAN DISHES	GOOD WINE LIST
MARGAUX (FRENCH) €€€€€ Unter den Linden 78. **Map** 6 E4, 15 A3. 22 65 26 11. The Michelin-starred Margaux represents the new Berlin better than any other gourmet restaurant. It is stylish and urban, in the classic yet creative French dishes, the sophisticated interior, the service and the patrons. noon–2pm 7–10:30pm Mon–Sat, 7–10:30pm Sun.		AE DC MC V		●	■
VAU (AUSTRIAN AND GERMAN) €€€€€ Jägerstrasse 54–55. **Map** 6 F4, 15 C4. 202 97 30. This restaurant stands out. The interior is elegant though unpretentious, and the excellent Austrian- and German-based dishes are created by well-known chefs. The service is welcoming and there is a selection of good wines. The small courtyard is used during lunch. noon–2:30pm & 7–10pm Mon–Sat.		AE DC MC V		●	■
MUSEUM ISLAND					
RAABE DIELE (GERMAN) €€ Märkisches Ufer 10. **Map** 7 C4. 27 58 29 99. A pleasant restaurant that specializes in Berlin cuisine and is based in the cellar of Ermeler-Haus (see pp84–5). The huge portions will satisfy any appetite. Pork knuckle with pureed peas and sauerkraut (Eisbein mit Erbsenpuree und Sauerkraut) is the speciality. Everything served is drowned in the heavy but tasty sauces typical of the region. 11:30am–2am daily.		AE DC MC V	■		
EAST OF THE CENTRE					
ZUM NUSSBAUM (GERMAN) € Am Nussbaum 3. **Map** 7 C3. 242 30 95. Situated in an alley off the Nikolaiviertel, this is a reconstruction of a 16th-century country inn, serving traditional Berlin cuisine, with tender pork knuckle and rollmops. In summer, dine in its garden. noon–2am daily.		MC V	■		
HISTORISCHE WEINSTUBEN (GERMAN) €€ Poststrasse 23. **Map** 7 C3. 242 41 07. This popular wine bar is located in Knoblauchhaus (see p91), one of the most decorative buildings of the Nikolaiviertel. Traditional dishes from Berlin are offered, and an amazing wine list. winter: noon–midnight; summer: 11am–1am.		AE MC V			■
OXYMORON (INTERNATIONAL) €€ Rosenthaler Strasse 40–41. **Map** 7 B2. 28 39 18 86. This fashionable restaurant, with its distinctive red and gold interior, has mainly Mediterranean dishes on the menu. For lunch, dine at a table in the courtyard, and enjoy a lighter dish at a reasonable price. 11–3am daily.		AE V	■	●	■
ZUR LETZTEN INSTANZ (GERMAN) €€ Waisenstrasse 16. **Map** 8 D3. 242 55 28. One of the oldest restaurants in Berlin, this used to be a meeting place for lawyers. It specializes in traditional German food, such as pork knuckle (Eisbein) and beef olive (Rinderroulade). noon–1am Mon–Sat, noon–11pm Sun.		AE DC V	■		
LA RIVA (ITALIAN) €€€ Spreeufer 2. **Map** 7 C4. 242 51 83. This restaurant, serving good-quality Italian food, is found on the bank of the Spree river. Different types of pasta and good Italian wines appear on the menu. In summer, diners can enjoy the terrace. 11am–11pm daily.		AE V	■	●	■
REINHARD'S (INTERNATIONAL) €€€ Poststrasse 28. **Map** 7 C3. 238 42 95. The interior of this enchanting place is decorated in the style of the Roaring Twenties. The food is excellent. The speciality is Das Geheimnis aus dem Kaiserhof (the secret of the Kaiser's court) – succulent steak served with a sauce that was apparently created for Max Liebermann. 9–1am.		AE DC V	■	●	■

<table>
<tr><td>

Price categories for a three-course meal per person, including tax and service but not alcohol:

€ up to €18
€€ €19–€25
€€€ €26–€36
€€€€ €37–€51
€€€€€ over €51

</td><td>

CREDIT CARDS
Indicates which credit cards are accepted: AE American Express; DC Diners Club; MC Master Card/Access; V Visa; JCB Japan Credit Bureau.

TABLES OUTSIDE
Weather permitting, meals can be served outside.

VEGETARIAN DISHES
The restaurant offers a good selection of meat-free and vegetarian dishes.

GOOD WINE LIST
Denotes a wide selection of good wines.

</td></tr>
</table>

	CREDIT CARDS	TABLES OUTSIDE	VEGETARIAN DISHES	GOOD WINE LIST
NORTH OF THE CENTRE				
KURVENSTAR (INTERNATIONAL) € Kleine Präsidentenstrasse 3. **Map** 7 B2, 16 F1. 📞 *28 59 97 10.* An unusual place that links together a restaurant, a music club and a bar. The menu offers food from all over the world. Try the *sushi* or the *calaloo* (from the Caribbean). European dishes are also served. 🎵 🕐 *7pm–late daily.*	DC MC V		●	
YOSOY (SPANISH) € Rosenthaler Strasse 37. **Map** 7 B2. 📞 *283 912 13.* A pleasant and inexpensive restaurant with a large selection of Spanish wines and dishes. The *tapas* are excellent. 🕐 *11am–late daily.*	AE MC V	■	●	
BRAZIL (BRAZILIAN) €€ Gormannstrasse 22. **Map** 7 C1. 📞 *28 59 90 26.* The combination of good Brazilian food and friendly atmosphere ensures this place is always busy. Brazil is ideal for a relaxed supper. 🕐 *10–2am daily.*	DC MC V	■	●	
KAMALA (THAI) €€ Oranienburger Strasse 69. **Map** 7 A1. 📞 *283 27 97.* This small restaurant has simple furnishings, but the service is pleasant and prompt and the quality of food is high. The menu features excellent soups flavoured with delicate Thai flavours. 🕐 *noon–midnight daily.*	MC V	■	●	
KELLERRESTAURANT IM BRECHT-HAUS (AUSTRIAN) €€ Chausseestrasse 125. **Map** 6 E1. 📞 *282 38 43.* This restaurant is located in the cellar of the house where Bertolt Brecht used to live. Apparently, the dishes served here are prepared according to the recipes of Helene Weigel, the wife of this famous writer. 🕐 *noon–1am daily.*	AE MC	■		
ORANGE (INTERNATIONAL) €€ Oranienburger Strasse 32. **Map** 7 A1. 📞 *28 38 52 42.* Diners sit in a pleasant interior in the style of a café-restaurant, offering Italian dishes. Try a leisurely three-course meal or a snack. 🕐 *9am–late daily.*	AE MC V	■	●	
OREN (JEWISH AND MIDDLE EASTERN) €€ Oranienburger Strasse 28. **Map** 7 A1. 📞 *282 82 28.* A great option for vegetarians. Try the *falafel* (fried chickpea balls) or one of the excellent aubergine (eggplant) dishes. 🎵 🕐 *noon–1am daily (from 10am Sun).*	AE MC V	■	●	■
PAN ASIA (VIETNAMESE, THAI AND CHINESE) €€ Rosenthaler Strasse 38. **Map** 7 B1. 📞 *27 90 88 11.* Asian fusion cuisine at its best, with healthy vegetable dishes from Vietnam, Thailand and China served in a stylish 1960s retro ambiance. Mostly a young and hip urban crowd. 🍴 ♿ 🕐 *noon–1am Mon–Fri, noon–2am Sat, Sun.*	MC V	■	●	
STÄNDIGE VERTRETUNG (GERMAN) €€ Schiffbauerdamm 8. **Map** 6 F2. 📞 *282 39 65.* A friendly establishment serving regional food and drink from the Rhine. Dishes include *Flammekuchen*, a type of quiche with meat, vegetables and shrimp, and *Zander* (pike-perch) served on *sauerkraut*. 🕐 *10am–12:30am.*	AE MC V	■	●	
GANYMED (INTERNATIONAL) €€€ Schiffbauerdamm 5. **Map** 6 F2, 15 C1. 📞 *28 59 90 46.* A good-quality restaurant in pleasant surroundings. The chef favours fish dishes, including Berlin fish specialities. 🕐 *noon–1am Mon–Sat, 10–1am Sun.*	V	■	●	
HACKESCHER HOF (INTERNATIONAL) €€€ Rosenthaler Strasse 40/41. **Map** 7 B2. 📞 *283 52 93.* A very popular spot, this café-restaurant serves breakfast from early morning, followed by inexpensive fixed-price lunches and Italian dishes in the evenings. Book ahead. 🍴 🕐 *7–3am Mon–Fri, 9–3am Sat & Sun (last orders midnight).*	AE DC MC V	■	●	■

Mare Bê (International)
€€€   AE MC V

Rosenthaler Strasse 46–48. **Map** 7 B2. ☎ *283 65 45.*
The perfect place for fans of southern-French, Italian and Spanish cuisines, with a hint of Middle Eastern influence. In the summer, tables are placed in the quiet courtyard garden. ☐ *noon–1am Mon–Sat, 4pm–1am Sun.*

Schwarzen Raben (Italian, Mediterranean)
€€€€   AE MC V

Neue Schönhauser Strasse 13. **Map** 7 B2. ☎ *28 39 16 98.*
A fashionable venue with a bistro and a restaurant – the latter only open in the evening. Good Italian food, cheeses and wines. ☐ *10am–midnight daily.*

TIERGARTEN

Café Einstein (Viennese)
€€€   AE DC MC V

Kurfürstenstrasse 58. **Map** 10 F1. ☎ *261 50 96.*
Many tourists enjoy the delicious strawberry cake in this Viennese café, but don't return for dinner. West Berlin's intellectual crowd, however, comes here for Austrian classics such as Wiener Schnitzels or goulash. ☐ *9am–1am daily.*

Du Pont (French)
€€€   AE DC V

Budapester Strasse 1. **Map** 10 F1. ☎ *261 88 11.*
Good, classical French cuisine. The prices, however, are rather extravagant. The intimate room, charming atmosphere and pleasant service almost make up for it. ☐ *noon–3pm & 6pm–midnight Mon–Fri; 6pm–midnight Sat.*

Il Sorriso (Italian)
€€€   AE DC MC V

Kurfürstenstrasse 76. **Map** 11 A1. ☎ *262 13 13.*
Il Sorriso serves very good Italian cuisine with a large selection of traditional dishes. The menu changes according to the season and during the summer diners can sit outside. ☐ *noon–midnight Mon–Sat.*

Käfer im Bundestag (German and Italian)
€€€€   AE DC MC V

Reichstag, Platz der Republik 13. **Map** 6 D3. ☎ *22 62 990.*
A favourite dining place of the Mitte district, thanks to creative cooking, impeccable service and a breathtaking view. ☐ *9am–5pm, 6:30pm–midnight daily.*

Harlekin (International)
€€€€€   AE MC V

Lützowufer 15. **Map** 11 A1. ☎ *25 47 88 58.*
The pride of the Grand Hotel Esplanade is one of the best restaurants in town. The open kitchen allows guests to observe the chefs at work. All the dishes are well presented. Book ahead. ☐ *6:30–11pm Tue–Sat.*

Vox (International)
€€€€€   AE DC MC V

Marlene-Dietrich-Platz 2. **Map** 6 D5. ☎ *25 53 12 34.*
Situated within the Grand Hyatt hotel, the Vox is a gourmet establishment in a minimalist setting, where the German and Asian food is prepared in an open show kitchen. ☐ *noon–2pm (3pm Sun) 6:30pm–midnight daily.*

Zum Hugenotten (International)
€€€€€   AE DC MC V

Budapester Strasse 2. **Map** 10 F1. ☎ *26 02 12 63.*
The Inter-Continental hotel is the location of Zum Hugenotten, one of the best restaurants in Berlin. Unusual French dishes prepared with a German influence attract a steady clientele. Any fish or seafood dish proves the real mastery of the chef. Reservations necessary. ☐ *6–11:30pm Mon–Sat.*

KREUZBERG

Bar Centrale (Italian)
€€   MC V

Yorckstrasse 82. **Map** 12 F4. ☎ *786 29 89.*
A popular bistro with a modern-style interior, Bar Centrale is often frequented by younger diners. The Italian cuisine is experimental. ☐ *noon–1am daily (to 2pm Sat).*

Joe Peña's Cantina y Bar (Mexican)
€€   AE MC V

Marheinekeplatz 3. **Map** 13 A4. ☎ *693 60 44.*
If you like spicy-hot Mexican food, a range of tortillas, burritos and enchiladas, Corona beer served with a wedge of lemon, loud music and a relaxed atmosphere, you'll love this place. ☐ *5pm–late daily.*

Parlamento (Italian)
€€

Bergmannstrasse 3. **Map** 12 F4. ☎ *694 77 45.*
Delicious Italian dishes that taste like they were home-made and a pleasant atmosphere enable this place to compete easily with other restaurants in the Kreuzberg area. ☐ *6pm–midnight Wed–Sun.*

Price categories for a three-course meal per person, including tax and service but not alcohol:

€ up to €18
€€ €19–€25
€€€ €26–€36
€€€€ €37–€51
€€€€€ over €51

CREDIT CARDS
Indicates which credit cards are accepted: AE American Express; DC Diners Club; MC Master Card/Access; V Visa; JCB Japan Credit Bureau.

TABLES OUTSIDE
Weather permitting, meals can be served outside.

VEGETARIAN DISHES
The restaurant offers a good selection of meat-free and vegetarian dishes.

GOOD WINE LIST
Denotes a wide selection of good wines.

	CREDIT CARDS	TABLES OUTSIDE	VEGETARIAN DISHES	GOOD WINE LIST
GROSSBEERENKELLER (GERMAN) €€€			●	
Grossbeerenstrasse 90. **Map** 12 F3. 251 30 64. A charming cellar restaurant, with antlers on the walls, that offers traditional Berlin home cooking. Try the fried potatoes (flecked with bacon, onions and spices). ◖ 4pm (6pm Sat)–last customer Mon–Sat.				
ALTES ZOLLHAUS (GERMAN) €€€€	AE DC MC V			▦
Carl-Herz-Ufer 30. **Map** 13 B3. 692 33 00. This restaurant is situated on the picturesque bank of the Landwehrkanal in what used to be a border control point. Excellent gourmet-style German food is served here without the usual heavy sauces. ⑨◖ 6pm–1am Tue–Sat.				

AROUND KURFÜRSTENDAMM

	CREDIT CARDS	TABLES OUTSIDE	VEGETARIAN DISHES	GOOD WINE LIST
MARCHÉ (INTERNATIONAL) €	AE DC MC V JCB	▦	●	
Kurfürstendamm 14. **Map** 10 D1. 882 75 78. A self-service restaurant under the Mövenpick umbrella, Marché caters for the many tourists visiting Kaiser-Wilhelm-Gedächtniskirche. Choose from meat and fish dishes, plenty of desserts, beer and wine. ◖ 8am–midnight daily.				
SATYAM (INDIAN) €			●	
Goethestrasse 5. **Map** 3 C5. 312 90 79. If you don't mind a shabby interior, you will enjoy feasting (very inexpensively) on vegetarian Indian dishes, and many are not too spicy. Dishes made from *panir* (Indian fresh cheese) are the speciality. ◖ 9am–11pm daily.				
XII APOSTEL (ITALIAN) €		▦	●	
Bleibtreustrasse 49. **Map** 9 B1. 312 14 33. The Italian food served is available nearly 24 hours, but this place is always busy. The menu includes all types of pastas and pizzas. ◖ 7–5am daily.				
DON QUIJOTE (SPANISH) €€		▦	●	
Bleibtreustrasse 41. **Map** 9 B1. 881 32 08. The food in this restaurant is wonderfully prepared, the kitchen smells like a tavern in Spain and there is even a good, affordable Rioja. ◖ 4pm–1am daily.				
HAMLET (INTERNATIONAL) €€	AE DC MC V	▦	●	
Uhlandstrasse 47. **Map** 9 C3. 882 13 61. Do not be misled by the name – the menu offers mainly French and a few Oriental dishes, but nothing English or Danish. ◖ 8–2am daily.				
ISTANBUL (TURKISH) €€	AE DC MC V		●	
Pestalozzistrasse 84. **Map** 3 A5. 883 27 77. One of the best traditional Turkish restaurants in Berlin offering food from every region. Belly-dancing shows at weekends. ♫ ◖ noon–midnight daily.				
LUBITSCH (INTERNATIONAL) €€	AE MC V	▦	●	
Bleibtreustrasse 47. **Map** 9 B1. 882 37 56. This popular restaurant is in one of the liveliest streets around Savignyplatz. A wide variety of German and international dishes is on the menu, with very reasonable prices at lunchtime. ⑨◖ 9:30–1am daily.				
BOVRIL (INTERNATIONAL) €€€	AE MC V	▦	●	
Kurfürstendamm 184. **Map** 9 B2. 881 84 61. A popular bistro, although a bit elitist. During lunchtime, Bovril is usually visited by people working around the Ku'damm. Good, light food influenced by German cuisine. ⑨◖ 10–2am Mon–Sat.				
FLORIAN (INTERNATIONAL) €€€	V	▦	●	▦
Grolmannstrasse 52. **Map** 3 C5. 313 91 84. The daily specials in this restaurant vary with the seasons – the best dishes are created during the asparagus and wild mushroom seasons. Also on offer is a wide selection of wines. Reservations required. ◖ 6pm–3am daily.				

HEISING (FRENCH) €€€
Rankerstrasse 32. Map 10 E1. 213 39 52.
This is one of the most traditional restaurants in Berlin, with a Neo-Rococo interior and impeccable service. The food is straight classic French with no experiments. Would suit a demanding guest. 7pm–midnight Mon–Sat.

KASHMIR PALACE (INDIAN) €€€
AE DC MC V
Marburger Strasse 14. Map 10 E1. 214 28 40.
A good Indian restaurant. The food is authentic, but not overly spiced.
noon–3pm & 6pm–midnight Tue–Fri, noon–midnight Sat, 5pm–midnight Sun–Mon.

KUCHI (JAPANESE) €€€
AE DC MC V
Kantstrasse 30. Map 9 B1. 31 50 78 15.
Kuchi, one of the best-value Japanese restaurants in Berlin, offers excellent *sushi* and regional dishes. A simple, unpretentious interior and a welcoming service make it the ideal venue for a dinner for two. noon–midnight Mon–Fri, 12:30pm–12:30am Sat, Sun.

LE CANARD (FRENCH) €€€
AE DC V
Knesebeckstrasse 88. Map 3 C5. 312 26 45.
The wonderful, popular French food served in this classic bistro includes a magnificent dish of duck. 5pm–midnight daily.

PARIS BAR (FRENCH) €€€
AE
Kantstrasse 152. Map 9 C1. 313 80 52.
This is an exclusive bistro frequented by artists and politicians. Fairly expensive, but the food is excellent – the blood sausage with potatoes *(Blutwurst mit Kartoffeln)* is recommended. Book ahead. noon–1am daily.

PEPPINO (ITALIAN) €€€
AE MC DC V
Fasanenstrasse 65. Map 10 D2. 883 67 22.
A good-quality Italian restaurant serving mainly dishes from the region of Tuscany. Fish dishes, prepared exquisitely, are among the house specialities. The menu varies according to season. noon–midnight Mon–Sat.

BACCO (ITALIAN) €€€€
AE V
Marburger Strasse 5. Map 10 E1. 211 86 87.
An intimate restaurant, with a modern interior and marvellous food from Tuscany. Prices are fairly high and the portions are small, but the quality makes it worthwhile. noon–3pm & 6pm–midnight Mon–Fri, 6pm–midnight Sat.

OTTENTHAL (AUSTRIAN) €€€€
AE V
Kantstrasse 153. Map 10 D1. 313 31 62.
The simple interior is adorned by a clock from the Ottenthal Church in Austria and the background music is mainly Mozart. Fine Austrian cuisine is served with a fantastic wine list. Reservations required. 6pm–1am daily.

DIE QUADRIGA (FRENCH) €€€€€
AE DC MC V JCB
Eislebener Strasse 14. Map 10 E2. 21 40 56 50.
Hotel Brandenburger Hof's most obvious attraction is this gourmet restaurant (one of the best in Berlin). This cosy establishment serves unusual French dishes accompanied by perfect service. Book ahead. 7pm–late Mon–Fri.

FIRST FLOOR (FRENCH) €€€€€
AE DC MC V JCB
Budapester Strasse 42. Map 10 E1. 25 02 10 20.
An elegant restaurant of the highest-quality French cuisine. The menu offers traditional food as well as unrivalled creations with fish, crayfish and truffles. Book in advance. noon–3pm & 6–11pm Sun–Fri, 6–11pm Sat.

AROUND SCHLOSS CHARLOTTENBURG

WOOLLOOMOOLLOO (AUSTRALIAN) €€
Röntgenstrasse 7. Map 3 B3. 34 70 27 77.
As its Aboriginal name suggests, this place is situated "where rivers cross", here the Spree and Landwehrkanal. The menu includes kangaroo, ostrich and crocodile meat. Live Australian music on Sundays. 5pm–1am daily.

PONTE VECCHIO (ITALIAN) €€€
DC
Spielhagenstrasse 3. Map 2 F4. 342 19 99.
An unpretentious restaurant that specializes in dishes from Tuscany. Regular guests usually follow the chef's recommendations. However, food can be cooked to your own specifications. Book ahead.
6:30–11pm Wed–Mon.

For key to symbols see back flap

<table>
<tr><td colspan="2">

Price categories for a three-course meal per person, including tax and service but not alcohol:

€ up to €18
€€ €19–€25
€€€ €26–€36
€€€€ €37–€51
€€€€€ over €51

</td><td>

CREDIT CARDS
Indicates which credit cards are accepted: AE American Express; DC Diners Club; MC Master Card/Access; V Visa; JCB Japan Credit Bureau.

TABLES OUTSIDE
Weather permitting, meals can be served outside.

VEGETARIAN DISHES
The restaurant offers a good selection of meat-free and vegetarian dishes.

GOOD WINE LIST
Denotes a wide selection of good wines.

</td></tr>
</table>

	CREDIT CARDS	TABLES OUTSIDE	VEGETARIAN DISHES	GOOD WINE LIST
ANA E BRUNO (ITALIAN) €€€€€	AE			▨

ANA E BRUNO (ITALIAN) €€€€€
Sophie-Charlotten-Strasse 101. **Map** 2 D3. 〖 325 71 10.
One of the best Italian restaurants in Berlin. An elegant interior and quiet music create the perfect atmosphere to sample the magnificent creations prepared by the chef. Everything is delicious, including the roasted sturgeon in Mediterranean sauce. Menus given to women omit prices, but provide a calorie count for each dish. ¶ ◗ 6:30pm–midnight Tue–Sat.

GREATER BERLIN

	CREDIT CARDS	TABLES OUTSIDE	VEGETARIAN DISHES	GOOD WINE LIST
BLOCKHAUS NIKOLSKOE (BERLIN) €€	MC	▨	●	

BLOCKHAUS NIKOLSKOE (BERLIN) €€
Nikolskoer Weg 15 (Wannsee). 〖 805 29 14.
This restaurant is in an old *dacha* (Russian-style log cabin) built for Tsar Nicholas I. The terrace has views of the lake. The menu offers German dishes and tasty cakes. ◗ 16 Apr–31 Oct: 10am–10pm daily; 1 Nov–15 Apr: 10am–7pm daily.

	CREDIT CARDS	TABLES OUTSIDE	VEGETARIAN DISHES	GOOD WINE LIST
MAO THAI (THAI) €€	AE MC V	▨	●	

MAO THAI (THAI) €€
Wörtherstrasse 30. 〖 441 92 61.
This is one of the best Thai restaurants in Berlin, with an interior filled with beautiful antiques from Burma. The menu offers a full range of aromatic dishes toned down to better suit European tastes.
¶ ◗ noon–midnight daily.

	CREDIT CARDS	TABLES OUTSIDE	VEGETARIAN DISHES	GOOD WINE LIST
MERHABA (TURKISH) €€	AE V			

MERHABA (TURKISH) €€
Hasenheide 39. **Map** 13 C5, 14 E5. 〖 692 17 13.
People from all over Berlin come to this charming restaurant to join the local Turks and Germans who enjoy the food served here. There is outdoor dining in summer and belly dancing on Fridays and Saturdays.
♫ ◗ noon–midnight daily.

	CREDIT CARDS	TABLES OUTSIDE	VEGETARIAN DISHES	GOOD WINE LIST
NOLA (CALIFORNIAN) €€	MC V	▨	●	

NOLA (CALIFORNIAN) €€
Dortmunder Strasse 9 (Tiergarten). **Map** 4 E2. 〖 399 69 69.
The food here is a typical Californian-Mexican blend. However, the atmosphere is fantastic and booking is required at weekends. ◗ 4pm–1am daily.

	CREDIT CARDS	TABLES OUTSIDE	VEGETARIAN DISHES	GOOD WINE LIST
OSTWIND (CHINESE) €€		▨	●	

OSTWIND (CHINESE) €€
Husemannstrasse 13. 〖 441 59 51.
The interior is a bit garish but the food is great and there are many tasty dishes from different regions of China. ¶ ◗ 6pm–1am daily (from 10am Sun).

	CREDIT CARDS	TABLES OUTSIDE	VEGETARIAN DISHES	GOOD WINE LIST
RESTAURATION 1900 (INTERNATIONAL) €€	MC V	▨	●	

RESTAURATION 1900 (INTERNATIONAL) €€
Husemannstrasse 1. 〖 442 24 94.
This restaurant offers light cuisine with some dishes of German origin and a large selection for vegetarians. It is worth visiting for the excellent views over eastern Berlin from the terrace. ♫ ◗ 10–1am daily.

	CREDIT CARDS	TABLES OUTSIDE	VEGETARIAN DISHES	GOOD WINE LIST
WALDHAUS (GERMAN) €€		▨	●	

WALDHAUS (GERMAN) €€
Onkel-Tom-Strasse 50 (Zehlendorf). 〖 81 37 575.
This restaurant, set in leafy surroundings, is a pleasant place to spend an evening enjoying a barbecue. In winter, the menu offers German dishes such as duck, goose and venison. ◗ 5pm–1am Mon–Fri.

	CREDIT CARDS	TABLES OUTSIDE	VEGETARIAN DISHES	GOOD WINE LIST
WIRTSHAUS MOORLAKE (GERMAN) €€	AE DC MC V	▨		

WIRTSHAUS MOORLAKE (GERMAN) €€
Moorlakeweg 1 (Zehlendorf). 〖 805 58 09.
Situated on the bank of the Havel river, this restaurant serves German dishes. In summer, visitors to the nearby Schloss Glienicke stop for coffee and cake on the terrace. ¶ ◗ Daily. Summer: 11am–10pm; Winter: 11am–6pm.

	CREDIT CARDS	TABLES OUTSIDE	VEGETARIAN DISHES	GOOD WINE LIST
ABENDMAHL (VEGETARIAN) €€€			●	

ABENDMAHL (VEGETARIAN) €€€
Muskauer Strasse 9 (Kreuzberg). **Map** 14 F2. 〖 612 51 70.
This rather gaudy restaurant is loosely vegetarian, but fish is also included on the menu. Everything comes from organic farms and there is a large choice of salads. The food is healthy and tasty, but not cheap. ◗ 6pm–1am daily.

CHALET SUISSE (SWISS)
Clayallee 99. 832 63 62.
Occupying a picturesque wooden building, this is a perfect place for a
rest after walking in the Grunewald forest. There is a large selection of
Swiss and German dishes, including game. *11:30am–midnight daily.*

€€€

| AE DC MC V |

FORSTHAUS PAULSBORN (GERMAN)
Hüttenweg 90 (Grunewald). 818 19 10.
This former hunting palace is located deep in the forest. Now used as
a lodge, the ground floor is occupied by this excellent restaurant which,
in summer, extends into the garden. The food is magnificent.
Mar–Oct & Dec: 11am–11pm Tue–Sun; Jan–Feb & Nov: 11am–6pm Tue–Sun.

€€€

| AE DC MC V JCB |

GRUNEWALDTURM (GERMAN)
Havelchaussee 61. 300 07 30.
Combining a meal in this restaurant with a trip to the Grunewald forest is a
fine way to spend an afternoon. Lunch or supper with wonderful views
is an ideal end for this kind of outing. *10am–11pm daily.*

€€€

| AE MC V |

JOLESCH (AUSTRIAN AND GERMAN)
Muskauer Strasse 1. **Map** 14 F1. 612 38 51.
The most popular of the many new Austrian gourmet restaurants, Jolesch
offers hearty dishes, always with an unexpected twist, and fine wines in a
simple setting. *10am–1am daily.*

€€€

| AE MC V |

MAXWELL (INTERNATIONAL)
Bergstrasse 22 (Mitte). 280 71 21.
This highly regarded restaurant is known for its good food with
Mediterranean influences. There is a cheaper menu for lunch but
few affordable wines. *6–11:30pm daily.*

€€€

| AE DC V |

PASTERNAK (RUSSIAN)
Knaackstrasse 22–24. 441 33 99.
Comfortable armchairs and food from St Petersburg can be found here.
Specialities include: beetroot soup (*borshch*), *blinis* and beef strogonov.
Vodka and caviar are available for brunch. *noon–2am daily.*

€€€

SPREE-ATHEN (GERMAN)
Leibnizstrasse 60 (Charlottenburg). **Map** 9 B1. 324 17 33.
This is an excellent place to try typical Berlin dishes. There is a stylish
and nostalgic atmosphere inside and old German tunes are played in
the background. The menu changes daily. *6pm–late Tue–Sat.*

€€€

| AE DC V |

STORCH (ALSATIAN)
Wartburgstrasse 54 (Schöneberg). **Map** 11 A5. 784 20 59.
Highly esteemed restaurant specializing in dishes from the German-French
border. Sweet and savoury tarts are the specialities. Excellent service, but
large tables often require sharing with strangers. *6pm–1am daily.*

€€€

| AE MC V |

REMISE IM SCHLOSS KLEIN-GLIENICKE (GERMAN)
Königstrasse 36 (Klein-Glienicke). 805 40 00.
This is an ideal place for an elegant meal in the outskirts of Berlin. The
menu offers excellent German cuisine, with perch, crayfish and game
all prepared with a dose of imagination. *noon–midnight Wed–Sun.*

€€€€

| AE DC MC V |

ALT LUXEMBURG (FRENCH)
Windscheidstrasse 31. **Map** 2 E5. 323 87 30.
Food for a true gourmet set in a tastefully understated atmosphere. The
best of European cooking has been given a personal touch inspired by
aromatic flavours of the East. Book ahead. *5pm–1am Mon–Sat.*

€€€€€

| AE DC MC V |

BAMBERGER REITER (FRENCH)
Regensburger Strasse 7. **Map** 10 E3. 218 42 82.
One of the largest restaurants in Berlin, this is the domain of Austrian chef
Franz Raneburger. The intimate atmosphere and impeccable service guarantee
a perfect evening. Reservations required. *5:30–11:30pm Tue–Sat.*

€€€€€

| DC MC V |

VIVALDI (FRENCH)
Brahmsstrasse 10. 89 58 45 20.
A luxurious restaurant in Berlin's expensive Regent Schlosshotel. The
interior, designed by Karl Lagerfeld, features panelled walls, gold leaf and
chandeliers. Impeccable French food. Book ahead.
noon–2pm 6pm–late Tue–Sat.

€€€€€

| AE DC MC V JCB |

Light Meals and Snacks

THERE ARE MANY popular fast-food bars and restaurants in Berlin that serve the all-pervading burgers, French fries and pizzas, some of them run by well-known international chains. By way of contrast, many of the self-service places specialize in local foods. The city's cafés are ideal stopping places for a quick meal and always offer something on the menu that will fill you up. Even more convenient are the many bars on wheels or small kiosks – *Imbissbuden* – that serve the traditional Berlin *Currywurst (see p233)*.

IMBISSBUDEN AND SNACK BARS

THE CLASSIC *Imbissbude* is a simple little kiosk selling drinks and a few light snacks, such as *Currywurst* or French fries *(Pommes)* served with mayonnaise or ketchup (or both). The former is a genuine Berlin speciality consisting of grilled, sliced sausage *(Bratwurst)*, topped with a spicy sauce, and served on a paper plate with a plastic fork. These kiosks are usually located in convenient sites near the S-Bahn or U-Bahn stations, or on busy streets and junctions. **Ku'damm 195**, **Amtsgerichtsplatz** and **Konnopke** are considered the best places to experience traditional *Currywurst*, which is served with home-made spicy sauce instead of the now standard tomato ketchup sprinkled with curry powder and fiery paprika.

Other popular snacks sold on the streets include various grilled sausages, collectively referred to as *Bratwurst*. The most common types are frankfurters *(Wienerwurst)* and a thicker kind of sausage known as *Bockwurst*. These are heated in hot water. The German variation on the hamburger theme is called *Boulette*. Unfortunately there are few places similar to the *Imbissbude* that offer visitors the chance to try food from other regions of Germany. One of the exceptions is **Weizmann**, which can be found in an arcade under the S-Bahn railway bridge near Bellevue station. Short, thick noodles called *Spätzle* feature in many dishes on its typically southern German menu.

SPECIALITIES FROM AROUND THE WORLD

TRADITIONAL BERLIN specialities are facing stiff competition from further afield. Turkish restaurants serving excellent *Döner Kebab* are on every corner. Typically a kebab is a piece of warmed flat *pitta* bread stuffed with hot sliced meat, lettuce, cucumber, and tomatoes, and covered with a thick, aromatic, yogurt-based sauce. Obviously the best kebabs are made by the Turks living around Kreuzberg, but you can also have an excellent version of this dish in most of the other Berlin districts. The restaurants worth trying are **Kebab** or indeed any of the places around Kottbuser Tor or Oranienstrasse.

Although Turkish cuisine does have a reputation for not catering for vegetarians, **Kulinarische Delikatessen** goes some way to disprove this by offering many delicious kinds of vegetarian kebabs.

Also suitable for vegetarians are *falafel*, a Middle Eastern speciality widely available in Berlin. Balls of chickpeas and coriander or parsley are rolled in breadcrumbs and deep fried, then served stuffed inside flat bread with salad and yogurt sauce. The best places to try this excellent snack are around Winterfeldt-platz, for example, **Habibi**, **Dada Falafel** and **Baharat Falafel**, or **Hasir** in the eastern part of the city.

Fragrant Thai dishes are offered by **Fish & Vegetables** in Goltzstrasse, while those with a passion for Chinese food should eat at **Pagode** in Kreuzberg on Bergmann-strasse. If you wish to try

Korean cuisine, then go to **Kwang-Ju-Grill**, where the variety of dishes is quite over-whelming, or to **Korea-Haus**. A visit to **Vietnam Imbiss** is a good opportunity to try out some Vietnamese specialities, and if you fancy genuine Mexican tacos and burritos, visit **Viva Mexico!** which is managed by a Mexican family. There are also many restaurants offering Indian food, mainly along Grolmanstrasse. Nearby, in Wielandstrasse, the Italian **Briganti** deserves a special recommendation.

Berlin's Japanese restau-rants tend to be of the more exclusive type but still offer excellent soups and sushi. The best are **Sushi Bar Ishin**, **Cat Food sushi bar**, **Sushi-Bar**, **FUKU Sushi** and **Musashi**.

LIGHT SNACKS

THOSE WITH AN APPETITE for more traditional snacks are easily catered for in the establishments around S- and U-Bahn stations and along the main streets offering fresh baguettes filled with ham or cheese.

For an instant solution to hunger pangs, try one of the bakeries that offer delicious freshly baked croissants or excellent *Brezeln* (pretzels) covered with coarse salt. During lunchtime, the popular **Nordsee** chain of restaurants offers fish sandwiches to take away, as does the stylish **Gosch**. Some sandwich bars offer mouth-watering quiches and tarts alongside baguettes and rolls. If this is what you are looking for, it is worth visiting the snackbar **Fressco** in Kreuzberg.

If a traditional American-Jewish bagel bar is what you fancy, then **Bagels & Bialys** in Rosenthaler Strasse or **Salomon Luna Bagels** in Joachimstaler Strasse are the places to go, where the variety of fillings is quite staggering.

Some places also specialize in one particular kind of dish or food. For example **Soup-Kultur** serves only soup, but in a multitude of varieties – hot, cold, exotic, spicy or mild. Garlic lovers should visit **Knofel** in Prenzlauer Berg. **Diekmann im Weinhaus Huth** is an upscale bistro tucked away in the Weinhaus Huth, the only historic building still standing in the ultra-modern Potsdamer Platz. Also worth mentioning are **Deli** and **Deli 31**.

Another way to ensure a quick and inexpensive fill-up is to visit one of the self-service pizzerias such as **Piccola Italia**.

EATING IN SHOPPING CENTRES

ONE OF THE PROBLEMS for the dedicated shopper is that eating can seriously cut down on shopping time. Fortunately, many snack bars in shopping centres have put the emphasis on fast service. Some, however, such as **KaDeWe** manage this in stylish surroundings. A visit to this enormous shop features on most tourists' list of things to do, and its self-service café is therefore very popular. Lunch at one of the tables with a view of Wittenbergplatz is a very pleasant adjunct to a Berlin shopping trip.

Another equally busy venue is the self-service café situated in the basement of the chic **Galeries Lafayette** in Friedrichstrasse. If you are visiting the boutiques of Quartier 205, it is also worth taking a refreshing break from the shopping in a quality cup of coffee or tea in **E33**.

For those reluctant shoppers who put more emphasis on the food, a new oasis of bars and cafés has opened near to Potsdamer Platz, in the **Arkaden** shopping centre. As well as a branch of Salomon Bagels, this centre provides a taste of the Orient in Asia Pavillon, while fans of potatoes should pay a visit to Pomme de Terre. Here, the humble potato becomes the star of the meal and is served in a myriad of guises and with just as many different fillings.

For short stops, both the dedicated and the reluctant shopper should visit the classic **Wiener Café** for coffee and cakes and the **Caffè e Gelato** for delicious ice cream.

CAFÉS

BERLIN IS well served by cafés that provide a wide range of light snacks or cakes to suit everyone's budget and tastes. They are normally open from 9 or 10 in the morning until late at night. In the mornings they serve breakfast, either à la carte or as a buffet. After that the regular café menu comes into force, although breakfast items are often still available. Main meals on the menu might include several salads, several hearty soup-type stews *(Eintöpfe)* and a few simple hot dishes. Prices are quite reasonable, not greater than ten euros. Invariably, every café has a great choice of desserts, ice creams and cakes, as well as a range of alcoholic drinks.

Around the Ku'damm, **Café Adlon** is worth a visit, as is Café Möhring. Café Kranzler, a familiar landmark for many decades, has recently closed. Around the Technical University, **Café Hardenberg** is popular with students, and near Kantstrasse you can visit **Schwarzes Café**, which is open 24 hours a day. If you are on Savignyplatz you might want to try **Café Aedes**, which has two good branches, one by the architecture gallery and the other in the second courtyard of Hackesche Höfe in Mitte. **Café am Neuen See** is situated near the lake in the Tiergarten Park. **Patisserie Buchwald**, in Hansaviertel, offers a wide range of *Baumkuchen* (so-called "tree cakes" that resemble tree stumps).

Other renowned cafés include the charming **Café Wintergarten**, located in the Literaturhaus on Fasanenstrasse, and the Viennese-style **Café Einstein**. Here you can enjoy coffee made with beans fresh from their own roasting room. The original café, in Kurfürstenstrasse, has been joined by another branch in Mitte, on Unter den Linden, whose delicious cakes are in welcome competition with those of the nearby **Opernpalais** (see p259).

If you prefer Hungarian cakes and desserts then you should pay a visit to **Café Zsolnay**. While taking a walk around Checkpoint Charlie, you could drop in to **Sale e Tabacchi**, where, along with an excellent Italian restaurant, you will find the equally admirable **Café Adler**.

There are many places that offer light lunches and coffee around Oranienburger Strasse and Alte and Neue Schönhauser Allees. In the evening they attract livelier crowds in search of decent music and good beer. You can stop by **Die Eins**, an atmospheric café, and the **Café Cinema**, which is decorated with film ephemera. If that is not to your taste, **Café Zucca** serves Italian cuisine.

An interesting evening can be spent investigating the options in Prenzlauer Berg. You can join the in-crowd at **Anita Wronski** then move on to **Tantalus**, which serves excellent pancakes. If you prefer a cosier environment, then **Chagall** is the place to visit, with an open fire and Russian ballads. During hot days a good spot to enjoy the sun is on the terrace in **November** or at **Seeblick**, which is a good place to eat.

Other reliable cafés are **Atlantic**, **Café Berio**, **Keyser Soze**, **Rathauscafé**, **Telecafé**, **Voltaire** and **Café Savigny**, where the menu changes daily.

COFFEE BARS AND TEA ROOMS

THERE ARE NOT many coffee bars in Berlin, but they are easily spotted as they tend to be run by well-known coffee producers such as Eduscho or Tschibo. **Barcomi's** is a real treat, an American-style coffee bar with its own roasting room and a large selection of coffees. If you need more sustenance than coffee and muffins, try **Barcomi's Deli** where you can build your own sandwiches.

If you want a good cup of tea, then you should go to **Tadschikische Teestube**, or **TTT (Tee, Tea, Thé)**, where the choice is quite amazing – but smokers beware, it has a no-smoking policy. **Mittendrin** also has a wide choice of teas.

DIRECTORY

IMBISSBUDEN AND SNACK BARS

Amtsgerichtsplatz
Kantstrasse/Suarezstrasse.
Map 2 E5. ◷ 11:30am–
11pm Mon–Fri, 1pm–
11pm Sat & Sun. ● Tue.

Konnopke
Schönhauser Allee 44a
(U-Bahnhof Eberswalder Str).
€ 442 77 65.
◷ 6am–8pm Mon–Fri.

Ku'damm 195
Kurfürstendamm 195.
Map 9 B2.
◷ 6pm–1am Mon–Fri,
5pm–7am Sat & Sun.

Weizmann
Lüneburger Strasse.
Map 5 A3. € 394 20 57.
◷ 6–11pm daily.

SPECIALITIES FROM AROUND THE WORLD

Baharat Falafel
Winterfeldstrasse 37.
Map 11 B3. € 216 83 01.
◷ 11am–2pm Mon–Sat,
11am–late Sun.

Briganti
Wielandstrasse 15.
Map 9 B1. € 323 53 62.
◷ 11am–8pm Tue–Fri,
10am–2pm Sat.

Cat Food sushi bar
Körterstrasse 8.
Map 13 C4. € 693 02 27.
◷ 6pm–midnight daily.

Dada Falafel
Linienstrasse 132. **Map**
6 F1. € 27 59 69 27
◷ 10am–2am Sun–Wed,
10am–4am Thu–Sat.

Fish & Vegetables
Goltzstrasse 32. **Map** 11
A3. € 215 74 55. ◷
noon–midnight daily.

FUKU Sushi
Rosenthaler Strasse 61.
Map 7 B1. € 28 38 77
83. ◷ noon–midnight
Mon–Fri, 6pm–midnight
Sat, Sun.

Habibi
Goltzstrasse 24.
Map 11 A3. € 215 33
32. ◷ 11am–5am daily.

Hasir
Oranienburger Strasse 4.
Map 7 B2. € 28 04 16
16. ◷ 11:30am–1am
daily.

Kebab
Goltzstrasse 37a.
Map 11 A3, 11 A4.
◷ 10am–11pm daily.

Korea-Haus
Danziger Strasse 195.
€ 423 34 41.
◷ noon–11pm daily.

Kulinarische Delikatessen
Oppelner Strasse 4.
€ 618 67 58.
◷ 8:30am–2am daily.

Kwang-Ju-Grill
Emser Strasse 24.
Map 9 B3. € 883 97 94.
◷ noon–midnight daily.

Musashi
Kottbusser Damm 102.
Map 14 E3. € 693 20
42. ◷ noon–10:30pm
Mon–Sat, noon–10pm
Sun.

Pagode
Bergmannstrasse 88.
Map 13 A4. € 691 26 40.
◷ noon–midnight daily.

Sushi-Bar
Friedrichstrasse 115.
Map 6 F1. € 281 51 88.
◷ 11am–11pm daily.

Sushi Bar Ishin
Schlossstrasse 101.
Map 2 E4. € 797 10 49.
◷ 11am–8pm Mon–Fri,
11am–4pm Sat.

Sushi Imbiss
Pariser Strasse 44.
Map 9 B2. € 881 27 90.
◷ noon–midnight Mon–
Sat, 3pm–midnight Sun.

Vietnam Imbiss
Damaschkestrasse 30.
€ 324 93 44.
◷ noon–9pm Mon–Fri.

Viva Mexico!
Chausseestrasse 36.
Map 6 F1. € 280 78 65.
◷ noon–11pm Mon–Fri,
2pm–midnight Sat, 5pm–
midnight Sun.

LIGHT SNACKS

Bagels & Bialys
Rosenthaler Strasse
46–48. **Map** 7 B2.
€ 283 65 46.
◷ 24 hours daily.

Diekmann im Weinhaus Huth
Alte Potsdamer Str. 5.
Map 6 D5. € 25 29 75
24. ◷ noon–1am daily.

Deli
Kollwitzstrasse 44.
€ 442 05 60.
◷ 9am–7pm Mon–Fri,
9am–3am Sat.

Deli 31
Bleibtreustrasse 31. **Map**
9 B2. € 88 47 46 02.
◷ 8am–9pm Mon–Sat,
8am–8pm Sun.

Fressco
Stresemannstrasse 34.
Map 12 F2. € 25 29 93
09. ◷ 9am–midnight
Mon–Fri, 4pm–midnight
Sat & Sun.

Zossener Strasse 24.
Map 13 A4.
€ 69 40 16 13.
◷ 5:30pm–1am
Tue–Sun.

Knofel
Wichertstrasse 33.
€ 447 67 17.
◷ 6pm–late Mon–Thu,
2pm–late Fri, 1pm–late
Sat–Sun.

Nordsee
Spandauer Strasse 4.
Map 7 C3, 16 F2.
€ 24 26 881.
◷ 10am–9pm daily.

Piccola Italia
Oranienburger Strasse 6.
Map 7 B2. € 283 58 43.
◷ 11am–1am Mon–Thu,
11am–3am Fri–Sun.

EATING IN SHOPPING CENTRES

E33
Friedrichstadtpassage,
Friedrichstrasse 67.
Map 6 F4, 15 C4.
€ 20 94 50 20.
◷ 8am–8pm daily.

Galeries Lafayette
Französische Strasse 23.
Map 6 F4, 15 C3.
€ 20 94 80.
◷ 9:30am–8pm Mon–
Fri, 9am–4pm Sat.

KaDeWe
Tauentzienstrasse 21–24.
Map 10 E1. ◷ 9am–8pm
Mon–Fri, 9am–4pm Sat.

Potsdamer Platz Arkaden
Alte Potsdamer Strasse 7.
Map 6 D5.
◷ 9:30am–8pm
Mon–Fri, 9am–4pm Sat.

Wertheim
Kurfürstendamm 231.
Map 10 D1. € 880 030.
◷ 9:30am–8pm Mon–
Fri, 9am–4pm Sat.

CAFES

Anita Wronski
Knaackstrasse 26–28.
€ 442 84 83.
◷ 9am–2am Mon–Fri,
10am–2am Sat & Sun.

Atlantic
Bergmannstrasse 100.
Map 12 F4. € 691 92
92. ◷ 9am–late daily.

Buchwald
Bartningallee 29.
Map 4 F2. € 391 59 31.
◷ 9am–6pm Mon–Fri.
10am–6pm Sat & Sun.

Salomon Luna Bagels
Joachimstaler Strasse 13.
Map 10 D2. € 881 81
96. ◷ 8:30am–8pm
Mon–Fri, 10am–6pm Sat.

Soup-Kultur
Kurfürstendamm 224.
Map 10 D1. € 88 62 92
82. ◷ noon–8pm
Mon–Fri, noon–4pm Sat.

Café Adler
Friedrichstrasse 206.
C 251 89 65.
O 10am–midnight
Mon–Sat, 10am–
7pm Sun.

Café Adlon
Kurfürstendamm 100.
Map 9 A2.
C 883 76 82.
O 9am–midnight daily.

Café Aedes
Savignyplatz (arcade
under the S-Bahn bridge).
Map 9 C1.
C 31 50 95 35.
O 8am–10pm Mon–Fri,
9am–10pm Sat & Sun.

Rosenthaler Strasse 40–41
(Hackesche Höfe,
second courtyard).
Map 7 B2.
C 28 58 275.
O 10am–11pm daily.

Café am
Neuen See
Lichtensteinallee 1.
Map 4 F5. **C** 254 49 30.
O May–Sep: 10am–
midnight daily; Oct–Apr:
10am–11pm Mon–Fri,
10am–8pm Sat–Sun.

Café Ständige
Vertretung
Schiffbauerdamm 8.
C 282 39 65.
O 10am–1am daily.

Café Berio
Maassenstrasse 7.
Map 11 A2. **C** 216 19
46. **O** 8am–1am daily.

Café Cinema
Rosenthaler Strasse 39.
Map 7 B2. **C** 280 64 15.
O noon–3am daily.

Café Einstein
Kurfürstenstrasse 58.
Map 11 A2.
C 261 50 96.
O 9am–2am daily.

Unter den Linden 42.
Map 6 F3, 15 C3.
C 204 36 32.
O 7am–1am daily.

Café Ephraim's
Spreeufer 1. **Map** 7 C4.
C 24 72 59 47.
O noon–10pm daily.

Café Hardenberg
Hardenbergstrasse 10.
Map 3 C5.
C 312 26 44.
O 9am–1am daily.

Café Lebensart
Unter den Linden 69–73.
Map 6 E3, 15 B3.
C 229 00 18.
O 8am–8pm Mon–Fri,
10am–8pm Sat & Sun.

Café Möhring
Charlottenstrasse 55.
Map 7 A4.
C 20 30 92 240.
O 8am–midnight daily.

Café Savigny
Grolmanstrasse 51.
Map 3 C5, 9 C1.
C 312 81 95.
O 9am–1am daily.

Café Wellenstein
Kurfürstendamm 190.
Map 9 B2. **C** 88 17 850.
O 9am–1am daily.

Café Wintergarten
im Literaturhaus
Fasanenstrasse 23.
Map 10 D1.
C 882 54 14.
O 9:30am–1am daily.

Café Zsolnay
Karl-Liebknecht-Strasse 9.
Map 7 C2. **C** 241 57 15.
O noon–10pm daily.

Café Zucca
Am Zwirngraben 11–12
(in the S-Bahn arcade).
C 24 72 12 12.
O 9am–1am Mon–Fri,
10am–3am Sat & Sun.

Catherine's
Im Dussmann-Haus,
Friedrichstrasse 90.
Map 6 F3.
C 20 25 15 55.
O 11am–10pm Mon–Sat.

Chagall
Kollwitzstrasse 2. **C** 441
58 81. **O** 11am–late daily.

Die Eins
Wilhelmstrasse 67A
(eingang Reichstagsufer).
Map 6 E3.
C 22 48 98 88.
O 9am–midnight Mon–
Sat, 10am–midnight Sun.

Eckstein
Pappelallee 73.
C 441 99 60.
O 9am–2am daily.

Filmbühne am
Steinplatz
Hardenbergstrasse 12.
Map 4 D5.
C 312 65 89.
O 9am–1am daily.

Gosch
Kurfürstendamm 212.
Map 9 C2.
C 88 68 28 00.
O 11am–midnight
Mon–Sat.

Kaffeestube
am Nikolaiplatz
Poststrasse 19.
Map 7 C3.
C 242 71 20.
O 9am–midnight daily.

Keyser Soze
Tucholskystrasse 33.
Map 7 A1.
C 28 59 94 89.
O 9am–late daily.

Kleine Orangerie
Spandauer Damm 20.
Map 2 E3.
C 322 20 21.
O 9am–9pm daily
(10am–8pm in winter).

November
Husemannstrasse 15.
C 442 84 25.
O 10am–2am Mon–Fri,
9am–2am Sat & Sun.

Operncafé
Unter den Linden 5.
Map 7 A3, 16 E3.
C 20 26 83.
O 8am–midnight daily.

Sale e Tabacchi
Kochstrasse 18.
C 252 11 55.
O 9am–2am Mon–Fri,
10am–2am Sat & Sun.

Schwarzes Café
Kantstrasse 148.
Map 9 C1.
C 313 80 38.
O 24 hours daily.

Seeblick
Rykestrasse 14.
C 442 92 26.
O 8am–2am daily.

Telecafé
Alexanderplatz (TV Tower).
Map 8 D2.
C 242 33 33.
O 10am–midnight daily.

Voltaire
Stuttgarter Platz 14.
C 324 50 28.
O 24 hours daily.

COFFEE BARS
AND TEA ROOMS

Barcomi's
Bergmannstrasse 21.
Map 13 A5.
C 694 81 38.
O 9am–midnight Mon–
Sat, 10am–midnight Sun.

Barcomi's Deli
Sophienstrasse 21
(second courtyard).
Map 7 B1. **C** 28 59 83
63. **O** 9am–10pm Mon–
Sat, 10am–10pm Sun.

Cafezeit
Kurfürstendamm 200
Map 9 C2. **C** 88 25
814. **O** 8am–midnight
Mon–Sat, 9am–10pm Sun.

Mittendrin
Sophienstrasse 19.
Map 7 B1.
C 28 49 77 40.
O noon–11pm Tue–Thu,
noon–1am Fri & Sat,
2–8pm Sun.

Tadschikische
Teestube
Am Festungsgraben 1.
Map 7 A3, 16 E2.
C 204 11 12.
O 5pm–midnight
Mon–Fri, 2pm–midnight
Sat & Sun.

Tomasa
Motzstrasse 60
Map 10 F3.
C 21 32 345.
O 8am–2am daily.

TTT – Tee,
Tea, Thé
Goltzstrasse 2.
Map 11 A4.
C 21 75 22 40.
O 9am–midnight Mon–
Sat, 10am–midnight Sun.

Bars and Wine Bars

TRYING TO MAKE a clear distinction between wine bars, bars, pubs and *Bierstuben* or giving a precise definition for the word *Kneipe* is practically impossible. However, regardless of the nuances behind all these names, they do share some basic characteristics: they are places where drinking is the primary activity, although eating is sometimes possible; they are usually open from late afternoon or early evening but do not close till late at night or even till morning, if the atmosphere is lively.

KNEIPEN

IN GENERAL TERMS, a *Kneipe* means a cosy sort of place which serves beer (although other drinks are available, too) and where you can have something to eat. The typical *Alberliner Kneipe* is a dark room with panelled oak walls, a big bar and buffet with snacks such as *Buletten* (made from pork), *Soleier* (pickled eggs), *Rollmöpse* (marinated herring) and a selection of cold meats, black pudding (blood sausage) and patés. This kind of traditional pub can still be found in the less affluent districts of Berlin – in Moabit, Kreuzberg and in Prenzlauer Berg, for example, but they are not as common in the city centre. Among the most popular are **Metzer Eck** in Prenzlauer Berg, **Zur Kneipe** and **Ranke 2**, as well as several *Kneipen* in Mitte around the Nikolaiviertel, including **Zum Nussbaum**.

Each *Kneipe* has its own character. More and more of them are choosing modern and inventive interiors, often specializing in less traditional kinds of food: Italian, French or Oriental. Whatever the blend, however, a relaxed atmosphere and a big choice of alcoholic beverages seem to be common features. Many *Kneipen* are evolving into a fashionable mix of *Kneipe*, bar, lounge and beer garden. One such is **Reingold** in Mitte. In Savignyplatz, you might want to visit **Dicke Wirtin**, where you can try a hearty *Eintopf* (a rich soup-type stew). The majority of these fashionable places are situated in Kreuzberg and in Prenzlauer Berg – especially around Kollwitzplatz, which is liberally dotted with all sorts of bars and pubs.

At **Ankerklause**, on the Landwehrkanal, students and political activists come together to drink, dance and put the world to rights.

BIERGARTEN

WHAT DISTINGUISHES a *Biergarten* from other hostelries is that it is an outdoor venue only open during the summer months, and usually located somewhere scenic, maybe in a park or by a lake. In addition to the usual food and drinks, it completes the outdoor experience with a barbecue. The **Loretta im Garten** and **Schleusenkrug** provide a much welcome breath of fresh air in the centre of Berlin; or if you are exploring Prenzlauer Berg, try the **Prater**. After enjoying the views or, for the more active, the water sports at Wannsee, the **Loretta am Wannsee** is a pleasant place to end the day.

WINE BARS

BERLIN WINE BARS tend to have a Mediterranean feel to them. Interiors are often quite rustic in style, but there are exceptions. They open from early evening and stay open late. As for food, menus feature predominantly Italian, Spanish and French cuisine, while the bar serves a huge selection of wines by the glass, bottle or carafe. **Le Bar du Paris Bar** – a wine bar with an established reputation, features French food and wine, as does **Il Calice**. If you are visiting Prenzlauer Berg you might want to try **Weinstein** which offers French and Spanish food and wine. By way of contrast, at **Lutter & Wegener** in Mitte you can match German-Austrian food with appropriate, native wines, although they too serve a wide variety of wines from vineyards all over Europe.

BARS

A BERLIN BAR IS a good place to finish your evening, and the dedicated barfly is spoiled for choice. You should not count on food but you can drink till late, as most bars do not open until 8pm or later. Although there is no strict dress code, scruffy clothes are not really appropriate. The **Riva Bar**, one of the city's most elegant and hip bars, is tucked away under the S-Bahn viaduct, and serves some of the best cocktails in town. A Latin American atmosphere is created at **Roter Salon** by tango, salsa and all the fantastic dancers. You might step in to **Zoulou-Bar** to try one of its huge range of cocktails in a pre-war movie setting. Don't forget to visit some of the hotel bars which are among the best late-night venues in the city. Two worthy of mention are **Harry's New York Bar** (the later the better), in the Hotel Esplanade and the **Newton Bar**.

GAY AND LESBIAN BARS

BERLIN HAS A unique tradition of nightlife for homosexuals, dating back to the 1920s, when its cabarets and bars, especially around Nollendorfplatz, were the most outrageous in Europe. Today that hardcore legacy remains, but there are also bars to suit every taste. Some, like **Café Seidenfaden**, are for women only, while **Roses** is exclusively for men. Many, like **Anderes Ufer** and **Die Busche** are frequented by both gays and lesbians. The friendly attitude of bars such as **Lenz** or **So 36** means they are popular with both gay and straight visitors alike.

DIRECTORY

KNEIPEN

Ankerklause
Maybachufer 1.
Map 14 E3.
[693 56 49.

Le Bateau
Europa-Center
(cellar bar).
Map 10 E1.
[261 36 09.

Dicke Wirtin
Carmerstrasse 9.
Map 3 C5.
[312 49 52.

Diener Tattersall
Grolmanstrasse 47.
Map 9 C1.
[881 53 29.

**Gerichtslaube mit
Bierschenke und
Ratsherren-Stube**
Poststrasse 28.
Map 7 C3.
[241 56 97.

Meilenstein
Oranienburger Strasse 7.
Map 7 B2, 16 F1.
[282 89 95.

Metzer Eck
Metzer Strasse 33.
[442 76 56.

Mutter
Hohenstaufenstrasse 4.
Map 11 A3.
[216 49 90.

Oberwasser
Zionskirchstrasse 6.
[448 37 19.

Ranke 2
Rankestrasse 2.
Map 10 E1.
[883 88 82.

Reingold
Novalisstrasse 11.
Map 6 F1.
[21 75 16 45.

Slumberland
Goltzstrasse 24.
Map 11 A3.
[216 53 49.

Titanic
Winsstrasse 30.
[442 03 40.

Zum Nussbaum
Am Nussbaum 3.
Map 7 C3.
[242 30 95.

Zum Patzenhofer
Meinekestrasse 26.
Map 10 D1.
[882 11 35.

Zur Kneipe
Rankestrasse 9.
Map 10 D2.
[883 82 55.

BIERGARTEN

**Loretta
am Wannsee**
Kronprinzessinnenweg 260.
[803 51 56.

Loretta im Garten
Lietzenburger Strasse 87.
Map 9 C2.
[882 33 54.

Prater
Kastanienallee 7–9.
Map 1 A5, 1 B3.
[448 56 88.

Schleusenkrug
Müller-Breslau-Strasse/at
Tiergartenschleuse.
Map 4 E4.
[313 99 09.

WINE BARS

Le Bar du Paris Bar
Kantstrasse 152.
Map 10 D1.
[31 01 50 94.

Lutter & Wegener
Gendarmenmarkt 56.
Map 7 A4, 16 D4.
[202 95 40.

Weinstein
Lychener Strasse 33.
[441 18 42.

BARS

Ballhaus Berlin
Chausseestrasse 102
Map 6 F1.
[282 75 75.

**Bar am
Lützowplatz**
Lützowplatz 7.
Map 11 A1.
[262 68 07.

b-flat
Rosenthaler Strasse 13.
Map 7 B1.
[280 63 49.

Blue Note Bar
Courbièrestrasse 13.
Map 11 A2.
[69 50 50 17.

c.itho
Lychener Strasse 43.
[46 79 66 18.

Green Door
Winterfeldtstrasse 50.
[215 25 15.

Haifischbar
Arndtstrasse 25.
Map 13 A5.
[691 13 52.

**Harry's New
York Bar**
Lützowufer 15 (in Hotel
Esplanade). **Map** 11 A1.
[25 47 88 21.

Kumpelnest 3000
Lützowstrasse 23.
Map 11 B1.
[26 16 918.

Newton Bar
Charlottenstrasse 57.
Map 16 D4.
[20 29 54 21.

Riva Bar
Dircksenstrasse,
S-Bahnbogen 142.
Map 7 C2.
[24 72 26 88.

Roter Salon
Rosa-Luxemburg-Platz.
Map 7 C1.
[24 06 58 06.

**Times Bar
(cigar bar)**
Fasanenstrasse 9–10.
Map 10 D1.
[31 10 30.

Trompete
Lützowplatz 9.
Map 11 A1.
[23 00 47 94.

Zoulou-Bar
Hauptstrasse 4.
Map 11 B4.
[78 46 894.

**Zur weissen
Maus**
Ludwigkirchplatz 12.
Map 9 C3.
[886 792 88.

GAY AND LESBIAN
BARS

**Anderes
Ufer**
Hauptstrasse 157.
Map 11 B4.
[784 15 78.

**Café
Seidenfaden**
Dircksenstrasse 47.
Map 7 C3.
[283 27 83.

Die Busche
Mühlenstrasse 11–12.
[296 08 00.

Hafenbar
Motzstrasse 19.
Map 11 A2.
[211 41 18.

Lenz
Eisenacher Strasse 3.
Map 11 A2.
[217 78 20.

Roses
Oranienstrasse 187.
Map 14 E2.
[615 65 70.

So 36
Oranienstrasse 190.
Map 13 B1, 14 D1.
[61 40 13 06.

SHOPPING IN BERLIN

WITH A SHOPPING CENTRE in every district, each selling a wide variety of merchandise, Berlin is a place where almost anything can be bought, so long as you know where to look. The most popular places are Kurfürstendamm and Friedrichstrasse, but the smaller shops in Wedding, Friedrichshain, Schöneberg and the Tiergarten are also worth a visit. Small boutiques selling flamboyant Berlin-style clothes crop up in unexpected courtyards, while the top fashion houses offer the latest in European elegance. Early on Saturday morning is often the best time to visit the city's various markets, the most popular of which – with their colourful stalls full of hats, bags and belts – can be found on Museum Island and at the Tiergarten. The Galeries Lafayette, KaDeWe and any of the city's numerous bookshops all make ideal venues for a pleasant afternoon's window shopping.

Inside the modern, multi-level Europa-Center (see p150)

OPENING HOURS

THE MAJORITY of shops are open Monday to Friday from 10am to 8pm (10am to 4pm on Saturday), but some department stores open as early as 9am, and some smaller shops open in the afternoons only. Generally, there are no lunch-breaks unless the shop is a one-person business. During the six weeks before Christmas, shops stay open until 8pm on Saturdays and the local transport authority, the Berliner Verkehrs-Betriebe, or BVG *(see pp294–5),* runs a useful service for shoppers. You can leave your bags in a special Weihnachtsgeschenke-Bus (Christmas-gift bus) and shop without dragging all your purchases around with you.

DEPARTMENT STORES

KAUFHAUS DES WESTENS, better known as **KaDeWe** at Wittenbergplatz *(see p155),* is undoubtedly the biggest and the best department store in Berlin.

Only products of the highest quality are sold in these luxurious halls, where virtually everything you need is on sale – from unusual perfumes and elegant underwear to *haute couture*, all sold in a system of shops-within-shops. The food hall on the sixth floor is legendary for its restaurant overlooking Tauentzienstrasse.

Galeries Lafayette on Friedrichstrasse is nothing less than a slice of Paris placed in the heart of Berlin. Perfumes, domestic accessories and clothing attract an enormous clientele, many of whom also visit the food counter which offers a wide range of French specialities. An extraordinary glass cone rises through the middle of the store, reflecting the interiors of the shops.

Another very popular store is **Wertheim** on the Ku'damm.

A typical street-side stall, brimming with souvenirs for visitors

Although its range of goods is not as broad as the range at Galeries Lafayette, there is still an enormous choice and the top-floor restaurant offers excellent views over the city.

SHOPPING CENTRES

IN ADDITION TO the two biggest shopping districts in town – Ku'damm and Friedrichstrasse – new shopping

The well-stocked toy department of KaDeWe (see p155)

Elegantly displayed china and table linen

DIRECTORY

DEPARTMENT STORES

Wertheim
Kurfürstendamm 231.
Map 10 D1.
(88 00 30.

KaDeWe
Tauentzienstrasse 21.
Map 10 F2. **(** 21 21 00.

Galeries Lafayette
Französische Strasse 23.
Map 7 A4.
(20 94 80.

SHOPPING CENTRES

Galleria
Schlossstrasse 101. **Map** 2 E3.

Gesundbrunnencenter
Gesundbrunnen S-Bahn.

**Potsdamer Platz
Arkaden**
Debis Gelände. **Map** 6 E5.

Shopping Guide
Claudia Barthel
(28 59 86 22.

centres are constantly being built, usually conveniently situated close to S-Bahn stations. These massive three-level structures, resembling huge arcaded passageways, contain an enormous number of shops, ranging from super-markets and chemists to bars, high-street fashion and book-shops. Like most of the shops in Berlin they stay open until 8pm during the week. They also do business on Sundays. One of the newest shopping centres is the **Potsdamer Platz Arkaden**. Built in October 1998 it is very popular both as a shopping mall and a meeting place. It is visited by thousands of tourists and Berliners every day.

Of a similar character, although built on a slightly smaller scale, is **Galleria** on Schlossstrasse in Steglitz. Here, under one roof, you can browse through an extra-ordinary selection of goods. **Gesundbrunnencenter** is the biggest shopping passage in Berlin, and has countless stalls and tables offering every kind of bargain. A large number of bars also makes this a popular place to meet friends for a beer or a coffee.

SEASONAL SALES

A LL SHOPS IN BERLIN empty their racks and shelves in the sale, or *Schlussverkauf*, which takes place twice a year. At the end of January, before the new year's collec-tions are displayed in shop windows, you can buy winter clothes for as little as 50 per cent of their original price. During the summer sales *(Sommerschlussverkauf)*, which take place at the end of July, you can find similarly-reduced summer outfits. Goods bought in a sale are officially non-returnable, but if you are really keen to take an item back, there is no harm in at least trying to negotiate with the shop assistant.

A number of shops sell a variety of articles marketed as "second season" items. These are always new articles, albeit stocked for the previous season, and they are offered at often generously-reduced prices. You will also find that various shops specialize in top-brand jeans, selling them at much-reduced rates owing to what are often very minor defects. These represent excellent value for money.

HOW TO PAY

W HEN IT COMES to paying for goods you may find that some small shops still insist on cash. In the centre of Berlin there should be a suitable cash machine not too far away *(see p284)*. Larger shops and department stores will also accept most major credit cards.

SHOPPING GUIDE

I F YOU ARE planning to do some serious shopping in Berlin, and are worried about getting lost among the many possibilities, you may want to use the services of a "shopping guide". These are specialists who will tell you what is currently on offer in both the big department stores and in the smaller boutiques.

A stand offering cosmetics for sale in Galeries Lafayette *(see p65)*

Clothes and Accessories

THERE ARE MANY SHOPPING centres in Berlin, and nearly every district has its own high street where residents do their shopping. If it's luxury, elegance and a wide variety of goods you are after, however, then head for the shops on Kurfürstendamm, Friedrichstrasse and Potsdamer Platz. This is where all the major fashion houses and perfume makers have their shops, right in the heart of the city. Alternatively, if you want to explore the smaller boutiques of some lesser-known designers, make your way to Hackescher Markt in the Mitte district, or to Prenzlauer Berg.

WOMEN'S FASHIONS

THE MOST FAMOUS fashion houses are on the Ku'damm (Kurfürstendamm) and its side streets, particularly in the area around the quietly elegant Fasanenstrasse. Among the many famous names doing business here are **Yves Saint Laurent**, **Max Mara**, **Sonia Rykiel**, **Gianni Versace**, **Horn Modehaus**, **ESCADA**, **Chanel**, **Jean-Paul Gaultier** and **Gucci**. Simplicity is the order of the day in the **Jil Sander** shop, making it the ideal place to buy a straight-forward dress with exquisite accessories. Gucci has two shops in the area, one in Fasanenstrasse and another in the fashionable Quartier 206 on Friedrichstrasse. The latter shares the street with many other fashion houses that specialize in women's clothes: **Evelin Brandt**, **Department Store 206**, **Strenesse**, **Strenesse Blue** and **ETRO**, to name a few.

MEN'S FASHIONS

FOR THE FULL RANGE of the latest in fashion for men, on or near Kurfürstendamm is the place to go shopping, for this is where various retailers sell clothing straight from Europe's best-known fashion houses. **Patrick Hellmann** is certainly worth a visit with its wide choice of the best designer labels around. Clothes by Giorgio Armani, Helmut Lang, Christian Dior and Dolce E Gabbana can all be found here. Also very popular is **Mientus**, which has a second outlet on Wilmersdorfer Strasse.

Peek & Cloppenburg, Germany's second largest speciality store, sells its own budget labels as well as high-end designer clothes by Boss, Armani, Joop and others.

CHILDREN'S CLOTHING

SHOPS SELLING children's clothes can generally satisfy any taste, depending on how much you are willing to spend. **Sonia Rykiel's Kinder Boutique** offers clothes by the Parisian designer for up to 8-year-olds, as well as dolls and cuddly toys. **Boom** has a wide range of clothes for children up to 14, while **Cinderella** offers *haute couture* for all ages, including Armani Junior, Pinco Pallino, Simonetta, DKNY, Miss Blumarine and Young Versace. The needs of children whose parents have a more restricted budget can be met in **H&M Kinder**, which sells fashionable items at relatively moderate prices.

YOUNG DESIGNERS

A NUMBER OF GALLERIES, studios and boutiques specialize in the so-called Berlin style, the collections on sale usually consisting of short-series items that are produced in strictly limited numbers. At one time it was possible to find shops like this across the whole of the city, but now they are concentrated mainly in the northern part of the Mitte area, where a unique fashion centre is firmly established. **NIX** offers timeless clothes made from heavy, dark fabrics and cut in

classical fashion, while **Stephanie Schenk** offers high-quality knitted goods. A great selection of clothing by 19 very different designers is on offer in **Tagebau** in Rosenthaler Strasse 19, where just about every kind of item can be bought, from evening dresses and luxury wedding gowns to elegant hats and other fashion accessories.

Among the other shops in Mitte, **Fishbelly** on Sophienstrasse is noted for its unique range of erotic underwear, designed by Jutta Teschner. At **Molotow**, in Kreuzberg, the choice is more classical than the trendy name might suggest. Another very popular place to buy clothes is **Chapeaux**, in Charlottenburg.

SHOES AND ACCESSORIES

ONE OF THE largest shoe shops in Berlin is **Schuhtick**, which has three branches in the city, though the highest quality can be found in the **Budapester Schuhe** chain. A good selection can also be found at the **Görtz** outlets around Kurfürstendamm. The latest Italian designs are available at **Riccardo Cartillone**.

Penthesileia on Tucholskystrasse offers an amusing range of handbags, which come in all kinds of shapes and sizes. If it's a hat you are after, then you need go no further than **Hut Up**, in the Heckmannhöfen. All kinds are headgear are available here, from typical Russian *shlapas* to party hats with Rastafarian dreadlocks.

PERFUMES

ALL OF THE LARGE department stores, including **KaDeWe** and **Galeries Lafayette**, offer a sizeable selection of the best-known perfumes, but there are also a number of specialist shops dotted around the city. The **Douglas** chain, which has numerous outlets, has a wide range of perfumes at very reasonable prices. **Quartier 206** has a good selection of the better-known perfumes, but if you are looking for something unusual, then **Harry Lehmann** is the place to visit. This unique store is a perfume-lover's paradise, where Mr Lehmann himself continues an 80-year-long family tradition of mixing your very own perfume from a variety of 50 scents. He also stocks long-forgotten brands. The **Body Shop** group is popular in Berlin. Natural perfumes of all kinds can be bought here, and its policy of no animal testing is popular with customers. It also encourages the return of its containers for recycling.

DIRECTORY

WOMEN'S FASHION

Chanel
Fasanenstrasse 30.
Map 9 C3. 885 13 24.

Department Store 206
Friedrichstrasse 23.
Map 6 F4. 20 94 80.

ESCADA
Kurfürstendamm 186/187.
Map 10 D1.
881 16 36.

ETRO
Friedrichstrasse 71.
Map 6 F3.
20 94 61 20.

Evelin Brandt
Savignyplatz 6.
Map 9 C1. 313 80 80.

Gianni Versace
Kurfürstendamm 185.
Map 10 D1.
885 74 60.

Gucci
Fasanenstrasse 73.
Map 9 C2. 885 63 00.

Friedrichstrasse 71.
Map 6 F3.
201 70 20.

Horn Modehaus
Kurfürstendamm 213.
Map 9 A2.
881 40 55.

Jean Paul Gaultier
Französische Strasse 23.
Map 15 C3.
20 94 79 38.

Jil Sander
Kurfürstendamm 185.
Map 10 D1.
886 70 20.

Max Mara
Kurfürstendamm 178.
Map 10 D1.
885 25 45.

Sonia Rykiel
Kurfürstendamm 186.
Map 9 A2.
882 17 74.

Strenesse & Strenesse Blue
Friedrichstrasse 71.
Map 6 F3.
20 94 60 35.

Yves Saint Laurent
Kurfürstendamm 52.
Map 9 A2.
883 39 18.

MEN'S FASHIONS

Mientus
Wilmersdorfer Strasse 73.
Map 2 F3, 3 A5, 9 A1.

Kurfürstendamm 52.
Map 9 A2.
323 90 77.

Patrick Hellmann
Fasanenstrasse 26.
Map 10 D2.
882 42 01.

Peek & Cloppenburg
Tauentzienstrasse 19.
Map 10 E1.
21 29 00.

CHILDREN'S CLOTHING

Boom
Uhlandstrasse 170.
Map 9 C1.
883 72 12.

Cinderella
Kurfürstendamm 46.
Map 10 D1.
881 28 63.

H&M Kinder
Schlossstrasse 1 (Steglitz).
Map 2 E3, E4.

Sonia Rykiel's Kinder-Boutique
Kurfürstendamm 186.
Map 10 D1.
88 21 774.

YOUNG DESIGNERS

Chapeaux
Bleibtreustrasse 51.
Map 9 B1.
20 38 81 10.

Fishbelly
Sophienstrasse 7a.
28 04 51 80.

Molotow
Gneisenaustrasse 112.
Map 13 A4.
693 08 18.

NIX
Oranienburger Strasse 32.
Map 7 A2. 281 80 44.

Stephanie Schenk
Gipsstrasse 9. **Map** 7 B1.
28 39 07 85.

Tagebau
Rosenthaler Strasse 19.
Map 7 B1.
28 39 08 90.

SHOES AND ACCESSORIES

Budapester Schuhe
Kurfürstendamm 199.
Map 10 D1.
88 11 707.

Bleibtreustrasse 24.
Map 9 B1.
88 62 95 00.

Friedrichstrasse 81.
Map 6 F3.
20 38 81 10.

Görtz
Kurfürstendamm 13-14.
Map 10 D1.
88 68 37 52.

Hut Up
Oranienburger Strasse 32.
Map 7 A2.
28 38 61 05.

Penthesileia
Tucholskystrasse 31.
Map 7 A2, 16 D1.
282 11 52.

Riccardo Cartillone
Savignyplatz 4.
Map 9 C1.
31 50 33 27.

Schuhtick
Savignyplatz 11. **Map** 9 C1. 315 93 80.

Tauentzienstrasse 5.
Map 10 E1.
214 09 80.

PERFUMES

Body Shop
(in the main hall of Zoologischer Garten railway station). **Map** 10 D1.
31 21 391.

Douglas
Kurfürstendamm 216.
Map 10 D1.
881 25 34.

Galeries Lafayette Parfümerie
Franzözische Strasse 23.
Map 6 F4.
20 94 80.

Harry Lehmann
Kantstrasse 106.
Map 9 A1.
324 35 82.

KaDeWe Parfümerie
Tauentzienstrasse 21–24.
Map 10 E1.
21 210.

Quartier 206
Friedrichstrasse 71.
Map 6 F3.
20 94 68 00

Gifts and Souvenirs

U NLIKE LONDON, PARIS OR ROME, where whole industries are devoted to providing mementos for travellers and tourists, Berlin doesn't have a great variety of typical souvenirs. But this doesn't mean you won't be able to find an interesting gift – a browse through any of the major markets or a trip along one of the main shopping thoroughfares should be sufficient for you to buy whatever you need. Posters and CDs are easy to find, but if you're looking for something elegant, then a piece of china made by Königliche Porzellan-Manufaktur Berlin *(see p133)* might be a good idea. For a child, a teddy bear is always an option, particularly in this city, where it is part of the official insignia. For hand-made jewellery or contemporary art, head for Strasse des 17 Juni during one of its Sunday markets *(see p256)*.

BOOKS AND MUSIC

T HE BEST PLACES to buy books on art are the shops at major museums, where you will also find a good selection of cards, posters and general souvenirs. The best of these are in **Hamburger Bahnhof** *(see pp110–11)*, **Gemälde-galerie** *(see pp122–25)*, **Sammlung Berggruen** *(see p164)*, **Schloss Charlotten-burg** *(see pp160–61)* and **Altes Museum** *(see p75)*.

The **Bücherbogen** chain offers a huge choice of books and has several outlets in the city; the one under the S-Bahn bridge near Savignyplatz has the largest stock. Other good stores include **Autorenbuch-handlung** or, if you want to combine shopping and art appreciation, **Artificium** has a gallery attached. The biggest stores also have sections on Berlin art such as the huge **Hugendubel**, which sells CDs as well as books, and **Kulturkaufhaus Dussmann**.

For English-language books or papers, **Books** and **Buch-express** are the places to go with their choice of both English and American literature. **Prinz Eisenherz** also has a good selection of gay literature. In all of these shops the staff are very helpful.

Music lovers should head for **Artificium** in Schloss-strasse, **Cover Music** near the Ku'damm or any of the **WOM** (World of Music) stores which offer a wide variety of CDs. If it is classical music you are after then **L & P Classics** has one of the finest selections, while for something avant-garde don't miss **Gelbe Musik** on Schaperstrasse. If you happen to be short of funds there is always the option of flicking through the second-hand CDs on offer at the Sunday antique market on Strasse des 17 Juni *(see p256)*. The market is always crammed with souvenirs and is a great hunting-ground for collectors of old vinyl records.

TOYS

Y OU WON'T HAVE to travel far to buy a typical Berlin teddy bear – you can find them in stores all over the city, especially the gift shops in the Nikolaiviertel. If you're after a wider variety of toys, then **KaDeWe** *(see p155)* is the place to go. Like all the major department stores, KaDeWe *(see p155)* offers a whole range of toys for children of all ages, but its teddy bear section is second to none in Berlin. From the highly portable half-inch bear to the life-size 2-metre model, every kind of bear you can imagine is on sale here, so you shouldn't be disappointed. Also, the store can arrange a delivery to your home, so if your child has always dreamed of having an enormous teddy bear, this is a perfect opportunity to fulfil the dream.

Small manufacturers still make old-style wooden toys, from doll's house furniture to traditional jigsaw puzzles, and these make excellent gifts to take home. **Heidi's Spiel-zeugladen** on Kantstrasse, **Johanna Petzoldt** on Sophienstrasse and **Spielen** on Hufelandstrasse are the best places to go for souvenirs of this kind. Train lovers hoping to extend their tracks and build more depots and stations should visit **Michas Bahnhof** on Nürnberger Strasse, the city's top provider of model train set accessories. An amazing range of goods is available here.

As an old Prussian capital, Berlin is also a good place to find Germanic lead soldiers; the best places to look are **Berliner Zinnfiguren Kabinett** and **Zinnsoldaten**. While most of the soldiers available are designed for children, collecting them is a popular hobby among adults, and the rarities often fetch very high prices.

FLOWERS

I T IS VERY EASY to find a nice bouquet in Berlin. Flower shops stand on nearly every street corner and the majority of them are open for business on Sundays. **Blumenhaus Finger** in Prenzlauer Berg is famous for its bouquets of exotic flowers which are always arranged and wrapped with real artistry. Similarly, **Blumen-Koch** in Wilmersdorf offers an amazing selection of beautiful and colourful plants. However, if you want to arrange a surprise delivery then **Fleurop** on Kurfürsten-damm will send a bouquet of flowers to a given address.

CHINA AND CERAMICS

T HE HISTORY of European china started in Germany in 1708. The alchemist Böttger, while searching for the secret of making gold, discovered instead how to make Chinese-style porcelain. Berlin soon became a major producer. **KPM (Königliche Porzellan-Manufaktur Berlin)** *(see p133)* is still in operation, and its products will satisfy even the most choosy of porcelain collectors. Plenty of newly made china is available, but if you are looking for something older, then an afternoon could be spent in some of the city's antique shops *(see pp256–7)*. Currently manufactured pieces can be bought in the KPM factory shop or in the elegant salon on the ground floor of the Kempinski hotel *(see p226)*. Those who prefer Meissen porcelain will be able to find it in several shops along the Ku'damm.

While porcelain is expensive, an equally precious gift can be made of a ceramic dish or breakfast set, traditionally manufactured in Thuringia.

With their characteristic blue and white patterns, a wide choice of exquisite Thuringian ceramics can be found in **Bürgel-Haus** on Friedrichstrasse.

SPECIALIST SHOPS

IF YOU ARE determined to find something unique, or even quirky, you might want to visit some of the interesting specialist shops – like **Knopf Paul**, which specializes in extraordinary buttons, or **Bären-Luftballons**, which

offers a delightful variety of colourful and amusing balloons. There are also a number of shops which specialize in teas and tea-time accessories. **King's Teagarden** and **TeeHaus** offer the best selection in this field.

Smart letter paper and good pens can be bought in **Papeterie**, but if you're still stuck for ideas, there's no harm in browsing through the specialist departments in **KaDeWe** *(see Toys)* where there's always something guaranteed to catch the eye.

DIRECTORY

BOOKS AND MUSIC

Artificium
Rosenthalerstrasse 40/41.
Map 7 B1.
📞 *30 87 22 80.*

Schlossstrasse 101.
Map 7 B1.
📞 *797 36 12.*

Autorenbuchhandlung
Carmerstrasse 10.
Map 3 C5.
📞 *313 01 51.*

Books
Goethestrasse 69.
Map 3 B5.
📞 *31 31 233.*

Buchexpress
Unter den Eichen 97.
📞 *831 40 04.*

Bücherbogen
Savignyplatz.
Map 9 C1.
📞 *31 86 95 11.*

Kochstrasse 19.
Map 12 F1.
📞 *251 13 45.*

Cover Music
Kurfürstendamm 11.
Map 10 D1.
📞 *88 55 01 30.*

Gelbe Musik
Schaperstrasse 11.
Map 10 D2.
📞 *211 39 62.*

Gemäldegalerie
Matthäikirchplatz 8.
Map 5 C5.
📞 *20 90 55 55.*

Hamburger Bahnhof
Invalidenstrasse 50/51.
Map 6 D1.
📞 *397 83 40.*

Hugendubel
Tauentzienstrasse 13.
Map 10 E1.
📞 *21 40 60.*

Kulturkaufhaus Dussmann
Friedrichstrasse 90.
Map 15 C2.
📞 *202 50.*

L & P Classics
Knesebeckstrasse 33-34.
Map 9 C1.
📞 *88 04 30 43.*

Prinz Eisenherz
Bleibtreustrasse 52.
Map 9 C1. 📞 *313 99 36.*

Sammlung Berggruen
Schlossstrasse 1.
Map 2 E3.
📞 *20 90 55 55.*

WOM
Augsburger Strasse 36–42.
Map 10 D1.
📞 *885 72 40.*

TOYS

Berliner Zinnfiguren Kabinett
Knesebeckstrasse 88.
Map 3 C5. 📞 *313 08 02.*

Heidi's Spielzeugladen
Kantstrasse 61.
Map 2 F5.
📞 *323 75 56.*

Johanna Petzoldt
Sophienstrasse 9.
Map 7 B1.
📞 *282 67 54.*

KaDeWe
Tauentzienstrasse 21.
Map 10 E1.
📞 *212 10.*

Michas Bahnhof
Nürnberger Strasse 24.
Map 10 E2, 10 F2.
📞 *218 66 11.*

Zinnsoldaten
Skalitzer Strasse 81.
📞 *618 38 15.*
By appointment only.

FLOWERS

Blumen Damerius
Potsdamerplatz Arkaden.
📞 *45 38 005.*

Blumen-Koch
Westfälische Strasse 38.
Map 9 A4.
📞 *896 69 00.*

Blumenhaus Finger
Schönhauser Allee 10-11.
📞 *242 63 96.*

Fleurop Blankenberg
Kurfürstendamm 69.
Map 9 A2. 📞 *881 91 23.*

CHINA AND CERAMICS

Bürgel-Haus
Friedrichstrasse 154.
Map 6 F3, 15 C3.
📞 *204 45 19.*

KPM
Strasse des 17 Juni 100.
📞 *39 00 92 15.*

Fasanenstrasse 27.
Map 10 D1.
📞 *886 72 10.*

SPECIALIST SHOPS

Bären-Luftballons
Kurfürstenstrasse 31/32.
Map 9 C1.
📞 *261 92 99.*

Kings Teagarden
Kurfürstendamm 217.
Map 10 D1.
📞 *883 70 59.*

Knopf Paul
Zossener Strasse 10.
Map 13 A4.
📞 *692 12 12.*

Papeterie
Uhlandstrasse 28.
Map 9 C2.
📞 *881 63 63.*

TeeHaus
Krumme Strasse 35.
Map 3 A5.
📞 *31 50 98 82.*

Antiques and Objets d'Art

THE ANTIQUE AND ART MARKETS in Berlin are booming. New galleries are opening all the time, particularly in the eastern areas of town. Spandauer Vorstadt is full of antique shops and contemporary art galleries, but the northern part of Mitte (the area around East of the Centre) is the focus of the Berlin art market. Constantly raising their standards, the galleries attract numerous art dealers and collectors, while non-commercial exhibitions organized by art societies like NGbK, NBK and Kunst-Werke add to the creative atmosphere. As for the antique trade, a walk through any of the city's main thoroughfares should show that it is active in just about every district.

AUCTION HOUSES

BERLIN'S OLDEST and most prestigious auction houses are **Gerda Bassenge** and **Villa Grisebach**, both of which organize sales at the start of the year and in the autumn. Bassenge specializes in graphic art, and a month before each sale an auction of books and autographs is held. A photographic auction takes place a few days after the main sale of graphic art. The prices are usually higher at Grisebach which deals mainly in 19th-century paintings. Expressionists and modern classics often go under the hammer here. Another good auctioneer is **Kunst-Auktionen Leon Spik** on Ku'damm; top London auction house **Christie's** has facilities on Fasanenstrasse.

GALLERIES

IF YOU ARE pressed for time, Spandauer Vorstadt in the northern part of Mitte might be the place to go. Since the fall of the Berlin Wall, some 30 galleries have been established in the Linienstrasse, Auguststrasse, Sophienstrasse and Gipsstrasse areas. Among these are **Arndt & Partner** and **Eigen & Art**, both on Augststrasse, **Contemporary Fine Arts**, **Gebauer**, **Max Hetzler**, **Mehdi Chouakri** and **Wohnmaschine**. **Wiens Laden & Verlag** and **Neugerriemenschneider** are both on Linienstrasse. So-called "open days" take place three or four times a year when all the galleries open at the same time to exhibit the new collections. One is always in early

October, when the Art Forum Berlin fair is held, providing a chance to spot the changing trends in contemporary art.

The galleries near Kurfürstendamm, such as **Brusberg**, offer high-quality art in a quieter atmosphere. Other galleries include **Hartmann & Noé** and **Fine Art Rafael Vostell**, both on Knesebeckstrasse, as well as **Anselm Dreher**, **Barbara Weiss**, **Franck & Schulte** and **Poll**.

ANTIQUE SHOPS

ANTIQUE SHOPS can be found in every district of Berlin. Near Kurfürstendamm and around Ludwigkirchplatz there are a number of high-class shops offering expensive *objets d'art*, from Chinese furniture in **Alte Asiatische Kunst** to Secession trinkets in **ART 1900** and glass from different periods in the **Galeries Splinter**.

Furniture specialists can be found in Suarezstrasse in Charlottenburg, where original Thonets can be bought as well as modern steel items by well-known designers. For a slightly lower grade of antique, the best place to go is Bergmannstrasse in Kreuzberg. In its mildly Oriental atmosphere you can often find valuable pieces among masses of junk. **Das Zweite Büro** in Zossener Strasse specializes in trading old desks, cupboards and filing cabinets, which don't come cheap, but the quality of the merchandise is excellent. Standing opposite Das Zweite Büro is **Radio Art** with its extensive collection of old radios and record

players. Some other interesting shops to try are **Antiklampen**, **Bleibtreu Antik** and **Art Déco**.

There's a real market atmosphere in the arcades of the S-Bahn railway bridge near Friedrichstrasse where a host of street traders sell all kinds of knick-knacks, from clothes and books to cutlery and domestic accessories.

FLEA MARKETS

MANY BERLINERS spend their Saturday and Sunday mornings at flea markets, and after a coffee go for a walk in the Tiergarten or take a stroll to a museum. Trödel- und Kunstmarkt, on Strasse des 17 Juni near Tiergarten S-Bahn station, is the most popular market in town. It is divided into two parts, and the antique section deals with books and magazines as well as pricey rarities. If you have the time and patience to sift through the enormous amount on offer, you are likely to find some great bargains. Arts and crafts trading takes place on the other side of Charlottenburger Brücke, and the goods on offer range from leather items and ceramics to colourful silk clothes and jewellery. Shops from all over Berlin are usually represented here.

From **Berliner Kunst-und Nostalgiemarkt an der Museumsinsel**, it is only a few steps to the museums. The stalls along Kupfergraben stand opposite the Pergamon- and Altes Museum, and art objects, books, records and other antiques are always on display around the Zeughaus.

The flea market operating in the car park near the Fehrbelliner Platz U-Bahn station opens at the weekends at 8am. If you are interested in going, you would do well to get there as early as possible as it is full of experienced collectors who only need a few minutes to spot something valuable. Another flea market can be found on Arkonaplatz, in the centre of a residential district in the eastern part of the town. If you are after memorabilia from the former GDR, you should try the stalls around Potsdamer Platz and Leipziger Platz. However the quality and authenticity of what is on sale is often questionable.

Another great market is the **Treptower Hallentrödel** on Eichenstrasse, which offers everything under one roof. Old telephones and army boots can be found beside bathroom

accessories and piles of very cheap books (5 for 2 euros). The hall itself, a former bus depot, is worth visiting for its interesting architecture alone.

Other flea markets to visit include **Antik & Trödelmarkt am Ostbahnhof**, **Kunstmarkt Mulackstrasse** and **Kiezmarkt am Moritzplatz**.

Berliner Stadtreinigungsbetriebe is an organization responsible for disposing of rubbish, and a number of "BSR" shops sell old furniture which is still in good condition. They are ideal places to pick up a bargain, although you are often in competition with small traders.

DIRECTORY

AUCTION HOUSES

Christie's
Giesebrechtstrasse 10.
Map 9 A2.
885 69 50.

Gerda Bassenge
Erdener Strasse 5a.
89 38 02 90.
9am–6pm Mon–Fri.

Kunst-Auktionen Leo Spik
Kurfürstendamm 66.
Map 10 D1.
883 61 70.

Villa Grisebach
Fasanenstrasse 25.
Map 10 D2.
885 91 50.

GALLERIES

Anselm Dreher
Pfalzburger Strasse 80.
Map 9 C2.
883 52 49.
2–6:30pm Tue–Fri,
11am–2pm Sat.

Arndt & Partner
Zimmerstrasse 90–91.
Map 7 B1.
280 81 23.
11am–6pm Tue–Sat.

Barbara Weiss
Potsdamer Strasse 93.
Map 11 C2.
262 42 84.
11am–6pm Tue–Sat.

Brusberg
Kurfürstendamm 213.
Map 9 C1.
882 76 82.
10am–6:30 pm Tue–Fri,
10am–2pm Sat.

Contemporary Fine Arts
Sophienstrasse 21.
Map 7 B1.
28 87 870.
11am–6pm Tue–Sat.

Eigen & Art
Auguststrasse 26.
Map 7 B1.
280 66 05.
11am–6pm Tue–Sat.

Eva Poll
Lützowplatz 7.
Map 11 A1.
261 70 91.
11am–1pm Mon,
11am–6:30pm Tue–Fri,
11am–3 pm Sat.

Fine Art Rafael Vostell
Schönhauser Allee 175.
885 22 80.
noon–6pm Tue–Sat.

Gebauer
Holzmarktstrasse 15–19,
S-Bahn-Bogen 51–52.
Map 6 F1.
280 81 10.
11am–6pm Tue–Sat.

Hartmann & Noé
Knesebeckstrasse 32.
Map 9 C1.
881 28 95.
11am–6:30pm Tue–Fri,
11am–2pm Sat.

Max Hetzler
Zimmerstrasse 90–91.
Map 6 F5.
229 24 37.
11am–6pm Tue–Sat.

Mehdi Chouakri
Gipsstrasse 11.
Map 7 B1.
28 39 11 53.
11am–6pm Tue–Sat.

Michael Schultz
Mommsenstrasse 34.
32 41 591.
11am–7pm Tue–Fri,
10am–2pm Sat.

Neugerriemenschneider
Linienstrasse 155.
Map 7 A1.
30 87 28 10.
11am–6pm Tue–Sat.

Thomas Schulte
Mommsenstrasse 56.
Map 7 A1.
324 00 44.
11am–6pm Mon–Fri,
11am–3pm Sat.

Wiens Laden & Verlag
Linienstrasse 158.
Map 7 C1.
28 38 53 52.
2–7pm Wed–Fri,
noon–6pm Sat.

Wohnmaschine
Tucholskystrasse 35.
Map 7 A2, 16 D1.
30 87 20 15.
11am–6pm Tue–Sat.

ANTIQUE SHOPS

Alte Asiatische Kunst
Fasanenstrasse 71.
Map 10 D1.
883 61 17.

Antiklampen
Motzstrasse 32.
Map 10 F3.
213 72 27.

Art Déco
Grolmanstrasse 51.
Map 3 C5.
31 50 62 05.

ART 1900
Kurfürstendamm 53.
Map 9 B2.
881 56 27.

Bleibtreu Antik
Schlüterstrasse 54.
Map 9 B1.
883 52 12.

Das Zweite Büro
Zossener Strasse 6.
Map 13 A3. 693 07 59.

Galerie Splinter
Sophienstrasse 20–21.
Map 7 B1.
28 59 87 37.

Lakeside Antiques
Neue Kantstrasse 14.
Map 2 E5.
25 45 99 30.

Radio Art
Zossener Strasse 2.
Map 13 A3.
693 94 35.
noon–6pm Thu & Fri,
10am–1pm Sat.

FLEA MARKETS

Antik & Trödelmarkt am Ostbahnhof
Erich-Steinfurth-Strasse.
9am–3pm Sat,
10am–5pm Sun.

Berliner Kunst- und Nostalgiemarkt an der Museumsinsel
Museumsinsel
& Kupfergraben.
Map 7 A2, 16 D1.
11am–5pm Sat & Sun.

Kunstmarkt Mulackstrasse
Mulackstrasse 12.
2pm–9pm Sat & Sun.

Kiezmarkt am Moritzplatz
Moritzplatz.
8am–4pm Sat & Sun.

Treptower Hallentrödel
Puschkinallee.
10am–6pm Sat & Sun.

Food Products

FOOD SPECIALITIES from all over the world can be found in Berlin, a fact which is due partly to the city's own lack of traditional cuisine. Gone are the days when local fare was restricted to pork knuckle with cabbage, cutlets, *Currywurst* and potatoes. Today the side-streets and thoroughfares are teeming with the shops and restaurants of many nationalities – Italian, Greek, Turkish, Spanish and French as well as Mexican, American, Japanese, Chinese and Thai. As befits any major European capital, the food is of the highest quality, and there are more and more shops providing organic products, from vegetables and wholemeal bread to various wines and beers.

PATISSERIES AND SWEET SHOPS

BERLINERS CERTAINLY have a sweet tooth for there are plenty of patisseries and sweet shops all over the city, and a wide range of cakes is available. A typical speciality is a doughnut known simply as a *Berliner*, but the majority of places offer a whole range of cakes along with French pastries and fruits. **Buchwald** is renowned for producing some of the best cakes in town, mainly to take away, but there are also a number of patisseries, or *Konditoreien*. Among the best of these is **Opernpalais**.

Delicacies from Vienna can be bought in **Wiener Konditorei Caffeehaus**, while **Leysieffer** shops, with their exquisite chocolates and pralines, are a serious temptation for chocoholics. Visitors with a sweet tooth should also try the large stores: **KaDeWe's Feinschmecker Etage** and **Galeries Lafayette's Gourmet** departments both have a wonderful range of confectioneries.

CHEESES

THE LARGEST SELECTION of cheeses in Berlin can be found at **Galeries Lafayette** which has a particularly broad choice from France. **KaDeWe**'s cheese department also offers a wide variety, while **Maître Philipe** sells only select cheeses from small producers. You won't find any fridges here but the whole shop is air-conditioned and the aroma whets the appetite. Italian cheese can be bought in **Südwind** on Akazienstrasse, together with Italian wines and oils, and **Grand Vignoble, Wein & Delicatessen** specializes in French products, mainly wines and cheeses. **Lindner** and **Salumeria** are also a must for cheese lovers.

WINES

BETWEEN THEM, **KaDeWe** and **Galeries Lafayette** have the biggest wine cellars, while smaller businesses usually specialize in wines from a particular region. **Der Rioja-Weinspezialist**, for example, sells only wines originating from northern Spain, while **Vendemmia** specializes in Tuscan wines. A wide selection of German wines is available at **Viniculture**.

MEATS, COLD CUTS AND FISH

BERLINERS EAT QUITE a lot of meat and meat products – the latter in particular are real German specialities. So if you are not vegetarian you should try something from the bewildering range of sausages and meat rolls. As well as the well-stocked departments in the big stores **KaDeWe** and **Galeries Lafayette**, small shops offer excellent quality products. **Fleischerei Bachhuber** is good, and **Alternative Fleischerei** specializes in chemical- and hormone-free meats, while a broad selection of fish (both fresh- and salt-water) and game is offered in **KaDeWe's** delicatessen. **Rogacki** is another good fishmonger and in **Schlemmermeyer** you can find good quality cold meats.

FOOD HALLS

THE OLD 19TH-CENTURY food halls are not as important today as they were before World War II, when they were the chief source of produce. The biggest of them all was on Alexanderplatz. The place used to teem with people 24 hours a day, but the hall wasn't rebuilt after sustaining damage during World War II. The GDR authorities had no use for such a large food hall, and with the advent of supermarkets, there was no need for it.

Today there are only three food halls in operation; **Arminiushalle** in Moabit, the **Markthalle am Marheineke-platz** and **Eisenbahnhalle**, both in Kreuzberg. All of these are usually open all day six days per week – Monday to Saturday. Typically, Berliners use the food halls to pick up the one or two speciality items they can't find in the supermarkets. Shopping in these halls is a good opportunity to try traditional German *Currywurst*: the outlets in these food halls are regarded as the best in town.

MARKETS

MARKETS OFFER an additional way of shopping for food. They take place twice a week, and one of the best is the **Winterfeldtmarkt** which takes place on Wednesdays and Saturdays from 7am till 2pm. On Saturdays the opening hours are extended if the crowd is big, which it often is. You can buy everything from high quality fruits, through vegetables and cheeses from all over the world to clothing and domestic accessories. Fast-food outlets offer *falafel* or grilled sausages, and the place is surrounded by bars and cafés full of clients and traders relaxing with a glass of beer. The atmosphere and range of goods on offer is truly international.

Türken Markt am Maybachufer is a big Turkish market which opens on Tuesdays and Fridays until 6:30pm. It is popular with Turks living in Kreuzberg and Neukölln. The stalls offer all kinds of Turkish specialities. There are also markets in the city centre on Wittenbergplatz – **Wochenmarkt Wittenbergplatz** on Tuesdays and Fridays, Winterfeldtmarkt on Wednesdays and Saturdays and the **Bauernmarkt Wittenbergplatz** on Thursdays. In fact, Thursday is the day when Wittenbergplatz is invaded by farmers from all over the region offering a variety of products.

You won't find any exotic fruits at these, but if you have had enough of tasteless supermarket tomatoes and apples then they should provide a good alternative. Depending on the season, you can buy pickled gherkins (*Salzgurken*) from the Spreewald, asparagus from the Beelitz region and delicious, sweet aromatic strawberries.

DIRECTORY

DEPARTMENT STORES WITH FOOD HALLS

Feinschmecker Etage at KaDeWe
Tauentzienstrasse 21.
Map 10 E2.
21 21 00.

Gourmet in Galeries Lafayette
Friedrichstrasse 23.
Map 6 F4.
20 94 80.

PATISSERIES AND SWEET SHOPS

Berliner Bonbonmacherei
Heckmann Höfe,
Oranienburger Strasse 32.
Map 7 A1.
612 73 37.

Buchwald
Bartningallee 29.
Map 4 F3.
391 59 31.

Fassbender & Rausch
Charlottenstrasse 60.
Map 7 A4.
20 45 84 40.

Konditorei Am Hagenplatz
Hagenplatz 3.
826 16 38.

Leysieffer
Kurfürstendamm 218.
Map 10 D1.
885 74 80.

Leysieffer
at Hotel Adlon
Unter den Linden 77.
Map 6 E3, 15 A3.
22 67 98 65.

Opernpalais
Unter den Linden 5.
Map 7 A3, 16 E3.
20 26 83.

Wiener Konditorei Caffeehaus
Hohenzollerndamm 92.
89 59 69 20.

Wiener Konditorei Caffeehaus
Reichsstrasse 81.
304 55 35.

CHEESES

Grand Vignoble, Wein & Delicatessen
Joachim-Friedrich-Strasse 37.
893 59 82.

Lindner
Olivaer Platz 17
(near Kurfürstendamm).
Map 9 B2.
881 35 53.

Maître Philipe
Emser Strasse 42.
Map 9 B3, 9 C3.
88 68 36 10.

Salumeria
Windscheidstrasse 20.
Map 2 E5.
324 33 18.

Südwind
Akazienstrasse 7.
Map 11 A5.
782 04 39.

WINES

Der Rioja-Weinspezialist
Akazienstrasse 13.
782 25 78.

Vendemmia
Akazienstrasse 20.
784 27 28.

Viniculture
Grolmanstrasse 44–45.
883 81 74.

MEATS, COLD CUTS AND FISH

Alternative Fleischerei
Körtestrasse 20.
Map 13 C4.
691 64 86.

Fleischerei Bachhuber
Güntzelstrasse 47.
Map 9 C4.
873 21 15.

Rogacki
Wilmersdorfer Strasse 145–146. Map 2 F4.
343 82 50.

Schlemmermeyer
Schlossstrasse 6
Map 2 E3.
793 31 38

FOOD HALLS

Arminiushalle
Arminiusstrasse.
Map 4 E1. 8am–6pm Mon–Thu, 8am–7pm Fri, 8am–2pm Sat.

Eisenbahnhalle
Pücklerstrasse. Map 14 E2. 8am–7pm Mon–Fri, 8am–2pm Sat.

Markthalle am Marheinekeplatz
Marheinekeplatz. Map 13 A5. 8am–7pm Mon–Fri, 8am–2pm Sat.

Markthalle Tegel-Center
Gorkistrasse 13–17.
43 43 849. 8am–7pm Mon–Fri, 8am–3pm Sat.

MARKETS

Bauernmarkt Wittenbergplatz
Wittenbergplatz.
Map 10 F1.
10am–7:30pm Thu.

Winterfeldtmarkt
Wittenbergplatz.
Map 11 A3.
8am–noon Wed & Sat.

Türken Markt am Maybachufer
Maybachufer. Map 14 E3, F4. noon–6:30pm Tue & Fri.

Wochenmarkt Wittenbergplatz
Wittenbergplatz.
Map 10 F2.
8am–2pm Tue & Fri.

ENTERTAINMENT IN BERLIN

WITH SO MUCH on offer, from classical drama and cabaret to variety theatre and an eclectic nightclub scene, it is possible to indulge just about any taste in Berlin. During the summer months many bars and restaurants set up outdoor tables, and the area around Unter den Linden, the Kurfürstendamm, Kreuzberg and Prenzlauer Berg in particular, seems to turn into one large social arena. The city really comes into its own at night, when its clubs, all-night cafés and cocktail bars give you

Flute player in costume

the chance to dance till dawn. The city has many night-life centres, each with a slightly different character. Prenzlauer Berg is best for mainstream bars, cafés and clubs, while Friedrichshain is more exclusive, and Kreuzberg has a vibrant gay scene. The Mitte district (see East of the Centre) offers a true mixture, its opera house and classical theatre surrounded by lively and inexpensive bars. On a Sunday, a quiet trip down the river or along the canals offers a pleasant way to unwind.

The Berlin Philharmonic Orchestra

PRACTICAL INFORMATION

THERE ARE so many things going on in Berlin that it can be difficult to find what you're looking for. The Information Centre offers basic information (see p279), but for greater detail you can buy a copy of the listings magazines *Tip* or *Zitty* which offer the widest range of suggestions. Information on festivals, sports events, cinema programmes, theatre schedules, cabarets and concerts can be found on the following websites: berlinonline.de and berlin.de

But if you've only just arrived in town and haven't made it yet to an internet café or a kiosk, the chances are the bar you're sitting in, or your hotel foyer, has leaflets on the wall to point you in the right direction. And there is no end of posters around town telling you what's on offer.

GUIDES

YOU WON'T BE short of cultural guides in Berlin. The fortnightly listings magazines *Tip* and *Zitty*, which cover the widest choice of events, are issued on Wednesdays, while the daily newspaper *Berliner Morgenpost* has a supplement, *"bm Live"*, which is available each Thursday. The Thursday supplement to *Tagesspiegel* is called *Ticket*, and *Taz* publishes cinema programmes every other Thursday in *Cinemataz*. All of these can be bought at news kiosks.

Berlin Programm provides details of the month ahead and *Berlin Magazin*, issued by Berlin Tourismus Marketing GmbH, contains quarterly information. The free magazine *Flyer* is full of news about nightclubs and discos, and it should be available in restaurants.

If you want general information about the whole range of cultural events on offer, including current exhibitions in galleries and museums, then turn to the monthly *Kunstkalender* which is available in most bookshops, museums and galleries.

TICKETS

TICKETS CAN USUALLY be bought two weeks before an event, and you can buy them directly at theatre box

Prokofiev's *The Love of Three Oranges* staged at the Komische Oper

The Love Parade, a festival of techno music

offices or make a telephone booking. Reserved tickets have to be picked up and paid for at least half an hour before a show. Students, pensioners and the disabled are entitled to a 50 per cent discount, but you will need to present appropriate documentation. You can also pre-book tickets at special outlets all over Berlin but they charge a 20 per cent commission. All the major theatres and concert halls have special wheelchair access, but the number of places for the disabled is limited; make it clear when buying a ticket that you want an appropriate place. Tickets to some theatres include a pass for public transport.

If a performance has sold out, you can always try to find tickets just before the show, for some of the pre-booked tickets may not have been collected. One agency which specializes in these last-minute purchases is called **Hekticket Theaterkassen**. You can buy tickets on the day, even an hour before a performance. If someone has already returned their ticket, you might be able to buy it at a 50 per cent discount.

Other agencies to contact for tickets are **Fullhouse Service**, on Budapester Strasse, and **Showtime Konzert- und Theaterkassen**.

INFORMATION FOR THE DISABLED

I N ALL THE GUIDES to theatres and concert halls the availability of wheelchair access is noted by a distinctive blue sign. The majority of the bigger theatres, halls and opera houses have special places for wheelchairs and seats reserved for people with walking difficulties. When buying a ticket you must specify your need as the number of places is limited.

If you are disabled you should be able to commute without restriction on public transport, as the majority of U- and S-Bahn stations have lifts, and they are clearly marked on maps of the underground. Many buses now have special ramps and facilities for wheelchairs, but if you experience any difficulty members of the BVG staff will always help.

PUBLIC TRANSPORT AT NIGHT

T HE LAST U-BAHN TRAINS run at around 1am, but buses and trams continue running every half an hour, making

Elephant Gate at the Zoologischer Garten *(see p150)*

Berlin's night-time transport one of the most efficient in Germany. Bus and tram time-tables are linked, and there are two major interchange points: one on Hardenberg-platz, near the Zoo railway station, and the other on Hackescher Markt. On Friday and Saturday nights you can also use lines 1 and 9 of the U-Bahn which operate every 15 minutes. Some S-Bahn lines also work at night over the weekend. Every ticket office and information point in town has brochures with all the relevant details about night-time public transport.

Afternoon with the children in the Museumsdorf Düppel *(see p180)*

DIRECTORY

TICKET AGENTS

Fullhouse Service
Unter den Linden 36–38/ZDF-Shop. **Map** 6 F3.
[C] 308 78 56 85.

Hekticket Theaterkassen
Hardenbergstrasse 29a.
Map 10 D1. [C] 230 99 30.

Karl-Liebknecht-Strasse 12.
Map 7 C2. [C] 24 31 24 31.

Showtime Konzert- und Theaterkassen
KaDeWe department store (6th floor), Tauentzienstrasse 21.
Map 10 F2. [C] 217 77 54.

Wertheim department store (ground floor), Kurfürstendamm 181. **Map** 10 D1. [C] 882 25 00.

Theatres

THANKS TO REINHARDT AND BRECHT, Berlin became a
landmark in the European theatre scene in the
1920s, and its success continues to this day. During the
years of Nazi rule, many people working in the business
were killed or forced to emigrate as the stage became a
propaganda machine, but after World War II a revival
spread through Berlin's theatres. At the heart of this
revival were Bertolt Brecht and his Berliner Ensemble,
and Peter Stein who ran the Schaubühne.

MODERN HISTORY

FOLLOWING THE construction
of the Berlin Wall, the number of venues doubled as each
part of the divided city worked
to build its own theatres. The
Volksbühne in the East had its
equivalent in the West called
the Freie Volksbühne, and the
eastern acting school, the
Academy, was matched by a
second Academy in the west.

The economic difficulties
caused by the reunification of
Germany forced a number of
places to shut down, but the
theatres of East Berlin
managed to survive. In the
west, the Freie Volksbühne
and the Schiller-Theater (the
largest stage in Germany) had
to close, but the Volksbühne,
under Frank Castorf, and the
Deutsches Theater, led by
Thomas Langhoff, continued
to do well. Independent
theatres have fared equally
well in both parts of the city.

The theatre season runs from
September to July, with its
peak in May during Berliner
Theatertreffen (Berlin Theatre
Forum), when many other
German theatre groups are
invited to stage their plays.
There are also a number of
youth theatres which produce
the work of young writers,
and these follow the seasons
of the major venues.

Repertoires are published in
the listings magazines *Tip* and
Zitty, and also displayed on
yellow posters in U-Bahn
stations and throughout Berlin.
Leaflets are available in many
restaurants around the city.

MAJOR STAGES

THE **Deutsches Theater**
and its small hall **Kammerspiele** on Schumannstrasse is
a top-class theatre and offers

a varied repertoire of productions with very professional
modern stagings. From the
Greek classics to the modern
classics and contemporary
plays, the Deutches Theater
has successfully staged them
all. Tickets for these plays can
be difficult to obtain, but it is
worth persevering.

At **Volksbühne** you can
see interesting performances
of classical plays in modern
settings, as well as adaptations
of books or films or pieces
written by young writers.
Concerts, lectures and dance
evenings are organized in the
Red and Green Salon of the
theatre, and with so much
going on at the Volksbühne now
seems more of a cultural
centre with a multimedia
character than just a stage.

Although it was particularly
important for German theatre
in the 1970s and 80s, **Schaubühne am Lehniner Platz** is
no longer as popular as it was,
which is a shame, for production values don't get any higher
than this. The close attention to
detail – on everything from the
sets and scenery to the choice
of music and the editing of the
printed programme – is extraordinary, and distinguishes it
from the other theatres in town;
every performance is an event.

The **Berliner Ensemble**
(or BE for short) has been
managed by such influential
dramatists as Bertolt Brecht
from 1949 and then Heiner
Müller in 1970. The spectacles
created by these two are still
performed today. The whole
theatre is magnificent, and it
has some superb architecture
including the stage; after each
performance you can meet
the actors in the canteen in
the courtyard, behind the
building. Another venue well
worth visiting is the **Hebbel-**

Theater – an ambitious place
with a programme that in-
cludes contemporary plays
from all over the world and
works of modern dance.

Other major venues include
the **Maxim Gorki Theater**,
the **Renaissance-Theater** and
the **Schlosspark Theater**.

SMALL STAGES AND ALTERNATIVE THEATRE

THERE ARE a number of alternative theatres in Berlin,
each enthusiastically playing
the works of what are generally
lesser known authors. **Theater
am Halleschen Ufer** is devoted to avant-garde theatre and
dance and is considered to be
the city's best alternative stage.
The smaller boulevard theatres,
like **Theater am Kurfürstendamm**, **Komödie am Kurfürstendamm** or **Berlins Volkstheater Hansa**, offer different,
lighter programmes.

Among other small theatres
are **Bat-Studiotheater** and
Kleines Theater. There are
many other notable venues,
including **Theater zum
Westlichen Stadthirschen**,
Hackesches-Hoftheater,
Theater 89, **Theater
Zerbrochene Fenster**,
Theater Kreatur, and the
Vagantenbühne.

MUSICALS, REVIEWS AND CABARETS

THERE ARE THREE main
musical theatres in Berlin,
in addition to the many small
venues which fit musicals into
their more general repertoire.
Friedrichstadtpalast, in the
eastern part of the city, stages
many of the new major shows
as well as classical musicals,
and a smaller stage is reserved for cabaret. The **Theater
des Westens** in Charlottenburg is more traditional, while
the **Stella Musical Theater
Berlin am Potsdamer Platz**
is a modern theatre established
in the newly built city on
Potsdamer Platz in 1999.

As for cabaret, there are
probably as many acts in
Berlin today as there were in
the 1920s. They are usually
performed by small itinerant
groups which rely on the hospitality of theatres for a venue.

Distel, in Friedrichstrasse, continues its success from GDR times, and **Stachelschweine** celebrates its popularity in western Berlin.

There are many more venues for musicals, reviews and cabarets. Among these are **Bar jeder Vernunft**, **Chamäleon Variété**, **Dr Seltsam Kabarett**, **Musical-Zelt**, **Scheinbar**, **Wintergarten Variété** and **Wühlmäuse**.

TICKETS

IT IS USUALLY POSSIBLE to pre-book tickets two weeks before a performance. You can buy them directly from the box office of the theatre or by telephone booking. There are also ticket vendors all over town, but they usually charge a 15–22 per cent commission. Even if the theatre or concert has been sold out, there is still a chance of buying something just before the performance, provided that not all pre-booked tickets have been collected.

Hekticket Theaterkassen specializes in this kind of last-minute ticket. If you are lucky enough to pick up a ticket on the day of performance, you may find it has been returned and reduced to half its former price.

DIRECTORY

MAJOR STAGES

Berliner Ensemble
Bertold-Brecht-Platz 1.
Map 6 F2, 15 C1.
C 28 408 155.

Deutsches Theater
Schumannstrasse 13.
Map 6 E2, 15 A1.
C 28 44 12 25.

Hebbel-Theater
Stresemannstrasse 29.
Map 12 F2.
C 25 90 04 27.

Kammerspiele
Schumannstrasse 13a.
Map 6 E2, 15 A1.
C 28 44 12 26.

Maxim Gorki Theater
Am Festungsgraben 2.
Map 7 A3, 16 E2.
C 20 22 11 29.

Renaissance-Theater
Hardenbergstrasse 6.
Map 3 C5.
C 312 42 02.

Schaubühne am Lehniner Platz
Kurfürstendamm 153.
C 89 00 23.

Schlosspark Theater
Schlossstrasse 48
Map 2 E4.
C 793 15 15.

Volksbühne
Rosa-Luxemburg-Platz.
Map 8 D1.
C 247 67 72.

SMALL STAGES AND ALTERNATIVE THEATRE

Bat-Studiotheater
Belforter Strasse 15.
C 44 01 89 12.

Berlins Volkstheater Hansa
Alt-Moabit 48.
C 39 90 99 09.

Hackesches-Hoftheater
Rosenthaler Strasse 40.
Map 7 B2.
C 283 25 87.

Kleines Theater
Südwestkorso 64.
C 821 30 30.

Komödie am Kurfürstendamm
Kurfürstendamm 206.
Map 9 C2.
C 88 59 11 88.

Sophiensaele
Sophienstrasse 18.
Map 7 B1.
C 283 52 66.

Theater 89
Torstrasse 216.
Map 6 F1.
C 282 37 27.

Theater am Halleschen Ufer
Hallesches Ufer 32.
Map 12 F2.
C 251 09 41.

Theater am Kurfürstendamm
Kurfürstendamm 206.
Map 9 C2.
C 88 59 11 88.

Theater am Ufer
Tempelhofer Ufer 10.
Map 12 F2.
C 251 31 16.

Theater Zerbrochene Fenster
Schwiebusser Strasse 16.
Map 12 F5.
C 691 29 32.

Theater zum Westlichen Stadthirschen
Kreuzbergstrasse 37.
Map 12 D4.
C 785 70 33.

Vagantenbühne
Kantstrasse 12a.
Map 10 D1.
C 312 45 29.

MUSICALS, REVIEWS & CABARETS

Bar jeder Vernunft
Schaperstrasse 24.
Map 10 D2.
C 883 15 82.

Chamäleon Variété
Rosenthaler Strasse 40–41.
Map 7 B2.
C 282 71 18.

Distel
Friedrichstrasse 101.
Map 6 F2, 15 C1.
C 204 47 04.

Friedrichstadtpalast
Friedrichstrasse 107.
Map 6 F2, 15 C1.
C 23 26 23 26.

Kalkscheune
Johannisstrasse 2 (behind Friedrichstadtpalast).
Map 6 F2.
C 59 00 43 40.

Scheinbar
Monumentenstrasse 9.
Map 11 C5.
C 784 55 39.

Stachelschweine
Europa-Center.
Map 10 E1.
C 261 47 95.

Stella Musical Theater Berlin am Potsdamer Platz
Marlene-Dietrich-Platz 1.
C (0180) 544 44.

Theater des Westens
Kantstrasse 12.
Map 2 E5, 9 A1, 10 D1.
C (0180) 599 89 99.

Wintergarten Variété
Potsdamer Strasse 96.
Map 11 C2.
C 25 00 88 88.

Wühlmäuse am Theo
Pommernallee 2–4.
Map 1 B5.
C 30 67 30 11.

TICKETS

Hekticket Theaterkassen
Hardenbergstrasse 29a.
Map 10 D1. **C** 23 09 930.

Karl-Liebknecht-Strasse 12.
Map 7 C2.
C 24 31 24 31.

Cinema

BERLIN HAS ALWAYS been the capital of German cinema, and it is likely to remain so. In November 1895, exactly two months after the Lumière Brothers presented their first moving pictures in France, brothers Emil and Max Skladanowsky showed a series of short films to a spellbound German public. Wintergarten Varieté-theater was the place where you could go to see those famous pioneering films of kangaroos fighting, acrobats tumbling and children performing folk dances. By 1918 there were already some 251 cinemas with 82,796 seats available in Berlin, and by 1925 the number of people involved in the film industry had reached 47,600. The history of UFA (Universal Film AG), established in 1917, is intimately linked to that of Berlin, for the company has its two studios here.

BIG SCREENS AND BIG FILMS

THE MAJORITY of cinemas can be found in the western part of town, around Breitscheidplatz, near the Ku'damm and Tauentzienstrasse, and this is where the big American and German blockbusters are shown. After the fall of the Berlin Wall, many new multiplex cinemas were built, the biggest being the **CinemaxX Potsdamer Platz** and the **Cinestar Sony Center**. Mainstream Anglo-American movies are dubbed, rather than subtitled, but you can also see films in their original language here.

Next door to CinemaxX is the **IMAX** cinema – the biggest screen in Germany. It can only show films that are shot with an Imax camera, but the spectacle is always breathtaking. Its huge curved screen is 27 m (89 ft) across and covers approximately 1000 sq m (10,750 sq ft). It shows a range of films including natural history, travel and underwater features, as well as a selection of 3D films that require special viewing glasses. There are three other areas of Berlin that are known as cinema centres: East of the City, in Friedrichshain and in Prenzlauer Berg.

The **International** on Karl-Marx-Allee is typical of cinemas built in the communist era. It was built in 1963 and may be of interest to anyone curious about the days of the GDR, but it's pretty austere and only has 551 seats. Another venue on Karl-Marx-Allee is the **UFA-Palast Kosmos**. It is is now a modern multiplex with ten screens, but it was originally very small; only the exterior of the building provides hints of its GDR-era origins.

STUDIO CINEMAS

THERE ARE PLENTY of small studio cinemas scattered across town, and it is in these that new independent films and retrospectives of particular actors and directors are shown. Cinemas like **Hackesche Höfe Kino** or **Central**, situated near Hackescher Markt, offer a pleasant break from the bustle of modern city life, and most have bars of their own. The café at Hackesche Höfe Kino is noteworthy as it offers light snacks as well as a wonderful 5th-floor view over the neighbourhood.

The **Arsenal**, on Potsdamer Platz, belongs to the Freunde der Deutschen Kinemathek (Friends of German Cinema), and is ideal for lovers of German film for this is where you can see all the national classics. The venue has a detailed monthly programme which includes four screenings per day, many of which come with a small introductory lecture. Copies of the programme are distributed in bars all over town.

If you're interested in original language movies, **Cinéma Paris** in Charlottenburg is the place to go for French films, while the **Odeon** in Schöneberg specializes in English and American films.

OPEN-AIR CINEMA

OPEN-AIR cinemas start operating as soon as the weather allows. The biggest is **Waldbühne** – a concert hall with seating for an audience of 20,000. Others can be found in Hasenheide, Künstler Haus Bethanien garden, in Friedrichshain or in UFA-Fabrik. All of these outdoor venues show a selection of current first-run films as well as the established classics. Screenings start at around 9pm, which is when it starts to grow dark during summer.

NON-COMMERCIAL FILMS

ALTHOUGH MOST people tend to go to the cinema nowadays to see the latest blockbuster movie from Hollywood, it is still possible to track down some of the venues which show less popular films including documentaries and other non-commercial films.

The **Zeughauskino**, which has recently reopened its doors, specializes in non-commercial films. It coordinates its interesting and informative repertoire with exhibitions in the Deutsches Historisches Museum (the German Historical Museum), as well as showing its òwn series of documentaries.

What used to be known as the Museum für Völkerkunde (the Museum of Mankind) in Dahlem (see p170), but now goes under the new name of the **Ethnologisches Museum**, also organizes various film showings, usually in conjunction with exhibitions of non-European culture. As at Zeughauskino, a ticket is very reasonably priced.

PRICES

CINEMA TICKETS usually cost between 5–8 and students and senior citizens don't always receive a discount. Many cinemas declare Tuesday or Wednesday as Cinema

Day, when tickets are 1–2 cheaper. Some cinemas also organize so-called "Blue Mondays" when tickets are reduced to as little as 4.

In most cinemas there are usually three shows per evening, the first starting at 6pm, the last at around 10pm. All cinemas accept telephone bookings, but you have to turn up to pay for your ticket at least half an hour before a show, otherwise it may go to somebody else. Most ticket offices don't take credit cards, so have cash in hand.

Twenty minutes of commercials tend to precede the screenings of most films, although some venues use this time to show short films by up-and-coming directors.

THE FILM BUSINESS

IF YOU'RE INTERESTED in the business of film production then you will want to visit Studio UFA in Babelsberg, Potsdam. A must for all cinema fans, the **Studiotour Babelsberg** allows you to see a live film crew working on a

current production *(see p205)*. You will also get a chance to see some classic film sets – some going back to the days of Marlene Dietrich – as well as samples of the latest technical wizardry.

A wide variety of books, in many different languages, about cinema and film can be found in **Bücherbogen** under the arcade of the S-Bahn railway bridge at Savignyplatz. Alternatively you can try **Bücherstube Marga Schoeller** at 33 Knesebeckstrasse, near Kurfüstendamm.

DIRECTORY

BIG SCREENS AND BIG FILMS

CinemaxX Potsdamer Platz
Potsdamer Strasse 1–19.
Map 6 D5.
(0180) 524 63 62 99.

Cinestar Sony Center
Potsdamer Strasse 4.
Map 6 D5.
26 06 62.

IMAX
Marlene-Dietrich-Platz 4.
26 06 62.

International
Karl-Marx-Allee 33
(corner of Schillingstrasse).
Map 8 E3.
24 75 60 11.

UFA-Palast Kosmos
Karl-Marx-Allee 131a.
Map 8 E3.
42 28 40.

STUDIO CINEMAS

Arsenal 1–2
Potsdamer Platz/Sony Center. **Map** 10 F2.
26 95 51 00.

Central
Rosenthaler Strasse 39.
Map 7 B1.
28 59 99 73.

Cinéma Paris
Kurfürstendamm 211.
Map 9 A2, 10 D1.
881 31 19.

Hackesche Höfe Kino
Rosenthaler Strasse 4041.
Map 9 C2.
283 46 03.

Odeon
Hauptstrasse 116.
Map 11 B5.
78 70 40 19.

OPEN-AIR CINEMA

Waldbühne
Glockenturmstrasse 1.
23 08 82 30 (tickets).

NON-COMMERCIAL FILMS

Ethnologisches Museum
Filmbuehne Museum, Lanssrasse 8.
830 14 38.
during festivals.

THE FILM BUSINESS

Bücherbogen am Savignyplatz
Stadtbahnbogen 593.
31 86 95 11.

Studiotour Babelsberg
August-Bebel-Str. 26–53, Potsdam (entrance Grossbeerenstrasse).
(0331) 721 27 55.

FAMOUS FILMS ABOUT BERLIN

Berlin Alexanderplatz
Germany 1931, directed by Phillip Jutzi, based on Alexander Döblin's book.

Berlin Alexanderplatz
GDR 1980, directed by Rainer Werner Fassbinder.

Berlin, Chamissoplatz
GDR 1980, directed by Rudolf Thome.

Berlin – Ecke Schönhauser
GDR 1957, directed by Gerhard Klein.

Berliner Ballade (Berlin Ballad)
American Occupied Zone 1948, directed by Robert Stemmle.

Berlin, die Symphonie einer Grossstadt (Berlin, Symphony of a Great City)
Germany 1927, directed by Walter Ruttmann.

Coming Out
GDR 1988/1989, directed by Heiner Carow.

Der Himmel über Berlin (The Sky Above Berlin)
GDR/France 1987, directed by Wim Wenders.

Die Legende von Paul und Paula (The Legend of Paul and Paula)
GDR 1973, directed by Heiner Carow.

Eins, zwei, drei (One, two, three)
USA 1961, directed by Billy Wilder.

Kuhle Wampe
Germany 1932, directed by Slatan Dudow, script by Bertolt Brecht.

Menschen am Sonntag (Men on Sunday)
Germany 1930, directed by Robert Siodmak and Edgar G Ulmer.

Lola rennt (Run, Lola, Run)
Germany 1998, directed by Tom Tykwer.

Sonnenallee
Germany 1998, directed by Leander Haußmann.

Classical Music

BERLIN HAS one of the world's finest orchestras (the Berlin Philharmonic Orchestra) as well as one of the most beautiful concert halls (the Philharmonie). The Berlin Philharmonic has long been pre-eminent among the city's three symphonic orchestras, all of which perform regularly in Berlin. There are three major opera houses to choose from and a smaller one for lovers of the avant-garde. Apart from regular concerts the city offers many festivals, two of the most popular being the Musik-Biennale and the Open Air Festival on Gendarmenmarkt. Smaller concerts are organized year-round in the city's many churches, halls and palaces.

CONCERT HALLS

THE **Philharmonie** is one of Europe's grandest concert halls, with excellent acoustics. The Berlin Philharmonic Orchestra itself was founded in 1882 by a group of 54 ambitious musicians, and it achieved great popularity under the conductor Herbert von Karajan, who stayed at the helm from 1954 through to 1989. The orchestra was taken over by Claudio Abbado, a worthy successor, and since 2002 it has been directed by Sir Simon Rattle, an acclaimed British conductor. Tickets for popular programmes quickly sell out, but the more obscure concerts will usually have some seats available. It is easier to obtain tickets when other orchestras such as the Berlin Symphony Orchestra and the Berlin Radio Symphony Orchestra are playing in the Philharmonie.

Chamber orchestras perform special chamber pieces in the smaller **Kammermusiksaal** attached to the bigger hall.

Konzerthaus Berlin, formally known as the Schauspielhaus (*see p65*), is another important venue for classical music. The building was restored after World War II and now contains a large concert hall and a smaller room for chamber music. It is one of the best places to hear classical music in elegant surroundings. Two unusual places that also sometimes put on musical concerts are the **Universität der Künste** on Hardenbergerstrasse and the **Staatsbibliothek** (State Library) on Potsdamer Strasse.

Many churches in Berlin also open their doors for concerts throughout the year. For a guide to all these events, look up the listings magazines *Tip* or *Zitty* (*see p260*).

OPERA

AMONG BERLIN'S three major opera houses, the **Staatsoper Unter den Linden** (*see p63*), under the leadership of Daniel Barenboim, is a gem. In this beautiful building, painstakingly restored according to Knobelsdorff's original design, performances take place in the Grosser Saal and the Apollo-Saal. The repertoire includes the traditional German classics, Italian opera and to a lesser extent, contemporary pieces.

Komische Oper (*see p68*), managed by Harry Kupfer, is known for its broad range of lighter opera. Its operas usually have a long run, so you can nearly always find tickets. The ballet produced here is particularly innovative.

Deutsche Oper Berlin on Bismarckstrasse is the only one of the three main opera houses to be a modern building. The interior is a rather plain 1960s style, but the repertoire includes all kinds of music from different periods ranging from major Italian operas and Mozart to Wagner and Saint Saëns. There is often an exhibition organized in the foyer so the waiting time passes quickly.

A fourth opera house is the **Neuköllner Oper** in the Neukölln district. Less famous than the others, it is known for its unconventional approach.

CONTEMPORARY MUSIC

THE BERLIN organization **Initiative Neue Music Berlin e.V.** publishes a bulletin every two months containing information about current performances of contemporary music. It always includes **BKA** near Mehringdamm with its **Unerhörte Music** series. The **Akademie der Künste** and **Sender Freies Berlin (SFB)** initiated a project designed to promote contemporary music; it is called *Insel Music* and one of its achievements is a series of concerts organized each November in the Haus des Rundfunks.

FESTIVALS

THE **Berliner Festwochen** takes place throughout the month of September, and every year there is a different theme. Each festival promises a range of exhibitions, theatrical events and concerts, and the most famous orchestras and soloists from around the world come to take part each year.

Every other year in March you can also experience the **Musik-Biennale Berlin**, where contemporary music dominates. At this international festival numerous world premieres are made, both of music by new names and that of established composers.

A real treat for opera lovers is the summer festival of opera – Classic Open Air – which is organized on an open stage on Gendarmenmarkt, specially built for the occasion. Another musical feast well worth volunteering for is the Bach-Tage festival, a charming showcase of Baroque music, which takes place every year in July.

OPEN AIR CONCERTS

THERE ARE TWO open stages in Berlin and during the summer months a number of classical concerts are staged. **Waldbühne**, located near the Olympia Stadion, has seating for 20,000, and is the venue for concerts by European youth orchestras. The atmosphere is relaxed and informal, very often with children running around while their parents eat and drink during the shows. After sunset, when the crowds light the candles they have brought for the occasion, the atmosphere becomes quite magical.

Although the concerts organized the **Parkbühne Wuhlheide** are every bit as good as the ones held in Waldbühne, the audiences tend to be smaller.

MUSIC IN PALACES AND NOTABLE BUILDINGS

DURING MUSIC FESTIVALS, recitals are often held in Berlin's beautiful historic buildings, and a concert in the Berliner Dom *(see p77)*, the Eichengallerie in Schloss Charlottenburg *(see pp160–61)* or Schloss Friedrichsfelde *(see p174)* can be an unforgettable

experience. The **Universität der Künste** *(see Concert Halls)* has very good acoustics, but if you prefer a more modern environment, try one of the rooms in **Staatsbibliothek** *(see Concert Halls)* or the concert hall in the **Akademie der Künste** *(see Contemporary Music)*. Occasionally classical concerts are also held in venues that are normally reserved for popular music.

VARIOUS

THE **Musikinstrumenten-Museum** offers concerts on selected Sunday mornings, and as a part of the Alte Musik Live scheme you can listen to the music of old masters played on their original instruments. A special booklet covering all the museum's events is published

twice a year and is available from all theatres, concert halls and music shops.

The **Kulturkaufhaus Dussmann** shop offers the widest range of music in Berlin, with a stock of over 50,000 titles, and competent staff always ready to help you find what you are after. They also stage literary readings, lectures, and other special cultural events at the store. **Gelbe Musik** on Schaperstrasse is also more than a shop; it has a gallery specializing in contemporary music and co-ordinates many concerts and recitals. **Schöne Künste Exkursionen** organizes walks around the city under the theme of Musikstadt Berlin; these take place on Saturday and set off from Bebelplatz, at the back of the opera building on Unter den Linden *(see p57)*.

DIRECTORY

CONCERT HALLS

Konzerthaus Berlin (Schauspielhaus)
Gendarmenmarkt 2.
Map 7 A4, 16 D4.
☎ 203 09 21 01/02.
w www.konzerthaus.de

Philharmonie Kammermusiksaal
Herbert-von-Karajan-Strasse 1. **Map** 6 D5.
☎ 25 48 81 32.

Staatsbibliothek
Potsdamer Strasse 33.
☎ 26 62 303.

Universität der Künste
Hardenbergstrasse 33.
Map 4 E3.
☎ 31 85 23 74.

OPERA

Deutsche Oper Berlin
Bismarckstrasse 34–37.
Map 3 A4.
☎ 34 10 249.

Komische Oper
Behrenstrasse 55–57.
Map 6 F4, 15 C3.
☎ 47 99 74 00.

Neuköllner Oper
Karl-Marx-Str. 131–133,
Neukölln.
Map 14 F5.
☎ 688 90 777.

Staatsoper Unter den Linden
Unter den Linden 7.
Map 7 A3, 16 D3.
☎ 20 35 45 55.

CONTEMPORARY MUSIC

Akademie der Künste
Hanseatenweg 10.
Map 4 F3.
☎ 390 76 0.

Initiative Neue Musik Berlin e.V.
Klosterstrasse 68–70.
Map 8 D3.
☎ 242 45 34.

Sender Freies Berlin (SFB)
Masurenallee 8–14.
Haus des Rundfunks.
Map 1 B5.
☎ 30 31 0.

Unerhörte Musik (BKA)
Mehringdamm 34.
Map 12 F3, 12 F4.
☎ 202 20 07.

FESTIVALS

Berliner Festwochen
Berliner Festspiele GmbH
Schaperstrasse 4. **Map** 10
D2. ☎ 25 48 91 00.

Musik-Biennale Berlin
Berliner Festspiele GmbH
Schaperstrasse 4.
Map 10 D2. ☎ 25 48 90.

OUTDOOR CONCERTS

Parkbühne Wuhlheide
An der Wuhlheide.
w www.wuhlheide.de

Waldbühne
Glockenturmstrasse 1.
☎ 23 08 82 30.

VARIOUS

Gelbe Musik
Schaperstrasse 11. **Map**
10 D2. ☎ 211 39 62.

Kulturkaufhaus Dussmann
Friedrichstrasse 90.
☎ 202 50.

Musik-instrumenten-Museum
Tiergartenstrasse 1.
Map 6 D5.
☎ 20 90 55 55.

Schöne Künste Exkursionen
☎ 782 12 02.

TICKETS

Fullhouse Service
Unter den Linden 36–38.
Map 15 B3.
☎ 308 78 56 85.

Showtime Konzert- und Theaterkassen
KaDeWe department store
(6th floor)
Tauentzienstrasse 21.
Map 10 F2.
☎ 217 77 54.

Wertheim department store (ground floor)
Kurfürstendamm 181.
Map 10 D1.
☎ 882 25 00.

Rock, Jazz and World Music

To MUSIC LOVERS Berlin can mean anything from techno to the Berlin Philharmonic Orchestra, for the city has a thriving and multi-faceted music industry. Between its classical and ultra-modern extremes the full spectrum of musical taste is catered for, from bar-room blues to rock'n'roll and international pop. Whether it's a major event by a world-famous band or a small-scale evening of jazz improvization, you needn't look far to find what you want. The biggest events take place in sports halls and stadiums, but most of the action can be found in discos, bars and the city's various clubs (see pp270–71). There are also a number of cultural centres where you can stop by to listen to modern music. The best way to find something for yourself is to get hold of a copy of the listings magazines *Zitty* or *Tip*, and look out for flyers and leaflets in bars.

BIG CONCERTS

BERLIN IS ALWAYS high up on the list when major pop, rock or jazz bands go on tour. While people flock from all over the country to attend these events, there are a number of smaller events which attract an equally devoted audience. Since the closure of the huge Deutschlandhalle, the big events take place in **Max-Schmeling-Hall** and the Velodrom (see p273). For the really big crowds, events are usually held at the **Olympia Stadion** (see p184) which has seating for 100,000. The **Waldbühne** next door has a capacity of 20,000 and hosts both classical orchestras and rock bands. **Parkbühne Wuhlheide** is another equally flexible venue. For detailed information about what's on and where, consult the websites berlinonline.de and berlin.de or the listings magazines *Zitty* and *Tip*.

OTHER MUSICAL EVENTS

THERE ARE PLENTY of smaller venues in Berlin where concerts are held. Among them are the **Loft** in Metropol on Nollendorfplatz, nearby **Café Swing**, and the famous **SO 36** in Kreuzberg. Schöneberg was notorious in the 1980s for its punk rock scene, but while those days are now over, there are still plenty of exciting things on offer here today. One of the most popular places in town is

Tempodrom (check listings magazines for details).

Columbiahalle, which is located near Columbiadamm, is a well-known location for medium-size events, and so is the **Knaack Club**, a multi-sited venue on Greifswalder Strasse. If you are looking for particularly atmospheric concerts, try the **Passionskirche**, a church in Kreuzberg. For a whole range of cultural events the **Palais Podewils** (see p97) is the place to go. Everything is on offer here from theatrical performances to dance and evenings of jazz improvization – and all in a truly modern style.

Concerts and plays are also organized at the popular **Arena** in Treptow – a very large music hall, dating from the 1920s, which used to be a local bus depot.

JAZZ

JAZZ lovers from all over the world descend on Berlin for the **Jazzfest Berlin**, and its accompanying **Total Music Meeting**, both of which are held each year. The former is more traditional, but the latter is devoted to modern experimental work. "Jazz across the Border" takes place in July; it is a festival at which all kinds of borders are crossed, not least those of musical inhibition.

As far as regular clubs are concerned, jazz is still very popular in Berlin, in spite of the pull of its perhaps better known electronic and techno discotheques. The **A Trane** and **b-flat** are classical jazz bars where you can listen to small bands just about every night of the week, and **Flöz**, on the ground floor and basement of a place in Nassauische Strasse, is famous for its excellent acoustics.

Another great venue is **Quasimodo** on Kantstrasse, but its concerts only start after 10pm when performances at Theater des Westens have finished; the vibrations would otherwise disturb the neighbouring audience. The acoustics at Quasimodo are also excellent, which is perhaps just as well as little can be seen through the clouds of cigarette smoke. Two other venues which fit evenings of jazz into their otherwise varied programmes are **Kalkscheune** on Johannisstrasse and **Palais Podewil** on Klostestrasse. Another good venue for enjoying jazz is **Bilderbuch**, on Akazienstrasse.

Apart from the typical, classical jazz clubs, jazz can also be heard in many of the city's smaller bars, like **Schlot** on Kastanienallee or **Harlem** in Prenzlauer Berg. If it's a mixture of soul, rap and jazz you want to listen to then head for the **Junction Bar** in Kreuzberg. The **pipapo**, near Nollendorfplatz, is a worthy choice on Sunday. The **Badenscher Hof Jazzclub** on Badensche Strasse is another great place for jazz.

WORLD MUSIC

As A BROADLY cosmopolitan city with an increasingly multi-national population, Berlin is home to a wide variety of music. The SFB4 MultiKulti radio station and Weltmusikfestival Heimaklänge were established here in 1988, and the presence of music from all parts of the world is never that far away.

The **Haus der Kulturen der Welt** on John-Foster-Dulles-Allee is an institution set up by the Berlin Upper Chamber to support this cosmopolitanism, and its main aim is to make non-European cultures more accessible to Germany. As music is one of the best ways of bridging cross-cultural differences, the Haus der Kulturen der Welt organizes all kinds of concerts at its own **Café Global** – one of the best Saturday evening venues for listening to and dancing to music from all over the world. Details of the bands on offer can be found in a booklet which should be available in bookshops and restaurants around town.

A similar organization is the **Werkstatt der Kulturen** on Wissmannstrasse which has been staging all kinds of cultural events for some years now. These include regular concerts and music festivals. Between them, the Haus der

Kulturen der Welt and the Werkstatt are the most reliable providers of world music in town, but you can also find a number of bars and clubs that specialize in the music of one particular nation. Details of these can be found in the listings magazines *Zitty* and *Tip*, and on flyers all over town.

Latin American discos are becoming ever more popular throughout Berlin – **El Barrio** in Tiergarten is one of the city's most popular and best.

Irish music is also well represented in the city, and all you have to do is visit a few pubs. Live music is played in **Wild at Heart** on almost every night of the week. However, if it's Russian ballads you want then head for the ever popular **Chagall**.

TICKETS

THE PRICE OF TICKETS for major pop concerts can be astronomical, particularly if you want to secure a good seat. At the other extreme, you should be able to get into smaller clubs for €5–12, but again, if a famous person or band is playing you will have to pay a good deal more. Often you will find the ticket price includes a drink at the bar.

Tickets for major events are likely to sell out quickly and should be booked well in advance; there are numerous ticket offices in the busier parts of town *(see p261)*.

If you just want to spend the night at a club you should have no trouble buying a ticket at the door.

DIRECTORY

BIG CONCERTS

Parkbühne Wuhlheide
An der Wuhllheide.
w www.wuhlheide.de

Tränenpalast
Friedrichstrasse 17.
Map 6 F2.
℡ 20 61 00 11.

Waldbühne
Glockenturmstrasse 1.
℡ 23 08 82 30.

OTHER MUSIC EVENTS

Arena
Eichenstrasse 4.
℡ 533 73 33.

Columbiahalle
Columbiadamm 13–21.
℡ 69 80 980.

Knaack Club
Greifswalder Strasse 224.
℡ 442 70 60.

Loft (Metropol)
Nollendorfplatz 5.
Map 11 A2.
℡ 217 36 80.

Palais Podewils
Klosterstrasse 68–70.
Map 8 D3.
℡ 24 74 97 77.

Passionskirche
Marheineckeplatz.
Map 13 A5.
℡ 69 40 12 41.

SO 36
Oranienstrasse 190.
Map 14 E2.
℡ 61 40 13 06.

Tempodrom
Am Anhalter Bahnhof,
Möckernstrasse 10. **Map**
12 E1. ℡ 69 53 38 85.

tipi-das Zelt
Grosse Queralle,
Tiergarten. **Map** 5 C3.
℡ (0180) 327 93 58.

JAZZ

A Trane
Pestalozzistrasse 105.
Map 3 C5.
℡ 313 25 50.

Badenscher Hof Jazzclub
Badensche Strasse 29.
Map 10 D5.
℡ 861 00 80.

b-flat
Rosenthaler Strasse 13.

Map 7 B1.
℡ 280 63 49.

Bilderbuch
Akazienstrasse 28.
Map 11 A5.
℡ 78 70 60 57.

Flöz
Nassauische Strasse 37.
Map 9 C5.
℡ 861 10 00.

Musik-Café Harlem
Rodebergstrasse 37.
℡ 444 56 54.

Jazzfest Berlin
Schaperstrasse 24.
Map 10 D2.
℡ 25 48 90 .

Junction Bar
Gneisenaustrasse 18.
℡ 694 66 02.

Kalkscheune
Johannisstrasse 2.
Map 6 F2.
℡ 59 00 43 40.

Palais Podewils
Klosterstrasse 68–70.
Map 8 D3.
℡ 24 74 97 77.

pipapo
Grossgörschenstrasse 40.
Map 11 C4.
℡ 216 15 43.

Quasimodo
Kantstrasse 12a.
℡ 312 80 86.

Schlot
Chausseestrasse 18.
Map 1 A4. ℡ 448 21 60.

Soultrane
Kantstrasse 17 (at Stilwerk).
Map 9 C1.
℡ 315 18 60.

WORLD MUSIC

Chagall
Kollwitzstrasse 2.
℡ 441 58 81.

El Barrio
Potsdamer Strasse 82.
Map 11 B3.
℡ 262 18 53.

Haus der Kulturen der Welt & Café Global
John-Foster-Dulles-Allee 10.
Map 5 C3.
℡ 39 78 71 75.

Werkstatt der Kulturen
Wissmannstrasse 31–42.
Map 14 E5.
℡ 609 77 00.

Wild at Heart
Wiener Strasse 20
(Kreuzberg).
℡ 61 17 010.

Classical and Modern Dance

WITH SO MUCH ON OFFER in the arts, Berlin is a place where you can spend the early evening watching a ballet or musical, and later go out dancing yourself. The three opera houses have interesting ballet programmes built into their repertoires, and these are performed largely by resident dance companies. The city also attracts international ballet groups, not only during the May and August festivals but throughout the year. These productions are usually held in the Hebbel-Theater on Stresemannstrasse, although in recent years the Tanzfabrik in Kreuzberg has become a centre of contemporary dance. Berlin also has a thriving techno scene, which spills out on to the streets for the annual Love Parade *(see p49)*, and a plethora of dance clubs.

CLASSICAL BALLET

ALL THREE BALLET groups working within Berlin's opera houses regularly stage new performances which appeal to a wide variety of audiences. To provide a balance, ballet evenings are often arranged to combine elements of classical and ballet with modern choreography. The Komische Oper *(see p68)* has a more modern repertoire, while the Staatsoper Unter den Linden *(see p63)* has a programme that focuses on classical work, such as *Swan Lake* with its traditional choreography.

MODERN DANCE

THE **Hebbel-Theater** is the customary venue that welcomes foreign avant-garde dance companies. In return for its hospitality, its own productions are staged in co-operation with other dance groups all over the world. Together with **Theater am Halleschen Ufer**, it organizes the dance festival called "Tanz", which takes place every August. As the seating capacity for both theatres is limited, buying a ticket can be difficult; it is worth booking well in advance.

The **Sophiensaele**, a theatre now mainly used for drama, also features contemporary and avant-garde dance companies from time to time. **Tanzfabrik**, based on Möckernstrasse in Kreuzberg, is an excellent stage for all kinds of modern dance, and it also organizes dance workshops as well as popular body-work courses.

The International Choreographic Theatre of Johann Kresnik, in the Volksbühne on Rosa-Luxemburg-Platz *(see p263)*, has earned a great reputation, with many outstanding performances of their productions of *Frida Kahlo*, *Hotel Lux* and *Malinche*.

TANGO

YOU CAN DANCE the tango in Berlin every day of the week. A full schedule could incorporate the **Checkpoint** on Monday, **Kalkscheune** on Tuesday, the Red Salon on Wednesday and the Grüner Salon on Thursday (both at Volksbühne) and Friday at the **Walzerlinksgestrickt**. For the grand finale on Saturday you can always improve your dance moves at one of the many dance schools. But if that still hasn't satisfied your appetite, Saturday lessons can even be extended to Sunday to fully prepare yourself for the week ahead.

TECHNO

AMONG ITS MANY artistic claims, Berlin is also the techno capital of Europe, with over a million devotees celebrating the genre at the annual Love Parade. The festival is held at the beginning of July and most of the action takes place around the Tiergarten, but even over the following weekend, after the event has ended, streets all over Berlin are still packed with people dancing. Parties and discos are organized throughout Berlin, and the areas around clubs turn into meeting areas where people exchange news about what's going on elsewhere in the city.

The Love Parade lasts only one weekend, but techno fans can spoil themselves all year round at any of countless clubs, most of which stay open through the night until noon the following day. **Tresor** is at the very heart of it all, situated in the old vault of a defunct department store (Wertheim on Leipziger Platz). This is where the best DJs in town can be heard.

Few clubs specialize in a particular kind of music, but most reserve certain days of the week for different styles. Find out where the latest techno outfits can be heard – a good way to start is to get hold of a copy of the free publications *Flyer* or *Partysan*, both of which are distributed widely in bars.

The clubs **Matrix** and **ColumbiaFritz** are guaranteed to provide what you're after, and so too is the special techno-room known as Subground, which is located in the subways of **Pfefferbank**. Techno dominates the menu here, but Subground also caters for music lovers of all kinds.

DISCOS AND OTHER CLUBS

IF IT'S A GOOD old-fashioned disco you're looking for, with happy tunes and a little less of the techno, then **Far Out** and **Metropol** are the places to go. It was famous before the fall of the Wall and attracts a teenage crowd every weekend. Tuesdays are devoted to thirtysomethings, who come here to dance to classic funk, soul and pop. For a crowded house with 2000 Watts for 2000 people, head for the **Loft** *(see p268)* which is always packed, but, if you're no longer a teenager and fancy a bit of retro, then a night at the **Tränenpalast** could be the choice; it's based in the pavilion that served as the former passport control between East and West Berlin *(see p39)*. The **Privat Club** is known for arranging a good disco or two, aside from its customary repertoire of jazz.

During the summer, you can dance to pop music in the open air at **Golgatha** in Kreuzberg's Viktoriapark, or in **Die Insel**, a café built on an island in Treptow.

Delicious Doughnuts is one of the best places in town for ambient, house and acid-jazz. If it's Latin-American rhythms you are looking for, then **Salsa** *(see p269)*, **Havanna** and **Cueva Buena Vista** are the best places to go. The **Akba-Lounge** is another good choice of venue. Many

smaller bars have a space for itchy feet. Lovers of soul and reggae should head for **Fat Cat** or **Lumumba Tanzcafé**, while pop music can be heard in the **Mitte Bar**. For something a little more intimate, the romantic atmosphere of **Sophienclub** might be worth investigating.

There are also a few places where you can waltz and step back in time to experience the ambience of the old dance halls. Among the oldest is **Clärchens Ballhaus**.

GAY AND LESBIAN CLUBS

BERLIN GENERALLY maintains a very tolerant attitude to people with different sexual orientations.

A big day for the gay community is the gigantic parade on Christopher Street Day, which takes place annually at the end of June. On a daily basis, homosexual men and women meet in their own clubs and discos, or during special evenings organized by places normally frequented by heterosexuals.

The city's most popular gay discos are **SchwuZ**, on Mehringdamm, **Connection**, on Fuggerstrasse and **Ostgut**. Gay-only discos are also held regularly in Stellwerk *(see Techno)* and other clubs around town.

For lesbians the best clubs in Berlin are **Ackerkeller** and **So 36**. The latter also admits gay men.

DIRECTORY

MODERN DANCE

Hebbel-Theater
Stresemannstrasse 29.
Map 12 F2.
[25 90 04 27.

Sophiensaele
Sophienstrasse 18.
Map 7 B1. [283 52 66.

Tanzfabrik
Möckernstrasse 68.
Map 12 E4.
[786 58 61.

Theater am Halleschen Ufer
Hallesches Ufer 32.
Map 12 E2, 12 F2.
[251 09 41.

TANGO

Checkpoint
Leipziger Strasse 55.
Map 16 F5.
[20 89 29 95.

Kalkscheune
Johannisstrasse 2.
Map 6 F2.
[59 00 43 40.

Walzerlinks-gestrickt
Am Tempelhofer Berg 7e.
Map 12 F5.
[69 50 50 00.

TECHNO

ColumbiaFritz
Columbiadamm 9–11
(Kreuzberg).

Matrix
Warschauer Platz 18.

Pfefferbank
Schönhauser Allee 176.
[281 83 23.

Tresor
Leipziger Strasse 126a.
Map 6 F5.

DISCOS AND OTHER CLUBS

90 Grad
Dennewitzstrasse 37.
Map 12 D2.
[23 00 59 54.

Akba-Lounge
Sredzkistrasse 64.
[441 14 63.

Clärchens Ballhaus
Auguststrasse 24. **Map** 7
A1, 7 B1. [282 92 95.

Cox Orange
Dircksenstrasse 40.
Map 7 C2.
[281 05 08.

Cueva Buena Vista
Andreasstrasse 66.
[24 08 59 51.

Delicious Doughnuts
Rosenthaler Strasse 9.
Map 7 B1.
[28 09 92 74.

Die Insel
Alt Treptow 6.
[53 60 80 20.

Far Out
Kurfürstendamm 156.
Map 9 A2.
[32 00 07 23.

Golgatha
Dudenstrasse 48–64.
Map 12 D5, 12 E5.
[785 24 53.

Havanna
Hauptstrasse 30. **Map** 11
A5. [784 85 65.

Lumumba Tanzcafé
Steinstrasse 12. **Map** 7
C1. [28 38 54 65

Metropol
Nollendorfplatz 5.
Map 11 A2.
[217 36 80.

Mitte Bar
Oranienburger Strasse 46.
Map 6 F1. [283 38 37.

Privat Club
Markthalle Pücklerstrasse
34. **Map** 14 F2.
[617 55 02.

Sage-Club
Köpenicker Strasse 76–78.
Map 8 D5.
[278 98 30.

Sophienclub
Sophienstrasse 6.
Map 7 B1.
[282 45 52.

Tränenpalast
Reichstagufer 17.
Map 6 D2, 6 F3.
[20 62 00 11.

GAY & LESBIAN DISCOS

Ackerkeller
Ackerstrasse 12 (Mitte).

Connection
Fuggerstrasse 33.
Map 10 F2.
[218 14 32.

Ostgut
Mühlenstrasse 26–30
(Friedrichshain).

SchwuZ
Mehringdamm 61.
Map 12 F4.
[693 70 25.

So 36
Oranienstrasse 190.
Map 14 E2.
[61 40 13 06.

Sport and Recreation

BERLIN IS A sports-loving town, and every year the major sports events attract a growing number of fans and competitors. The Berlin Marathon, run in September, is now the third largest in the world, its 42-km (26-mile) distance tackled by runners and roller-skaters – able-bodied and disabled alike. The Bundesliga (German football league) cup final takes place in May in the Olympia Stadion. Crowds of each team's supporters converge on the city a few days before the game, and after the match they all join a huge party for the winners along the Ku'damm. The world tennis élite battle it out during the German Open championship every April.

CYCLING

THE FLAT TERRAIN, numerous parks and countless special routes for cyclists – which reach a total of 850 km (530 miles) – make Berlin a cycle-friendly city. Outside rush hour you can take your bike on S- or U-Bahn trains, which provide easy access to the three most popular routes – along the Havel river, around the Grunewald forest, and around the Müggelsee.

There are many places all over Berlin where you can rent a bike for €5–12 per day (*see p293*), provided you leave a deposit, either as cash or a cheque. The best hotels in town also hire out their own bikes for guests. The route from the historic centre of Mitte to the Ku'damm via Tiergarten can be an unforgettable experience.

In January those lovers of two wheels meet during Berliner Sechs-Tage-Rennen in the newly built **Velodrom** on Paul-Heyse-Strasse. You might have some problems buying a ticket as the event is very popular, so give them a call beforehand. For information concerning routes, events, tours, or anything else you may need to know about cycling in Berlin, contact the **ADFC (Allgemeiner Deutscher Fahrrad-Club)**.

GOLF

JUST ABOUT EVERY sporting discipline is catered for in Berlin, and golfing is no exception. The Driving Range golf club is situated in the centre of the town on Chausseestrasse, and during spring and summer it is open from noon until sunset. Entrance to the course is free, but you have to leave a deposit on hiring golf clubs. A bucket of 30 balls costs only €1.50. Golf coaching is available either for individuals or in a group.

There are two golf courses within Berlin: the **Golf und Landclub Berlin-Wannsee**, which has a large 18-hole course and a smaller one with 9 holes, and **Berliner Golfclub-Gatow** which only has a 9-hole course. There are a total of 15 golf clubs around Berlin, most of which have excellent restaurants and are situated close to hotels.

SWIMMING POOLS

PUBLIC SWIMMING FACILITIES in Berlin are extremely clean and you can always swim there safely. Some of the best places to try are on the Havel river and the city's lakes. Swimming on natural beaches is free, but there are no changing rooms or toilet facilities.

Berlin also has a number of artificial beaches which are all manned by lifeguards. The best known is the **Strandbad Wannsee**, which was built in the 1920s and remains very popular today. Another excellent spot is the **Strandbad Müggelsee**, which also has an area for nude bathing. The entrance fee to these beaches is similar to that of swimming pools – usually around €3.

One of the most beautiful swimming pool complexes is **Olympia Stadion** (*see p184*) which was a venue for the 1936 Berlin Olympic Games. A special pool for diving has a 10-m (33-ft) tower with a lift. Alternatively, you can simply sunbathe on the steps and admire the view.

The three most beautiful swimming pools are situated in Mitte, Neukölln and Wilmersdorf. **Stadtbad Mitte**, on Gartenstrasse, is a painstakingly restored building which dates from the 1930s. It has a 50-m (164-ft) pool designed for sporting events as well as recreational swimming. **Stadtbad Charlottenburg**, on the other hand, offers a smaller pool which is more appropriate for relaxation than serious swimming; it is also beautifully decorated with Secessionist paintings. But if it's a swim in luxurious surroundings you want, then take a dive at the **Stadtbad Neukölln**; the extraordinary decorative mosaics, frescos, and marble-and-bronze ornamentation is enough to make you forget why you came here in the first place.

A good day out for the whole family can be had at **"blub" Badeparadies**, situated on Buschkrugallee in the southern part of town. More than simply a pool, this is an aquapark with a 120-m (394-ft) long slide, a wave-pool and diving boards, as well as several saunas.

BADMINTON, SQUASH AND TENNIS

YOU WON'T HAVE to travel far in Berlin to find facilities to play badminton, squash or tennis as numerous courts are scattered all over town, from local parks to sophisticated sports centres. It is customary to bring your own sports shoes, but rackets are almost always available to rent.

The entrance fee in most cases includes the use of a sauna. **Fit-Fun Squash und Fitness Center** has 14 courts for squash, and at **Sportoase** there are 18 badminton courts in addition to 8 squash courts. **Tennis & Squash City** offers an opportunity to play tennis on any of its five courts. Other addresses can be found in the telephone directory.

OTHER SPORTS

EVERY WEEKEND in August, John-Foster-Dulles-Allee in Tiergarten is closed to traffic to become a genuine paradise for rollerblade and in-line skaters. If you fancy trying this yourself, there are plenty of shops in the area offering skates and safety equipment at reasonable rates.

If you fancy a boat trip, rowing boats are available for hire at many places along the banks of the lakes. In the Tiergarten you can rent them near Café am Neuen See and around Schlachtensee; the price is usually somewhere around €7–€10 per hour.

FITNESS

THERE ARE ALWAYS new gyms opening and others closing down in Berlin, so your best bet is to check the telephone directory for the most up-to-date listings. At many gyms you can buy a daily card, rather than becoming a member. But if your visit to Berlin is a long one, it may be worth joining. **Ars Vitalis** is the best

independent fitness club and spa for men and women. **Jopp-Frauen-Fitness-Berlin** is one of the best options for women; it has five studios across the city and they are all large and well equipped. The main one is on Tauentzienstrasse and has a pleasant terrace overlooking town. A one-day ticket costs €25.

SPECTATOR SPORTS

AS A RULE, Berlin's sports teams tend to be among the country's best, and rank highly in each of their respective leagues. Football matches of Hertha BSC take place in the Olympia Stadion and tickets are usually available at approximately €6–€18.

Alba Berlin is among the top basketball teams in Germany, and its matches in **Max-Schmeling-Halle** can be attended by up to 8,500 fans. For international events it's best to pre-book tickets well in advance, and these can vary between €10 and €52, depending on the match. Berlin has two very good hockey teams: Berlin-Capitals

and Eisbären Berlin – both of whose matches always sell out of tickets very quickly.

HORSE RACING

LOVERS OF HORSE RACING have two tracks to choose from in Berlin. **Trabrennbahn** in Mariendorf is open all year and the races held here are strictly commercial. **Galopprennbahn Hoppegarten**, on the other hand, has a more approachable feel.

MARATHON

MARATHON RUNNING isn't everyone's cup of tea, but when you see the enormous crowds gathered to run the **Berlin-Marathon** in August, you may well wish you were one of the pack.

The route is one of the fastest in the world, attracting top sponsors and athletes alike; the world record was broken here in 1998. Thousands of viewers gather en route to cheer the runners, rollers and disabled athletes – the latter having their own group which starts before the others.

DIRECTORY

CYCLING

ADFC
Brunnenstrasse 28.
℡ 448 47 24.

Velodrom
Paul-Heyse-Strasse.
℡ 44 30 44 30.

GOLF

Berliner Golfclub-Gatow
Kladower Damm 182–288, Gatow.
℡ 365 53 35.

Golf und Landclub Berlin-Wannsee
Golfweg 22.
℡ 806 70 60.

SWIMMING

"blub" Badeparadies
Buschkrugallee 64.
℡ 609 06 0.

Stadtbad Charlottenburg
Krumme Strasse 9–10.
℡ 34 38 38 65.

Stadtbad Mitte
Gartenstrasse 5.
Plan 7 A1.
℡ 30 88 09 10.

Stadtbad Neukölln
Ganghoferstrasse 3.
℡ 68 24 98 12.

Strandbad Müggelsee
Fürstenwalder Damm 838.
℡ 64 87 777.

Strandbad Wannsee
Wannseebadweg 25.
℡ 80 40 45 55.

BADMINTON, SQUASH, TENNIS

FitFun Squash und Fitness Center
Uhlandstrasse 194.
℡ 312 50 82.

Sportoase
Stromstrasse 11–17.
Plan 4 F1, 4 F2.
℡ 394 50 94.

Tennis & Squash City
Brandenburgische Strasse 53.
Map 9 A3, 9 B5.
℡ 873 90 97.

MARATHON

Berlin-Marathon
Informations Bureau
Waldschulallee 34.
℡ 30 12 88 10.

SPECTATOR SPORTS

Max-Schmeling-Halle
Am Falkplatz.
℡ 44 30 44 30.

FITNESS

Ars Vitalis
Hauptstrasse 19.
Map 11 A5.
℡ 788 35 63.

Jopp-Frauen-Fitness-Berlin
Tauentzienstrasse 13.
Map 10 E1.
℡ 21 01 11
(central switchboard).

HORSE RACING

Galopprennbahn Hoppegarten
Goetheallee 1.
℡ (03342) 389 30.
🕐 4–10pm Sat & Sun.

Trabrennbahn Mariendorf
Mariendorfer Damm 222, Tempelhof.
℡ 740 12 12.
🕐 1pm Sun.

Children in Berlin

WHEN IT COMES to entertainment, people of all ages are catered for in Berlin, and children are no exception. There are numerous shops, theatres and cinemas to keep them occupied, not to mention circuses and zoological gardens. Additionally, there is the Deutsches Technikmuseum

One of Berlin's young roller skaters

(German Museum of Technology), the Museumsdorf Düppel, or the Kinder- und Jugendmuseum, all of which encourage children to take part in the displays. Tickets for children under 14 are almost always reduced, and very young children are often admitted for free. Restaurants often have special areas for toddlers.

The Potsdam train, always a favourite among children

INFORMATION

BERLIN IS VERY welcoming to its younger visitors. Families with children are entitled to public transport discounts, and children can travel free or at a reduced rate, depending on their age. For detailed information on the discounts and opportunities for children, contact **Berlin Tourismus Marketing GmbH**. From this organization you can obtain the so-called Ferienpass, valid for the whole summer, which entitles the holder to all kinds of reductions around town. For girls there is a special pocket diary on offer, called Berta, which has much information and advice about current events.

ZOOLOGICAL GARDENS

ONE OF BERLIN'S zoological gardens can be visited the moment you arrive in town, as it is located opposite the Zoo railway station. The **Zoologischer Garten** offers extensive parkland and many animal enclosures, as well as an excellent aquarium with the biggest collection of aquatic fauna in the world.

The second zoo, **Tierpark Berlin** in Friedrichsfelde, isn't quite so convenient but it is much bigger and can still be reached by U-Bahn. Covering a wide area around Schloss Friedrichsfelde, the Tierpark is the largest park in Europe.

Apart from these zoological gardens, a lot of the parks in Berlin contain mini-zoos where many different kinds of animals can be seen. In a garden behind the Märkisches Museum, for example, you can see a family of bears.

As well as the more exotic animals, however, it is also possible to see the familiar favourites. Small children will love the **Kinderbauernhof Görlitzer Bauernhof**, which has a collection of domestic animals. Here geese, pigs and rabbits run happily around the Görlitzer Park.

MUSEUMS

GENERALLY SPEAKING, Berlin's museums are well set up for children. Perhaps the most entertaining is the **Deutsches Technikmuseum** (see p144) where children can take part in all kinds of experiments. The **Ethnologisches Museum** (see p178) also prepares special exhibitions for children. On some days you can take part in a game with Mexican papier-mâché dolls, on others you can participate in a Japanese ceremonial bath. A visit to the **Museumsdorf Düppel** is an excellent way to show a child the workings of a medieval village. The Museum für Naturkunde (see p109) is another fun place for children, particularly the dinosaur sections and the dioramas of animals in their natural habitats. The **Kindermuseum Labyrinth** is another favourite.

Another great place to visit is the **Puppentheatermuseum**, which is always lively, and offers a chance for children to take part in minor performances. For more information about museum events try to get hold of the brochure Museumpädagogischer Dienst. Exhibitions and events change regularly, but you are bound to find something of interest. The website **Kinder-Berlin** also offers information about children's activities and events.

Children admiring Neptune's Fountain by the Town Hall

A visit to the medieval village at Museumsdorf Düppel

THEATRES

ESTABLISHED IN 1969, **Grips Theater** is probably the most interesting theatre for children and teenagers. Its independent and ambitious programme attracts many spectators and one of its performances, *Linie 1*, was made into a film. Other venues worth trying are the **carrousel-Theater an der Parkaue**, **Theater o.N.**, **Zaubertheater Igor Jedlin** and the **Puppentheater Berlin**. Another option is to go to one of the city's many circuses, all of which prepare their programmes with children in mind.

SPORTS

ICE-SKATING IN WINTER and roller-skating in summer are popular in Berlin, and football and swimming are popular year-round. You can swim in rivers, lakes and swimming pools (Hotline **Berliner Bäderbetriebe** offers useful information) but "blub" Badeparadies *(see p273)* is the best place for children. Each district has its own ice-skating rink, but the **Eisstadion Berlin Wilmersdorf** is outstanding with its 400-m (1,312-ft) run and large ice-hockey rink. **FEZ Wuhlheide** offers a special daily programme for kids.

OTHER ENTERTAINMENT

AN ASCENT OF the Fernsehturm (television tower) at Alexanderplatz *(see p93)* is a great way to treat a child, perhaps for afternoon tea. You will also be able to buy cake and juice in the tower's rotating café. A lift in the Funkturm (radio tower) in the Messegelände *(see p183)* offers an excellent view of the city, from a slightly lower height.

The Story of Berlin is a fun way for both parents and children to experience the history of Berlin in a thrilling multimedia exhibit. And the **Berliner Gruselkabinett** (Room of Fear) is enough to frighten anybody.

For an out-of-the-ordinary experience, you can't go wrong at either the **Zeiss-Planetarium** or the **Planetarium am Insulaner**. A fascinating programme of wonderful shows allows you to explore the known universe and to have a good look at the stars.

DIRECTORY

INFORMATION

Berlin Tourismus Marketing GmbH
Am Karlsbad 11.
25 00 25.
w www.btm.de

Kinder-Berlin
w www.kinder-berlin.de

ZOOLOGICAL GARDENS

Kinderbauernhof a Görlitzer Park
Wiener Strasse 59
611 74 24.

Tierpark Friedrichsfelde
Am Tierpark 125,
Lichtenberg.
51 53 10.

Zoologischer Garten
Hardenbergplatz 9,
Charlottenburg.
25 40 10.

MUSEUMS

Kindermuseum Labyrinth
Osloer Strasse 12.
49 30 89 01.
◐ 2–6pm Mon–Fri, 1–6pm Sat, 11am–6pm Sun.

Museumsdorf Düppel
Clauertstrasse 11.
802 66 71 or 802 33 10.
◐ Apr–Oct: 3–7pm Thu, 10am–5pm Sun and holidays .

Puppentheater-Museum Berlin
Karl-Marx-Strasse 135.
687 81 32.
◐ 9am–4pm Mon–Fri, 11am–5pm Sun.

THEATRES

carrousel-Theater an der Parkaue
Parkaue 29.
55 77 52 52.

Grips Theater
Altonaer Strasse 22.
39 74 74 77.

Puppentheater Berlin
Haubachstrasse 26.
342 19 50.

Theater o.N.
Kollwitzstrasse 53.
440 92 14.

Zaubertheater Igor Jedlin
Roscherstrasse 7.
323 37 77.

SPORTS

Berliner Bäderbetriebe
(01803) 10 20 20.

Eisstadion Berlin Wilmersdorf
Fritz-Wildung-Strasse 9.
824 10 12.

FEZ Wuhlheide
An der Wuhlheide,
Köpenick.
53 07 15 04.

OTHER ENTERTAINMENT

Berliner Gruselkabinett
Schöneberger Strasse 23a.
Map 12 E1.
26 55 55 46.

Planetarium am Insulaner
Munsterdamm 90.
790 09 30.

The Story of Berlin
Kurfürstendamm 207–208.
Map 9 A2.
88 72 01 00.

Zeiss-Groß Planetarium
Prenzlauer Allee 80.
42 18 45 12.

SURVIVAL
GUIDE

PRACTICAL INFORMATION

BERLIN IS A tourist-friendly city, so you shouldn't have too much difficulty getting around. Many Germans speak English and Berliners as a rule are welcoming to newcomers. Cash machines, telephones and parking meters all have clear instructions, and public transport is of the highest standard *(see pp292–3)*. For reduced fares on public transport, buy

Berlin tourist information sign

yourself a daily or weekly travel card, or a Welcome Card which also gives you reduced access to many museums. There are plenty of information centres in the busiest areas of town, and a number of different listings magazines and brochures are available for tourists. If you have access to the Internet, BerlinOnline will point you in the right direction.

Entrance tickets for some of Berlin's historic buildings

MUSEUMS AND HISTORIC BUILDINGS

THERE ARE OVER 150 museums and galleries in Berlin, but exhibitions change and collections move continually. This guide covers the most important places, but plenty of information is also available on lesser-known museums and galleries. A tourist information office could be your first port of call, but better still is the museum information centre itself, run by **Museumpädagogischer Dienst Berlin**. Details of current and forthcoming exhibitions can be picked up here, including

information on seasonal events, like the bi-annual Lange Nacht der Museen, when museums stay open until midnight. A good information line is the **Info-Telefon der Staatlichen Museen zu Berlin** and there are also information centres devoted to the Pergamonmuseum and the Sanssouci complex in Potsdam. Contact the **Besucherbetreuung der Schlösser und Gärten Potsdam-Sanssouci** for more details.

Museums and historic buildings are usually open Tuesday to Sunday, from 10am to 5pm (sometimes 6pm). Some museums, however, close on another day instead of Mondays. For reduced entrance prices, you may want to get hold of the Museums-Pass, which allows three days' unlimited access to the major museums. This pass is sold in the **Europa-Center** and **Brandenburg Gate** information centres. It can be used at all the national museums, including the whole Museum

Island complex, the Kulturforum, Museumszentrum Dahlem and four additional institutions in Charlottenburg (Ägyptisches Museum, Galerie der Romantik, Sammlung Berggruen, Museum für Vor- und Frühgeschichte). In this case, the Museums-Pass is like a one-day ticket, allowing you to visit all the sites in the same complex.

Another option is the Welcome Card. This entitles you to free public transport for three days within Berlin and Potsdam, and a discount on many museums. Each Welcome Card is valid for one adult and up to three children.

OPENING HOURS

OFFICES IN BERLIN usually open from 9am until 6pm, with an hour's lunch break, but many people in the east of the city still work to the old timetable of 8am till 4 or 5pm. Smaller shops open from 9:30 or 10am until 8pm, and on Saturdays most shops close at 4pm. The majority of shops are also open on Sundays in the period leading up to Christmas, and opening hours are extended during the week. Bank hours are 9am until 3pm (Monday and Wednesday), 6pm (Tuesday and Thursday) and 1pm (Friday).

TOURIST INFORMATION

THERE ARE MANY excellent tourist information centres in Berlin. The two biggest are at the **Europa-Center** and the **Brandenburg Gate**, but others can be found at **Tegel Airport**, in the KaDeWe department store

A modern rickshaw providing alternative transport on Berlin's streets

(see p155) and in a new information café on the ground floor of the TV tower in Alexanderplatz. The **Potsdam Information** office is in the centre of Potsdam, on Friedrich-Ebert-Strasse.

For up-to-the-minute news, turn to the Internet; **Berlin-Online**, which is managed by **Berlin Tourismus Marketing** is a very reliable source of information for tourists.

ENTERTAINMENT

THE THREE BEST magazines devoted to cultural events are *Zitty*, *Tip* and *Berlin-Programm*, all of which cover the major (as well as minor) concerts, exhibitions and lectures held throughout Berlin. The very latest news can also be obtained from tourist information centres and the Internet, the most popular site being Berlin-Online. There are many ticket offices all over town where you can pre-book tickets (see p261), some of them offering excellent bargain deals. On-the-day tickets can often be bought at half price.

Popular listings magazines

Guided bus tour offering an overview of Berlin and its environs

GUIDED TOURS

THERE ARE MANY bus tours available in Berlin, each of which, in 3 or 4 hours, introduces you to the city's chief historic buildings. A single ticket usually allows you to get off at any stage and rejoin the tour at different stops. However, if you want to save some money, the public transport bus No. 100 follows a similar route (see p295). If you would rather go on foot, walking tours are also possible – these provide a more intimate tour of the city, stopping at all the major landmarks and museums. Organized trips to buildings just nearing completion can also be arranged. For information on these and other tours, visit the red Info-Box, currently on the corner of Leipziger and Postdamer Platz. If you are in Potsdam you can ride a train around town, starting outside the Kutscherhaus Inn in Sanssouci.

DISABLED VISITORS

NOT ALL OF BERLIN'S streets and shops have been altered to cater for the disabled, but the majority of theatres and galleries do have the required facilities. Detailed information can be obtained from the **Informations-und Beratungsgruppe für Behinderte** on Landesamt für Zentrale Soziale Aufgaben. Two other organizations to turn to are the **Berliner Behindertenverband** and **Deutscher Service-Ring**. Give them a call if you want to hire a wheelchair, a special bus, or someone to help you for the day.

(see p155), (see p261), (see p295)

DIRECTORY

MUSEUM INFORMATION

Besucherbetreuung der Schlösser und Gärten Potsdam-Sanssouci
(0331) 969 42 02.

Info-Telefon der Staatlichen Museen zu Berlin
20 90 55 55.

Museumpädagogischer Dienst Berlin
28 39 74 44.

TOURIST INFORMATION

Berlin Tourismus Marketing
Am Karlsbad 11.
(0190) 01 63 16 (24-hour).
FAX 25 00 24 24.
W www.berlin.de and www.btm.de

BerlinOnline
W www.berlinonline.de

Brandenburg Gate
Pariser Platz. **Map** 6 E3, 15 A3.
9:30am–6pm.

Europa-Center
Entrance from Budapester Strasse.
Map 10 E1. 8:30am–8:30pm Mon–Sat, 10am–6:30pm Sun.

Info Café at Fernsehturm
Alexanderplatz.
Map 7 C2. 10am–6pm daily.

Potsdam Information
Friedrich-Ebert-Strasse 5.
(0331) 27 55 80.
FAX (0331) 275 58 29.

Tegel Airport
Main hall. 5am–10:30pm.

DISABLED VISITORS

Berliner Behindertenverband
Jägerstrasse 63d. 204 38 47.

Behinderten-beauftragter des Landes Berlin
Oranienstrasse 106.
90 28 29 17.

Deutscher Service-Ring e.V
859 40 10.

Additional Information

A typical kiosk selling newspapers, drinks and cigarettes

VISAS AND CUSTOMS

A VALID PASSPORT IS necessary for all visitors to Germany. Visas are not required for citizens of EU countries. A list, available from all German embassies, specifies other countries whose nationals do not need a visa for visits of less than 90 days. Non-EU citizens wishing to stay in Germany for longer than three months will need a special visa, available from German consulates. These need to be obtained in advance. All visitors should however check requirements before travelling.

On arrival in Germany, you will not be charged duty on personal articles. As in other European countries, no drugs or weapons may be brought across the border. The amount of cigarettes and alcohol allowed in or out of the country is restricted. Adults resident outside the EU can bring up to 200 cigarettes (50 cigars, or 250g of tobacco), and one litre of spirits (or two litres of wine).

VAT REFUND

I F YOU BUY non-edible goods in Berlin you are entitled to a VAT refund *(Mehrwertsteuer)*, unless you are a citizen of another EU country. Individual shops differ on the minimum taxable amount, but it is usually somewhere around €50. If you enter a shop with a Tax-Free sign outside, ask for a special form or Tax-Free cheque (you will need to present your passport). This form must be stamped when you go through Customs – but do be prepared to show your goods, which must still be in their original packing (you won't be able to claim a refund on anything that has been opened or which has been used). The tax is refunded either at the border or sent to the address on the envelope containing the cheque. Make sure you leave the right details with Customs staff – chasing old claims is a time-consuming and often fruitless task.

Antique pump

A Welcome Card with a small information brochure

B EFORE YOU ARRIVE in Berlin it is worth getting hold of an ISIC card (or International Student Identity Card). This entitles you to a 50 per cent reduction in some museums, and to occasional discounts on theatre, plane and rail tickets. For similar reasons you might want to have a GO25 or EURO<26 card, both of which entitle you to a variety of reductions. These cards are only valid in Europe, but can earn you up to 300,000 different discounts.

A selection of Berlin's most popular daily newspapers

NEWSPAPERS

N EWSPAPERS CAN BE bought in shops all over Berlin, but mostly they are sold by the city's numerous street vendors. In the evenings you will also find them on sale in bars and cafés. The most popular titles are the *Berliner Zeitung, Der Tagesspiegel*, the *Berliner Morgenpost* and *BZ*. Foreign language papers can be found all over the city, especially at airport and railway kiosks. Some of the major department stores also sell newspapers and magazines. A whole range of English-language books and newspapers is available at the British Bookshop at Mauerstrasse No. 83–4 in Mitte.

Theatre ticket office and an old-fashioned post with posters

TELEVISION AND RADIO

YOU MAY find yourself spoiled for choice when it comes to television channels in Germany. Apart from the national ARD and ZDF there are many regional and private channels (Berlin has its own, alongside RTL, RTL2, SAT1 and PRO7). You can also pick up special interest channels, like DSF for sport and VIVA or MTV for music. In addition to these there is even an option for Turkish programmes in Berlin, and thanks to cable and satellite television you can easily tune into foreign programmes in English, American, French and many other languages. In hotels the channels mainly cover the news, music and sport. For radio news in English, you can tune into Info-Radio (93.1 MHz), the BBC World Service (90.2 MHz), or the very popular SFB4 Multi-Kulti (106.8 MHz), which transmits in a number of different languages.

TIME

GERMANY IS IN the Central-European time zone, which means that Berlin is one hour ahead of Greenwich Mean Time; six hours ahead of US Eastern Standard Time, and 11 hours behind Australian Eastern Standard Time.

ELECTRICAL EQUIPMENT

MOST ELECTRICAL sockets carry 220V, although in bathrooms the voltage may be slightly lower for safety reasons. Plugs are all of the standard continental type, with two round pins. A European travel adaptor (buy it before you leave home), will allow you to use electric appliances.

EMBASSIES AND CONSULATES

UNTIL THE UNIFICATION of Germany, many countries had an Embassy in Eastern Berlin and a Consulate in the West. Currently, because of the government's move from Bonn to Berlin, many countries have employed top architects to build luxurious embassies in the central part of the town; as a result, the addresses listed here are liable to change. If you are in any doubt, check at a tourist information point or in the telephone directory.

PUBLIC CONVENIENCES

THERE ARE PLENTY of public toilets in Berlin, but you can also use the facilities in museums, stores and cafés. In some places the convenience comes with a charge, usually around 25 cents. Men's toilets are marked by the word *"Herren"* or a triangle with the vertex pointing downwards; ladies', by the word *"Damen"* or *"Frauen"*, or a triangle with its vertex pointing upwards.

A refurbished antique public convenience in Kreuzberg

Security and Health

Berlin police insignia

GONE ARE THE DAYS when demonstrations were held against the influx of foreign nationals, for Berlin is now a broadly cosmopolitan city. Nevertheless, as with all major European destinations, you should always be careful with your wallet, particularly on public transport during rush hours. If you do run into trouble, or simply need advice, you can always get help from the police. For minor health problems, which don't require a doctor, advice from a competent pharmacist is often sufficient.

Policeman   Policewoman

PERSONAL PROPERTY

UNFORTUNATELY, TOURISTS are more frequently targeted by thieves than any other group, which is why all valuables should be kept in a hotel safe. Major robberies are rare in Berlin, but pick-pockets are active, particularly on the U-Bahn. If you are travelling by car, don't leave photographic equipment or luggage in open view, and try to use a parking lot or hotel garage when possible. Zoo railway station is notorious for its drug pushers, so be careful there late at night. Like most big cities, few of the S- and U-Bahn stations are pleasant after dark, but these are often patrolled by guards – if you need assistance, don't hesitate to turn to them. There are also panic buttons installed on each platform, to be used in the event of emergency.

Before you set off for Berlin, it is advisable to buy insurance, and, if you are unlucky enough to be the victim of street crime, you must report it to the police straight away. Remember to obtain a statement confirming what was stolen – you will need this when it comes to making your insurance claim.

If you spot a fire, phone the **Fire Brigade**, or *Feuerwehr*, or use one of the bright-red public fire alarms placed strategically around Berlin.

LOST PROPERTY

THERE IS ONE central bureau for lost property in Berlin (the **Zentrales Fundbüro**), and this is where anything left in public is deposited. It is worth noting, however, that the BVG (Berliner Verkehrs-Betriebe) has its own office (the **Fundbüro der BVG**) for items left on buses or trams or in the U-Bahn. Some items left on S-Bahn trains may also be sent to the new **Zentrales Fundbüro der Deutschen Bahn AG** in Wuppertal.

WOMEN TRAVELLING ON THEIR OWN

IN BERLIN IT IS quite normal for women to go to theatres, bars and restaurants on their own. You won't find yourself in danger during the day, but some basic precautions should be taken late at night, when it is preferable to avoid empty platforms or S-Bahn and U-Bahn trains. Night buses are a much safer option, and if something should go wrong the driver can always call the **police** with his radio. The safest, and

A public fire alarm

Police boats patrolling the water 24-hours a day

An independent chemist in Berlin's city centre

most expensive, way to travel is by taxi. If you are determined to walk alone in a park or in one of the quieter districts, is is best to do so during daylight hours only. For all kinds of advice there is a **Confidential Help-Line for Women**.

MEDICAL CARE AND INSURANCE

Citizens of the EU do not have to buy special insurance to cover emergency treatment, but non-EU visitors should do so. In case of sudden illness you can call an **ambulance**, but if the state of the patient allows, then drive them to the nearest Emergency Room. If the complaint is minor, a chemist should be able to help. Chemists, such as **Bären-Apotheke**, usually keep the same hours as other shops, but there are always a few places open overnight. There is a special telephone line offering **Information about Chemists**. Other telephone helplines include a **Narcotics Emergencies** service and a **Confidential**

Symbol for *Apotheke* (pharmacy)

Help-Line for Spiritual and Religious Support. There is also the English-speaking **Helpline International**. Another option is to contact your embassy which should be able to inform you which doctors are able to speak your language.

German police van, a common sight around the city

Rettungswagen or ambulance bearing the red cross

DIRECTORY

EMERGENCY SERVICES

Fire Brigade and Ambulance
☎ 112.

Police
☎ 110.

DRK-Rettungsdienst (German Red Cross)
☎ 85 00 55.

Ambulance
☎ 31 00 31.

Narcotics Emergencies
☎ 192 37.

Confidential Help-Line for Women
☎ 615 42 43.

Confidential Help-Line for Religious Support (Telefon-Seelsorge)
☎ (0800) 111 02 22 (Catholic) or (0800) 111 0 111 (Protestant).

Helpline International
☎ 44 01 06 07.
◷ 6pm–midnight daily.

CHEMISTS

Information about Chemists
☎ 11 880.

Bären-Apotheke
☎ 40 91 11 12.

LOST PROPERTY

Zentrales Fundbüro
Platz der Luftbrücke 6.
☎ 69 93 64 44.

Fundbüro der BVG
Potsdamer Strasse 180–82.
☎ 25 62 30 40.

Zentrales Fundbüro der Deutschen Bahn AG
Döppersberg 37, 42103 Wuppertal. ☎ (0180) 599 05 99.

Banking and Local Currency

Reise Bank

Logo of ReiseBank

ONLY A FEW years ago, some credit cards, like VISA, were far less popular in Germany than they were in other countries, but recently things have started to change. Now, on the whole, tourists have few problems using credit cards. There are plenty of cash machines available, as well as numerous banks and Bureaux de Change for exchanging foreign currencies.

CHANGING MONEY

THERE ARE NO restrictions on the amount of cash you can bring into Germany, but most visitors use travellers' cheques or debit cards for safety.

Cash can be exchanged at banks and Bureaux de Change (*Wechselstuben*). The major banks, such as **Berliner Bank** and **ReiseBank**, usually have similar rates of exchange, but some charge a commission; be sure to ask how much before commencing your transaction. Banks have limited office hours, so try to get to one immediately on arrival at the airport or station.

Bureaux de Change are often located close to railway stations and other places frequented by tourists. **Thomas Cook Foreign Exchange** and **American Express** are among the best known places for exchanging travellers' cheques. Other Bureaux de Change can be found near the Bahnhof Zoo railway station on Joachimstaler Strasse, between Hardenbergstrasse and Kurfürstendamm.

You can also exchange cash at hotel reception desks, but this should be a last resort as their rates tend to be poor.

A typical cash machine

TRAVELLERS' CHEQUES

TRAVELLERS' CHEQUES are a secure method of carrying money, with the advantage that you can change as much or as little as you need. Keep your receipts separate from the cheques themselves for added security. It may be convenient to carry cheques denominated in euros.

At many of the larger hotels you can pay for your room with travellers' cheques. For most other purchases, however, it is easier to use cash.

DEBIT AND CREDIT CARDS

CREDIT CARDS can be used in most larger hotels, shops and restaurants. A sign on the door should tell you which are accepted - **American Express, VISA, MasterCard** and **Diners Club** are most frequently used. Some cafés and restaurants require a minimum purchase to use a credit card. If you are only ordering a snack, check that you have some cash in case your card is not accepted.

DIRECTORY

BANKS AND BUREAUX DE CHANGE

American Express
Bayreuther Strasse 37.
(214 98 30.

American Express
Friedrichstrasse 172.
(20 17 400.

Berliner Bank
Kurt-Schuhmacher-Platz.
(417 78 10.
🕐 9am–5pm Mon, Wed, Fri,
9am–6pm Tue–Thu.

ReiseBank
Bahnhof Zoo.
(881 71 17.
🕐 7:30am–10pm daily.

ReiseBank
Ostbahnhof, Friedrichshain.
(296 43 93 or 426 70 29.
🕐 7am–10pm Mon–Fri,
8am–8pm Sat & Sun.

Thomas Cook Foreign Exchange
Friedrichstrasse 56.
(20 16 59 16.

LOST CARDS AND CHEQUES

American Express
((069) 97 97 10 00.

Diners Club
((05921) 86 12 34.

MasterCard
((069) 74 09 87.

VISA
((0800) 814 91 00.

One of the city's many Bureaux de Change

THE EURO

THE DEUTSCHMARK (German mark) was the sole German currency until the end of 2001. But on 1 January 2002 the euro (the common currency of the European Union) was introduced into general circulation. Before this, it was already quoted in non-cash transactions. A transition period allowed the euro and the Deutschmark to be used simultaneously, but the Deutschmark (both notes and coins) was finally phased out by mid-2002. Now only the euro is accepted in Germany.

The euro was issued in 11 European Union countries in addition to Germany: Austria, Belgium, Finland, France, Greece, Holland, Ireland, Italy, Luxembourg, Portugal and Spain.

Bank Notes
Euro bank notes have seven denominations. The 5-euro note (grey in colour) is the smallest, followed by the 10-euro note (pink), 20-euro note (blue), 50-euro note (orange), 100-euro note (green), 200-euro note (yellow) and 500-euro note (purple). All notes show the 12 stars of the European Union.

5 euros

10 euros

20 euros

50 euros

100 euros

200 euros

500 euros

2 euros

1 euro

50 cents

20 cents

10 cents

5 cents

2 cents

1 cent

Coins
The euro has eight coin denominations: 2 euros and 1 euro; 50 cents, 20 cents, 10 cents, 5 cents, 2 cents and 1 cent. The 2- and 1-euro coins are both silver and gold in colour. The 50-, 20- and 10-cent coins are gold. The 5-, 2- and 1-cent coins are bronze.

Communications

Logo for Deutsche Telekom

THE POSTAL AND telecommunications services in Germany are both very efficient. You may have to wait a minute or two at the post office, but letters addressed within the country are usually delivered within 24 hours. Making a telephone call certainly shouldn't be difficult: public telephones stand on just about every street corner, and many restaurants and cafés have phone booths of their own. U-Bahn and S-Bahn stations always have a telephone or two, and often a mailbox to post your letters.

A typical Deutsche Telekom public telephone booth in Berlin

USING THE TELEPHONE

THERE ARE VARIOUS types of public phone booths in Berlin, all of which are owned by Deutsche Telekom. The oldest is the coin-operated telephone. If you make a call that costs less than the amount of coins inserted, then the telephone will retain only those coins required to cover the cost of the call and will return the rest.

Telephone cards are far more convenient to use, and these are sold at all post offices. When using a card-operated telephone, your credits are displayed on a panel beside the receiver, so you should have plenty of warning before your card runs out and you need to buy a new one.

There are also some public phones which accept credit cards. Most of these are in the busy centre of town. As with a phone card, all you have to do is place your credit card in the phone, which will then ask you for your PIN (personal identification number).

Many public phones have their own numbers and accept incoming calls, so you can be called back if your card or money runs out. Every public phone should also have a set of phone directories.

Charges depend on the type of call (local or international) and the time of day. Early mornings, evenings and weekends have the cheapest rates.

If you are staying in a hotel, making telephone calls from your room is usually the least economical option.

USING A COIN TELEPHONE

1 Lift the receiver and wait for the dial tone.

2 Insert coins into the slot.

3 Dial number and wait to be connected.

4 Add another coin when requested to do so.

5 When you have finished your call, replace the receiver and press the button above the slot to collect any unused coins.

USING A CARD TELEPHONE

1 Lift the receiver and wait for the dial tone.

2 Choose an appropriate language.

3 Insert your card and the display will show your balance.

4 Dial number and wait to be connected.

5 When you have finished, replace the receiver, press the green button and remove your card.

One of many telephone cards available, complete with instructions

Entrance to a post office (Deutsche Post) in the centre of Berlin

THE INTERNET AND E-MAIL

THE INTERNET AND e-mail have become increasingly popular and are especially useful for people who are abroad on holiday or business. As a result, many hotels now offer guests access to these facilities. Internet cafés can be found in most towns and cities, while computers can often be hired by the hour in commercial centres.

POSTAL SERVICES

GERMAN POST OFFICES are difficult to miss with their distinctive yellow Deutsche Post signs. Mailboxes, too, are an eye-catching yellow.

As in other European countries, you can send registered letters, parcels, telegrams and money orders from the post office. In addition to stamps, a number of products are sold here, too, including telephone cards and the usual variety of postal stationery. Local postcards are also available, as are limited-edition German stamps.

SENDING A LETTER

STAMPS FOR LETTERS and cards can be bought at the post office, but sometimes they are sold together with cards, and there are also special stamp machines around town. When posting a letter, always check the signs on the mailbox. Some boxes are divided, with one side accepting only mail for within Berlin, and the other accepting everything else.

POST OFFICES

POST OFFICES IN Berlin usually open from 8am until 6pm weekdays, and until noon on Saturdays. Those with extended hours, including Sundays, are at the airports

MAIN POST OFFICES

Joachimstaler Strasse 7
◻ 8am–midnight Mon–Sat,
10am–10pm Sun.

Flughafen Tegel
◻ 8am–6pm Mon–Fri,
8am–1pm Sat.

Bahnhof Friedrichstrasse
◻ 6am–10pm Mon–Fri,
8am–10pm Sat & Sun.

and major railway stations, such as **Flughafen Tegel** and **Bahnhof Friedrichstrasse**. Poste restante letters can be collected from **Joachimstaler Strasse** post office, which is open daily until midnight.

A rare antique mailbox, predating the contemporary yellow boxes

Operating instructions

Buttons for different kinds of stamp

Slot for collecting stamps

Street vending machine for buying postage stamps as well as telephone cards

Information about collection times

Slot for local letters

Slot for other letters

Typical Berlin-style mailbox found on street corners

IMPORTANT NUMBERS

- Germany country code 49.
- Berlin area code 030.
- Potsdam area code 0331.
- National directory inquiries 11 8 33.
- International directory inquiries 11 8 34.
- Operator 1 11 41.
- Police 110.

- To make an international call, dial 00 followed by the country code, area code and number, omitting the initial 0. Country codes: UK 44; Eire 353; Canada and US 1; Australia 61; South Africa 27; New Zealand 64.

GETTING TO BERLIN

BERLIN LIES at the heart of Europe and has excellent rail and air links with the rest of the continent. Its three airports receive regular flights from major European cities as well as North America, the Middle East and southeast Asia. Likewise Lufthansa, the German national carrier, offers flights to destinations around the world. The railway network is as good as

A Lufthansa aeroplane

anywhere in Europe, and takes you right to the centre of Berlin. One of the cheapest ways to travel to the city is by international coach, although this is usually the slowest form of transport. If you are travelling by car, the *Autobahn* (motorway) leads to the Berliner Ring (Berlin Circular Road), from where a number of exits are signposted to the city centre.

Airport information signs, directing passengers to various services

ARRIVING BY AIR

ALTHOUGH BERLIN receives numerous flights from destinations in Europe, Asia and North America, Frankfurt is still Germany's chief intercontinental airport. However, expansion at Schönefeld, formerly East Berlin's airport, may change this, and low-cost carrier **Ryanair** has started a service three times daily to Schönefeld from London Stansted. For the time being, however, Tegel Airport is still Berlin's busiest terminal. The most frequent flights are by **Lufthansa** and **British Airways**, but the airport is also used by many other carriers, offering flight connections from all over Europe and beyond. From North America, Lufthansa flies

non-stop to Tegel from Washington DC. **Air Berlin** flies twice daily from London Stansted to Tegel, and Lufthansa also has flights from London's City Airport to Tempelhof, Berlin's third, and most central, airport.

TICKETS AND FARES

WHEN PLANNING your trip to Berlin, it is always worth shopping around for a ticket as prices can vary enormously. Some of the best deals are offered by inclusive tour operators; see your local press or travel agent for details. Air fares are usually cheaper when booked well in advance, and discounts are available for children and students. Low-cost airlines, such as Ryanair, can only be booked via the Internet. It is also worth checking other airlines' websites; a useful source of up-to-date information on schedules and fares to Berlin can be found at www.opodo.com which is a site operated by a consortium of European airlines including Lufthansa.

Destinations listings on the departures board

If you are willing to travel at short notice, you can occasionally find a last-minute bargain.

TEGEL AIRPORT

TEGEL AIRPORT is located conveniently within Berlin, only 5 miles (8 km) from the city centre. It has one terminal, designed for maximum convenience. In the main hall you can find an information point, a bank with Bureau de Change and a post office, as well as a number of shops for gifts, souvenirs and newspapers.

The city centre can be reached easily by bus or taxi, both of which stop in front of the main hall. Bus No. 109 stops at Bahnhof Zoologischer

Tegel Airport, the main international airport serving Berlin

The busy main hall at Tegel Airport

Garten and several other places in the centre before terminating at Budapester Strasse. Bus No. 128 links the airport with U-Bahn Kurt-Schumacher-Platz, while No. X9 takes you to Kurfürstendamm. TXL buses are a little more expensive, but they take you quickly to Unter den Linden. A journey by bus from the airport to the centre of Berlin usually takes between 25 and 30 minutes.

Taxi ranks are located in front of the lower exit leading from the arrivals hall and on the inner square at the back of the main hall. A taxi from the airport to the city centre is not very expensive; the journey to Bahnhof Zoologischer Garten costs around €12–15 and takes about 15 minutes.

SCHÖNEFELD AIRPORT

LOCATED ABOUT 12 miles (20 km) south of the city centre, Schönefeld Airport

used to be the main airport of East Berlin. Bus No. 171 can take you from the airport to Flughafen Berlin Schönefeld railway station, from where you can catch the S-Bahn 9 or S-Bahn 45 train (or any of the long-distance trains which stop here) straight to the city centre. Another option is to take bus No. 171 to Rudow U-Bahn station. A taxi ride from Schönefeld to the centre of Berlin is quite expensive.

TEMPELHOF AIRPORT

THE OLDEST AIRPORT in Berlin, Tempelhof is also the least busy of the three. It is located close to the city centre, at the border of Kreuzberg and Tempelhof. The easiest way to get from Tempelhof Airport to the centre of Berlin is by U-Bahn train from Platz der Luftbrücke station. Otherwise, bus No. 119 will take you to Kurfürstendamm.

DIRECTORY

AIRPORTS

Tegel Airport
[(01805) 00 01 86.

Schönefeld Airport
[(01805) 00 01 86.

AIRLINES

Air Berlin
Saatwinkler Damm 42. [(01801) 73 78 00. W www.airberlin.com

British Airways
Budapesterstrasse 18b. [(01805) 26 65 22. W www.ba.com

Lufthansa
Kurfürstendamm 21. [(01803) 80 38 03. W www.lufthansa.com

Ryanair
W www.ryanair.com

Airport check-in counter for First-Class passengers

TEGEL AIRPORT

Tegel Airport is relatively small and easy to use. A series of circular corridors leads to the departure gates. Shops and other services are situated in the main hall on two levels.

Parking at ground level

AIRPORT

☐	Arrivals
☐	Departures
☐	Main hall
☐	Round corridor
🚗	Taxi
🚌	Bus stop
🍴	Restaurant

Leaflets offering special deals on international train travel

TRAVELLING BY TRAIN

THE STANDARDS of European public transport are generally very high, particularly in central Europe, so whichever rail link you take to Berlin your journey is bound to be comfortable. The city has excellent connections with most major German and European cities. There are direct services between Berlin and Zürich, Brussels, Prague, Amsterdam, Paris, and Warsaw. Besides these lines, there are many convenient international routes to choose from, via other German cities.

If you are thinking of staying in Germany for quite a while, and are keen to travel around a lot by train, one of the cheapest options is an InterRail card. This can be bought by persons of any age, from any European country, Morocco or Turkey, and gives the traveller unlimited access to rail transport in a selection of European countries. North American visitors can enquire into Eurail cards, available through travel agents. The prices differ depending on your age and the number of countries you want to visit; the younger the visitor, and the more limited number of countries you wish to visit, the cheaper the card.

At various times of the year, but especially in summer, there are often special deals offering discounted travel. Among these are weekend tickets and family tickets. It pays to visit the information desk and ask about the different fares currently on offer.

What promises to be the biggest railway station in Berlin is currently under construction near the Lehrter Bahnhof S-Bahn station, but for the time being the majority of Germany's long-distance trains arrive at **Bahnhof Zoo** (Zoo station) – a small-scale station in which it is impossible to get lost. The trains stop at platforms from which you descend to reach the main hall. This hall contains a small shopping precinct with a restaurant, a left-luggage office, a bank *(see p284)*, a hotel reservation point and a car rental kiosk.

Logo of Deutsche Bahn (German Railways)

Deutsche Bahn railway workers wearing the distinctive uniform

One downside to the station is the number of drug pushers, pickpockets and other strange characters who tend to hang around. Police patrols make sure that the area is safe for travellers, but be careful here, particularly late at night.

Bahnhof Zoo is situated in the centre of old West Berlin and has excellent connections with the other districts via five U-Bahn and three S-Bahn lines. There is also a taxi rank located outside the station and a number of bus stops, for both day and night buses.

The best place to obtain information about public transport is the BVG pavilion on Hardenbergplatz *(see p295)*. You can also buy tickets from the pavilion.

Some trains coming from destinations in the south or east arrive in **Ostbahnhof** (the former Hauptbahnhof), a convenient station where you can easily exchange money, send mail and use the tourist information office. Ostbahnhof is linked to other districts in Berlin via S-Bahn.

Some international trains arriving in Berlin from the east terminate at **Bahnhof Berlin Lichtenberg**, but from there you can get to the Alexanderplatz or Bahnhof Zoo by S-Bahn lines S5, S7 or S75 or U-Bahn line U5.

Always remember that the ticket for your journey to Berlin is also valid on all S-Bahn connections to other stations, providing you use it immediately upon arrival. For details of train times and destinations telephone the **Railway Information** line.

Main hall of Zoo railway station (Bahnhof Zoo)

COACH TRAVEL

WHEREVER YOU CAN travel by train, the chances are you can also travel by coach, and Germany is no exception. On international routes, the fast network of *Autobahnen* (motorways) enables coaches to nearly match the speed of the trains. Some try to raise the level of comfort by showing videos and serving light refreshments; but coaches generally are less roomy and less comfortable than trains. It often a question of cost. Coach (bus) travel is nearly always cheaper than rail travel.

After you have visited Berlin, you may decide to take a coach trip to another German city or further afield. If so, the place to go is the **Zentral-Omnibus-Bahnhof**, situated near the Funkturm between Masurenallee and Messedamm. This is the city's largest long-distance bus station, and you will find connections to towns all over Germany, as well as links to other major European cities. Some coach companies, on overnight journeys, offer more comfortable sleeper seats for a small extra charge.

Information signs for passengers at a railway station

TRAVELLING BY CAR

BERLIN is surrounded by a circular *Autobahn* or motorway (the Berliner Ring), which is linked to *Autobahnen* leading to Dresden, Nürnberg, Munich, Hannover, Hamburg and beyond. Numerous exits from the ring road are signposted into the city centre, but the road is so long that it is sometimes quicker to cut through town to get to wherever you're going (although not during rush hour).

While driving around the city, keep an eye on your speed; the police are extremely vigilant at doing speed checks. Less experienced drivers may feel a little uneasy on the *Autobahn* (motorway) as German drivers tend to zoom along at speeds reaching 125 mph (200 km/h). Keep to the right, unless you are overtaking. Always remember to check your side- and rearview mirrors before switching to a left-hand lane. If you want to overtake, make sure there's nobody coming up behind. The speed at which fast cars come up behind you can be surprising. On some stretches of the *Autobahn* speed limits are imposed depending on weather and road conditions.

Driving licences from all European countries are valid in Germany. Visitors from other countries need an international licence. You must also carry your passport and the standard documentation (including insurance certificate or "green card") if driving your own car. To rent a car you will need a credit card. There are several places to rent vehicles around the city, including the major train stations and airports *(see p293)*.

As in most countries, German law is tough on drinking and driving. In the event of an accident, or being pulled over by the police, you may find yourself in serious trouble if alcohol is found in your bloodstream. It is better not to take the risk in the first place, and abstain from drinking.

Typical road signs indicating the *Autobahn* and sights within Berlin

DIRECTORY

USEFUL NUMBERS

Bahnhof Zoo
Hardenbergplatz.
Map 4 E5.
29 70.

Ostbahnhof
Strasse der Pariser Kommune.
29 70.

Bahnhof Berlin Lichtenberg
Travel Office, Weitlingstrasse 22.
29 70.

Railway Information
(01805) 996 633 (24 hours).

Zentral-Omnibus-Bahnhof
Am Funkturm,
Masurenallee 4–6.
Map 1 C5.
301 03 80.

One of the many express coaches available in Berlin

The engine of an ICE (Inter-City Express) train

GETTING AROUND BERLIN

Taxi rank sign

BERLIN ISN'T the easiest of cities to move around in, largely because of the endless work being done to the roads. Building sites are scattered all over the city, and the number of parking spaces is still inadequate, so congestion is bad and driving should be avoided if possible. The centre of town (Mitte) can easily be seen on foot, but more peripheral areas should be reached by public transport. The U- and S-Bahn are by far the quickest way to travel, but the buses are very reliable – and if you happen to get a double-decker, they are excellent for sightseeing. Cyclists are exremely well catered for, so you may well want to hire a bike; there are many cycling routes around the city and further afield.

Lights at a pedestrian crossing

BERLIN ON FOOT

GERMAN DRIVERS are generally careful and watch out for pedestrians, but it always pays to be vigilant. Cyclists travelling at speed can be dangerous as many cycle routes run along the pavements (sidewalks), only marked by a line

or by a different colour. You may not be aware of a cyclist coming up behind you, so be warned; you can easily be hit, or at least scolded for being in the wrong lane.

When walking in Berlin one thing worth remembering is that street numbers sometimes increase along one side of the street and then "turn round" at the end and continue on the other side. Usually, for example along Unter den Linden, the numbers increase equally on both sides, with odd and even numbers separated. If you are looking for a particular address, always make a note of where the street ends – although finding the right house is also made much easier by the street signs on every corner. These include the name of the street, as well as the numbers within that particular block.

Disabled tourists should get in contact with **Telebus-Zentrale** for transport details.

DRIVING

ALTHOUGH CONGESTION is often quite bad in the centre of town, driving around Berlin is not as difficult as it is in some European capitals, for the town doesn't have a typical old centre with narrow, winding streets. You can drive to Unter den Linden and Museum Island along the wide boulevards with few delays.

Local drivers are usually very careful and don't break speed limits or enter junctions on yellow lights; you are legally allowed to turn right on a red light if there is also a green arrow showing.

You won't have a problem hiring a car in Berlin, as long as you show your passport and a valid driving licence; a credit card is the preferred method of payment. There are many international hire companies with offices at the airports, railway stations and

Stopping and parking prohibited from Monday to Friday

Various old-fashioned local street signs in Berlin

Parking permitted during working hours and Saturday mornings only with a ticket

Parking Meter
Parking meters are used on most streets. You have to pay for parking between 9am and 7pm on weekdays and 9am and 2pm on Saturdays.

Clock indicating date and time

Slot for inserting coins

Information in different languages

Ticket is dispensed here

Some of the best known and most reliable car hire companies

in the city centre, some of which require the driver to be over 21 years of age. **Hertz**, **Sixt** and **AVIS** are three of the most reliable – and if you experience any trouble on the road, you should telephone **ADAC Auto Assistance**.

Taxis are also a very reliable and convenient method of transport around Berlin, three of the best companies being **Funk Taxi Berlin**, **Würfelfunk** and **Spree Funk**.

German road sign indicating various locations

PARKING

Finding a parking place won't always be easy, especially during lunchtime, but with a bit of luck you should be able to leave your car, free of charge, in the middle lane of the Ku'damm or in Alexanderplatz. There are also parking meters situated on just about every street, and many multi-storey car parks around West Berlin. Parking your car illegally certainly is not worth the risk; Berlin traffic wardens are constantly on the prowl, and apart from giving you a ticket, they can arrange to have your vehicle towed away. Retrieving an impounded car from the police is expensive and can be very inconvenient as these places are usually located out of town.

When using a parking meter, always check its time limit. These vary from area to area, so you may have to return after an hour or two to feed more money into the meter.

CYCLING

Cycling is very popular in Berlin, so most of the main roads have separate cycling lanes and even special traffic lights at intersections. Many offices, schools and banks have bicycle racks outside, but make sure your bike is securely locked and don't leave it there for too long.

You can also take your bike on S-Bahn trains, but you must enter the carriage by a marked door and leave your bike in a designated place. There are various places around town where you can hire a bike; one of the most reliable is **Fahrradstation**, with several outlets in the city.

A cycling lane between the pavement and the main road

DIRECTORY

CAR RENTAL

AVIS
23 09 370.
(0180) 55 577.
(International booking).
w www.avis.com

Europcar
(01805) 22 11 22.
w www.europcar.com

Hertz
26 11 053.
w www.hertz.com

Sixt
w www.sixt.com

BICYCLE RENTAL

Fahrradstation
Hackesche Höfe/Rosenthaler
Strasse 40–41.
10am–7pm Mon–Fri,
10am–4pm Sat. 28 38 48 48.

ROAD ASSISTANCE

ADAC Auto Assistance
(01802) 22 22 22.

DISABLED VISITORS

Telebus-Zentrale (Special bus)
Esplanade 17 9am–6pm
Mon–Fri. 41 02 00.

TAXI

Funk Taxi Berlin
261 026.

Würfelfunk
210 101.

Taxi Funk Berlin
690 22 or 44 33 22.

Buses, Trams and Taxis

Travelling by bus in Berlin can be something of a trial during rush hour, but at other times of the day it is highly recommended. Most of the major roads have special bus lanes so buses are punctual even when the main roads are getting congested. A double-decker bus is worth taking if you're new in town and want to have a good look round. Trams are another option in the eastern part of the centre; like the buses and S-Bahn lines they are part of BVG and accept the same tickets.

BVG pavilion on Hardenbergplatz provides transport information

TICKETS

The whole of Berlin is divided into three travel zones: A, B and C. Zone A covers the city centre, Zone B the outskirts of town, while Zone C includes Potsdam and its environs. Travel between the zones is very simple, with tickets for each combination of zones. The most expensive option is to travel by buying single tickets, which come in two kinds, the normal ticket *(Normal-tarif)* and the cheaper ticket *(Kurzstrecke)*. The former is valid for two hours and gives you access to all methods of public transport, including S- and U-Bahn trains, with as many changes as you need, while the latter can only be used for three stops on trains and

Three-day Welcome Card

six stops on buses. Single tickets can be bought from ticket offices at U- or S-Bahn stations, or from the bus driver. You must validate your ticket before you start your journey by inserting it in a red machine *(Entwerter)* found on the train platforms or in the bus, where it will be punched with the date and time. Children under 14 years old are entitled to a discount *(Ermässigungstarif)* and those under 6 can travel for free. No fee is charged for bringing a pram or a dog on board.

At most stations there are machines selling tickets and cards. The One-Day Ticket *(Tageskarte)* is valid from the moment it is punched until 3 o'clock the following morning. Weekly cards *(7-Tage-Karte)* are valid for seven days until midnight and are transferable. The three-day Welcome Card is another good option, giving unlimited travel in Berlin and Potsdam. Cheap tickets are also made available on special occasions. During the Love Parade *(see p49)*, for example, people are allowed to use all kinds of transport at a cheaper rate for two days.

Tram Stop

Every tram stop displays the appropriate tram numbers, timetables and maps. Buses sometimes also use the stops and are listed accordingly.

Tram stop symbol: Haltestelle

Bus numbers and names of destinations

Public transport map

Timetable of each route

For information about tickets and public transport in general, telephone **BVG Information (BVG-Kundendienst)** or the **Ticket Information** line – or the **U-Bahnhof Turmstrasse** for information about trains. If you think you may have mislaid something on a bus or a tram, give the **BVG Lost Property** number a call.

TRAVELLING BY BUS

All bus routes have a detailed timetable on display at each stop. Apart from its number, a bus will also have its destination on show, and it is important to pay attention to this as many buses shorten their routes outside rush hour. In the more modern buses you have to press a button to open the door. Until 8pm you can use all the doors to enter the bus, but after 8pm you should

A typical double decker bus

only use the front door near the driver; you will have to show him or her your ticket. The driver usually calls out the next stop, which may also be displayed electronically. Outside the city centre, however, the electronic display is something of a rarity. When travelling in the suburbs (and in the city centre outside rush hour) you need to press the *"Halt"* ("Stop") button as necessary, since most stops are made "on request" only.

TYPES OF BUS SERVICE

THERE ARE SEVERAL different bus services operating in Berlin. Buses run frequently throughout the week, but somewhat less often on Saturdays and Sundays. Apart from the regular buses, marked by three-digit numbers, there are also some slightly more expensive "express" buses. These carry a two digit number preceded by an X, amd stop less frequently than other services. The regular daytime bus services start to wind down at around 11pm, but their place is taken by a very reliable network of night buses. These are marked by the letter N and require special tickets which can be bought from the driver.

ROUTES 100 AND 200

THESE SPECIAL ROUTES are served by double-deckers and include the most

attractive parts of town. The buses operate between Bahnhof Zoo and Prenzlauer Berg, passing most of the city's interesting historic sites. Using a one-day ticket you can get off at any bus stop and visit Museum Island, Unter den Linden, the Brandenburg Gate, the Reichstag, the Tiergarten or Kaiser-Wilhelm-Gedächtniskirche. An extremely useful map and leaflet with descriptions (in German and English) of the route can be obtained from the **BVG Pavillon** on Hardenbergplatz.

TRAMS

TRAMS OPERATE mainly within the area of former East Berlin; only one route was extended to Wedding. They can be relied upon to depart on time as they never have traffic jams to deal with. A tram ticket can also be used on buses, S- and U-Bahn trains.

TAXIS

TAXIS ARE a comfortable but expensive way of getting around Berlin. Regardless of the make of car, all taxis are of the same cream colour and have a big TAXI sign on the roof. You can easily hail one on the street or arrange a cab by phone *(see p293)*. You can also get a taxi at a taxi rank, though these are quite rare. If the taxi rank is empty, you can use the rank telephone to

Modern tram operating in the former East Berlin quarter

call a cab directly, as each car has its own phone. The fare is calculated by a meter on the driver's dashboard. The cheapest fares are charged on weekdays in the centre of town (night-time and weekend rates are higher). There is also a special rate called *Kurzstreckentarif*: if you flag down a taxi and the journey is less than 2 km (1¼ miles), you pay a fixed rate of €3. It is generally a good idea to find out the name and telephone number of the taxi company nearest to your hotel.

DIRECTORY

USEFUL NUMBERS

BVG Information (BVG-Kundendienst)
☎ 194 49.

Ticket Information S-Bahn Berlin
Bahnhof Alexanderplatz.
☎ 29 72 06 48. ◷ 8am–9pm Mon–Fri, 9am–6pm Sat, Sun.

U-Bahnhof Turmstrasse
Service Centre
◷ 5:30am–8:30pm Mon–Fri, 8:45am–4pm Sat.

BVG Pavillon
Hardenbergplatz.
◷ 5:30am–10pm daily.

BVG Lost Property
U-bahn station Kleistpark.
☎ 25 62 88 74.
W www.bvg.de

A typical Berlin bus stop during rush hour

U-Bahn and S-Bahn

U-Bahn information sign

U-Bahn display board with U-Bahn platform *(Gleis)*, and destination

WHILE IN THEORY Berlin has two separate train networks – the U-Bahn and S-Bahn systems – in practical terms there is not much difference between them, and commuters use the same tickets for both. Strictly speaking, the U-Bahn operates as a metro system, with trains running underground, while the S-Bahn is a longer-distance commuter service. In practice however, there is a great deal of overlap between the two systems, and many stations have both S- and U-Bahn platforms. The U-Bahn is owned by BVG and the S-Bahn by the independent S-Bahn GmbH.

only valid for three stops. Vending machines stand at the entrance to each station, selling single tickets, returns, and one- and seven-day travel cards. The red machines that punch your ticket are usually behind the vending machines at the entrance to each platform. You may notice that there are no gates to stop free-riders trying their luck on the trains, but attempting to travel free of charge is a rather risky business in Berlin. Trains are patrolled by ticket inspectors who always work in plain clothes. They go on their rounds as soon as the train starts moving, and tend not to accept any excuses; fines for not having a ticket are high.

Trains arriving and departing at a station on U-Bahn line 6

U-Bahn

THE U-BAHN network is very dense, with numerous stations very close together, many of them on lines which do not connect. During rush hours trains are very frequent, usually arriving every minute or two. There are ten U-Bahn lines in all, although one of them (number 15) has no branches, while number 12 uses partly the same rails as U1 and U2. Most of the service closes down between midnight and 5am. There are two exceptions to this: U1 and U9, which run an overnight service during the weekends.

S-Bahn

TRAIN ROUTES ARE usually a bit longer on the S-Bahn, which doesn't have as dense a network as the U-Bahn. As many as five lines go along the same route between Ost- and Westkreuz, but the stations are spaced much further apart than U-Bahn

stops, and trains run every ten or 20 minutes. There are a total of 17 S-Bahn lines, all running well beyond the confines of the city.

Tickets

TICKETS FOR S- and U-Bahn trains are the same as the tickets used on local buses and trams. The *Kurzstrecke* (short stretch) single ticket is also acceptable, although it is

Signs

THERE'S NO MISTAKING a U-Bahn station with its large rectangular sign and trademark white U on a blue background; similarly for S-Bahn stations, which have a round sign with a large white S on a green background. On metro maps each line is marked by a different colour. The direction of the train is noted by the displays which always give the final destination of the train. White ovals or circles on the map indicate where you can change to another line. All stations have maps of the local area as well as maps of the

Buying an S-Bahn ticket from a machine on the platform

An S-Bahn line 5 train heading out to Pichelsberg

entire metro system. Maps of the network are also on view in the train carriages. When embarking, always check both the line number and the final destination of the train as it is very easy to confuse your direction.

Older-style carriages have manually-opened doors which will close behind you automatically. Newer ones are fully automatic. A station attendant on each platform is responsible for co-ordinating departures. When you hear *"Zurück bleiben!"* you must not enter the train as this means it is ready to depart. During the journey the next station is often announced inside the carriage – on more modern trains information about your journey is given on an electronic screen.

Information and emergency help point for the S-Bahn and U-Bahn

JOURNEY BY U- AND S-BAHN

1 Find the station you want on a map and see which line runs there. Do not forget to make a note of the final destination of the line so you can be sure of travelling in the right direction.

Map of U- and S-Bahn lines
(see inside back cover)

2 Find the button showing the type of ticket you require. After making your selection, the price is displayed and you can insert your coins in the slot.

3 A ticket from the machine looks different from one bought at the counter, but it will always contain information about its type and price.

Weekly travel card and one–day travel card

4 After entering the station you must validate your ticket in one of the red stamping machines located on the platform.

5 Follow the signs to the appropriate platform and choose the correct side by checking the destinations of departing trains.

An information board indicating the destinations of departing trains

6 After leaving a train, proceed to the exit marked by the *Ausgang* sign. If there are several exits from the station additional signs will tell you the names of the streets outside.

A typical exit sign

Getting Around by Boat

THE RIVER ROUTES of Berlin may not be as dense as those of Amsterdam or Venice, but the Spree and the Havel offer more than just a pleasure cruise in the sun. An extensive system of canals and lakes links the city centre with Potsdam, Spandau, Charlottenburg and the area of Müggelsee. All kinds of transport are available, from rowing boats to catamarans and barges.

A ship's bell

One of many tourist boats on the Spree river

Timetable and routes of various boats near the Nikolaiviertel

GETTING AROUND BERLIN ON THE WATER

ONE OF THE MOST relaxing ways to spend the afternoon in Berlin is to take a leisurely three- or four-hour journey by boat along the Spree river and the Landwehrkanal. There is no shortage of companies offering this kind of trip. Four of the most reliable are **Reederei Bruno Winkler**, **Stern und Kreis**, **Reederei Hartmut Triebler** and **Reederei Riedel**. Each has its own dock, but the routes they follow are similar. You can admire the historic buildings of Mitte as the boat passes by the Berliner Dom along Museum Island, before heading off to the new government district and the Reichstag. You would have a good view of the Haus der Kulturen der Welt and the new city in Moabit shortly before entering the Landwehrkanal. This runs alongside the Zoological Garden and new city buildings on Potsdamer Platz, and passes through Kreuzberg on its way to the junction with the Spree at Oberbaumbrücke. Most of the boats available along this

route have closed lower decks and open upper decks, with a bar serving snacks and drinks. All the sights are explained by a guide along the way; the commentary is usually in German, but some companies can arrange for an English speaker.

TRIPS ALONG THE SPREE AND HAVEL RIVERS

IF YOU WANT TO try something a little more adventurous there are longer trips to choose from, some of which cover the

western lakes as well as the city centre. A particularly nice route takes you along the Spree, past the Mitte district, to Treptow, Charlottenburg and Spandau. From here you can carry on along the Havel river to the Grunewald and the Wannsee, then take a trip past Pfaueninsel to Potsdam. To do this, enquire at Stern und Kreis. Companies Reederei Bruno Winkler and Reederei Hartmut Triebler offer similar trips starting at Spandau and Charlottenburg.

Other options include a trip from Tegel port to Spandau and Wannsee, or a journey from Treptow to Köpenick. If you really want to, you can cover the whole of Berlin by boat, starting from Tegel in the north and finishing at Köpenick in the southeast, all within five or six hours.

Boat moored along the river in the summer

One of the larger boats available on the Spree

LONGER JOURNEYS AROUND BERLIN

FOR EVEN LONGER TOURS, you may decide to take a whole day exploring the rivers, canals and lakes of Berlin. From Treptow you can take a boat to Woltersdorf which takes you through the charming lakeland area of Müggelsee. This region really is one of Berlin's greatest

A sight-seeing boat negotiating a lock on a canal

treasures, and is ideal for anyone searching for a quiet place to relax. There are many man-made beaches to choose from, as well as summer gardens and cafés - and a large white fleet of ships to show you around the area. Müggelsee is best visited on a warm summer's day when you can easily spend a few hours on one of its beaches.

Another adventurous idea is to take a voyage along the Teltowkanal from Treptow to Potsdam, from where **Weisse Flotte Potsdam** can take you not only to Wannsee and the other familiar routes around town, but also to Caputh, Werder and to many other sights to the south and west of Potsdam. For the absolute die-hards of the waterways, there is still one other option, which is to

Reederei Riedel company logo

take a boat all the way to Szczecin in Poland. You will need to allow a whole day to reach Szczecin, so be prepared to stay the night there as well. Perhaps the best idea is to leave your boat at the docks, spend a restful day exploring the city, and return by coach to Berlin.

DIRECTORY

TOUR BOAT COMPANIES

Reederei Bruno Winkler
Mierendorffstrasse 16.
349 95 95.
www.ReedereiWinkler.de

Reederei Hartmut Triebler
Bratringweg 29. 371 16 71.

Reederei Riedel
Planufer 78.
691 37 82, 693 46 46,
FAX 694 21 91.
www.reederei-riedel.de

Stern und Kreis
Schiffahrt GmbH Berlin
Puschkinallee 16/17.
53 63 60 0.
FAX 53 63 60 99.
www.STERNundKREIS.de

Weisse Flotte Potsdam
Lange Brücke.
(0331) 275 92 10.

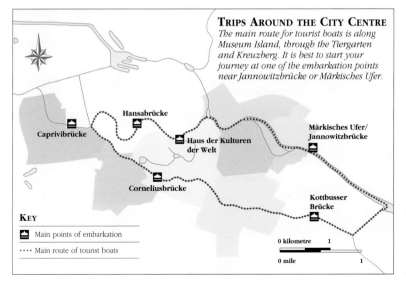

TRIPS AROUND THE CITY CENTRE

The main route for tourist boats is along Museum Island, through the Tiergarten and Kreuzberg. It is best to start your journey at one of the embarkation points near Jannowitzbrücke or Märkisches Ufer.

Hansabrücke

Caprivibrücke

Haus der Kulturen der Welt

Märkisches Ufer/ Jannowitzbrücke

Corneliusbrücke

Kottbusser Brücke

KEY

⚓ Main points of embarkation

···· Main route of tourist boats

0 kilometre 1

0 mile 1

STREET FINDER

M AP REFERENCES given for historic buildings, hotels, restaurants, bars, shops and entertainment venues refer to the maps included in this section of the guidebook. A complete index of street names and all places of interest can be found on the following pages. The key map below shows the area of Berlin covered by the *Street Finder*. The maps include all the major sightseeing areas, historic attractions, railway stations, bus stations and the suburban stations of the U-Bahn and S-Bahn, as well as the ferry embarkation points. The names of the streets and squares in the index and maps are given in German. The word Strasse (Str.) indicates a street, Platz a square, Brücke a bridge and Bahnhof a railway station.

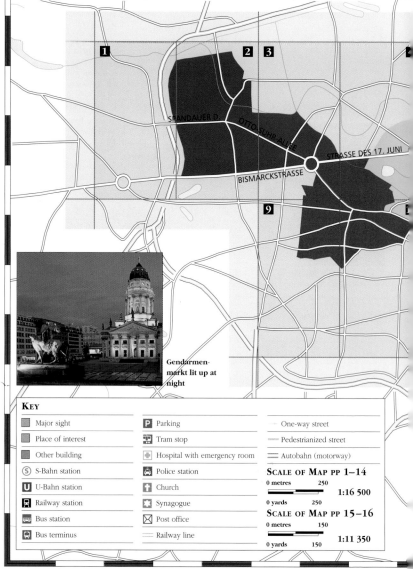

Gendarmenmarkt lit up at night

KEY

▢ Major sight	P Parking	— One-way street
▢ Place of interest	Tram stop	— Pedestrianized street
▢ Other building	Hospital with emergency room	Autobahn (motorway)
S S-Bahn station	Police station	**SCALE OF MAP PP 1–14**
U U-Bahn station	Church	0 metres 250
Railway station	Synagogue	**1:16 500**
Bus station	Post office	0 yards 250
Bus terminus	Railway line	**SCALE OF MAP PP 15–16**
		0 metres 150
		1:11 350
		0 yards 150

Palm house in the Botanischer Garten

Rococo Chinesisches Teehaus in Park Sanssouci, Potsdam

UNTER DEN LINDEN

KARL-MARX-ALLEE

LEIPZIGER STRASSE

POTSDAMER STRASSE

TEMPELHOFER DAMM

Modern business centre of
Potsdamer Platz

Street Finder Index

6

A B C

6

1

SCHUMANNSTRASSE

UNTERBAUMSTRASSE

KARLPLATZ

REINHARDTSTRASSE

CHARITÉSTRASSE

SCHIFFBAUERDAMM

MARIENSTRASSE

LUISENSTRASSE

ALBRECHTSTRASSE

REINHARDTSTRASSE

AM ZIRKUS

Friedrichstadtpalast

ZIEGELSTRASSE

BERTOLT-BRECHT-PLATZ

Berliner Ensemble

Weidendammer Brücke

PLANCKSTRASSE

Admiralspalast

2

BECHSTAGUFER

SCHIFFBAUERDAMM

Bahnhof Friedrichstrasse

S

⊠

🚉

U P
Friedrichstrasse

Spree

Marschallbrücke

REICHSTAGUFER

SCHIFFBAUERDAMM

NEUSTÄDTISCHE KIRCHSTRASSE

GEORGENSTRASSE

P

EBERTSTRASSE

Reichstag

DOROTHEENSTRASSE

WILHELMSTRASSE

BUNSENSTRASSE

SCHADOWSTRASSE

DOROTHEENSTRASSE

P

MITTELSTRASSE

FRIEDRICHSTRASSE

3

Brandenburger Tor

PARISER PLATZ

PLATZ VON DEM BRANDENBURGER TOR

P

S
Unter den Linden

Hotel Adlon

BEHRENSTRASSE

UNTER DEN LINDEN

Russische Botschaft

GLINKASTRASSE

Komische Oper

BEHRENSTRASSE

Französische Strasse **U**

P

⊠
FRANZÖSISCHE STRASSE

MAUERSTRASSE

JÄGERSTRASSE

Friedrichstadt-Passagen

4

Holocaust Denkmal

WILHELMSTRASSE

EBERTSTRASSE

AN DER KOLONNADE

TAUBENSTRASSE

Mohrenstrasse **U**

MOHRENSTRASSE

GLINKASTRASSE

Stadtmitte **U**

FRIEDRICHSTRASSE

KRONENSTRASSE

P

5

Potsdamer Platz

S

POTSDAMER PLATZ

LEIPZIGER PLATZ

VOSS STRASSE

LEIPZIGER STRASSE

P

Bundesrat

MAUERSTRASSE

Museum für Post und Kommunikation

KRAUSENSTRASSE

P

U **Potsdamer Platz**

6

A B C

ORANIENBURGER STRASSE

HACKESCHER MARKT

MONBIJOUPARK

MONBIJOU-PLATZ

GR. PRÄSIDENTENSTRASSE

NEUE PROMENADE

Univ.-Klinik

ZIEGELSTRASSE

TUCHOLSKYSTRASSE

MONBIJOUSTRASSE

Univ.-Frauenkl.

Ebert-brücke

AM WEIDENDAMM

Monbijou-brücke

Spree

Hackescher Markt

P

P

ROSENSTRASSE

1

GESCHWISTER-SCHOLL-STRASSE

AM KUPFERGRABEN

Bodemuseum

BURGSTRASSE

Pergamon-museum

Alte Nationalgalerie

BURGSTRASSE

Friedrich-brücke

SPANDAUER STRASSE

GEORGENSTRASSE

Kupfergrabenkanal

MUSEUMSTRASSE

BAUHOFSTRASSE

Neues Museum

BODESTRASSE

Heiliggeistkapelle

PLANCKSTRASSE

HEGEL-PLATZ

P

DOROTHEENSTRASSE

Maxim-Gorki-Theater

H. D. GIEBHAUS

Altes Museum

Eiserne Brücke

AM LUSTGARTEN

Berliner Dom

KARL-LIEBKNECHT-STRASSE

2

Staats-bibliothek

UNIVERSITÄTSSTRASSE

Humboldt-Universität

Zeughaus Deutsches Historisches Museum

AM ZEUGHAUS

LUSTGARTEN

Liebknecht-brücke

Marx-Engels-Forum

CHARLOTTENSTRASSE

Neue Wache

Schlossbrücke

Palast der Republik

Rathaus-brücke

UNTER DEN LINDEN

Reiter Denkmal

Kronprinzen-palais

SCHLOSSPLATZ

P

Marstall

3

Altes Palais

Deutsche Guggenheim

BEBEL-PLATZ

Staatsoper Unter den Linden

NIEDERLAGSTRASSE

Schleusenbrücke

WERDERSTRASSE

BREITE STRASSE

Alte Bibliothek

BEHRENSTRASSE

Friedrichs-werdersche Kirche

P

St.-Hedwigs-Kathedrale

OBERWALLSTRASSE

WERDERSCHER MARKT

Auswärtiges Amt

UNTERWASSERSTRASSE

FRANZÖSISCHE STRASSE

Französischer Dom

JÄGERSTRASSE

P

KURSTRASSE

SPERLINGSGASSE

FRIEDRICHSGRACHT

Nicolai Haus

BRÜDERSTRASSE

JÄGERSTRASSE

GENDARMEN-MARKT

TAUBENSTRASSE

Hausvogteiplatz

U

Galgenhaus

SCHARRENSTRASSE

P

PETRI-PLATZ

4

Konzert-haus

HAUSVOGTEI-PLATZ

OBERWASSERSTRASSE

GERTRAUDENSTRASSE

CHARLOTTENSTRASSE

Deutscher Dom

MOHRENSTRASSE

MARKGRAFENSTRASSE

JERUSALEMER STRASSE

NIEDERWALLSTRASSE

KURSTRASSE

P

Gertrauden-brücke

KRONENSTRASSE

⊠

U Spittelmarkt

SPITTEL-MARKT

WALLSTRASSE

LEIPZIGER STRASSE

Spittelkolonnaden

SEYDELSTRASSE

5

KRAUSENSTRASSE

KRAUSENSTRASSE

P

BEUTHSTRASSE

MARKGRAFENSTRASSE

JERUSALEMER STRASSE

LINDENSTRASSE

SCHÜTZENSTRASSE

KOMMANDANTENSTRASSE

P

7 ▶

SCHÜTZENSTRASSE

Index   <small>Page numbers in bold type refer to main entries</small>

Acknowledgements

DORLING KINDERSLEY would like to thank the following people whose contributions and assistance have made the preparation of this book possible.

MANAGING ART EDITOR
Kate Poole

EDITORIAL DIRECTOR
Vivien Crump

ART DIRECTOR
Gillian Allan

CONSULTANT
Gordon McLachlan

FACT CHECKERS
Paul Otto Schulz, Margaret Schulz-Wenzel, Jürgen Scheunemann

TRANSLATORS
Magda Hannay, Anna Johnson, Ian Wisniewski

PROOFREADER
Stewart Wild

INDEXER
Hilary Bird

DESIGN AND EDITORIAL ASSISTANCE
Gillian Andrews, Brigitte Arora, Tessa Bindloss, Arwen Burnett, Lucinda Cooke, Jessica Hughes, Franziska Marking, Simon Ryder, Sands Publishing Solutions, Andrew Szudek

DTP
Samantha Borland, Lee Redmond

ADDITIONAL ILLUSTRATIONS
Paweł Pasternak

ADDITIONAL PHOTOGRAPHY
Jürgen Scheunemann

SPECIAL ASSISTANCE
DORLING KINDERSLEY would like to thank the staff at the featured museums, shops, hotels, restaurants and other organizations in Berlin for their invaluable help. Special thanks go to the following for providing photographs and pictures: Heidrun Klein of the Bildarchiv Preussischer Kulturbesitz; Frau Betzker and Ingrid Jager of the Bröhan Museum; Margit Billeb of the Centrum Judaicum; Brucke-Museum; Deutsche Press Agency (DPA); Renate Forster of the Deutsches Technikmuseum Berlin; Andrei Holland-Moritz of Forschung- und Gedenkstätte Normannenstrasse (Stasi-Museum); Matthias Richter of Konzerthaus Berlin and the Berlin Symphony Orchestra; Georg Kolbe Museum; Carl Kamarz of Stiftung Preussische Schlösser und Gärten Berlin and the Berlin and Potsdam Palaces; Thomas Wellmann of the Museum of the City of Berlin; Hamburger Bahnhof; Annette Jäckel of DeragHotels for providing photographs of the interiors of DeragHotel Grosser Kurfürst; Reinhard Friedrich; Hans-Jürgen Dyck of Haus am Checkpoint Charlie; Gaby Hofmann of Komische Oper Berlin; Gesine Steiner of Museum für Naturkunde; Ute Grallert of Deutsches Historisches Museum; Elke Pfeil of the Brecht-Weigel-Museum; Ingrid Flindell of the Käthe-Kollwitz-Museum; Sylvia U Moller of Villa Kastania; Manuel Volsk of the Savoy Hotel; Sabine Rogge of the Grand Hotel Esplanade Berlin; Claude Borrmann of the Hotel Palace Berlin; Gerald Uhligow of the Einstein Café; Hotel Adlon; Hotel Brandenburger Hof and Restaurant Die Quadriga; Hotel Kempinski; Rockendorf's Restaurant; The Westin Grand Hotel.

PHOTOGRAPHY PERMISSIONS
DORLING KINDERSLEY would like to thank the following for their kind permission to photograph at their establishments: Margaret Hilmer of the Berliner Dom; Kaiser-Wilhelm-Gedächtniskirche; Galeries Lafayette; KaDeWe; Frau Schneider of BVG (Berlin Underground system); Deutsche Bundesbahn for allowing photography of the Zoo railway station; Dorotheenstädtischer Friedhof for allowing photographs of the tombs; Flughafen Schönefeld for allowing photography of the airfield; Annie Silbert of the Zoologischer Garten Berlin for allowing photography of the animals and attractions; Hilton Hotel; Carlos Beck of the Sorat Art'otel, Berlin; Manuel Volsk of the Savoy Hotel, Berlin; Sabine Rogge of the Grand Hotel Esplanade; Claude Borrmann of the Hotel Palace Berlin; Gerald Uhligow of the Einstein Café; the Olive restaurant; the Bamberger Reiter restaurant; Sklepo for allowing photography of its interiors and porcelain.

Particular thanks to Hans-Gunter Harms, chef at the Hilton Hotel, for preparing the dishes for photography; Manfred Duhatschko for preparing cakes and desserts; Hilton Hotel for allowing photography of the interiors and the preparation of the food.

Count Lehmann of Senatsverwaltung für Bauen, Wohnen und Verkehr for providing cartographic information as well as copyright for the use of maps; Ms Grazyna Kukowska of ZAIKS for her help in securing permission to reproduce works of art.

Picture Credits

t=top; tl= top left; tc=top centre; tr= top right; cla=centre left above; ca= centre above; cra= centre right above; cl=centre left; c=centre; cr=centre right; clb=center left below; cb= center below; crb=centre right below; bl=bottom left; bc=bottom centre; br=bottom right; b=bottom.

Every effort has been made to trace the copyright holders and we apologize in advance for any unintentional omissions. We would be pleased to insert the appropriate acknowledgements in subsequent editions of this publication.

The publisher is grateful to the following individuals, companies and picture libraries for their permission to reproduce their photographs. The works of art have been reproduced with the consent of the copyright owners.

John Cage *Not Wanting to Say Anything About Marcel* (1969) 111c; Sandro Chia *Genova* (1980) 110cl; Keith Haring *Untitled* (1983) © The Estate of Keith Haring 110bl; Bernhard Heligerd, sculpture near Brücke-Museum © Bild-Kunst 179tr; Oskar Kokoschka *Pariser Platz in Berlin* (1925–26) 67bl; Pablo Picasso *Head of the Faun* (1937) 32tr, *Woman in a Hat* (1939) 159tl, all © Succession Picasso 2000; Robert Rauschenberg *First Time Painting* (1961) © Robert Rauschenberg 111bl; Karl Schmidt-Rottluff *Farm in Danger* (1910) © Bild-Kunst 126tl; Andy Warhol *Mao* (1973) © 2000 Andy Warhol Foundation for the Visual Arts/ARS, New York 111br.

ALLSTAR: cinetext 141t; AMJ HOLDING GMBH & CO. KG: Steffen Janicke 65br; ANA E BRUNO 231cr; AKG LONDON: Dieter E Hoppe front cover cl and 166, Lothar Peter front cover cbr; ANTHONY BLAKE PHOTO LIBRARY front cover ccr; BERGER + PARKKINEN ARCHITEKTEN ZIVILTECHNIK GMBH: 40br; BILDARCHIV PREUSSISCHER KULTURBESITZ 9c, 20–21c, 29tr, 30tr, 30br, 32tr, 32br, 33t, 33b, 54cb, 67b, 73ca, 80ca, 82tl, 82b, 83tl, 85b, 115cra, 118tl, 118tr, 122cb, 123clb, 126t, 158cra, 162t, 163cl, 165tl, 178tr, 178b; Jorg P Anders 20tc, 20cl, 21t, 29cl, 30cl, 73cra, 114c, 114b, 117t, 122tl, 122tr, 122ca, 122b, 123t, 123cr, 123b, 124t, 124ca, 124b, 125t, 125cb, 125cb, 187b; Hans-Joachim Bartsch 118cla, 118c, 120tl, 121cr; Margarete Busing 32c; Ingrid Geske-Heiden 30tl, 75tr, 121b; Klaus Goken 60t, 31crb, 78t, 80b, 81b; Dietmar Katz 41crb; Johannes Laurentius 75b; Erich Lessing 72t, 80t, 81cb; Jürgen Liepe 31cra, 75cla, 80cb, 82t, 83b, 118b, 164bl; Saturia Linke 32tl; Georg Niedermeiser 80t, 81ca; Arne Psille 18tc, 119t, 119b, 120c, 120b; Steinkopf 114tr; G Stenzel 83tr; Jens Ziehe 110t, 111c; Jürgen Zimmermann 29tl; BRIDGEMAN ART LIBRARY 47c,

175b; BRECHT-WEIGEL-GEDENKSTÄTTE 46t, 109b; BRÖHAN-MUSEUM 165cb; CENTRUM JUDAICUM 102t; DEUTSCHES HISTORISCHES MUSEUM (Zeughaus) 8–9, 22cb, 22bl, 23tr, 23b, 23clb, 24–25b, 25tr, 26tl, 26cr, 26cb, 26dp, 27tr, 27bl, 46br, 47cra, 58tl, 58tr, 58ca, 58cb, 58br, 59t, 59ca, 59cb, 59b; DEUTSCHES TECHNIKMUSEUM BERLIN 31bl, 136; DEUTSCHE PRESS AGENCY (DPA) 46ca, 46cb, 46bl, 47t, 47crb, 47b, 48tc, 48cla, 48b, 50t, 50b, 67t, 151br, 199b; EUROPEAN COMMISSION 285; FILMPARK BABELSBERG: 205 cla/crb/bl; FIT TO PRINT, BERLIN: 283tl; GEDENKSTÄTTE UND MUSEUM SACHSENHAUSEN 169b; GEORG KOLBE MUSEUM 183tr; GRAND HOTEL ESPLANADE 216b; HAMBURGER BAHNHOF 110ca, 110cb, 110b, 111t, 111cra, 111crb, 111b; HAUS AM CHECKPOINT CHARLIE 39br; HOTEL ADLON 68t; HOTEL PALACE 219tr; HAYDER ADAM 233br; IMAGEWORKSHOP BERLIN: Vincent Mosch 131br; JEWISH MUSEUM BERLIN: 143 br; Deutsches Technikmuseum Berlin 143cl; Jens Ziehe, Berlin 142cl; Leo Baeck Institute, New York 142tr; KÄTHE-KOLLWITZ-MUSEUM 148b; KOMISCHE OPER MONIKA RITTERSHAUS 49b, 68b; KONZERTHAUS BERLIN 65t; MEYER NILS 27cr, 38tr; MUSEUM FÜR NATURKUNDE 109t; PRESS ASSOCIATION PICTURE LIBRARY 261tl; PRESSE- UND INFORMATIONSAMT DES LANDES BERLIN: BTM 294c; BTM/Drewes 43bl; BTM/Koch 43tl, 129 tl; G. Schneider 51c; Landesarchive Berlin 129br; Meldepress/Ebner 126b; Partner fuer Berlin: FTB-Werbefotografie 128cl, 143cr, 143br; RAINER KIEDROWSKI: Nils Koshofer 28, 112; ROBERT HARDING PICTURE LIBRARY 52–53, 274tc, Walter Rawlings 208cl; SCHNEIDER, GUENTER: 39tr, 52–53; SCHIRMER, KARSTEN: 260cl; STAATLICHE MUSEEN ZU BERLIN-PREUSSISCHE KULTURBESITZ/KUNSTGEWERBEMUSEUM: Hans-Joachim Bartsch 119cl; Irmgard Mues-Funke 121 tl; STADTMUSEUM BERLIN 21tr, 22t, 24cla, 133tr; Hans-Joachim Bartsch 16, 17b, 18c, 19tl, 19br, 25br, 85t; Christel Lehmann 18tl, 18cb; Peter Straube 88b, 90tr; STASI-MUSEUM 174cr; STIFTUNG PREUSSISCHE SCHLÖSSER UND GÄRTEN BERLIN 14t, 19c, 160t, 160c, 161ca, 161c, 161b, 188clb, 194tl, 194cla, 194clb, 194br, 195cra, 195br, 195bl, 198t, 200cla, 200b, 201cra, 201crb, 201bl, 201br; TELEGRAPH COLOUR LIBRARY: Bavaria-Bildagentur front cover cbc, Messerschmidt front cover t; TONY STONE IMAGES: Doug Armand 214; VIEW PICTURES: William Fife 41bl; VILLA KASTANIA 217b; THE WESTIN GRAND 218b; WÓJCIK PAWEŁ 235bl.

JACKET Front - DK PICTURE LIBRARY: Dorota Mariusz Jarymowicz cb, bl, clb; GETTY IMAGES: Hans Wolf main image. Back - DK PICTURE LIBRARY: Dorota Mariusz Jarymowicz t, b. Spine - GETTY IMAGES: Hans Wolf.

All other images © Dorling Kindersley. For further information see: www.dkimages.com

---

DORLING KINDERSLEY SPECIAL EDITIONS

Dorling Kindersley books can be purchased in bulk quantities at discounted prices for use in promotions or as premiums. We are also able to offer special editions and personalized jackets, corporate imprints, and excerpts from all of our books, tailored specifically to meet your own needs.

To find out more, please contact: (in the United Kingdom) – Sarah.Burgess@dk.com OR SPECIAL SALES, DORLING KINDERSLEY LIMITED, 80 STRAND, LONDON WC2R 0RL;

(in the United States) – SPECIAL MARKETS DEPARTMENT, DK PUBLISHING, INC., 375 HUDSON STREET, NEW YORK, NY 10014.

Phrasebook

IN AN EMERGENCY

Where is the telephone?	Wo ist das Telefon?	voh ist duss tel-e-fone?
Help!	Hilfe!	hilf-uh
Please call a doctor	Bitte rufen Sie einen Arzt	**bitt**-uh **roof**'n zee ine-en artst
Please call the police	Bitte rufen Sie die Polizei	**bitt**-uh **roof**'n zee dee poli-**tsy**
Please call the fire brigade	Bitte rufen Sie die Feuerwehr	**bitt**-uh **roof**'n zee dee **foyer**-vayr
Stop!	Halt!	hult

COMMUNICATION ESSENTIALS

Yes	Ja	**yah**
No	Nein	**nine**
Please	Bitte	**bitt**-uh
Thank you	Danke	dunk-uh
Excuse me	Verzeihung	fair-**tsy**-hoong
Hello (good day)	Guten Tag	**goot**-en tahk
Goodbye	Auf Wiedersehen	owf-**veed**-er-zay-ern
Good evening	Guten Abend	goot'n **ahb**'nt
Good night	Gute Nacht	goot-uh **nukht**
Until tomorrow	Bis morgen	biss **morg**'n
See you	Tschüss	chooss
What is that?	Was ist das?	voss ist duss
Why?	Warum?	var-**room**
Where?	Wo?	**voh**
When?	Wann?	**vunn**
today	heute	**hoyt**-uh
tomorrow	morgen	**morg**'n
month	Monat	**mohn**-aht
night	Nacht	**nukht**
afternoon	Nachmittag	**nahkh**-mit-tahk
morning	Morgen	**morg**'n
year	Jahr	yar
there	dort	**dort**
here	hier	**hear**
week	Woche	**vokh**-uh
yesterday	gestern	**gest**'n
evening	Abend	**ahb**'nt

USEFUL PHRASES

How are you? (informal)	Wie geht's?	vee gayts
Fine, thanks	Danke, es geht mir gut	dunk-uh, es gayt meer goot
Until later	Bis später	biss **shpay**-ter
Where is/are?	Wo ist/sind…?	voh ist/sind
How far is it to…?	Wie weit ist es…?	vee **vite** ist ess
Do you speak English?	Sprechen Sie Englisch?	shpresh'n zee **eng**-glish
I don't understand	Ich verstehe nicht	ish fair-**shtay**-uh nisht
Could you speak more slowly?	Könnten Sie langsamer sprechen?	**kurnt**-en zee **lung**-zam-er **shpresh**'n

USEFUL WORDS

large	gross	**grohss**
small	klein	**kline**
hot	heiss	**hyce**
cold	kalt	**kult**
good	gut	**goot**
bad	böse/schlecht	**burss**-uh/**shlesht**
open	geöffnet	g'**urff**-nett
closed	geschlossen	g'**shloss**'n
left	links	**links**
right	rechts	**reshts**
straight ahead	geradeaus	g'**rah**-der-**owss**

MAKING A TELEPHONE CALL

I would like to make a phone call	Ich möchte telefonieren	ish **mer**-shtuh tel-e-fon-**eer**'n
I'll try again later	Ich versuche es später noch einmal	ish fair-zookh-uh es **shpay**-ter nokh ine-mull
Can I leave a message?	Kann ich eine Nachricht hinterlassen?	kan ish **ine**-uh nakh-risht hint-er-**lahss**-en
answer phone	Anrufbeantworter	an-roof-be-**ahnt**-vort-er
telephone card	Telefonkarte	tel-e-**fohn**-kart-uh
receiver	Hörer	**hur**-er
mobile	Handy	han-dee
engaged (busy)	besetzt	b'zetst
wrong number	Falsche Verbindung	falsh-uh fair-**bin**-doong

SIGHTSEEING

library	Bibliothek	bib-leo-**tek**
entrance ticket	Eintrittskarte	ine-tritz-**kart**-uh
cemetery	Friedhof	**freed**-hofe
train station	Bahnhof	**barn**-hofe
gallery	Galerie	**gall**-er-ree
information	Auskunft	**owss**-koonft
church	Kirche	**keersh**-uh
garden	Garten	**gart**'n
palace/castle	Palast/Schloss	pallast/shloss
place (square)	Platz	**plats**
bus stop	Haltestelle	**hal**-te-shtel-uh
national holiday	Nationalfeiertag	nats-yon-**ahl**-fire-tahk
theatre	Theater	tay-**aht**-er
free admission	Eintritt frei	ine-tritt fry

SHOPPING

Do you have/ Is there…?	Gibt es…?	geept ess
How much does it cost?	Was kostet das?	voss **kost**'t duss?
When do you open/ close?	Wann öffnen Sie? schliessen Sie?	vunn **off**'n zee **shlees**'n zee
this	das	duss
expensive	teuer	**toy**-er
cheap	preiswert	**price**-vurt
size	Grösse	**gruhs**-uh
number	Nummer	**noom**-er
colour	Farbe	**farb**-uh
brown	braun	brown
black	schwarz	**shvarts**
red	rot	**roht**
blue	blau	**blau**
green	grün	**groon**
yellow	gelb	**gelp**

TYPES OF SHOP

antique shop	Antiquariat	antik-**var**-yat
chemist (pharmacy)	Apotheke	appo-**tay**-kuh
bank	Bank	**bunk**
market	Markt	**markt**
travel agency	Reisebüro	**rye**-zer-boo-roe
department store	Warenhaus	**vahr**'n-hows
chemist's, drugstore	Drogerie	droog-er-**ree**
hairdresser	Friseur	freezz-**er**
newspaper kiosk	Zeitungskiosk	tsytoongs-kee-osk
bookshop	Buchhandlung	**bookh**-hant-loong

English	German	Pronunciation
bakery	Bäckerei	beck-er-**eye**
post office	Post	posst
shop/store	Geschäft/Laden	gush-**eft/lard**'n
film processing shop	Photogeschäft	fo-to-gush-**eft**
self-service shop	Selbstbedienungsladen	selpst-bed-**ee**-nungs-lard'n
shoe shop	Schuhladen	shoo-lard'n
clothes shop	Kleiderladen, Boutique	klyder-lard'n boo-**teek**-uh
food shop	Lebensmittelgeschäft	**lay**-bens-mittel-gush-eft
glass, porcelain	Glas, Porzellan	glars, **Port-sellahn**

STAYING IN A HOTEL

Do you have any vacancies?	Haben Sie noch Zimmer frei?	harb'n zee nokh **tsimm**-er-fry
with twin beds?	mit zwei Betten?	mitt tsvy bett'n
with a double bed?	mit einem Doppelbett?	mitt ine'm **dopp**'l-bet
with a bath?	mit Bad?	mitt **bart**
with a shower?	mit Dusche?	mitt **doosh**-uh
I have a reservation	Ich habe eine Reservierung	ish **harb**-uh ine-uh rez-er-**veer**-oong
key	Schlüssel	**shlooss**'l
porter	Pförtner	**pfert**-ner

EATING OUT

English	German	Pronunciation
Do you have a table for...?	Haben Sie einen Tisch für...?	harb'n zee tish foor
I would like to reserve a table	Ich möchte eine Reservierung machen	ish **mer**-shtuh ine-uh rezer-**veer**-oong makh'n
I'm a vegetarian	Ich bin Vegetarier	ish bin vegg-er-**tah**-ree-er
Waiter!	Herr Ober!	hair **oh**-bare!
The bill (check), please	Die Rechnung, bitte	dee **resh**-noong bitt-uh
breakfast	Frühstück	**froo**-shtock
lunch	Mittagessen	**mitt**-targ-ess'n
dinner	Abendessen	**arb**'nt-ess'n
bottle	Flasche	**flush**-uh
dish of the day	Tagesgericht	**tahg**-es-gur-isht
main dish	Hauptgericht	**howpt**-gur-isht
dessert	Nachtisch	**nahkh**-tish
cup	Tasse	**tass**-uh
wine list	Weinkarte	vine-kart-uh
tankard	Krug	khroog
glass	Glas	**glars**
spoon	Löffel	**lerff**'l
teaspoon	Teelöffel	tay-lerff'l
tip	Trinkgeld	**trink**-gelt
knife	Messer	**mess**-er
starter (appetizer)	Vorspeise	**for**-shpize-uh
the bill	Rechnung	**resh**-noong
plate	Teller	**tell**-er
fork	Gabel	**gahb**'l

MENU DECODER

German	Pronunciation	English
Aal	**arl**	eel
Apfel	**upf**'l	apple
Apfelschorle	**upf**'l-shoorl-uh	apple juice with sparkling mineral water
Apfelsine	**upf**'l-seen-uh	orange
Aprikose	upri-**kawz**-uh	apricot
Artischocke	arti-**shokh**-uh	artichoke
Aubergine (eggplant)	or-ber-**jeen**-uh	aubergine
Banane	bar-**narn**-uh	banana
Beefsteack	**beef**-stayk	steak
Bier	beer	beer
Bockwurst	**bokh**-voorst	a type of sausage
Bohnensuppe	burn-en-zoop-uh	bean soup
Branntwein	brant-vine	spirits
Bratkartoffeln	brat-kar-toff'ln	fried potatoes
Bratwurst	brat-voorst	fried sausage
Brötchen	bret-tchen	bread roll
Brot	brot	bread
Brühe	bruh-uh	broth
Butter	**boot**-ter	butter
Champignon	**shum**-pin-yong	mushroom
Currywurst	**kha**-ree-voorst	sausage with curry sauce
Dill	**dill**	dill
Ei	**eye**	egg
Eis	**ice**	ice/ ice cream
Ente	**ent**-uh	duck
Erdbeeren	ayrt-**beer**'n	strawberries
Fisch	**fish**	fish
Forelle	for-**ell**-uh	trout
Frikadelle	Frika-**dayl**-uh	rissole/hamburger
Gans	ganns	goose
Garnele	**gar**-nayl-uh	prawn/shrimp
gebraten	g'**braat**'n	fried
gegrillt	g'**grilt**	grilled
gekocht	g'**kokh**t	boiled
geräuchert	g'**rowk**-ert	smoked
Geflügel	g'**floog**'l	poultry
Gemüse	g'**mooz**-uh	vegetables
Grütze	**grurt**-ser	groats, gruel
Gulasch	**goo**-lush	goulash
Gurke	**goork**-uh	gherkin
Hammelbraten	hamm'l-**braat**'n	roast mutton
Hähnchen	**haynsh**'n	chicken
Hering	**hair**-ing	herring
Himbeeren	him-**beer**'n	raspberries
Honig	**hoe**-nikh	honey
Kaffee	kaf-**fay**	coffee
Kalbfleisch	kalp-flysh	veal
Kaninchen	ka-**neensh**'n	rabbit
Karpfen	**karpf**'n	carp
Kartoffelpüree	kar-toff'l-**poor**-ay	mashed potatoes
Käse	**kayz**-uh	cheese
Kaviar	**kar**-vee-ar	caviar
Knoblauch	**k'nob**-lowkh	garlic
Knödel	**k'nerd**'l	noodle
Kohl	**koal**	cabbage
Kopfsalat	**kopf**-zal-aat	lettuce
Krebs	**krayps**	crab
Kuchen	**kookh**'n	cake
Lachs	**lahkhs**	salmon
Leber	**lay**-ber	liver
mariniert	mari-neert	marinated
Marmelade	marmer-**lard**-uh	marmalade, jam
Meerrettich	may-re-tish	horseradish
Milch	**milsh**	milk
Mineralwasser	minn-er-**arl**-vuss-er	mineral water
Möhre	**mer**-uh	carrot
Nuss	**nooss**	nut
Öl	**erl**	oil
Olive	o-**leev**-uh	olive
Petersilie	payt-er-**zee**-li-uh	parsley
Pfeffer	**pfeff**-er	pepper
Pfirsich	**pfir**-zish	peach
Pflaumen	**pflow**-men	plum
Pommes frites	pomm-**fritt**	chips/ French fries
Quark	kvark	soft cheese
Radieschen	ra-**deesh**'n	radish
Rinderbraten	**rind**-er-brat'n	joint of beef
Rinderroulade	**rind**-er-roo-lard-uh	beef olive
Rindfleisch	**rint**-flysh	beef
Rippchen	**rip**-sh'n	cured pork rib
Rotkohl	roht-koal	red cabbage
Rüben	**rhoob**'n	turnip
Rührei	**rhoo**-er-eye	scrambled eggs
Saft	**zuft**	juice
Salat	zal-aat	salad

Salz	**zults**	salt
Salzkartoffeln	zults-kar-toff'l	boiled potatoes
Sauerkirschen	zow-er-**keersh**'n	cherries
Sauerkraut	zow-er-krowt	sauerkraut
Sekt	**zekt**	sparkling wine
Senf	**zenf**	mustard
scharf	sharf	spicy
Schaschlik	shash-lik	kebab
Schlagsahne	shlahgg-zarn-uh	whipped cream
Schnittlauch	shnit-lowhkh	chives
Schnitzel	**shnitz**'l	veal or pork cutlet
Schweinefleisch	**shvine**-flysh	pork
Spargel	**shparg**'l	asparagus
Spiegelei	shpeeg'l-eye	fried egg
Spinat	shpin-art	spinach
Tee	**tay**	tea
Tomate	tom-art-uh	tomato
Wassermelone	vuss-er-me-lohn-uh	watermelon
Wein	**vine**	wine
Weintrauben	vine-trowb'n	grapes
Wiener Würstchen	veen-er voorst-sh'n	frankfurter
Zander	**tsan**-der	pike-perch
Zitrone	tsi-trohn-uh	lemon
Zucker	**tsook**-er	sugar
Zwieback	tsvee-bak	rusk
Zwiebel	**tsveeb**'l	onion

NUMBERS

0	null	**nool**
1	eins	**eye'ns**
2	zwei	**tsvy**
3	drei	**dry**
4	vier	**feer**
5	fünf	**foonf**
6	sechs	**zex**
7	sieben	**zeeb**'n
8	acht	**uhkht**
9	neun	**noyn**
10	zehn	**tsayn**
11	elf	**elf**
12	zwölf	**tserlf**
13	dreizehn	**dry**-tsayn
14	vierzehn	**feer**-tsayn
15	fünfzehn	**foonf**-tsayn
16	sechzehn	**zex**-tsayn
17	siebzehn	**zeep**-tsayn
18	achtzehn	**uhkht**-tsayn
19	neunzehn	**noyn**-tsayn
20	zwanzig	**tsvunn**-tsig
21	einundzwanzig	**ine**-oont-tsvunn-tsig
30	dreissig	**dry**-sig
40	vierzig	**feer**-sig
50	fünfzig	**foonf**-tsig
60	sechzig	**zex**-tsig
70	siebzig	**zeep**-tsig
80	achtzig	**uhkht**-tsig
90	neunzig	**noyn**-tsig
100	hundert	**hoond**'t
1000	tausend	**towz**'nt
1 000 000	eine Million	**ine**-uh **mill**-yon

TIME

one minute	eine Minute	**ine**-uh min-**oot**-uh
one hour	eine Stunde	**ine**-uh **shtoond**-uh
half an hour	eine halbe Stunde	**ine**-uh hullb-uh **shtoond**-uh
Monday	Montag	**mohn**-targ
Tuesday	Dienstag	**deens**-targ
Wednesday	Mittwoch	**mitt**-vokh
Thursday	Donnerstag	**donn**-ers-targ
Friday	Freitag	**fry**-targ
Saturday	Samstag/	**zums**-targ
	Sonnabend	zonn-ah-bent
Sunday	Sonntag	**zon**-targ
January	Januar	**yan**-ooar
February	Februar	**fay**-brooar
March	März	**mairts**
April	April	april
May	Mai	my
June	Juni	**yoo**-ni
July	Juli	**yoo**-lee
August	August	ow-**goost**
September	September	zep-**tem**-ber
October	Oktober	ok-toh-ber
November	November	no-**vem**-ber
December	Dezember	day-**tsem**-ber
spring	Frühling	**froo**-ling
summer	Sommer	**zomm**-er
autumn (fall)	Herbst	**hairpst**
winter	Winter	**vint**-er

Berlin U-Bahn and S-Bahn